The Core Knowledge™ Series

Resource Books for Children from Year 1 to Year 6

What Your Year 3 Child Needs to Know

PREPARING YOUR CHILD
FOR A LIFETIME OF LEARNING

Edited by **E. D. HIRSCH, JR**

General Editors for the Civitas UK edition:
ROBERT WHELAN & TANYA LUBICZ-NAWROCKA

Original illustrations for this edition by MARK BEECH

Published by

Civitas
55 Tufton Street
London SW1P 3QL

First edition published in the USA in 1991, revised 1998, as *What Your Second Grader Needs to Know*

UK edition published December 2012

ISBN: 978-1-906837-25-9

Book design and layout by Luke Jefford (www.lukejefford.com)

Printed in Great Britain by Berforts Group Ltd, Stevenage, SG1 2BH

Acknowledgements: US edition

Editor-in-Chief of the Core Knowledge Series: E. D. Hirsch, Jr

Editor, revised edition: John Holdren

Project Manager and Art Editor: Tricia Emlet

Writers: Diane Darst (Visual Arts); Tricia Emlet (Visual Arts); John Hirsch (Mathematics); Susan Tyler Hitchcock (Science); John Holdren (Language and Literature, History and Geography, Visual Arts, Music, Mathematics, Science); Mary Beth Klee (History and Geography); Janet Smith (Music)

Artists and Photgraphers: Jonathan Fuqua, Julie Grant, Steve Henry, Hannah Holdren, Sara Holdren, Philip Jones, Bob Kirchman, Gail Mcintosh, Jeanne Nicholson Siler, Nic Siler

Art and Photo Research, Art and Text Permissions: Jeanne Nicholson Siler

Research Assistant: Brandi Jordan Johnson

Computer Assistance: Barbara Fortsch

This series has depended on the help, advice and encouragement of two thousand people. Some of those singled out here already know the depth of our gratitude; others may be surprised to find themselves thanked publicly for help they gave quietly and freely for the sake of the enterprise alone. To helpers named and unnamed we are deeply grateful.

Advisers on Multiculturalism: Minerva Allen, Barbara Carey, Frank de Varona, Mick Fedullo, Dorothy Fields, Elizabeth Fox-Genovese, Marcia Galli, Dan Garner, Henry Louis Gates, Cheryl Kulas, Joseph C. Miller, Gerry Raining Bird, Connie Rocha, Dorothy Small, Sharon Stewart-Peregoy, Sterling Stuckey, Marlene Walking Bear, Lucille Watahomigie, Ramona Wilson

Advisers on Elementary Education: Joseph Adelson, Isobel Beck, Paul Bell, Carl Bereiter, David Bjorklund, Constance Jones, Elizabeth LaFuze, J. P. Lutz, Sandra Scarr, Nancy Stein, Phyllis Wilkin

Advisers on Technical Subject Matter: Marilyn Jager Adams, Diane Alavi, Richard Anderson, Judith Birsh, Cheryl Cannard, Paul Gagnon, David Geary, Andrew Gleason, Blair Jones, Connie Juel, Eric Karell, Joseph Kerr, Mary Beth Klee, Michael Lynch, Joseph C. Miller, Jean Osborne, Margaret Redd, Nancy Royal, Mark Rush, Janet Smith, Ralph Smith, Nancy Strother, Nancy Summers, James Trefil, Nancy Wayne, Linda Williams, Lois Williams

Conferees, March 1990: Nola Bacci, Joan Baratz-Snowden, Thomasyne Beverley, Thomas Blackton, Angela Burkhalter, Monty Caldwell, Thomas M. Carroll, Laura Chapman, Carol Anne Collins, Lou Corsaro, Henry Cotton, Anne Coughlin, Arletta Dimberg, Debra P. Douglas, Patricia Edwards, Janet Elenbogen, Mick Fedullo, Michele Fomalont, Mamon Gibson, Jean Haines, Barbara Hayes, Stephen Herzog, Helen Kelley, Brenda King, John King, Elizabeth LaFuze, Diana Lam, Nancy Lambert, Doris Langaster, Richard LaPointe, Lloyd Leverton, Madeline Long, Allen Luster, Joseph McGeehan, Janet McLin, Gloria McPhee, Marcia Mallard, William J. Maloney, Judith Matz, John Morabito, Robert Morrill, Roberta Morse, Karen Nathan, Dawn Nichols, Valeta Paige, Mary Perrin, Joseph Piazza, Jeanne Price, Marilyn Rauth, Judith Raybern, Mary Reese, Richard Rice, Wallace Saval, John Saxon, Jan Schwab, Ted Sharp, Diana Smith, Richard Smith, Trevanian Smith, Carol Stevens, Nancy Summers, Michael Terry, Robert Todd, Elois Veltman, Sharon Walker, Mary Ann Ward, Penny Williams, Charles Whiten, Clarke Worthington, Jane York

Schools: Special thanks to Three Oaks Elementary for piloting the original Core Knowledge Sequence in 1990. And thanks to the schools that have offered their advice and suggestions for improving the Core Knowledge Sequence, including (in alphabetical order): Academy Charter School (CO); Coleman Elementary (TX); Coral Reef Elementary (FL); Coronado Village Elementary (TX); Crooksville Elementary (OH); Crossroads Academy (NH); Gesher Jewish Day School (VA); Hawthorne Elementary (TX); Highland Heights Elementary (IN); Joella Good Elementary (FL); Mohegan School-CS 67 (NY); The Morse School (MA); Nichols Hills Elementary (OK); Ridge View Elementary (WA); R. N. Harris Elementary (NC); Southside Elementary (FL); Three Oaks Elementary (FL); Washington Core Knowledge School (CO). And to the many other schools teaching Core Knowledge – too many to name here, and some of whom we have yet to discover – our heartfelt thanks for 'sharing the knowledge'!

Benefactors: The Brown Foundation, The Challenge Foundation, Mrs. E. D. Hirsch, Sr, The Walton Family Foundation.

Our grateful acknowledgment to these persons does not imply that we have taken their (sometimes conflicting) advice in every case, or that each of them endorses all aspects of this project. Responsibility for final decisions must rest with the editors alone. Suggestions for improvements are very welcome, and we wish to thank in advance those who send advice for revising and improving this series.

Acknowledgements: UK edition

General Editors of the UK edition: Robert Whelan & Tanya Lubicz-Nawrocka

Contributing Editor and Editor of the Music chapter for the UK edition: Nigel Williams

Editor and author of the Visual Arts chapter of the UK edition: Jo Saxton

Editor of the Mathematics chapter of the UK edition: Nick Cowen

Editorial Assistant: Catherine Green

Author of British and European Geography and British History: Andrew Phemister

Design and typesetting of the UK edition: Luke Jefford

Original illustrations for the UK edition: Mark Beech

Maps: Ed Dovey and Richard Kelly

Owl illustrations: Mark Otton

Compiling the UK edition of a book that has already become an established classic in the United States has been both a privilege and a challenge. Our first thanks must go to E.D. Hirsch, Jr, Linda Bevilacqua and the team at the Core Knowledge Foundation for sharing with us the fruits of their labours over so many years. We fully share their view that all children deserve access to a first-class education, and we hope that the Civitas edition of the Core Knowledge texts will do as much for children in the UK as the US edition has done for thousands of children in the US and abroad.

Many people have helped us. We are especially grateful for the assistance given to the project by Jo Saxton in Visual Arts; Andrew Phemister in British and European History and Geography; Sean Lang, Chris Gray and Margaret Lenton in History; Chris Cull in Music; Peter Clarke in Mathematics; and Matthew Robinson in Language and Literature. Marilyn Brocklehurst of the Norfolk Children's Book Centre shared her passion for children's books and helped us to find titles for the suggested resources sections.

We are grateful to Gail McIntosh for permission to reproduce her excellent original illustrations from the US edition; to Paul Collicutt for adding the dimension of colour to illustrations that were originally black and white; and to all those generous authors, illustrators and copyright owners who have allowed us to reproduce material for this book because they share our passion for bringing to children the very best in words and images.

Thanks to our colleagues past and present at Civitas for their help, especially Emma Lennard, Curriculum Project Director; Nigel Williams for work on Maths and Science; Nick Cowen for work on Maths; Annaliese Briggs for help with the UK Sequence; and Janet Russell for help with the text. Special thanks are due to Anastasia de Waal, Head of Family and Education at Civitas, for her help and guidance.

A Note to Teachers

Throughout the book, we have addressed the suggested activities and explanations to 'parents', since you as teachers know your students and will have ideas about how to use the content of this book in relation to the lessons and activities you plan. To discuss using Core Knowledge UK materials in your school, please contact Civitas at 55 Tufton Street, London SW1P 3QL, 020 7799 6677. There are further activities and resources to supplement this book available on the website given below.

Email: coreknowledge@civitas.org.uk

Website: www.coreknowledge.org.uk

About the Editor

E.D. Hirsch, Jr is a professor at the University of Virginia and the author of *The Schools We Need* and the bestselling *Cultural Literacy* and *The Dictionary of Cultural Literacy*. He and his wife, Polly, live in Charlottesville, Virginia, where they raised their three children.

E. D. Hirsch, Jr receives no renumeration for editing the series nor any other renumeration from the Core Knowledge Foundation.

Contents

Acknowledgements — v
A Note to Teachers — viii
About the Editor — viii
Foreword to the UK Edition of the Core Knowledge Series — xv
Introduction to the UK edition of The Core Knowledge Curriculum for Year 3 — xvii
General Introduction to the Core Knowledge Series — xix

Language and Literature

Reading, Writing and Your Year 3 Child: A Note to Parents — 1
Beginner Readers for Children — 2

Literature
Introduction — 3

Poetry
Caterpillars — 4
Hurt No Living Thing — 5
Bee! I'm Expecting You! — 5
The Night Before Christmas — 6
Discovery — 9
Caracola/Conch Shell — 9
The Answer — 10
Something Told the Wild Geese — 11
Five Friendly Farmers — 12
Rickety Train Ride — 12
On the Ning Nang Nong — 13
There Was an Old Man with a Beard — 14
There Is a Young Lady, Whose Nose — 14

Stories
The Fisherman and His Wife — 15
Talk — 17
The Emperor's New Clothes — 19
The Magic Paintbrush — 21
A Christmas Carol — 23
Please Look After This Bear
   (From *A Bear Called Paddington*) — 28

How the Camel Got His Hump — 31
Beauty and the Beast — 34
The Tongue-Cut Sparrow — 38
The Story of the Seventh Daughter — 40
Peter Pan — 45

Tall Tales
Introduction — 49
Albion and Brutus — 50
King Arthur and the
   Knights of the Round Table — 52
Robin Hood and his Merry Men — 55
Robin Hood and the Butcher — 56
Dick Whittington,
   Lord Mayor of London — 61

Myths from Ancient Greece
Heroes and Monsters, Gods and
   Goddesses — 65
Same Gods, Different Names — 70
Gods of Nature
   and Mythical Creatures — 70
Prometheus Brings Fire,
   Pandora Brings Woe — 72
Oedipus and the Sphinx — 73
Theseus and the Minotaur — 74
Daedalus and Icarus — 76
Arachne the Weaver — 76
Swift-Footed Atalanta — 78

Demeter and Persephone 79
The Labours of Hercules 81

Learning About Language
Sentences 83
Two Rules for Writing Sentences 84
Nouns Name a Person,
   Place or Thing 84
Singular and Plural Nouns 85
Verbs: Action Words 86
Verbs: Past and Present 86
Adjectives Describe Things 88
More About Words:
   Antonyms and Synonyms 89
Contractions 89
Abbreviations 90
Using Capital Letters 90

Familiar Sayings
Back to the drawing board 92
Better late than never 92
Cold Feet 92
It's no use crying over spilt milk 93
Easier said than done 93
Eaten out of house and home 93
Get a taste of your own medicine 94
Two heads are better than one 94
Get out of the bed on the wrong side 94
Practise what you preach 95
In hot water 95
Turn over a new leaf 95
Where there's a will there's a way 96
Keep your fingers crossed 96
You can't teach an old dog new tricks 96
Suggested Resources 97

History and Geography

Introduction 99
A Note on the History
   of the World Religions 100
A Note on Geography 100

Geography
A Quick Geography Review 101
Geography of Western Europe 102
Where You Live 111
Rivers and Basins 114

Great Rivers of the World
Introduction 118
Some Geography Words 120
Rivers of Europe 120
Rivers of Africa 121
Rivers of Asia 122
Rivers of Australia 123
Rivers of South America 123
Rivers of North America 124

Civilisations in Asia
Long Ago in Asia:
Civilisation in the Indus Valley 125
Civilisation Along the Ganges 126
Hinduism 127
A Story from the Holy
   Books of Hinduism 129
Rama and Sita:
   A Tale from the Ramayana 129
Buddha: The Enlightened One 132
Buddha's Teachings 134
King Asoka: From War to Peace 134
A Wise Teacher in China: Confucius 135
China: Great Rivers
   and a Great Wall 136
An Important Invention 138
Smooth as Silk 138
Chinese New Year 139

Great Explorers: Marco Polo 140
Let's Visit Japan:
   The Land of the Rising Sun 142
Japanese Feudalism 144
Japanese Religions 145
Modern Japan 145

Ancient Greece
Birthplace of the Olympics
   and More 147
A Civilisation of City-States 148
Athens: Birthplace of Democracy 149
Rough, Tough Sparta 151
The Persian Wars 151
Battles That Live in Memory 153
Marathon 153
Thermopylae 154
Great Thinkers in Athens 155
Alexander the Great 157
The Gordian Knot 158
What Lies Beyond? 159

British History
A Quick Look Back 161
Norman Monarchs 163
The Rule of Law and
   Murder in the Cathedral 163
The Crusades 165
Restraints on Royal Power:
   Magna Carta 167
How the Crown Jewels
   Were Lost in the Wash 169
Restraints on Royal Power:
   de Montfort's Parliament 169
The Wars of the Roses 170
Plantagenet Monarchs 172
The Reformation 172
The English Reformation 173
Religious Conflicts: From Protestant
   to Catholic and Back Again 175
The Elizabethan Era 176
Tudor Monarchs 180
Suggested Resources 180

Visual Arts

Introduction 181
The Pleasure of Art 181
Taking a Line for a Walk 181
Activity 1: It's your turn! 183
Lines and Form 183
Lines and Movement 184
Lines and Symmetry 185
Activity 2: From half to whole! 186
Looking at Landscapes 186
Still Life 188
Activity 3: Multi-colour still-life 190
Mythology 190
Activity 4: Words for pictures 191
The Art of Designing Buildings:
Architecture 192
A Building of Lines 192
Activity 5: Soap stone 193
A Building of Curves 195
Taking a Different Line:
A Modern Museum 197
New Lines for Breaking
New Ground 198
Suggested Resources 199
Where to find the works of art
   in this chapter 200

Music

Introduction — 201
Many Kinds of Music — 201
Patriotic Music — 202
Chorus of the Hebrew Slaves — 203
Folk Music — 204
Classical Music — 205
Meet Some Great Composers — 206
Composers and their Music — 206
Families of Instruments:
  A Closer Look — 209
The String Family — 209
The Percussion Family — 211
Keyboard Instruments — 212

Mr Bach at the Keyboard — 212
Writing Music Down — 213
Follow the Notes — 214
Pitch: High and Low — 215
A Musical Scale — 217
Some Songs for Year 3
Clementine — 218
Bobby Shaftoe — 220
My Grandfather's Clock — 221
The Hippopotamus Song — 221
Oranges and Lemons — 222
Who Killed Cock Robin? — 222
The Happy Wanderer — 224
Suggested Resources — 225

Mathematics

Introduction — 227
Working with Numbers to 100
Skip-Counting — 228
Some Special Maths Words — 229
Between, One More and One Less — 229
Counting With a Tally — 230
Using Graphs — 230
Writing Numbers as Words — 231
Reading a Number Line — 232
Review: Addition and
  Subtraction Facts to 20 — 233
Review: Adding in Any Order
  and Adding Three Numbers — 233
Review: Checking Addition
  and Subtraction — 233
Review: Fact Families — 234
Doubles and Halves — 235
Sum of 10 — 237
Find the Missing Number — 237

Missing Number Problems with
  Greater Than and Less Than — 238
Working with Equations — 238
Tens and Ones — 240
Adding Numbers with Two Digits — 241
Checking Addition by Changing
  the Order of Addends — 242
Adding Three Numbers — 242
Subtracting Numbers
  with Two Digits — 243
Checking Two-Digit Subtraction — 245
Adding and Subtracting Horizontally,
  Vertically and in Your Head — 245
Adding and Subtracting
  9 in Your Head — 247
Estimating and Rounding
  to the Nearest Ten — 248
Fractions — 249
Working with Numbers to 1,000 — 251

The Hundreds 251
Counting Between Hundreds 252
Count On! 252
Place Value 253
Expanded Form 254
Comparing Three-Digit Numbers 255
Adding Three-Digit Numbers 255
Regrouping Tens as Hundreds 255
Subtracting from a
   Three-Digit Number 257
Subtraction and Regrouping
   Hundreds 258
Word Problems 259

Measurement
Measuring Length 260
Measuring Weight 262
Measuring Time: The Calendar 263
Clock Time to 5 Minutes 264

Half and Quarter Hours 266
How Much Time Has Passed? 267

Geometry
Plane Figures 268
Solid Figures 269
Points, Lines and Segments 270
Lines of Symmetry 272

Multiplication and Division
Multiplication 273
Multiplication Words 273
Multiplying Vertically 273
Showing Multiplication 273
The Multiplication Table 274
Brackets,
   Multiplying Three Numbers 275
Division 276
Division Word Problems 277
Remainders 277

Suggested Resources 280

Science

Introduction 281

The Cycle of Life and the Seasons
The Life Cycle 282
From Seed to Seed:
   A Plant's Life Cycle 284
From Frog to Frog:
   An Amphibian's Life Cycle 284
The Cycle of the Seasons 285
Spring 286
Summer 286
Autumn 287
Winter 287

The Water Cycle
Evaporation 288
Going Up, Going Down 289

Condensation and Precipitation 290
Putting It All Together:
   The Water Cycle 291

Insects
Insects Everywhere! 292
What Makes an Insect an Insect? 293
Are They Insects? 295
Insect Life Cycles 296
A Simpler Kind of Metamorphosis 297
Social Insects 298
An Ant Colony 298
In a Beehive 299

The Human Body
Cells: The Building Blocks
   of Living Things 302

Cells and Tissues,
  Organs and Systems 303
What Happens to the Food You Eat? 303
A Healthy Diet: The Food Pyramid 306
Vitamins and Minerals 307

Magnetism
That Special Magnetic Attraction 308
Magnetic Poles 309
Using a Compass 311

Simple Machines
Tools and Machines 312
Levers 313
Wheels 314

Friction 315
Pulleys 315
Inclined Planes 316
Wedges 316
Screws 317

Stories About Scientists
Aristotle 318
Archimedes 319
Antonij van Leeuwenhoek 320
The Curie Family 322

Suggested Resources 323

Illustration and Photo Credits 325
Text Credits and Sources 327
Index 329

Foreword to the UK Edition of the Core Knowledge Series

This is the third in a series of books for parents who want to help their children do well at school. It describes what every child should aim to have learnt by the end of the school year. It is not a description of everything that could be known but rather a guide to the knowledge that children will need to advance to the next stage of their education. Nor is it primarily a textbook, although it could be used as such – along with other teaching resources – if schools wish.

The Core Knowledge series gives parents the tools to judge how effectively their children are being taught. And it provides teachers with clear aims that can be shared with parents, thereby enlisting them in the common cause of getting the best from every child.

Why publish a British version of a book originally designed for American children? For the last 50 years in both Britain and America there has been no consensus about how and what children should be taught. Sometimes knowledge was dismissed as mere 'rote learning', which was contrasted unfavourably with 'critical thinking skills'. Others argued that education should be 'child centred' not 'subject centred'. Professor Hirsch, who inspired the Core Knowledge series, was among the first to see that the retreat from knowledge was misguided. Above all, he showed that to compare 'knowledge' with 'thinking skills' was to make a false contrast. They are not mutually exclusive alternatives. Thinking skills can be 'knowledge-rich' or 'knowledge-lite'. The purpose of a good education is to teach children how to think clearly – to see through dubious reasoning, to avoid being conned, to learn how to question their own assumptions, to discover how to be objective or to argue a case with clarity. Knowledge does not get in the way of reasoning: it's what we reason with.

The Core Knowledge approach has six main strengths.

- It helps parents to bring out the best in their children. It provides a guide to what young people should be learning and helps parents decide on the school best suited to their child.

- It helps teachers. By providing clear expectations that are shared with parents, teachers are better able to benefit every child. Schools are always at their best when parents and teachers work together.

- It helps children to learn on their own initiative. The books are written in language suitable for each year group, so that children can read alone or with their parents.

- It provides more equal opportunities for everyone. Some children do not receive effective support at home, perhaps because some of us did not ourselves get the best education. A good school can do much to make up for lost ground and the Core Knowledge series is designed for this very task. The books describe what every child can learn if given the chance. What's more, many parents find that they learn as much as their children!

- It encourages social cohesion. Britain today has more cultures, ethnic groups and religions than 50 years ago. If we all share in a common stock of knowledge, social solidarity based on mutual respect for our legitimate differences is more likely.

- It strengthens democracy. A free and democratic society depends on the mass of people being well-informed. We often say that modern societies are 'knowledge based'. It's true. People who do not share in the knowledge that is regularly used by television news programmes or in our newspapers are at risk of being misled.

We are keen to work with teachers who share our ideals and who hope to play a leading part in developing this new curriculum in Britain. In co-operation with teachers, we will be evolving model lesson plans and resource guides, and if any teachers would like their school to be one of the pioneers, please contact Civitas at *coreknowledge@civitas.org.uk*.

David G. Green
Director of Civitas

Introduction to the UK Edition of the Core Knowledge Series for Year 3

The concerns which led Professor Hirsch and others to set up the Core Knowledge Foundation in the USA in 1986 are shared by many in Britain. Civitas has acquired direct experience of the problem through its network of supplementary schools. Beginning with a group of Bengali children in the East End of London in 2005, Civitas now runs 20 supplementary schools for over 600 children in different parts of the UK. The children attend once a week, either on Saturdays or after school, for help with English and maths. The children are, for the most part, attending full-time schools in areas with higher-than-average indicators of social deprivation, where academic outcomes are not the best in the country. Some children join supplementary schools at the age of seven, eight or even older, unable to read properly and unable to handle simple addition and subtraction. Our approach in the Civitas Schools has been to employ dedicated teachers with high expectations and a commitment to providing solid learning foundations. Children are assessed annually and it has become quite usual to see them make two or three years of progress in their reading and maths ages over the course of one calendar year.

The concepts that Professor Hirsch mentions in his General Introduction such as 'critical thinking' and 'learning to learn' have been just as prevalent in the UK's schools, where the curriculum has become less knowledge-based and more focused on attaining 'skills', as if the two things can be separated. The acquisition of skills requires knowledge, and a knowledge-poor curriculum is one that condemns pupils – especially children from less advantaged backgrounds – to remain outside the mainstream of attainment and fulfilment. The Core Knowledge Foundation believes that all children should be able to unlock the library of the world's literature; to comprehend the world around them; to know where they stand (literally) on the globe; and to realise the heritage that the history of their country has bestowed on them.

Making a reality of this ideal has been the outstanding achievement of the Core Knowledge Foundation in the hundreds of schools across the USA where its curriculum is being taught, and it is why we so admire the work of Professor Hirsch and his colleagues at the Core Knowledge Foundation.

As Professor Hirsch explains in his General Introduction, the project operates within the overarching framework of the Core Knowledge Sequence, produced by dozens of educators over a gestational period of several years. To bring this sequence into the classroom or the home, the Sequence is fleshed out by a book for each year group. We at Civitas were honoured and delighted to be entrusted by the Core Knowledge Foundation with the task of adapting the books for teachers, parents and pupils in the UK. This has entailed some changes to reflect differences between our cultures, for example, we study the rivers flowing into the Humber where children in the US study the Mississippi; maths examples replace basketball games with cricket matches; and 'The Lincolnshire Poacher' replaces 'Working on the Railroad'. British musical nomenclature has been used in the Music chapter and metric rather than imperial measures in Science. In addition, we have illustrated the Visual Arts chapter mainly with works that can be seen in UK museums and galleries, and we have revised the lists of resources to include books and educational materials readily available in the UK. However, for the most part, the US text has been left intact – because knowledge is universal!

We have adapted the Core Knowledge Sequence for the UK and it is freely available online at http://www.coreknowledge.org.uk/sequence.php. This will enable parents and teachers to understand how the grammar of each subject is unrolled over six years of primary school education. The UK Sequence follows the US Sequence very closely, with a few obvious changes. Maths has been slightly revised to reflect the demands of the National Curriculum; the works of art illustrated in the Visual Arts chapters can almost all be found in British museums and galleries; and British history and geography replace American. (American history and geography will be covered under World History and Geography.)

We share the view of the Core Knowledge Foundation that knowledge is best conveyed through subjects, and so we have followed their division of each book into chapters covering Language and Literature, History and Geography, Visual Arts, Music, Mathematics and Science. We will be producing volumes for each year group up to Year 6, and these will tie in with the UK version of the Core Knowledge Sequence.

In most states of the USA, children start their full-time education in Kindergarten when they are five rising six, whereas in the UK children of that age would be starting Year 1, having already spent a year in Reception. For this reason, the first book in Civitas UK Core Knowledge series, *What Your Year 1 Child Needs to Know*, represented, with small alterations, the text of *What Your Kindergartner Needs to Know*. The second book, *What Your Year 2 Child Needs to Know*, followed the text of the next book in the US series, *What Your First Grader Needs to Know*, first published 1991 and substantially revised in a new edition of 1997. This volume follows the next book in the US series, *What Your Second Grader Needs To Know*, first published in 1991 and revised in 1998.

Robert Whelan
General Editor, Civitas Core Knowledge UK Project

General Introduction to the Core Knowledge Series

I. WHAT IS YOUR CHILD LEARNING IN SCHOOL?

A parent of identical twins sent me a letter in which she expressed concern that her children, who are in the same grade in the same school, are being taught completely different things. How can this be? Because they are in different classrooms; because the teachers in these classrooms have only the vaguest guidelines to follow; in short, because the school, like many in the United States, lacks a definite, specific curriculum.

Many parents would be surprised if they were to examine the curriculum of their child's elementary school. Ask to see your school's curriculum. Does it spell out, in clear and concrete terms, a core of specific content and skills all children at a particular grade level are expected to learn by the end of the school year?

Many curricula speak in general terms of vaguely defined skills, processes and attitudes, often in an abstract, pseudo-technical language that calls, for example, for children to 'analyse patterns and data', or 'investigate the structure and dynamics of living systems', or 'work cooperatively in a group'. Such vagueness evades the central question: what is your child learning in school? It places unreasonable demands upon teachers, and often results in years of schooling marred by repetitions and gaps. Yet another unit on dinosaurs or 'pioneer days'. *Charlotte's Web* for the third time. 'You've never heard of the Bill of Rights?' 'You've never been taught how to add two fractions with unlike denominators?'

When identical twins in two classrooms of the same school have few academic experiences in common, that is cause for concern. When teachers in that school do not know what children in other classrooms are learning in the same grade level, much less in earlier and later grades, they cannot reliably predict that children will come prepared with a shared core of knowledge and skills. For an elementary school to be successful, teachers need a common vision of what they want their students to know and be able to do. They need to have *clear, specific learning goals*, as well as the sense of mutual accountability that comes from shared commitment to helping all children achieve those goals. Lacking both specific goals and mutual accountability, too many schools exist in a state of curricular incoherence, one result of which is that they fall far short of developing the full potential of our children. To address this problem, I started the non-profit Core Knowledge Foundation in 1986. This book and its companion volumes in the Core Knowledge Series are designed to give parents, teachers – and through them, children – a guide to clearly defined learning goals in the form of a carefully sequenced body of knowledge, based upon the specific content guidelines developed by the Core Knowledge Foundation (see below, 'The Consensus Behind the Core Knowledge Sequence').

Core Knowledge is an attempt to define, in a coherent and sequential way, a body of widely used knowledge taken for granted by competent writers and speakers in the United States. Because this knowledge is taken for granted rather than being explained when it is used, it forms a necessary foundation for the higher-order reading, writing and thinking skills that children need for academic and vocational success. The universal attainment of such knowledge should be a central aim of curricula in our elementary schools, just as it is currently the aim in all world-class educational systems.

For reasons explained in the next section, making sure that all young children in the United States possess a core of shared knowledge is a necessary step in developing a first-rate educational system.

II. WHY CORE KNOWLEDGE IS NEEDED

Learning builds on learning: children (and adults) gain new knowledge only by building on what they already know. It is essential to begin building solid foundations of knowledge in the early grades when children are most receptive because, for the vast majority of children, academic deficiencies from the first six grades can *permanently* impair the success of later learning. Poor performance of American students in middle and high school can be traced to shortcomings inherited from elementary schools that have not imparted to children the knowledge and skills they need for further learning.

All of the highest-achieving and most egalitarian elementary school systems in the world (such as those in Sweden, France and Japan) teach their children a specific core of knowledge in each of the first six grades, thus enabling all children to enter each new grade with a secure foundation for further learning. It is time American schools did so as well, for the following reasons:

(1) Commonly shared knowledge makes schooling more effective.

We know that the one-on-one tutorial is the most effective form of schooling, in part because a parent or teacher can provide tailor-made instruction for the individual child. But in a non-tutorial situation – in, for example, a typical classroom with twenty-five or more students – the instructor cannot effectively impart new knowledge to all the students unless each one shares the background knowledge that the lesson is being built upon.

Consider this scenario: in third grade, Ms Franklin is about to begin a unit on early explorers – Columbus, Magellan and others. In her class she has some students who were in Mr Washington's second-grade class last year and some students who were in Ms Johnson's second-grade class. She also has a few students who have moved in from other towns. As Ms Franklin begins the unit on explorers, she asks the children to look at a globe and use their fingers to trace a route across the Atlantic Ocean from Europe to North America. The students who had Mr Washington look blankly at her: they didn't learn that last year. The students who had Ms Johnson, however, eagerly point to the proper places on the globe, while two of the students who came from other towns pipe up and say, 'Columbus and Magellan again? We did that last year.'

When all the students in a class *do* share the relevant background knowledge, a classroom can begin to approach the effectiveness of a tutorial. Even when some children in a class do not have elements of the knowledge they were supposed to acquire in previous grades, the existence of a specifically defined core makes it possible for the teacher or parent to identify and fill the gaps, thus giving all students a chance to fulfill their potential in later grades.

(2) Commonly shared knowledge makes schooling more fair and democratic.

When all the children who enter a grade can be assumed to share some of the same building blocks of knowledge, and when the teacher knows exactly what those building blocks are, then all the students are empowered to learn. In our current system, children from disadvantaged backgrounds too often suffer from unmerited low expectations that translate into watered-down curricula. But if we specify the core of knowledge that all children should share, then we can guarantee equal access to that knowledge and compensate for the academic advantages some students are offered at home. In a Core Knowledge school, *all* children enjoy the benefits of important, challenging knowledge that will provide the foundation for successful later learning.

(3) Commonly shared knowledge helps create cooperation and solidarity in our schools and nation.

Diversity is a hallmark and strength of our nation. American classrooms are usually made up of students from a variety of cultural backgrounds, and those different cultures should be honoured by all students. At the same time, education should create a school-based culture that is common and welcoming to all because it includes knowledge of many cultures and gives all students, no matter what their background, a common foundation for understanding our cultural diversity.

In the next section, I will describe the steps taken by the Core Knowledge Foundation to develop a model of the commonly shared knowledge our children need (which forms the basis for this series of books).

III. THE CONSENSUS BEHIND THE CORE KNOWLEDGE SEQUENCE

The content in this and other volumes in the Core Knowledge Series is based on a document called the *Core Knowledge Sequence*, a grade-by-grade sequence of specific content guidelines in history, geography, mathematics, science, language arts and fine arts. The *Sequence* is not meant to outline the whole of the school curriculum; rather, it offers specific guidelines to knowledge that can reasonably be expected to make up about *half* of any school's curriculum, thus leaving ample room for local requirements and emphases. Teaching a common core of knowledge, such as that articulated in the *Core Knowledge Sequence*, is compatible with a variety of instructional methods and additional subject matters.

The *Core Knowledge Sequence* is the result of a long process of research and consensus building undertaken by the Core Knowledge Foundation. Here is how we achieved the consensus behind the *Core Knowledge Sequence*.

First we analysed the many reports issued by state departments of education and by professional organisations – such as the National Council of Teachers of Mathematics and the American Association for the Advancement of Science – that recommend general outcomes for elementary and secondary education. We also tabulated the knowledge and skills through grade six specified in the successful educational systems of several other countries, including France, Japan, Sweden and West Germany.

In addition, we formed an advisory board on multiculturalism that proposed a specific knowledge of diverse cultural traditions that American children should all share as part of their school-based common culture. We sent the resulting materials to three independent groups of teachers, scholars and scientists around the country, asking them to create a master list of the knowledge children should have by the end of grade six. About 150 teachers (including college professors, scientists and administrators) were involved in this initial step.

These items were amalgamated into a master plan, and further groups of teachers and specialists were asked to agree on a grade-by-grade sequence of the items. That sequence was then sent to some one hundred educators and specialists who participated in a national conference that was called to hammer out a working agreement on an appropriate core of knowledge for the first six grades.

This important meeting took place in March 1990. The conferees were elementary school teachers, curriculum specialists, scientists, science writers, officers of national organisations, representatives of ethnic groups, district superintendents and school principals from across the country. A total of twenty-four working groups decided on revisions in the *Core Knowledge Sequence*. The resulting provisional *Sequence* was further fine-tuned during a year of implementation at a pioneering school, Three Oaks Elementary in Lee County, Florida.

In only a few years, many more schools – urban and rural, rich and poor, public and private – joined in the effort to teach Core Knowledge. Based largely on suggestions from these schools, the *Core Knowledge Sequence* was revised in 1995: separate guidelines were added for kindergarten, and a few topics in other grades were added, omitted or moved from one grade to another, in order to create an even more coherent sequence for learning. Revised editions of the books in the Core Knowledge Series reflect the revisions in the *Sequence*. Based on the principle of learning from experience, the Core Knowledge Foundation continues to work with schools and advisors to 'fine-tune' the *Sequence*, and is also conducting research that will lead to the publication of guidelines for grades seven and eight, as well as for preschool. (*The Core Knowledge Sequence UK* can be downloaded from the Civitas Core Knowledge UK website www.coreknowledge.org.uk/sequence.php)

IV. THE NATURE OF THIS SERIES

The books in this series are designed to give a convenient and engaging introduction to the knowledge specified in the *Core Knowledge Sequence*. These are resource books, addressed primarily to parents, but which we hope will be useful tools for both parents and teachers. These books are not intended to replace the local curriculum or school textbooks, but rather to serve as aids to help children gain some of the important knowledge they will need to make progress in school and be effective in society.

Although we have made these books as accessible and useful as we can, parents and teachers should understand that they are not the only means by which the *Core Knowledge Sequence* can be imparted. The books represent a single version of the possibilities inherent in the *Sequence*, and a first step in the Core Knowledge reform effort. We hope that publishers will be stimulated to offer educational software, games, alternative books and other imaginative vehicles based on the *Core Knowledge Sequence*.

These books are not textbooks or workbooks, though when appropriate they do suggest a variety of activities you can do with your child. In these books, we address your child directly, and occasionally ask questions for him or her to think about. The earliest books in the series are intended to be read aloud to children. Even as children become able to read the books on their own, we encourage parents to help their children read more actively by reading along with them and talking about what they are reading. You and your child can read the sections of this book in any order, depending on your child's interests or depending on the topics your child is studying in school, which this book may complement or reinforce. You can skip from section to section and re-read as much as your child likes.

We encourage you to think of this book as a guidebook that opens the way to many paths you and your child can explore. These paths may lead to the library, to many other good books and, if possible, to plays, museums, concerts and other opportunities for knowledge and enrichment. In short, this guidebook recommends places to visit and describes what is important in those places, but only you and your child can make the actual visit, travel the streets and climb the steps.

V. WHAT YOU CAN DO TO HELP IMPROVE EDUCATION

The first step for parents and teachers who are committed to reform is to be sceptical about oversimplified slogans like 'critical thinking' and 'learning to learn'. Such slogans are everywhere and, unfortunately for our schools, their partial insights have been elevated to the level of universal truths. For example: 'What students learn is not important; rather, we must teach students to learn *how* to learn.' 'The child, not the academic subject, is the true focus of education.' 'Do not impose knowledge on children before they are developmentally ready to receive it.' 'Do not bog children down in mere facts, but rather, teach critical-thinking skills.' Who has not heard these sentiments, so admirable and humane, and – up to a point – so true? But these positive sentiments in favour of 'thinking skills' and 'higher understanding' have been turned into negative sentiments against the teaching of important knowledge. Those who have entered the teaching profession over the past 40 years have been taught to scorn important knowledge as 'mere facts', and to see the imparting of this knowledge as somehow injurious to children. Thus it has come about that many educators, armed with partially true slogans, have seemingly taken leave of common sense.

Many parents and teachers have come to the conclusion that elementary education must strike a better balance between the development of the 'whole child' and the more limited but fundamental duty of the school to ensure that all children master a core of knowledge and skills essential to their competence as learners in later grades. But these parents and teachers cannot act on their convictions without access to an agreed upon, concrete sequence of knowledge. Our main motivation in developing the *Core Knowledge Sequence* and this book series has been to give parents and teachers something concrete to work with.

It has been encouraging to see how many teachers, since the first volume in this series was published, have responded to the Core Knowledge reform effort.

Parents and teachers are urged to join in a grassroots effort to strengthen our elementary schools. The place to start is in your own school and district. Insist that your school clearly state the core of *specific* knowledge and skills that each child in a grade must learn. Whether your school's core corresponds exactly to the Core Knowledge model is less important than the existence of some core – which, we hope, will be as solid, coherent, and challenging as the *Core Knowledge Sequence* has proven to be. Inform members of your community about the need for such a specific curriculum, and help make sure that the people who are elected or appointed to your local school board are independent-minded people who will insist that our children have the benefit of a solid, specific, world-class curriculum in each grade.

Share the knowledge!

E. D. Hirsch, Jr
Charlottesville, Virginia

Language and Literature

Reading, Writing and Your Year 3 Child:
A Note to Parents

In the Core Knowledge UK books for Year 1 and Year 2, we described some features of an effective reading and writing programme in schools. We described how a good programme is not only rich in literature but also presents varied opportunities for children to work and play with letters and sounds. An effective programme presents important skills sequentially, with plenty of practice and review. It includes phonics; opportunities for decoding and encoding; as well as practice in spelling, handwriting, punctuation and grammar.

By the end of Year 2, a reasonable goal is for children to become independent readers and writers. By this we don't mean that children should be able to read any book in the library or write a perfectly polished essay, but that they should be able to read books appropriate for their age, and write legibly.

Nothing is more important in a child's schooling than learning to read and write by the end of Year 2, or more important than extending that confident ability by the end of Year 3.

Based on authoritative advice from mainstream scientific research, the Core Knowledge Foundation and Civitas have compiled a description of reading and writing goals that a school should work to achieve with all students in Year 3. Those goals are included in the Core Knowledge Sequence UK, the curriculum guidelines upon which this book is based. Parents who wish to have some benchmarks by which to gauge the adequacy and effectiveness of the reading and writing programmes in their child's school can access the Core Knowledge Sequence UK at www.coreknowledge.org.uk/sequence.php

In addition, as a parent you can do many things to help your child, such as:

- read aloud regularly and talk with your child about what they are reading
- take your child to your local library

- help your child write thank-you notes, letters and emails to relatives and friends

- play word games like Hangman or Scrabble Junior

- check on your child's progress with homework

- encourage and support your child's efforts to learn more about the English language and, possibly, other languages

Readers for Year 3 Children

Egmont's Bananas series are delightful books to share. Three levels of complexity at green, blue and red allow you to offer a variety of experiences to your child. Authors such as Linda Newbery, Michael Morpurgo and Julia Donaldson provide strong, lively stories with lots of humour. Look for titles such as *Conker, A Dog Called Whatnot* and *The Quick Brown Fox Cub*.

Ronda and David Armitage's Lighthouse Keeper Stories have been reintroduced by Scholastic as a series of short chapter books which children really enjoy. Nice big print and lots of speech bubbles, lists and notices add to the fun.

The Federation of Children's Book Groups produces *Carousel* three times a year. This magazine is an invaluable guide to new story books and emerging authors and illustrators. It is aimed at parents who are interested in introducing their children to excellent books. Their website www.carouselguide.co.uk has all the details.

Literature

Introduction

For your Year 3 child, we offer a selection of poetry, stories and myths. The poetry includes traditional rhymes as well as a few favourites by modern writers. We encourage you to read many more poems with your child, to delight in the play of language and occasionally to encourage your child to memorise a favourite poem and perhaps 'perform' it for friends or family members.

The stories presented here are mostly traditional tales that have stood the test of time. Some of the selections from other lands may not be familiar to British readers, but by including them here we hope to make them so. Parents and teachers may want to connect the folktales we include from China, Japan and India with the introductions to those lands in the World History section of this book. We also offer a selection of Greek myths, which you can tie in with the discussion of Ancient Greece in the World History section of this book.

The stories here are meant to complement, not replace, stories with controlled vocabularies and syntax that children may be given in school as part of their instruction in reading. While some Year 3 children may be able to read the stories in this book on their own, those who find the language too complex can readily understand and enjoy these stories when the words are read aloud and talked about with an adult. You may also want to try some 'shared reading' in which you read aloud parts of a story and your child reads aloud parts to you.

Many of these stories convey traditional values such as honesty, courage, generosity and diligence. Those parents who hope that schooling will instil ethical values can feel somewhat reassured if their child is being taught good literature. For, next to human role models who exemplify the desired virtues, good literature is one of the best means of instilling ethical values. Plato said that stories are the most important part of early education, and he advised parents and teachers to take great care in choosing the right stories: 'Let them fashion the mind with such tales even more fondly than they mould the body.'

We offer the stories in this book as a good starting point, and we encourage you and your child to explore further. Your local library has a treasury of good books, fiction and nonfiction. Some illustrated picture books are deceptively simple but offer a great deal for children to think about and discuss with you. Have a look at such titles as *Something Else* by Kathryn Cave which is concerned with celebrating difference, or *Billy's Bucket* by Kes Gray and Garry Parsons in which a little boy finds untold treasures in an ordinary plastic bucket. Beverley Naidoo's retelling of *Aesop's Fables* allows children to explore the idea that actions have consequences; while Oliver Jeffers has produced picture books like *The Great Paper Caper* and *The Incredible Book Eating Boy* that explore moral dilemnas.

Poetry

Caterpillars

by Aileen Fisher

What do caterpillars do?
Nothing much but chew and chew.

What do caterpillars know?
Nothing much but how to grow.

They just eat what by and by
will make them be a butterfly,

But that is more than I can do
however much I chew and chew.

Learn more about how caterpillars grow into butterflies on page 296.

Hurt No Living Thing

by Christina Rossetti

Hurt no living thing:
Ladybird, nor butterfly,
Nor moth with dusty wing,
Nor cricket chirping cheerily,
Nor grasshopper so light of leap,
Nor dancing gnat, nor beetle fat,
Nor harmless worms that creep.

Bee! I'm Expecting You!

by Emily Dickinson

Bee! I'm expecting you!
Was saying Yesterday
To Somebody you know
That you were due –

The Frogs got Home last Week –
Are settled, and at work –
Birds, mostly back –
The Clover warm and thick –

You'll get my Letter by
The seventeenth; Reply
Or better, be with me –
Yours, Fly.

What season do you think it is in this poem? See more on pages 285–288, and read more about bees on pages 299–301.

The Night Before Christmas

**Originally called *A Visit from St Nicholas*
by Clement C. Moore**

'Twas the night before Christmas, when all through the house
Not a creature was stirring, not even a mouse.
The stockings were hung by the chimney with care,
In hopes that St Nicholas soon would be there.

The children were nestled all snug in their beds,
While visions of sugar-plums danced in their heads.
And Mamma in her 'kerchief, and I in my cap,
Had just settled our brains for a long winter's nap,

When out on the lawn there arose such a clatter,
I sprang from my bed to see what was the matter.
Away to the window I flew like a flash,
Tore open the shutters and threw up the sash.

The moon on the breast of the new fallen snow,
Gave the lustre of midday to objects below.
When what to my wondering eyes should appear,
But a miniature sleigh and eight tiny reindeer.

With a little old driver so lively and quick,
I knew in a moment it must be St Nick.
More rapid than eagles his coursers they came,
And he whistled, and shouted, and called them by name:

'Now, Dasher! Now, Dancer! Now, Prancer and Vixen!
On, Comet! On, Cupid! On Donder and Blitzen!
To the top of the porch! To the top of the wall!
Now dash away! Dash away! Dash away all!'

As dry leaves that before the wild hurricane fly,
When they meet with an obstacle, mount to the sky,
So up to the housetop the coursers they flew,
With a sleigh full of toys and St Nicholas, too.

And then, in a twinkling, I heard on the roof
The prancing and pawing of each little hoof.
As I drew in my head and was turning around...
Down the chimney St Nicholas came with a bound!

He was dressed all in fur from his head to his foot,
And his clothes were all tarnished with ashes and soot;
A bundle of toys he had flung on his back,
And he looked like a pedlar just opening his pack.

His eyes – how they twinkled, his dimples how merry!
His cheeks were like roses, his nose like a cherry!
His droll little mouth was drawn up like a bow,
And the beard on his chin was as white as the snow.

The stump of a pipe he held tight in his teeth,
And the smoke it encircled his head like a wreath.
He had a broad face and a little round belly,
That shook when he laughed like a bowl full of jelly.

St Nicholas is also known as Santa Claus or Father Christmas. There is a film about him called *Miracle on 34th Street* that you can watch on DVD.

He was chubby and plump, a right jolly old elf,
And I laughed when I saw him in spite of myself!
A wink of his eye and a twist of his head
Soon gave me to know I had nothing to dread.

He spoke not a word, but went straight to his work,
And filled all the stockings – then turned with a jerk...
And laying his finger aside of his nose,
And giving a nod, up the chimney he rose!

He sprang to his sleigh, to his team gave a whistle,
And away they all flew like the down of a thistle.
But I heard him exclaim, 'ere he drove out of sight...
'Happy Christmas to all, and to all a good night!'

Discovery

by Harry Behn

In a puddle left from last week's rain,
A friend of mine whose name is Joe
Caught a tadpole, and showed me where
Its froggy legs were beginning to grow.

Then we turned over a musty log,
With lichens on it in a row,
And found some fiddleheads of ferns
Uncoiling out of the moss below.

We hunted around, and saw the first
Jack-in-the-pulpits beginning to show,
And even discovered under a rock
Where spotted salamanders go.

I learned all this one morning from Joe,
But how much more there is to know!

Caracola/Conch Shell

**by Federico García Lorca;
translated by Will Kirkland**

They have brought me a conch shell.

Within it sings
a map sized sea.
My heart
fills up with water
and little fish
of shadow and silver.

They have brought me a conch shell.

The Answer
by Allan Ahlberg

We're looking for the answer,
We're searching high and low,
We're doing what we can, Sir –
We really want to know.

We've ransacked desk and drawer, Sir,
Basket, bowl and bin.
We've scrutinised the floor, Sir –
You couldn't hide a pin.

We've been out in the street, Sir;
We've been up on the roof.
And even when we cheat, Sir,
This question's answer-proof.

We've cudgelled all our brains, Sir,
And still we're in the dark.
Got nothing for our pains, Sir,
Except a question mark.

We've thought ourselves to death, Sir,
With 'What?' and 'Where?' and 'Who?'
We're beat and out of breath, Sir,
So how about a clue?

The teacher tapped his forehead.
At last! The children cried.
The answer, Sir's, in your head…
What a perfect place to hide.

Something Told the Wild Geese

by Rachel Field

Something told the wild geese
It was time to go.
Though the fields lay golden
Something whispered, – 'Snow.'

Leaves were green and stirring,
Berries, lustre-glossed,
But beneath warm feathers
Something cautioned, – 'Frost.'

All the sagging orchards
Steamed with amber spice,
But each wild breast stiffened
At remembered ice.

Something told the wild geese
It was time to fly, –
Summer sun was on their wings,
Winter in their cry.

Learn more about the cycle of the seasons starting on page 285, and how certain birds migrate south.

Five Friendly Farmers

Five friendly farmers

Wake up with the sun,

For it is early morning

And the chores must be done.

The first friendly farmer

Goes to milk the cow.

The second friendly farmer

Thought he'd better plough.

The third friendly farmer

Feeds the hungry hens.

The fourth friendly farmer

Puts the piggies in their pens.

The fifth friendly farmer

Picks the ripe corn.

And waves to the neighbour

When he blows his horn.

When the work is finished

And the evening sky is red

Five tired farmers

Tumble into bed!

Rickety Train Ride

by Tony Mitton

I'm taking the train to Ricketywick.

Clickety clickety clack.

I'm sat in my seat.

With a sandwich to eat.

As I travel the trickety track.

It's an ever so rickety trickety train,

And I honestly thickety think.

That before it arrives

At the end of the line

It will tip up my drippety drink.

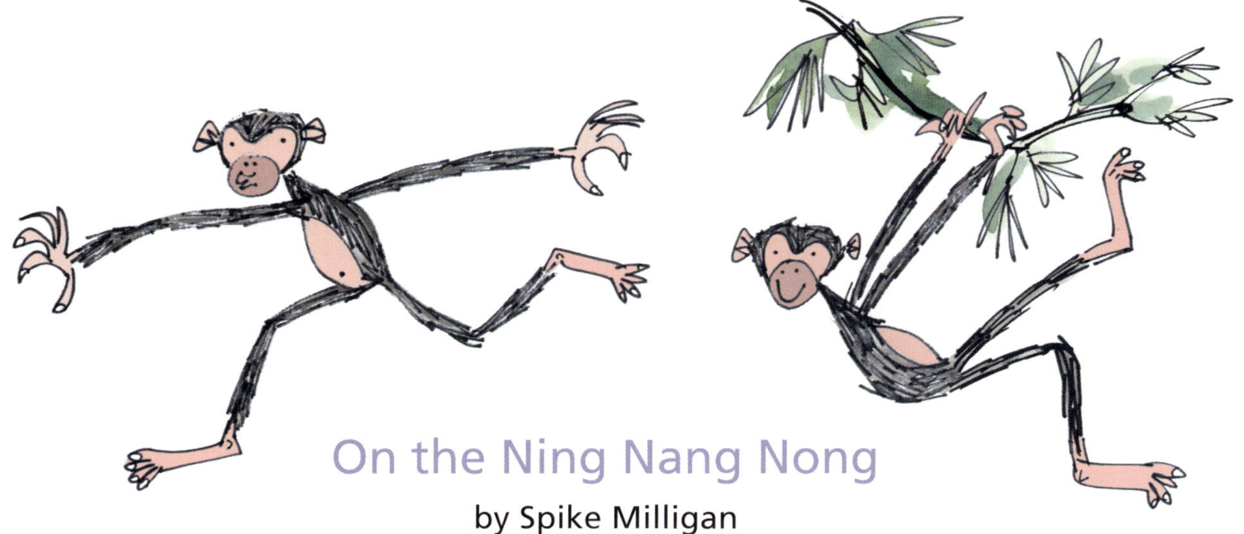

On the Ning Nang Nong

by Spike Milligan

On the Ning Nang Nong

Where the cows go Bong!

and the monkeys all say BOO!

There's a Nong Nang Ning

Where the trees go Ping!

And the tea pots jibber jabber joo.

On the Nong Ning Nang

All the mice go Clang

And you just can't catch 'em when they do!

So it's Ning Nang Nong

Cows go Bong!

Nong Nang Ning

Trees go Ping

Nong Ning Nang

The mice go Clang

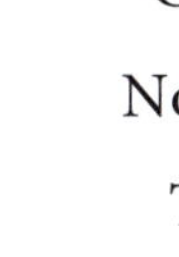

What a noisy place to belong

is the Ning Nang Ning Nang Nong!!

Edward Lear, an English artist and writer, was a master of the kind of humorous poem called a limerick. Edward Lear himself has illustrated the limericks below. A limerick has five lines: the first two lines rhyme, then the next two lines rhyme and the last line rhymes with the first two lines. The first line of a limerick often begins 'There was a...' or 'There once was a...'. Limericks are fun to read aloud, and to make up: try it!

There Was an Old Man with a Beard

by Edward Lear

There was an Old Man with a beard,

Who said, 'It is just as I feared! –

Two Owls and a Hen,

Four Larks and a Wren,

Have all built their nests in my beard!'

There Is a Young Lady, Whose Nose

by Edward Lear

There is a young lady, whose nose,

Continually prospers and grows;

When it grew out of sight,

She exclaimed in a fright,

'Oh! Farewell to the end of my nose!'

Stories

The Fisherman and His Wife

(A tale from the Brothers Grimm)

There was once a fisherman who lived with his wife in a little old run-down hut by the sea. Every day he went down to the sea to fish. One day, as he sat looking into the clear, shining water, he felt a strong tug on his line. He pulled and pulled with all his might, and out flopped a great big fish.

The fish spoke. 'Please let me go,' said the fish. 'I am not an ordinary fish but an enchanted prince. Put me back in the water and let me live.'

'Swim away!' said the fisherman. 'I would not eat a fish that can talk!'

Then the fisherman went back to his wife in the little old run-down hut. He told her about the fish that could talk. She said: 'You foolish man, that was a magic fish! Go back and ask him to change this hut into a pretty cottage.' The fisherman did not want to go, but his wife demanded it. So he walked slowly back to the sea. The water was no longer clear and shining but dull and green. The fisherman called:

Hear me, please, o magic fish,
My wife has sent me with a wish.

The fish swam up and asked: 'What do you want?'

'My wife wishes to live in a pretty cottage,' said the fisherman.

'Go home,' said the fish. 'She has her cottage.'

The fisherman went home.

Sure enough, there was his wife standing in the yard of a pretty cottage. 'Now you shall be happy!' said the fisherman. And she was – for about a week. Then the wife said: 'Husband, I am tired of this tiny little cottage. I want to live in a big castle built of stone. Go and ask the fish to give us a castle.'

The fisherman walked slowly to the sea. The water had turned from dull green to dark purple and grey. The fisherman called:

> *Hear me, please, o magic fish,*
> *My wife has sent me with a wish.*

The fish swam up. The fisherman said:
'My wife wishes to live in a big castle built of stone.'

'Go home,' said the fish. 'You will find her in a castle.'

When the fisherman got back, he could hardly believe his eyes. There stood a big castle built of stone. Inside, he saw servants and golden chairs and tables heaped with delicious foods.

'Now, indeed, you will be happy,' said the fisherman to his wife.

And she was – until the next morning.

As the sun rose, the fisherman's wife poked him and said: 'Husband, get up. Go to the fish at once and tell him that I wish to be queen of all the land.'

'Alas!' cried the fisherman. 'The fish cannot do that!'

'Go and ask him,' said his wife.

So the sad fisherman walked to the sea. The water was black and the waves roared and crashed. The fisherman called:

> *Hear me, please, o magic fish,*
> *My wife has sent me with a wish.*

The fish swam up and asked: 'Now what does she want?'

With his head hung low, the fisherman said: 'My wife wishes to be queen of all the land.'

'Go home,' said the fish. 'She is already queen.'

The fisherman hurried home and found his wife sitting on a high throne of gold and diamonds. She wore a long silk dress and a golden crown. Servants and ladies hurried here and there to do whatever she wished.

'Now,' said the fisherman, 'you must be truly happy.'

And she was – until that evening. As the moon began to rise in the sky, the wife said, 'Husband, I order you to go to the fish and tell him to give me the power to make the sun and the moon rise and set whenever I choose.'

The fisherman walked back to the sea. Thunder roared and lightning flashed. Huge dark waves crashed around him. The fisherman had to shout:

Hear me, please, o magic fish,
My wife has sent me with a wish.

The fish swam up and asked: 'What does she want?'

The fisherman replied: 'My wife wants the power to make the sun and the moon rise and set whenever she chooses.' The fish only said: 'Go home.' And so he did. And there he found his wife sitting in the little, old, run-down hut. And there they live, to this very day.

> Does this story remind you of 'It Could Always Be Worse' from Year 2?

Talk

(Retold by Harold Courlander and George Herzog)

'Talk' is a folktale from the Ashanti people (also called Asante) who live in West Africa, in what is now the country of Ghana. Many Ashanti are farmers, and their major crops include cacao (a main ingredient in chocolate) and, as you'll see in the story, yams. To appreciate the end of this story, it may help to know about an Ashanti tradition: almost every Ashanti man and woman once owned a carved wooden stool. Besides being useful, the stool, according to tradition, embodied the owner's spirit.

Once, not far from the city of Accra on the Gulf of Guinea, a country man went out to his garden to dig up some yams to take to market. While he was digging, one of the yams said to him:

'Well, at last you're here. You never weeded me, but now you come around with your digging stick. Go away and leave me alone!'

The farmer turned around and looked at his cow in amazement. The cow was chewing her cud and looking at him.

'Did you say something?' he asked.

The cow kept on chewing and said nothing, but the man's dog spoke up.

'It wasn't the cow who spoke to you,' the dog said. 'It was the yam. The yam said leave him alone.'

The man became angry because his dog had never talked before, and he didn't like his tone besides. So he took his knife and cut a branch from a palm tree to whip his dog. Just then the palm tree said:

'Put that branch down!'

The man was getting very upset about the way things were going, and he started to throw the palm branch away, but the palm branch said:

'Man, put me down softly!'

He put the branch down gently on a stone, and the stone said:

'Hey, take that thing off me!'

This was enough and the frightened farmer started to run for his village. On the way he met a fisherman going the other way carrying a fish trap on his head.

'What's the hurry?' the fisherman asked.

'My yam said: "Leave me alone!" Then the dog said: "Listen to what the yam says!" When I went to whip the dog with a palm branch the tree said: "Put that branch down!" Then the palm branch said: "Do it softly!" Then the stone said: "Take that thing off me!"'

'Is that all?' the man with the fish trap asked. 'Is that so frightening?'

'Well,' the man's fish trap said, 'did he take it off the stone?'

'Wah!' the fisherman shouted. He threw the fish trap on the ground and began to run with the farmer, and on the trail they met a weaver with a bundle of cloth on his head.

'Where are you going in such a rush?' he asked them.

'My yam said: "Leave me alone!"' the farmer said. 'The dog said: "Listen to what the yam says!" The tree said: "Put that branch down!" The branch said: "Do it softly!" And the stone said: "Take that thing off me!"'

'And then,' the fisherman continued, 'the fish trap said: "Did he take it off?"'

'That's nothing to get excited about,' the weaver said, 'no reason at all.'

'Oh yes it is,' his bundle of cloth said. 'If it happened to you, you'd run too!'

'Wah!' the weaver shouted. He threw his bundle on the trail and started running with the other men. They came panting to the ford in the river and found a man bathing. 'Are you chasing a gazelle?' he asked them. The first man said breathlessly: 'My yam talked at me and it said: "Leave me alone!" And my dog said: "Listen to your yam!" And, when I cut myself a branch, the tree said: "Put that branch down!" And the branch said: "Do it softly!" And the stone said: "Take that thing off me!"'

The fisherman panted: 'And my trap said: "Did he?"'

The weaver wheezed: 'My cloth spoke too!'

'Is that why you're running?' the man in the river asked.

'Well, wouldn't you run if you were in their position?' the river said.

The man jumped out of the water and began to run with the others. They ran down the main street of the village to the house of the chief. The chief's servants brought his stool out, and he came and sat on it to listen to their complaints. The men began to recite their troubles.

'I went out to my garden to dig yams,' the farmer said, waving his arms. 'Then everything began to talk! My yam said: "Leave me alone!" My dog said: "Pay attention to your yam!" The tree said: "Put that branch down!" The branch said: "Do it softly!" And the stone said: "Take it off me!"'

'And my fish trap asked: "Well, did he take it off?"' the fisherman said.

'And my cloth said: "You'd run too!"' the weaver said.

'And the river said the same,' the bather said hoarsely.

The chief listened to them patiently, but he couldn't refrain from scowling.

'Now this is really a wild story,' he said at last. 'You'd better all go back to your work before I punish you for disturbing the peace.' So the men went away, and the chief shook his head and mumbled to himself: 'Nonsense like that upsets the community.'

'Fantastic, isn't it?' his stool said. 'Imagine, a talking yam!'

The Emperor's New Clothes

(Based on the story by Hans Christian Andersen)

There was once an emperor who loved fine clothes. He had a different coat for every hour of the day. He loved to walk about and show off his fancy outfits.

One day two strangers arrived in town. They were thieves but they said they were weavers. They told the emperor they could weave the most beautiful cloth in the world. They told him it was a magic cloth, because only the most intelligent people could see it.

The emperor gave them a lot of money and told them to begin weaving the magic cloth right away. Day and night the two men pretended to be weaving. But they had nothing at all on their looms.

The emperor grew curious to see the cloth. But then he remembered that only intelligent people could see it. What if he could not see it? Just to be safe, he sent his prime minister instead.

The prime minister found the two men hard at work. 'Do you like the cloth?' they asked. 'Isn't it beautiful?' The prime minister did not dare to admit that he could not see any cloth. That would mean he was stupid! So he pretended to see the cloth. He said it was beautiful.

Now the emperor went to look for himself. After all, if his prime minister had seen the cloth, surely he could see it, too. But the emperor saw nothing on the looms. 'This is terrible!' he thought. 'Am I stupid?' But out loud he said: 'It is magnificent!' He told the weavers to make him a new suit out of that cloth as soon as possible.

For days, the dishonest weavers pretended to cut and sew their invisible cloth. All those who saw them pretended to admire their work, for they did not wish to appear stupid.

At last the day came for the emperor to wear his new clothes in public. In his dressing room, the emperor took off his clothes, and the weavers pretended to help him put on the make-believe clothes. The emperor looked at himself in the mirror.

'How handsome you look, your majesty!' said the cunning weavers.

The emperor stepped out of the palace, followed by many courtiers and servants. The streets were lined with great crowds. Everyone said: 'The emperor's new clothes are lovely! How well they fit!' No one would admit he or she could see nothing, for no one wanted to appear stupid.

But then a little child cried out: 'He hasn't got anything on!'

A hush fell over the crowd. Then everyone began to whisper: 'The child is right. The emperor isn't wearing a thing!' Then people began to giggle and laugh as they cried out: 'He hasn't got anything on!'

At last the emperor knew he had been tricked. He tried to march back in to the palace as proudly as ever. But he was blushing from head to toe, as everyone could plainly see.

The Magic Paintbrush

(A folktale from China)

Once upon a time, long ago in the land of China, there lived a poor orphan named Ma Liang. He had no one to care for him or protect him. So, to make a living, he gathered bundles of firewood to sell. But what he really wanted to do, more than anything else in the world, was paint. Ma Liang was so poor, however, that he could not buy even a single paintbrush.

One day, as Ma Liang passed by the village school, he saw the children busily painting pictures. 'Please, sir,' said Ma Liang to the teacher, 'I would like to paint, but I have no brush. Will you lend me one?'

'What!' cried the teacher. 'You are only a little beggar boy. Go away!'

'I may be poor,' said Ma Liang, 'but I will learn to paint!'

The next time he went to gather firewood, Ma Liang used a twig to draw birds on the ground. When he came to a stream, he dipped his hand in the water and used his wet finger to draw a fish on the rocks. That night, he used a piece of burned wood to draw animals and flowers.

Every day Ma Liang found time to make more pictures.

People began to notice. 'How lifelike the boy's pictures look!' they said. 'That bird he has drawn looks as though it's ready to fly away. You can almost hear it sing!'

Ma Liang enjoyed hearing the people's praise, but still he thought: 'If only I had a paintbrush!'

One night, after Ma Liang had worked hard all day, he fell into a deep sleep. In a dream, he saw an old man with a long white beard and a kind face. The old man held something in his hand. 'Take this,' he said to Ma Liang. 'It is a magic paintbrush. Use it with care.'

When Ma Liang awoke, he found his fingers wrapped around a paintbrush. 'Am I still dreaming?' he wondered. Quickly he got up and painted a bird. The picture flapped its wings and flew away!

He painted a deer. As soon as he had put the last spot on the animal's coat, it brushed its nose against Ma Liang and then ran into the woods.

'It is a magic brush!' said Ma Liang. He ran to where his poor friends lived. He painted toys for the children. He painted cows and tools for the farmers. He painted bowls full of food for the hungry.

No good thing can remain a secret forever. Soon, news of Ma Liang and the magic paintbrush reached the ears of the greedy emperor. 'Bring me that boy and his brush!' the emperor commanded. His soldiers found Ma Liang and brought him back to the palace.

With a scowl, the emperor looked at Ma Liang. 'Paint me a dragon!' he yelled. Ma Liang began to paint. But instead of painting a lucky dragon, he painted a slimy toad that hopped right onto the emperor's head!

'Stupid boy!' said the emperor. 'You will regret that!' He grabbed the magic paintbrush and ordered his soldiers to throw Ma Liang in jail.

Then the emperor called for his royal painter. 'Take this brush and paint me a mountain of gold,' he commanded. But when the royal painter finished the picture, all the gold turned into rocks.

'So,' said the emperor, 'this brush will only work for the boy. Bring him to me!' Ma Liang was brought to the emperor. 'If you will paint for me,' said the emperor, 'I will give you gold and silver, fine clothes, a new house, and all the food and drink you want.'

Ma Liang pretended to agree. 'What do you want me to paint?' he asked.

'Paint me a tree that has gold coins for leaves!' said the emperor with greed in his eyes.

Ma Liang took the magic paintbrush and began to paint. He painted many blue waves, and soon the emperor saw an ocean before him.

'That is not what I told you to paint!' he barked.

But Ma Liang just kept painting. In the ocean he painted an island. And on that island he painted a tree with gold coins for leaves. 'Yes, yes, that's more like it,' said the emperor.

'Now, quickly, paint me a boat so that I can get to the island.'

Ma Liang painted a big sailing boat. The emperor went on board with many of his highest officials. Ma Liang painted a few lines and a gentle breeze began to blow. The sailing boat moved slowly toward the island.

'Faster! Faster!' shouted the emperor. Ma Liang painted a big curving stroke, and a strong wind began to blow. 'That's enough wind!' shouted the emperor. But Ma Liang kept painting. He painted a storm, and the waves got higher and higher, tossing the boat like a little cork on the water. Then the waves broke the boat to pieces. The emperor and his officials were washed up on the shore of the island, with no way to get back to the palace.

And as for Ma Liang, people say that for many years, he went from village to village, using his magic paintbrush to help the poor wherever he went.

> Visit your local library to discover wonderful traditional tales such as Mary Hoffman's collection of animal stories from around the world called *A Twist in the Tale* (Frances Lincoln). *The Emperor's New Clothes* translated by Naomi Lewis with beautiful illustrations by Angela Barrett is a treat (Walker), as is Hugh Lupton's retelling of the Hebridean folktale *Pirican Pic and Pirican Mor* (Barefoot).

A Christmas Carol

(Based on the story by Charles Dickens)

Long ago, in the great old City of London, there lived a merchant named Ebenezer Scrooge. Scrooge was very rich and he was very mean. He loved money and he cared nothing for people. Money was his only source of happiness and he pitied other people who could be content with little. He thought them fools. He particularly hated the season of Christmas, when he saw people made happy by exchanging presents and sharing meals together. It was all a waste of time to Scrooge. He just wanted to get on with making money.

On a cold, bleak Christmas Eve, when the fog swirled thick in the streets of old London, Scrooge's poor clerk, Bob Cratchit, sat keeping his ledgers in the small outer office, shivering beside a fire that had only one piece of coal in it.

Scrooge frowned at Bob Cratchit and growled: 'I suppose you'll be wanting the whole day off tomorrow.'

'Yes sir,' the clerk replied meekly. 'If it's convenient.'

'It's not convenient,' said Scrooge. 'Be here even earlier the next morning!'

'Thank you sir,' said Bob Cratchit. 'And a Merry Christmas to you, sir.'

'Christmas! Bah, humbug!' grumbled Scrooge as he left the office.

Through the frost and fog, he made his way home. As he approached his front door, he stopped and stared. Where he expected to see the door knocker, he saw a face! It was the face of his old business partner, Jacob Marley. But Marley had been dead now for seven years. Scrooge blinked his eyes, and the face vanished.

'Bah, humbug!' said Scrooge as he walked in. He put on his dressing gown and slippers and made himself a bowl of thin porridge for his dinner. As he sat eating it, he heard a great noise. There was a howling of wind through the house, then a terrible clanking sound of chains being dragged up the staircase and towards the room he was sitting in. Suddenly, he saw a man – or the shade of a man – walking through the very door he had closed behind him. He recognised immediately his partner Jacob Marley – or what was left of him. He dragged behind him a long chain made of cash-boxes, keys, padlocks and account books.

'Hear me!' said the ghost of Jacob Marley. 'I wear the chain I forged in life and I can never rest. I cared only about money. And you are making your own chain now, Ebenezer. You care too much for money, and too little for your fellow man. You must change, before it is too late! There is still a chance for you to escape my fate. You will be visited by three spirits before this night is done.' Then, with a fearful groan, the ghost vanished.

'Bah, humbug,' said Scrooge, and he went to sleep in his huge and dirty old four-poster bed, with the curtains drawn tight around him.

When the clock struck one, a pale hand drew back the curtain that hung around Scrooge's bed. It was the first spirit. It looked like a child but at the

same time like an old man. 'I am the Ghost of Christmas Past,' said the spirit. Then the spirit took Scrooge's hand. Together they flew through the air and back into the past. Suddenly Scrooge found himself in an old school room. All the children had gone home for the Christmas holidays – all but one. One neglected child sat at his desk. 'Why, that's me,' said Scrooge. And he sobbed as he recalled his sad, lonely childhood. Then the scene changed, and Scrooge saw himself as a young man, working as a clerk in a warehouse where he was already showing what a good businessman he was, and how much he knew about making money. He saw himself again in a small room with a beautiful young lady, who looked sad. Scrooge recognised her as the love of his life. They had fallen in love when they were very young, and promised to marry each other. But she had come to tell him that she knew he only cared for money now, and not for her at all. She would not hold him to his promise.

Scrooge had a dim sense of being back in his bed again. He felt tired and sad. He heard the clock striking and saw a bright light shining all around the door to his bedroom. He went into the next room and he scarcely recognised it as a room in his own house. It was full of delicious food and hung with beautiful Christmas decorations. Seated on a great heap of roast turkeys, pies, apples, oranges, cakes and puddings was a large man wearing a loose robe of green, trimmed with white fur, and a crown of holly.

'I am the Ghost of Christmas Present,' said the spirit. 'Touch my robe!' Scrooge did so and found himself moving through the busy city streets on a Christmas morning. He saw

smiling faces and heard people wishing each other a merry Christmas. As the spirit took him from house to house, they could see people enjoying their Christmas dinners. Then they came to the home of Bob Cratchit, Scrooge's clerk.

The Cratchit family was sitting down to a small turkey and a small plum pudding. Scrooge felt ashamed that he paid his clerk so little that he could not put a bigger meal on the table for his family on Christmas Day, but they seemed as happy as if they had a great feast before them. The happiest of all was the youngest child, a small, frail boy called Tiny Tim, who walked with a crutch.

Scrooge saw Bob Cratchit lift his glass and say: 'A Merry Christmas to us all, my dears!'

'And God bless us, everyone,' said Tiny Tim. Scrooge saw how Bob held his little son close by his side, as if he feared he might lose him.

'Spirit,' said Scrooge, 'tell me if Tiny Tim will live.'

'I see an empty seat,' said the spirit, 'and a crutch without an owner. If things remain as they are, the child will die.'

'Oh, no, kind Spirit!' said Scrooge. 'Say he will be spared.' But the Ghost of Christmas Present was disappearing before Scrooge's eyes. And in his place, Scrooge saw a dark, hooded phantom.

'Am I in the presence of the Ghost of Christmas Yet to Come?' asked Scrooge.

The spirit did not answer but pointed onward with its hand. Scrooge found himself in a dark house. On the bed, beneath a sheet, lay something cold, still and lifeless. Scrooge knew that it was a dead body. He wanted to pull back the sheet and see whose it was, but he didn't dare. Scrooge heard people talking outside.

'When did he die?' asked a man.

'Last night,' said another.

'It's likely to be a very cheap funeral,' said a third, 'because nobody will come!' And they all laughed in a rather cruel way.

The silent spirit spread its dark robe like a wing, and suddenly Scrooge was at Bob Cratchit's house. It was quiet. Too quiet. The noisy Cratchit children now sat still as statues in a corner. Near the wall a crutch leaned against an empty chair. Then Scrooge heard Bob Cratchit's voice. 'I am sure that we shall never forget poor Tiny Tim,' he said, and then he began to weep. 'Oh, my little, little child!'

Again the spirit waved its dark robe, and now Scrooge found himself in a graveyard choked with weeds. The spirit stood among the graves and pointed to one. Scrooge crept toward the grave. And there he read upon the stone his own name, EBENEZER SCROOGE. So his was the body on the bed!

'No, Spirit!' cried Scrooge. He clutched at the spirit's robe. 'I am not the man I was. Please tell me I may yet change what you have shown me. Tell me that these are the shadows of things that might be, not the shadows of things that must be.' The spirit began to pull away but Scrooge held on tight. 'Good Spirit,' he cried, 'I will honour Christmas in my heart, and try to keep it all the year!'

Scrooge tried to grasp the spirit's hand, but suddenly the phantom was gone. Scrooge found himself sitting in his own bed with his arms around the bedpost. Yes, the bed was his own, and the room was his own. Best of all, his life was still his own, and there was still time to make himself a better man. Scrooge ran to the window and called to a boy passing in the street: 'What's today, my fine fellow?'

'It's Christmas day, of course!' said the boy.

'I haven't missed it!' said Scrooge. Then he said to the boy: 'Do you know that big prize turkey the butcher has in his window?'

'You mean the one as big as me?' said the boy.

'A remarkable boy!' cried Scrooge. 'Yes, that's the one. Run to the shop and tell the butcher to bring it here so that I can tell him where to deliver it. If you're back in ten minutes, I'll give you a reward.'

Scrooge dressed quickly and hurried into the street. He met the butcher, carrying the huge turkey that had been in his shop window. 'I want you to take this to the house of my clerk, Bob Cratchit,' said Scrooge. 'Here is his address,' he said, writing it on a piece of paper. 'And as it's rather a long way to go, you can take a cab at my expense!'

The butcher was astonished, as no one had ever heard Scrooge talk like this. 'Merry Christmas!' Scrooge cried to everyone he met. The sight of people hurrying to and fro in search of their families and friends on Christmas morning made him so happy that he seemed to glow. 'Merry Christmas!' he said to everyone, and they wished him a Merry Christmas in return.

The next morning, Scrooge arrived early at his office, before Bob Cratchit. When Bob entered, Scrooge tried very hard to put on his old voice and growled, 'Well, what do you mean by coming in eighteen-and-a-half minutes late?'

'I am very sorry, sir,' said Bob Cratchit.

'I am not going to stand for that sort of thing any longer!' barked Scrooge. 'And therefore,' he said, as he leaped down from his stool, 'I am going to raise your salary! A Merry Christmas to you, Bob Cratchit!'

From then on, Scrooge helped Bob Cratchit's family, and became like a second father to Tiny Tim, who did not die. Ebenezer Scrooge became as good a friend, as good a master, and as good a man as ever the good old City of London knew. And it was always said of him that he knew how to keep Christmas as well as anyone alive. May that be truly said of all of us. And, as Tiny Tim said: 'God bless us, every one!'

A Christmas Carol was one of the most popular books written by Charles Dickens, and it has been made into a film many times over. You can watch DVDs of some of the these films, such as the one with Alastair Sim which is just called *Scrooge* (Simply Media) or the one with Patrick Stewart which is called *A Christmas Carol* (Boulevard Entertainments). There is even a musical version with Albert Finney called *Scrooge* (Paramount Home Entertainment).

Please Look After This Bear

(From *A Bear Called Paddington* by Michael Bond)

Mr and Mrs Brown first met Paddington on a railway platform. In fact, that was how he came to have such an unusual name for a bear, for Paddington was the name of the station.

The Browns were there to meet their daughter Judy, who was coming home from school for the holidays. It was a warm summer day and the station was crowded with people on their way to the seaside. Trains were humming, loudspeakers blaring, porters rushing about shouting at one another, and altogether there was so much noise that Mr Brown, who saw him first, had to tell his wife several times before she understood.

'A bear? On Paddington station?' Mrs Brown looked at her husband in amazement. 'Don't be silly, Henry. There can't be!'

Mr Brown adjusted his glasses. 'But there is,' he insisted. 'I distinctly saw it. Over there – near the bicycle rack. It was wearing a funny kind of hat.'

Without waiting for a reply he caught hold of his wife's arm and pushed her through the crowd, round a trolley laden with chocolate and cups of tea, past a bookstall, and through a gap in a pile of suitcases towards the Lost Property Office.

'There you are,' he announced triumphantly, pointing towards a dark corner, 'I told you so!'

Mrs Brown followed the direction of his arm and dimly made out a small furry object in the shadows. It seemed to be sitting on some kind of suitcase and around its neck there was a label with some writing on it. The suitcase was old and battered, and on the side, in large letters, were the words WANTED ON VOYAGE.

Mrs Brown clutched at her husband. 'Why, Henry,' she exclaimed. 'I believe you were right after all. It is a bear!'

She peered at it more closely. It seemed a very unusual kind of bear. It was brown in colour, a rather dirty brown, and it was wearing a most odd-looking hat, with a wide brim, just as Mr Brown had said. From beneath the brim two large, round eyes stared back at her.

Seeing that something was expected of it, the bear stood up and politely raised its hat, revealing two black ears. 'Good afternoon,' it said, in a small, clear voice.

'Er… good afternoon,' replied Mr Brown, doubtfully. There was a moment of silence.

The bear looked at them inquiringly. 'Can I help you?'

Mr Brown looked rather embarrassed. 'Well… no. Er… as a matter of fact, we were wondering if we could help you.'

Mrs Brown bent down. 'You're a very small bear,' she said.

The bear puffed out its chest. 'I'm a very rare sort of bear,' he replied importantly. 'There aren't many of us left where I come from.'

'And where is that?' asked Mrs Brown.

The bear looked round carefully before replying. 'Darkest Peru. I'm not really supposed to be here at all. I'm a stowaway!'

'A stowaway?' Mr Brown lowered his voice and looked anxiously over his shoulder. He almost expected to see a policeman standing behind him with a notebook and pencil, taking everything down.

'Yes,' said the bear. 'I emigrated, you know.' A sad expression came into its eyes. 'I used to live with my Aunt Lucy in Peru, but she had to go into a home for retired bears.'

'You don't mean to say you've come all the way from South America by yourself?' exclaimed Mrs Brown.

The bear nodded. 'Aunt Lucy always said she wanted me to emigrate when I was old enough. That's why she taught me to speak English.'

'But whatever did you do for food?' asked Mr Brown. 'You must be starving.'

Bending down, the bear unlocked the suitcase with a small key, which it also had round its neck, and brought out an almost empty glass jar. 'I ate marmalade. And I lived in a lifeboat.'

'But what are you going to do now?' said Mr Brown. 'You can't just sit on Paddington station waiting for something to happen.'

'Oh, I shall be all right… I expect.' The bear bent down to do up its case again. As he did so Mrs Brown caught a glimpse of the writing on the label. It said, simply, PLEASE LOOK AFTER THIS BEAR. THANK YOU.

She turned appealingly to her husband. 'Oh, Henry, what shall we do? We can't just leave him here. There's no knowing what might happen to him. London's such a big place when you've nowhere to go. Can't he come and stay with us for a few days?'

Mr Brown hesitated. 'But Mary, dear, we can't take him… not just like that. After all…'

'After all, what?' Mrs Brown's voice had a firm note to it. She looked down at the bear. 'He is rather sweet. And he'd be such company for Jonathan and Judy. Even if it's only for a little while. They'd never forgive us if they knew you'd left him here.'

'It all seems highly irregular,' said Mr Brown, doubtfully. 'I'm sure there's a law about it.' He bent down. 'Would you like to come and stay with us?' he asked. 'That is,' he added hastily, not wishing to offend the bear, 'if you've nothing else planned.'

The bear jumped and his hat nearly fell off with excitement. 'Oooh, yes please. I should like that very much. I've nowhere to go and everyone seems in such a hurry.'

'Well, that's settled then,' said Mrs Brown, before her husband could change his mind. 'And you can have marmalade for breakfast every morning, and – ' she tried hard to think of something else that bears might like.

'Every morning?' The bear looked as if it could hardly believe its ears. 'I only had it on special occasions at home. Marmalade's very expensive in Darkest Peru.'

'Then you shall have it every morning starting tomorrow,' continued Mrs Brown. 'And honey on Sunday.'

A worried expression came over the bear's face. 'Will it cost very much?' he asked. 'You see, I haven't very much money.'

'Of course not. We wouldn't dream of charging you anything. We shall expect you to be one of the family, shan't we, Henry?' Mrs Brown looked at her husband for support.

'Of course,' said Mr Brown. 'By the way,' he added, 'if you are coming home with us you'd better know our names. This is Mrs Brown and I'm Mr Brown.'

The bear raised its hat politely – twice. 'I haven't really got a name,' he said. 'Only a Peruvian one which no one can understand.'

'Then we'd better give you an English one,' said Mrs Brown. 'It'll make things much easier.' She looked round the station for inspiration. 'It ought to be something special,' she said thoughtfully. As she spoke an engine standing in one of the platforms gave a loud wail and the train began to move. 'I know what!' she exclaimed. 'We found you on Paddington station so we'll call you Paddington!'

'Paddington!' The bear repeated it several times to make sure. 'It seems a very long name.'

'Quite distinguished,' said Mr Brown. 'Yes, I like Paddington as a name. Paddington it shall be.'

This is the beginning of a book called A Bear Called Paddington. *The book was such a success that Michael Bond wrote many more books about the friendly little bear from Darkest Peru. They have been turned into television programmes and you can watch them on DVD, as well as reading the books yourself.*

How the Camel Got His Hump

by Rudyard Kipling

PARENTS: Like all of Kipling's humorous *Just So Stories,* this tale comes alive when read aloud. Rudyard Kipling drew the illustrations himself.

In the beginning of years, when the world was so new-and-all, and the Animals were just beginning to work for Man, there was a Camel, and he lived in the middle of a Howling Desert because he did not want to work; and besides, he was a Howler himself. So he ate sticks and thorns and tamarisks and milkweed and prickles, most 'scruciating idle; and when anybody spoke to him he said 'Humph!' Just 'Humph!' and no more.

Presently the Horse came to him on Monday morning, with a saddle on his back and a bit in his mouth, and said:

'Camel, O Camel, come out and trot like the rest of us.'

'Humph!' said the Camel and the Horse went away and told the Man.

Presently the Dog came to him, with a stick in his mouth, and said: 'Camel, O Camel, come and fetch and carry like the rest of us.'

'Humph!' said the Camel; and the Dog went away and told the Man.

Presently the Ox came to him with the yoke on his neck and said: 'Camel, O Camel, come and plough like the rest of us.'

'Humph!' said the Camel; and the Ox went away and told the Man.

At the end of the day the Man called the Horse and the Dog and the Ox together, and said: 'Three, O Three, I'm very sorry for you (with the world so new-and-all); but that Humph-thing in the Desert can't work, or he would be here by now, so I am going to leave him alone, and you must work double-time to make up for it.'

That made the Three very angry (with the world so new-and-all), and they held a *palaver* and an *indaba,* and a *punchayet* and a *pow-wow*[1] on the edge of the Desert; and the Camel came chewing milkweed most 'scruciating idle, and laughed at them. Then he said 'Humph!' and went away again.

Presently there came along the Djinn [jin][2] in charge of All Deserts, rolling in a cloud of dust (Djinns always travel that way because it is Magic), and he stopped to palaver and pow-wow with the Three.

'Djinn of All Deserts,' said the Horse, 'is it right for anyone to be idle, with the world so new-and-all?'

'Certainly not,' said the Djinn.

'Well,' said the Horse, 'there's a thing in the middle of your Howling Desert (and he's a Howler himself) with a long neck and long legs, and he hasn't done a stroke of work since Monday morning. He won't trot.'

'Whew!' said the Djinn, whistling, 'that's my Camel, for all the gold in Arabia! What does he say about it?'

'He says "Humph!"' said the Dog, 'and he won't fetch and carry.'

'Does he say anything else?'

'Only "Humph!" and he won't plough,' said the Ox.

'Very good,' said the Djinn. 'I'll "humph" him if you will kindly wait a minute.'

---

[1] These words all mean a conference or discussion.
[2] A djinn is a genie or magical spirit.

The Djinn rolled himself up in his dust cloak, and took a bearing across the desert, and found the Camel most 'scruciatingly idle, looking at his own reflection in a pool of water.

'My long and bubbling friend,' said the Djinn, 'what's this I hear of your doing no work, with the world so new-and-all?'

'Humph!' said the Camel.

The Djinn sat down, with his chin in his hand, and began to think a Great Magic, while the Camel looked at his own reflection in the pool of water.

'You've given the Three extra work ever since Monday morning, all on account of your 'scruciating idleness,' said the Djinn; and he went on thinking Magics, with his chin in his hand.

'Humph!' said the Camel.

'I shouldn't say that again if I were you,' said the Djinn; 'you might say it once too often.'

And the Camel said 'Humph' again; but no sooner had he said it than he saw his back, that he was so proud of, puffing up and puffing up with a great big lolloping humph.

'Do you see that?' said the Djinn. 'That's your own humph that you've brought upon yourself by not working. Today is Thursday, and you've done no work since Monday, when the work began. Now you are going to work.'

'How can I,' said the Camel, 'with this humph on my back?'

'That's made a-purpose,' said the Djinn, 'all because you missed those three days. You will be able to work now for three days without eating, because you can live on your humph; and don't you ever say I never did anything for you. Come out of the Desert and go to the Three, and behave. Humph yourself!'

And the Camel humphed himself, humph and all, and went away to join the Three. And from that day to this the Camel always wears a humph (we call it 'hump' now, not to hurt his feelings); but he has never yet caught up with the three days that he missed at the beginning of the world, and he has never yet learned how to behave.

Here is the picture of the Djinn in charge of All Deserts guiding the Magic with his magic fan. The camel is eating a twig of acacia, and he has just finished saying 'Humph!' once too often (the Djinn told him he would) and so the Humph is coming. The long towelly-thing growing out of the thing like an onion is the Magic, and you can see the Humph on its shoulder. The Humph fits on the flat part of the Camel's back. The Camel is too busy looking at its own beautiful self in the pool of water to know what is going to happen to him.

Underneath the truly picture is a picture of the world-so-new-and-all. There are two smoky volcanoes in it, some other mountains and some stones and a lake, as well as a Noah's Ark. I couldn't draw all the deserts that the Djinn was in charge of, so I only drew one, but it is a most deserty desert.

We learned a bit about deserts in Year 2.

Beauty and the Beast

Once upon a time there lived a very rich merchant with his three daughters. But all at once the merchant lost his fortune, and nothing remained but a little cottage in the woods, far from town. He told his daughters they would have to move there and work hard and live simply. The older daughters complained bitterly, but the youngest daughter, who was called Beauty, tried to make the best of things.

One day, many months later, the merchant heard that one of his ships, which he had thought lost, had landed and was full of many valuable things. As he prepared to make the long trip to claim his goods, he asked his daughters what he might bring them. The older two asked for fancy gowns and jewels. But Beauty said: 'Dear father, please bring me a rose, for I have not seen one since we came here, and I love them so much.'

When the merchant finally reached his ship, he found that all his goods had been stolen. So he turned toward home, as poor as when he started his journey.

Not far from home, the snow began to fall and the wind blew so hard it almost knocked the merchant off his horse. Suddenly he came upon a palace with lights blazing. He found the door open, so he entered. 'Hello!' he called out, but no one answered. He came to a large dining hall, where there was a warm fire and a little table with a delicious meal just right for one person. After he had eaten, he looked for someone to thank, but no one appeared. He came upon a garden, blooming even in the middle of winter. He saw a beautiful rose bush and remembered Beauty's wish. He reached out to pluck a single rose. But just as the stem broke, he heard a loud roar behind him.

The startled merchant turned around to see a terrible creature, half man and half beast. 'How dare you!' snarled the Beast.

'Please forgive me,' said the frightened man, 'I only wanted a rose for my youngest daughter, Beauty. Her two older sisters asked for gowns and jewels, but Beauty longs to see a rose.'

'I will spare you, on one condition,' said the Beast. 'You must send one of your daughters to live with me here. Otherwise you must return here to die. Go and see if any of them loves you enough to save your life!'

When the sad father returned home and told what had happened, Beauty did not hesitate. 'I will go,' she said quietly.

'No, Beauty,' said her father. 'I am old, and have only a few years to live. I shall go back to the Beast.'

'You shall not return to that castle without me,' said Beauty. Her father tried to change her mind, but Beauty was determined.

Beauty and her father returned to the castle. When she first saw the Beast, she could not help shuddering but she tried to hide her fear. The Beast loaded a trunk filled with treasure onto Beauty's father's horse. As Beauty watched her father ride away, she began to cry.

'Beauty,' said the Beast, 'things are not as bad as you think. You have given yourself for your father's sake, and your goodness will be rewarded. Only listen to me and take this advice: do not be deceived by appearances. Trust your heart, not your eyes.'

The princess also learned the truth of the saying 'don't judge a book by its cover' when she encountered the frog prince, which we read about in Year 2.

As the days passed, Beauty walked in the lovely gardens, where the birds sang to her. She found a huge library filled with books she wanted to read.

At first the Beast's looks scared Beauty, but she soon grew used to them. The Beast treated her with great kindness. Every evening as she sat down to dinner, the Beast came in to talk with her as she ate. Soon she looked forward to their conversations because the Beast was kind and clever and could talk about so many things. But when the meal was over and it was time to say good night, the Beast always turned to her and asked: 'Beauty, will you marry me?' And though she cared for him more every day, Beauty always answered: 'No.'

One night, the Beast noticed a worried look on Beauty's face. 'Beauty,' he said, 'I cannot bear to see you unhappy. What is the matter?' She told him that she missed her family, and that she especially longed to see her father. 'But Beauty,' said the Beast, 'if you leave me, I fear that I will die of sadness.'

'Dear Beast,' said Beauty softly, 'I do not want to leave you. But I long to see my father. Only let me go for one month, and I promise to come back and stay for the rest of my life.'

'Very well,' sighed the Beast. 'But remember your promise. And take this magic ring. When you want to come back, turn the ring round upon your finger and say: "I wish to go back to my Beast."'

When Beauty awoke the next morning, she found herself back in her father's house – not the old country cottage, but a fine new house in town bought with the riches the Beast had given them. Her father hugged her and wept for joy. Soon her sisters came to visit with their new husbands. They pretended to be happy, but they were not. One sister had married a very handsome man who was so in love with his own face that he thought of nothing else. The other sister had married a man who was clever but cruel. He liked to make fun of people, especially his wife.

Day after day, Beauty enjoyed being with her father and doing whatever she could to help him. When the time came for her to return to the Beast, she found that she could not bring herself to say goodbye to her father. Every day she told herself: 'Today I will go back.' But every night she put it off again.

Then one night, she dreamed that she was wandering in the garden around the Beast's castle, when suddenly she heard painful groans. She looked down and saw the Beast lying on the ground. He seemed to be dying.

Beauty awoke with a start. 'Oh, how could I do this to my poor Beast?' she cried. 'Is it his fault he is ugly? Why did I refuse to marry him? I would be happier with him than my sisters are with their husbands. The Beast is honest and good, and that matters more than anything else.'

She turned the ring round on her finger and said firmly, 'I wish to go back to my Beast.' In an instant, she found herself at the castle. She ran through the rooms, calling aloud for the Beast. There was no answer. Then she remembered her dream. She ran to the garden, and there she found the Beast stretched on the ground.

'Oh, he is dead, and it is all my fault!' she cried. She fell to the ground and took him in her arms. As the Beast slowly opened his eyes, Beauty cried: 'Oh, Beast, how you frightened me! I never knew how much I loved you until now, when I feared it was too late.'

In a faint voice the Beast said: 'Beauty, I was dying because I thought you had forgotten your promise. But you have come back. Can you really love such an ugly creature as I am?'

'Yes,' said Beauty.

Then once again the Beast asked: 'Beauty, will you marry me?'

She answered: 'Yes, dear Beast.'

As she spoke, a blaze of light flashed around her. Beauty gasped and covered her eyes. When she opened them again, she no longer saw the Beast. But there, lying at her feet, was a handsome prince.

'What has happened to my Beast?' she asked.

'I was the Beast,' said the prince. 'A wicked fairy put a spell on me and changed me into a monster until a maiden would agree to marry me. You are the only one with goodness enough to see past my horrible appearance and into my heart.'

Beauty gave the young prince her hand to help him rise. Side by side they walked into the castle. And the very next day, with Beauty's father looking on, they were married. And they lived happily ever after.

The Tongue-Cut Sparrow

(A folktale from Japan)

Long, long ago in Japan, there lived an old man and his wife. The old man was good, kind and hard-working, but his wife was cross, mean and bad-tempered. They had no children, so the old man kept a tiny sparrow as a pet. Every day when he came home from working in the woods, he loved to pet the little bird, talk to her and feed her food from his own plate. The sparrow's sweet singing brought happiness into the old man's life. But his wife did not like the sparrow. She complained that her husband paid too much attention to a silly bird. One morning, the old man went away to cut wood and his wife prepared to wash clothes. On this day, she had made some starch for the washing, which she set out in a wooden bowl. While her back was turned, the sparrow hopped down on the edge of the bowl and pecked at some of the starch. When the old woman saw the sparrow, she became so angry that she grabbed a pair of scissors and cut off the sparrow's tongue. 'Go away, you greedy thing!' she shrieked, and the poor bird flew away to the woods.

When the old man returned home and heard what had happened, he felt very sad for his pet. The next morning, he went to the woods to look for the sparrow. Everywhere he went he cried: 'O sparrow, little sparrow! Where are you, my friend?'

The woods grew thick and dark, and the old man began to worry that he might never see the sparrow again. With little hope he called out: 'Little sparrow, please come home!' And just then he heard the fluttering of the sparrow's wings. And, to his great surprise, he heard the sparrow speak.

'Old man,' said the sparrow, 'you have been very kind to me. Now I wish to show you kindness in return.' She led the old man to a pretty little house with a bamboo garden and a tiny waterfall. 'Come in and meet my family,' said the sparrow.

The old man bowed, removed his shoes and entered the sparrow's house. Inside, many sparrows were singing sweet songs. They served the old man a delicious meal, with rice cakes, sweet candies and plenty of hot tea. Then they did a wonderful dance that brought

joy to his heart. 'This has been a magical day for me,' said the old man, 'and I thank you for your kindness. But I see that the sun is setting. Forgive me, but I must return home before my wife starts to worry.'

'Before you go,' said the sparrow, 'please accept a gift.' She placed two baskets before the old man. One was big and heavy, while the other was small and light. 'Please choose one of these,' said the sparrow, 'and do not open the basket until you reach home.'

The old man was not greedy, so he chose the small basket. With many thanks and goodbyes, he left the sparrow's house and returned home.

When the old man arrived at his home, he told his wife all that had happened. Then they opened the small basket. It spilled over with jewels, gold and silver coins and other treasures.

The old man was delighted, but his wife cried, 'You fool! Why didn't you take the big basket?' Then, without another word, she hurried into the woods to find the sparrow's home.

When she at last arrived at the sparrow's house, she called out, 'Sparrow! Let me in!' Of course the polite sparrow invited her into the house and served her some hot tea. She took one sip and then said: 'Enough of this. I am ready to leave.' The sparrow again brought out two baskets, one big and one small. 'Please choose one,' said the sparrow, 'and do not open it until you return home.' The old woman grabbed the big basket and ran out of the door.

'Good gracious,' she cried, 'this basket is so heavy!' She sat down to rest. She looked at the basket. 'Why should I wait to get home?' she said. 'One little peek won't hurt.'

She opened the basket. Instead of gold and silver, it was filled with toads that leaped into her hair, snakes that slithered around her arms and legs, and wasps that stung her all over.

The old woman screamed and ran as fast as she could. When she reached home, she fell into the old man's arms. He took care of her, and when she got better, she said to him: 'I was too greedy, and I am sorry that I hurt the sparrow.'

From that day forward, the old woman helped the old man feed any birds that came to their house, and their home was always filled with sweet songs.

The Story of the Seventh Daughter

(A folktale from Bengal)

Once upon a time there lived a certain merchant who had seven daughters. One day the merchant put to his daughters the question: 'By whose fortune do you get your living?'

The eldest daughter answered: 'Papa, I get my living by your fortune.' The same answer was given by the second daughter, the third, the fourth, the fifth and the sixth; but his youngest daughter said:

'I get my living by my own fortune.'

The merchant got very angry with the youngest daughter, and said to her:

'As you are so ungrateful as to say that you get your living by your own fortune, let me see how you fare alone. This very day you shall leave my house without a penny in your pocket.'

He immediately called his chairmen and ordered them to take away the girl in a sedan chair and leave her in the middle of a forest. The girl begged to be allowed to take her work-box containing her needles and threads, and she was allowed to do so. She then got into the sedan chair which the bearers lifted onto their shoulders. The bearers had not gone many hundred yards when an old woman bawled out to them and told them to stop. This old woman had been the nurse of the seventh daughter, and she loved her like a mother.

'Where are you taking away my beloved child?' she asked. The chairmen replied:

'The merchant has ordered us to take her away and leave her in the midst of a forest, and we are going to do his bidding.'

'I must go with her,' said the old woman. So she was put inside the sedan chair along with the seventh daughter. In the afternoon the chairmen reached a dense forest. They went far into it and towards sunset they put down the girl and the old woman at the foot of a large tree, then ran home as fast as their feet would carry them.

The situation of the merchant's youngest daughter was truly pitiable. She was scarcely 14 years old; she had been bred in the lap of luxury; and she was now here at sundown in the heart of what seemed to be an endless forest, with not a penny in her pocket and with no other protection than what could be given to her by a weak old woman. The very trees of the forest looked upon her with pity. The gigantic tree, at whose foot she was mingling her tears with those of the old woman, said to her (for trees could speak in those days):

'Unhappy girl! I much pity you. In a short time the wild beasts of the forest will come out of their lairs and roam about for their prey; they are sure to devour you and your companion. But I can help you. I will make an opening for you in my trunk. Go into it. I will then close it up and you will remain safe inside so the wild beasts cannot touch you.'

In an instant, the trunk of the tree was split into two. The merchant's daughter and the old woman went inside the hollow, whereupon the tree resumed its natural shape. When the shades of night darkened, the wild beasts of the forest came out of their lairs. The fierce tiger was there; the wild bear was there; the hard-skinned rhinoceros was there; the sly fox was there; the angry birds were there; and the horned buffalo was there.

They all growled round about the tree, for they could smell the scent of human blood. The merchant's daughter and the old woman heard from within the tree the growling of the beasts. The beasts came dashing against the tree. They broke its branches, they pierced its trunk with their horns, they scratched its bark with their claws, but in vain. The merchant's daughter and her old nurse were safe within. Towards dawn the wild beasts went away. After sunrise the good tree said to her two inmates:

'Unhappy women, the wild beasts have gone into their lairs after greatly tormenting me. The sun is up; you can now come out.'

The tree split itself into two, and the merchant's daughter and the old woman came out. They saw the extent of the damage done by the wild beasts to the tree. Many of its branches had been broken down; in many places the trunk had been pierced; and in other places the bark had been stripped off. The merchant's daughter said to the tree:

'Good mother, you are truly good to give us shelter at such a fearful cost. You must be in great pain from the torture to which the wild beasts subjected you last night.'

So saying she went to a pool that was near the tree, and scooped up some handfuls of mud to smear on the trunk of the tree, especially those parts that had been pierced and scratched. After she had done this, the tree said:

'Thank you, my good girl, I am now greatly relieved of my pain. I am, however, concerned not so much about myself as about you both. You must be hungry, not having eaten during the whole of yesterday. And what can I give you? I have no fruit of my own. Give to the old woman whatever money you have, and let her go into the city nearby and buy some food.'

The merchant's daughter said they had no money, but she searched her work-box and found five shells. The tree then told the old woman to go to the city with the shells and buy some rice crackers. The old woman went to the city, which was not far, and said to one shopkeeper:

'Please give me five shells' worth of rice crackers.'

The shopkeeper laughed at her and said:

'Be off, you old hag, do you think rice crackers can be had for five shells?'

She tried another shop and the shopkeeper, thinking the old woman to be in great distress, compassionately gave her a large quantity of rice crackers for the five shells. When the old woman returned with the rice crackers, the tree said to the merchant's daughter:

'Each of you must eat a few of the rice crackers, save half of them and scatter the rest on the banks of pool.'

They did as they were bidden, though they did not understand the reason why they were told to scatter the rice crackers on the banks of the pool. They spent the day bewailing their fate and, at night, they were housed inside the trunk of the tree as on the previous night. The wild beasts came as before, further mutilated the tree and tortured it as in the preceding night. However, during the night another scene was being acted out on the edge of the pool, but the two women only saw the outcome of this scene on the following morning when they emerged from the tree. Hundreds of peacocks with gorgeous feathers had come to the banks of the pool to eat the rice crackers that had been scattered there. As they competed against each other for the tempting food, many of their beautiful feathers had fallen off their bodies. The tree told the two women to gather the feathers together, and the merchant's daughter used them to make a beautiful fan. This fan was taken into the palace in the city, where the son of the king admired it greatly and paid a large sum of money for it. As each morning a quantity of feathers was collected, every day one fan was made and sold. In a short time, the two women became rich and the tree then advised them to employ men to build them a house where they could live. Accordingly, bricks were made, trees were cut down for beams and rafters, lime was mixed and, in a few months, a stately, palace-like house was built for the merchant's daughter and her old nurse. It was thought advisable to lay out the adjoining grounds as a garden and to dig a lake to supply them with water.

In the meantime, the merchant himself, with his wife and six remaining daughters, had been frowned upon by the goddess of wealth. By a sudden stroke of misfortune, he lost all his money. His house and his goods were sold, and he, his wife and six daughters were turned adrift penniless into the world. It so happened that they lived in a village not far from the place where everyone was talking about the strange lady who was building a palace and digging a lake. As the once-rich merchant was now supporting his family by the pittance which he obtained every day for his manual labour, he thought of working as a day labourer to dig the lake of the strange lady on the edge of the forest.

His wife said she would also go to dig the lake with him. One day the strange lady was amusing herself by looking from the balcony of her palace at the labourers digging her lake when, to her utter surprise, she saw her father and mother coming towards the palace, apparently to engage themselves as day labourers.

Tears ran down her cheeks as she looked at them, for they were clothed in rags. She immediately sent servants to bring them inside the house. The poor man and woman were frightened beyond measure. Why would such a rich lady want to talk to labourers like themselves? They feared they were in trouble. Their fears increased when they were given fine clothes to put on. They could not understand what was happening. Once they saw the strange lady of the palace, however, their fears were dispelled; they hugged and wept when they saw their seventh daughter. The rich daughter related her adventures and the father said she had been right when she said that she lived upon her own fortune and not on that of her father. She gave her father a large fortune which enabled him to go to the city in which he formerly lived and set himself up again as a merchant.

This is not the end of the story! The merchant's daughter marries a handsome prince called Prince Sobur, but her jealous sisters poison him. Two magical birds reveal to the merchant's daughter the cure for the poison, then carry her on their backs to his palace where she heals him. The Prince forgives his wicked sisters-in-law and lives happily with his Princess for ever afterwards. You can also read other Bengali tales in Folk Tales of West Bengal *by Swapna Dutta (Children's Book Trust).*

Peter Pan By J.M. Barrie

PARENTS: The character of Peter Pan, the boy who wouldn't grow up, was created by J.M. Barrie in the early 1900s. In 1904, Barrie wrote the famous play with Captain Hook, the pirates and the fairy Tinker Bell. For many years it was performed every Christmas. Barrie donated what he earned from the play to the Great Ormond Street Children's Hospital and, by a special act of parliament, it has been made perpetual. Children today are more likely to know the story from the Walt Disney film or from other film versions like *Hook* or *Finding Neverland*. Here we present the opening episodes, in which we meet the Darling family, their dog Nana and Peter Pan.

All children, except one, grow up. This is the story of that one…

Mr and Mrs Darling lived at Number 14 with their three children, Wendy, John and Michael. Mrs Darling loved to have everything just so, and Mr Darling had a passion for being exactly like his neighbours; so, of course, they had a nurse. As they were poor, this nurse was a Newfoundland dog called Nana. She escorted the children to school each day, walking by their side when they were well behaved, and butting them back into line if they strayed. There never was a simpler, happier family until the coming of Peter Pan.

He came from a wonderful place called the Neverland. Wendy told her mother that Peter Pan sat at the foot of her bed and played music on his pipes to her. Mrs Darling thought she must have been dreaming. Then one evening she saw him with her own eyes.

It was Nana's evening out, and Mrs Darling sat in the nursery putting the children to bed. Soon she fell asleep. The window blew open, and a boy dropped onto the floor. With him was a strange light that darted about the room.

Mrs Darling awoke and knew at once that the boy must be Peter Pan. She screamed, and at that moment Nana rushed in. She growled and sprang at the boy, who leapt lightly through the window. Poor Mrs Darling thought he must have been killed, for the window was three floors up. She looked for his body, but it was not there. She only saw what she thought was a shooting star in the black night sky. Then she saw that Nana had the boy's shadow in her mouth. When he had leapt out of the window, Nana had closed it quickly and it snapped the shadow off. Mrs Darling rolled it up and put it carefully in a drawer.

On Friday night a week later, Mr and Mrs Darling were getting ready to go out to a dinner party when Nana came in with Michael's bottle of medicine in her mouth. But he was naughty and refused to take it.

'Won't, won't,' he cried.

Mr Darling said he must be brave, and he offered to take a spoonful of *his* medicine, which was much nastier. But he only pretended to take it, and poured it into Nana's bowl. It looked like milk, and Nana began to lap it up. She knew at once that he had played a trick on her, and she gave him a sad look and crept into her kennel in the nursery.

The children were very upset. Mr Darling was ashamed at himself and furious with Nana.

'The proper place for you is the yard,' he said. He dragged Nana out, and tied her up in the backyard. So there was no Nana in the nursery that night to take care of the children after Mr and Mrs Darling had gone out.

Almost as soon as they had gone, the three nightlights in the nursery went out. Then another light appeared in the room, a thousand times brighter. When it came to rest for a second you could see it was a fairy: Tinker Bell. And Peter Pan was with her. Tinker Bell flashed about the room looking for Peter's shadow.

'Tinker Bell,' he called softly. 'Where is it?'

A tinkle of golden bells answered him. It was the fairy language, which children cannot understand. Tinker Bell told Peter that his shadow was in the chest of drawers. Peter jumped at it and pulled out his shadow, but he shut Tinker Bell in the drawer by mistake!

Then Peter tried to stick his shadow on, but it wouldn't stick. He tried and tried but everything failed. Peter sat on the floor and cried. His sobs woke Wendy and she sat up in bed.

'What is your name?' she asked, although she was quite sure she knew already.

'Peter Pan.'

'Where do you live?'

'Second star to the right,' said Peter, 'and then straight on till morning.'

'What a funny address!' said Wendy.

'No it isn't,' said Peter, but for the first time he felt that perhaps it was a funny address.

'I mean,' said Wendy politely, 'is that what they put on the letters?'

'Don't get any letters,' said Peter.

'But your mother gets letters?'

'Don't have a mother,' he said. Wendy felt sorry for him.

'Oh, Peter, no wonder you were crying,' she said.

'I wasn't crying about mothers,' said Peter. 'I was crying because I can't get my shadow to stick on. Besides, I wasn't crying.'

Wendy knew at once what to do, and she began to sew the shadow to his foot. Peter jumped about happily, quite forgetting what Wendy had done for him. He thought he had sewn on the shadow himself.

'How clever I am,' he boasted. In fact, there never was a cockier boy than Peter. Wendy was cross with him. He said he was sorry. Then he said, 'Wendy, one girl is more use than 20 boys.'

'Do you really think so, Peter?' asked Wendy.

'Yes, I do.'

Wendy asked Peter how old he was. 'I don't know,' he replied uneasily, 'but I am quite young. I ran away the day I was born because I heard father and mother talking about what I was to be when I grew up. I don't ever want to grow up. I always want to be a little boy and have fun. So I ran away to Kensington Gardens and lived amongst the fairies.'

He told Wendy about the beginning of fairies.

'You see, when the first baby laughed for the first time, its laugh broke into a thousand pieces, and they all went skipping about, and that was the beginning of fairies. There ought to be one fairy for every boy and girl, but children know such a lot now and they soon don't believe in fairies. Every time a child says "I don't believe in fairies", a fairy somewhere falls down dead.'

It struck him that Tinker Bell was keeping very quiet. 'I can't think of where she has gone to. You can't hear her, can you?' he said, and they both listened.

'The only sound I hear is something like a tinkle of bells. I think it's in the chest of drawers,' said Wendy. She was excited to think that there was a fairy in the room.

Peter let poor Tink out of the drawer, and she flew out screaming with fury.

'Oh Peter,' Wendy cried, 'if only she would stay still and let me see her!' At that moment, Tinker Bell came to rest on the cuckoo clock. 'Oh how lovely!' said Wendy. 'But what is she saying, Peter?'

Peter had to translate: 'She is not very polite. She says you are a great ugly girl.'

Peter and Wendy sat together in the armchair now, and he told her that he lived with the Lost Boys who have fallen out of their perambulators when their nurses were looking the other way. Peter said: 'If they are not claimed in seven days they are sent to Neverland. I am their captain!'

'What fun it must be!' said Wendy.

'Yes,' said Peter, 'but we are rather lonely because there are no girls. Girls, you know, are much too clever to fall out of their prams.'

Wendy asked Peter why he had been visiting the nursery, and he said it was to listen to stories, because the Lost Boys don't know any stories. 'Oh Wendy, I heard your mother telling you such a lovely story – about the prince who couldn't find the lady who wore the glass slipper.'

'That was Cinderella,' said Wendy, 'but there are so many wonderful stories. I know lots of them.'

Peter began to draw her towards the window, begging her to go with him and tell stories to the Lost Boys. 'I'll teach you how to fly,' he said. 'And, Wendy, there are mermaids, with such long tails.'

Wendy ran up to John and Michael and said: 'Wake up! Peter Pan has come and he is to teach us to fly.'

In the yard, Nana was barking furiously because she knew that something was wrong in the nursery. She eventually broke free from her chain and ran off to fetch Mr and Mrs Darling, who knew at once that something was happening in their nursery. By the time they arrived, ten minutes had passed, and Peter Pan can do a great deal in ten minutes. Peter Pan had shown the children how to fly. It looked very easy and they tried it, but they always went down instead of up. No one can fly unless fairy dust has been blown on him or her. Fortunately, Peter's hands were messy with it, and he blew some on Wendy, John and Michael.

Peter directed the children: 'Now just wiggle your shoulders this way, and let's go.'

Up and down they went, round and round, flying through the room. 'I say,' cried John. 'Why shouldn't we all go out?'

Of course Peter had been luring them to do this all the time, but Wendy hesitated.

'Mermaids!' said Peter again. 'And there are pirates.'

'Pirates,' cried John, seizing his Sunday hat. 'Let's go at once.' And so Peter Pan led Wendy, John and Michael through the bedroom window to the second star on the right, then straight on until morning.

Tall Tales

Britain is an old country with a long and rich history. So many amazing things have happened, and so many great men and women have lived there, that its history is one of the things that most interests people about Britain. Before the Romans arrived, history wasn't written down at all. Even after that, for hundreds of years only a few people were rich enough to own books. So how did people learn about their country's history in those days? They told stories. Storytellers were popular people, always welcome at fairs and in great people's houses. The more amazing their stories, the bigger their audiences – and the more they got paid. So perhaps it's not surprising that some of the stories became more like fairy stories than real history. In spite of that, these stories, which we call Tall Tales, still tell us a lot about Britain and its people. For example, there really was a man called Richard Whittington who became Lord Mayor of London three times, but he didn't really owe it to his cat! In Year 1 we read about St George, the patron saint of England, and about King Arthur and Merlin. Here we learn more about Arthur, and other stories that have become part of our history, even if they didn't happen exactly like this.

Albion and Brutus

(Adapted from *Our Island Story* by Henrietta Marshall)

Once upon a time there was a giant called Neptune. When he was still a boy, Neptune loved the sea. All day long he played in it, swimming, diving and laughing gleefully as the waves dashed over him.

As he grew older he came to know and love the sea so well that the sea and the waves loved him, too, and acknowledged him to be their king. At last, people said he was not only king of the waves but god of the sea.

Neptune was the ancient Roman name for the god the ancient Greeks called Poseidon. Learn more on page 66.

Neptune had a beautiful wife who bore him many sons. As each son became old enough to rule a kingdom, Neptune made him king over an island. Neptune's fourth son was called Albion. When it came to his turn to receive a kingdom, a great council was called to decide upon an island for him.

Now Neptune loved Albion more than any of his other children. This made it very difficult to choose which island should be his. The mermaids and mermen, as the wonderful people who live in the sea are called, came from all parts of the world with news of beautiful islands. But after hearing about them, Neptune would shake his head and say: 'No, that is not good enough for Albion.'

At last a little mermaid swam into the pink and white coral cave in which the council was held. 'O Father Neptune,' she said, 'let Albion come to my island. It is a beautiful little island. It lies like a gem in the bluest of waters. There the trees and the grass are green, the cliffs are white and the sands are golden. There the sun shines and the birds sing. It is a land of beauty. Let Albion come to my island.'

'Where is this island?' asked Neptune.

'Oh, come, and I will show it to you,' replied the mermaid. Then she swam away and Neptune followed, with all the mermaids and mermen. They swam and swam until they came to the little green island with the white cliffs and yellow sands.

As soon as it came in sight, Neptune raised himself on a big wave, and when he saw the little island lying before him like a beautiful gem in the blue water, just as the mermaid had said, he cried out in joy: 'This is the island of my love. Albion shall rule it and Albion it shall be called.'

So Albion took possession of the little island and called it by his own name. For seven years Albion reigned over his little island. At the end of that time he was killed in a fight

with the hero Hercules. This was a great grief to Neptune. But because of the love he bore to his son Albion, he continued to love and watch over the little green island which was called by his son's name.

For many years after the death of Albion, the little island had no ruler. At last, one day there came sailing from the far-off city of Troy a prince called Brutus. Seeing the fair island with white cliffs and golden sands, he landed with all his mighty men of war. He made himself king, not only over Albion, but over all the islands which lay around. He called them the kingdom of Britain or Britannia after his own name, Brutus, and Albion he called Great Britain because it was the largest of the islands.

Although, after this, the little island was no longer called Albion, Neptune still loved it. When he grew old and had no more strength to rule, he gave his sceptre to the islands called Britannia, and that is why the people there built a navy with many great ships to sail upon the waters of Neptune's seas. They wrote a song about this called 'Rule Britannia' which says that 'Britannia rules the waves'.

> 'Rule Britannia' is a patriotic song. Learn more about other patriotic songs starting on page 202.

This is a story of many thousand years ago. Some people think it is only a fairy tale. But however that may be, the little island is still sometimes called Albion, although it is nearly always called Britain.

King Arthur and the Knights of the Round Table

Of all the kings who have ruled over Britain, none was wiser or braver or kinder than King Arthur. He became king when he was only 15 years old. The old King Uther Pendragon had died and the nobles fell to fighting amongst themselves as each man tried to have himself crowned king in Uther's place. Then the wise man Merlin brought before them all a boy who had been born son to Uther Pendragon, and of whom it had been prophesied that he would be the greatest king ever to reign in Britain. Merlin had taken the child away soon after his birth to keep him safe from harm, and Arthur had been brought up by fairies in the land of Avalon.

The nobles refused to believe that this young boy could really be their king, so Merlin proved it by a wonderful test of strength. A sword appeared, deeply embedded in a huge stone, outside the great door of the cathedral. Its hilt glittered with brilliant jewels. Written on the stone were these words: 'Whoever can draw me from this stone is the rightful king of Britain.'

The nobles used all their strength to draw it out, but no one was strong enough. Then Arthur gave it the gentlest pull and drew it back out of the stone. All who saw it were amazed, and declared that Arthur must be the true king.

Arthur was not only brave and strong, he was kind and gentle. He taught his knights that they must use their strength to right wrongs and to protect the weak. When he discovered that his knights were arguing about which of them was the most important, and who should sit in the best places at the table, he told them that they must treat their fellow knights as brothers. He had a great Round Table made, so that no one should sit in a better place than anyone else. The knights were joined together by the fellowship of the Round Table, and they lived at King Arthur's court in Camelot.

Arthur married the Lady Guinevere, the beautiful daughter of another king, and when she came to live at Camelot all of the knights placed themselves at her service. They honoured Guinevere and promised to devote themselves to deeds of chivalry in her name.

Arthur led his knights in battle against the invading Saxons. The Saxons were great warriors, and had already defeated the native Britons in many parts of the country, but Arthur was the first leader who could hold them back. Arthur fought with a great sword called Excalibur. This is the strange tale of how he came to possess it.

The battles which Arthur was fighting against the Saxons were so fierce that Merlin was afraid Arthur might lose. He therefore took Arthur to the edge of a great lake and, in the middle of the lake, a hand rose out of the water, grasping a mighty sword. Then Arthur saw a beautiful lady coming towards him in a boat. He asked Merlin who she could be.

'That is the Lady of the Lake,' replied Merlin. 'Speak gently to her, and she will give you her sword.'

The boat approached the land and the Lady of the Lake greeted Arthur.

'Lady,' said Arthur, 'what mighty sword is that which the arm is holding aloft out of the water?'

'That is my sword,' replied the Lady of the Lake, 'and I will give it to you, Arthur, if you will promise me to use it to fight for the right and to defend the weak.'

'Gladly, my lady,' said the King, and he got into the boat and sailed to the middle of the lake. The mysterious hand gave him the sword, then sank beneath the water. The sword had its name – Excalibur – engraved on the shining steel of its blade, and Arthur would wield it in many battles to come.

✶ ✶

The bravest of all the knights of the Round Table was Sir Lancelot of the Lake. He was called that because, although he was the son of a king, he had been stolen away at birth and left beside a lake. The Lady of the Lake had found him there and brought him up as her own.

Sir Lancelot was the greatest of all the knights, not only in courage but in kindness and courtesy. Lancelot had never been defeated in combat. On horse or on foot, he was the champion. He served the weak and defenceless, and no lady in distress would be in need of a champion if Sir Lancelot were near. When Arthur brought Queen Guinevere to Camelot, all the knights pledged themselves to her service, but none was more devoted to the Queen than Lancelot. He did many mighty deeds and defeated many terrible foes, all in the name of the Lady Guinevere.

One night Lancelot was staying in a castle where an elderly couple had given him shelter. After dinner, Lancelot put his armour and his sword beside him and soon fell asleep in his room at the top of a tower.

During the night a violent knocking on the gate below woke him. He ran to the window and, by the light of the moon, he saw a knight being chased by three other knights. Lancelot put on his armour, tied his bedsheets to the window, and slid down to the ground. He strode right into the midst of the fighting knights where, to his surprise, he saw from the shield of the knight who was being attacked that he was Sir Kay, King Arthur's steward. Lancelot drew his sword and with seven mighty blows he felled the three attackers to the ground.

'Sir Knight,' they said, 'we yield to you as a champion of unmatched strength.'

He answered: 'I will not accept your yielding to me. You must yield to this knight or else I will kill you.'

'Fair knight, we cannot do that, because we would have beaten that knight if you had not come,' the three knights said.

'You can choose if you wish to live or die,' replied Sir Lancelot, 'but if you yield, it must be to that knight.'

So the three knights yielded to Sir Kay, and Sir Lancelot ordered them to go to the court at Camelot and beg the Queen for mercy, saying that Sir Kay sent them there as her prisoners.

Over the years Lancelot sent many a defeated knight to Camelot, commanding each to bow down before Guinevere. Eventually, however, the feelings of Sir Lancelot and Queen Guinevere for each other became too strong, and Lancelot and Arthur, who had been best friends, became enemies. The knights of the Round Table were divided, with some supporting Lancelot and some supporting Arthur. So the fellowship of the Round Table was broken, and the glorious chivalry of King Arthur's court became a thing of memory only.

The kingdom descended into fighting and chaos, and Arthur was killed on the battlefield. However, his body was never found, and there are those who say that he sleeps with the fairies in Avalon, waiting until his country needs him again.

Robin Hood and his Merry Men

**(Adapted and abridged from *Stories of Robin Hood
Told to the Children* by Henrietta Marshall)**

Very many years ago there ruled over England a king who was called 'Richard Coeur de Lion'. Coeur de Lion is French and means lion-hearted. It seems strange that an English king should have a French name. But more than a hundred years before this king reigned, a French duke named William came to England, defeated the English in a great battle at Hastings, and declared himself king of England.

Duke William, also known as William the Conqueror, brought with him a great many Frenchmen, or Normans as they were called from the name of the part of France over which this duke ruled. These Normans came with Duke William to help him fight because he promised to give them money and lands as a reward. Now Duke William had neither a great deal of money nor much land of his own. So when he had beaten the English, or Saxons as they were called in those days, he stole lands and houses from the Saxon nobles and gave them to the Normans. Many Saxon nobles themselves had to become the servants of these Normans. Thus it came about that two races lived in England, each speaking their own language and each hating the other.

Richard Coeur de Lion was a Norman who was a brave and noble man. He was ever ready to help the weak against the strong and, had he stayed in England after he became king, he might have done much good. But Richard did not stay in England. He went far over the seas to fight in a war which was known as a Crusade with armies from many other countries. Before he went away, he called two bishops whom he thought were good and wise men and said to them: 'Take care of England while I am gone. Rule my people wisely and well, and I will reward you when I return.' The bishops promised to do as he asked. Then Richard said farewell and sailed away.

You can see a statue of Richard Coeur de Lion outside the Houses of Parliament.

Now King Richard had a brother who was called Prince John. Prince John was quite different from King Richard in every way. He was not at all a nice man. He was jealous of Richard because he was king, and angry because he himself had not been chosen to rule while Richard was away. As soon as his brother had gone, John went to the bishop and said: 'You must let me rule while the King is away.' Deep down in his wicked heart, John meant to make himself king and never let Richard come back.

A very sad time now began for the Saxons. John tried to please the Normans, because he hoped they would help to make him king, so he took land from the Saxons and gave it to the Normans. Many Saxons became homeless beggars and lived a wild life in the forests which covered a great part of England at this time. Among the few Saxon nobles who still remained, there was one called Robert, Earl of Huntingdon. He had one son, also called Robert but known as Robin. Robin was a favourite with everyone. Tall, strong, handsome and full of fun, he kept his father's house bright with songs and laughter. He was brave and fearless too, and there was no better archer in the countryside who could reach his target with a bow and arrow. And with it all he was gentle and tender, never hurting the weak nor scorning the poor.

But Robert of Huntingdon was robbed of all his land and goods by Prince John's men, who burnt down his house and killed him and all of his followers. Only Robin was left alive, and he had to run for his life. He ran until he reached the forest, then he kept running, plunging deeper and deeper under the shadow of the trees. At last he threw himself down beneath a great oak, burying his face in the cool, green grass under it. Robin loved the forest. He felt as if it were a tender mother who opened her wide arms to him. The bitterness and anger melted out of his heart until only sorrow was left. In the dim evening light, Robin knelt bareheaded on the green grass to say his prayers:

'I swear to honour God and the King; to help the weak and fight the strong; to take from the rich and give to the poor; so God will help me with His power.'

And this is how Robin Hood first came to live in the Green Wood and have all his wonderful adventures.

* *

Robin Hood and the Butcher

The Sheriff of Nottingham was a very unkind man. He treated the poor Saxons very badly, and often took away their houses and all their money, leaving them to starve. The poor people used to go into the wood, and Robin would give them food and money. Sometimes they went home again, but very often they stayed with him and became his Merry Men.

The Sheriff knew this, so he hated Robin, and he was never so happy as when he had caught one of Robin's men and locked him in prison. But try how he might, he could not catch Robin Hood. Robin used to go to Nottingham very often, but he was so well disguised that the Sheriff never knew him. So he always escaped.

The Sheriff was too much afraid of Robin Hood to go into the forest and try to take him. He knew his men were no match for Robin's. Robin's men served him and fought for him because they loved him. The Sheriff's men only served him because they feared him.

One day Robin was walking through the forest when he met a butcher. The butcher was riding happily along to the market at Nottingham. He was dressed in a blue linen coat with a leather belt. On either side of his strong grey pony hung a basket full of meat. Suddenly Robin stepped from under the trees and stopped him.

'What have you there, my man?' he asked.

'Butcher meat,' replied the man. 'Fine prime beef and mutton for Nottingham market. Do you want to buy some?'

'Yes I do,' said Robin. 'I'll buy it all and your pony too. How much do you want for it? I should like to go to Nottingham and see what kind of butcher I will make.'

So the butcher sold his pony and all his meat to Robin. Then Robin changed clothes with him. Robin put on the butcher's blue clothes and leather belt and the butcher went off in Robin's suit of Lincoln green, feeling very grand indeed.

Then Robin mounted the pony and off he went to Nottingham to sell his meat at the market. When he arrived, he found the whole town in a bustle. In those days there were very few shops, so everyone used to go to market to buy and sell. The country people brought butter and eggs and honey to sell. With the money they got, they bought platters, mugs, pots, pans or whatever else they wanted and took it back to the country with them.

Robin laid out his meat and began to cry with the best of them: 'Prime meat, ladies. Come and buy. Cheapest meat in all the market, ladies. Come buy, come buy. Two pence a pound. Come buy, come buy!'

'What!' said everyone, 'beef at two pence a pound! I never heard of such a thing. Why, it is generally ten pence.'

When it became known that there was a new butcher who was selling his meat for two pence a pound, everyone came crowding round his stall eager to buy. All the other butchers stood idle until Robin had no more beef and mutton left to sell. These butchers began to talk amongst themselves and say: 'Who is this man? He has never been here before. We will never be able to sell anything as long as he comes here giving away beef at two pence a pound.'

'I tell you what,' said one old butcher who had been selling meat in Nottingham market for 50 years, 'it is no use standing here doing nothing. We had better go and talk to him and find out, if we can, who he is. We must ask him to come and have dinner with us and the Sheriff in the townhall today.' On market days, the butchers used to have dinner together in the townhall after market was over, and the Sheriff used to come and have dinner with them.

'Thank you,' said Robin when they asked him to dinner, 'I should like nothing better. I have had a busy morning and am very hungry and thirsty.'

At dinner the Sheriff sat at one end of the table and the old butcher at the other. Robin, as the stranger, had the place of honour on the Sheriff's right hand. At first the dinner was very dull. All the butchers were very sulky and cross, while only Robin was merry. He could not help laughing to himself at the idea of dining with his great enemy, the Sheriff of Nottingham. And not only dining with him, but sitting on his right hand and being treated as an honoured guest. If the Sheriff had only known, poor Robin would very soon have been locked up in a dark dungeon, eating dry bread instead of apple pie and custard and all the fine things they were having for dinner.

However, Robin was so merry that very soon the butchers forgot to be cross and sulky. Before the end of the dinner, all were laughing until their sides ached. Only the Sheriff was grave and thinking hard. He was a greedy old man, and he was saying to himself: 'This silly young fellow evidently does not know the value of things. If he has any cattle, I might buy them from him for very little. I could sell them again to the butchers for a good price. In that way I should make a lot of money.'

After dinner he took Robin by the arm and led him aside. 'See here, young man,' he said, 'I like your looks, but you seem new to this business. Now don't trust these men.' Pointing to the butchers, he said: 'They are all as ready as can be to cheat you. You take my advice. If you have any cattle to sell, come to me. I'll give you a good price.'

'Thank you,' said Robin, 'it is most kind of you. I have two or three hundred horned beasts and a hundred acres of good land. Would you like to see them?'

The Sheriff nearly danced for joy when he heard that. He had quite made up his mind that it would be very easy to cheat this silly young fellow. Already he began to count the money he would make. But there was a wicked twinkle in Robin Hood's eye.

'I start for home tomorrow morning,' said Robin. 'If you would like to go with me, I will show you the horned beasts and the land.'

'That night the Sheriff went into his counting-house and counted out three hundred pounds in gold. He tied it up in three bags, one hundred pounds in each bag. He put the gold underneath his pillow in case anyone should steal it during the night. Then he went to bed and tried to sleep, but he was too excited to sleep. Besides, the gold under his pillow made it so hard and knobby that it was most uncomfortable.

In the morning the sun shone and the birds sang as they merrily rode along. When the Sheriff saw that they were taking the road to Sherwood Forest, he began to feel a little nervous.

'There is a bold, bad man in these woods,' he said. 'He is called Robin Hood. He robs people. Do you think we will meet him?'

'I am quite sure we won't meet him,' replied Robin with a laugh.

'Well, I hope not,' said the Sheriff. 'I never dare to ride through the forest unless I have my soldiers with me.'

Robin only laughed as they rode on into the forest, until they came within sight of a large herd of deer.

'Look there,' he cried, 'look! What do you think of my horned beasts?'

'I think,' said the Sheriff in a trembling voice, 'I think I should like to go back to Nottingham.'

'What? And not buy any horned beasts? What is the matter with them? Are they not fine and fat? Are they not a beautiful colour? Come, come, Sheriff, when you have brought the money for them, too.'

At the mention of the money the Sheriff turned quite pale and clutched hold of his bags. 'Young man,' he said, 'I don't like you at all. I tell you I want to go back to Nottingham. This isn't money I have in my bags, it is only pebbles.'

Then Robin put his horn to his mouth and blew three blasts. One of his men immediately appeared, wearing Lincoln green.

'Good morning, Master Robin,' he said. 'What orders do you have for me today?'

'Well, in the first place I hope you have something nice for dinner, because I have brought the Sheriff of Nottingham to dine with us,' answered Robin.

'Yes,' replied the man, 'the cooks are busy already as we thought you might bring someone back with you. But we hardly expected so fine a guest as the Sheriff of Nottingham,' he added, making a low bow to him. 'I hope he intends to pay honestly.'

For that was Robin Hood's way. He always gave those wicked men who had stolen money from poor people a very fine dinner, and then he made them pay a great deal of money for it.

The Sheriff was very much afraid when he knew that he had really fallen into the hands of Robin Hood. He was angry, too, when he thought that he had actually had Robin in his power in Nottingham the day before and could so easily have put him in prison, if he had only known.

They had a very fine dinner, and the Sheriff began to feel quite comfortable and to think that he was going to get off easily, when Robin said: 'Now, Master Sheriff, you must pay for your dinner.'

'Oh! Indeed I am a poor man,' said the Sheriff. 'I have no money.'

'No money! What have you in your saddle bags, then?' asked Robin.

'Only pebbles, nothing but pebbles, as I told you before,' replied the frightened Sheriff. Robin told his men to search the Sheriff's saddle bags, where they found three hundred pounds in gold coins.

'Sheriff,' said Robin sternly, 'I shall keep all this money and divide it among my men. It is not half so much as you have stolen from them. If you had told me the truth about it then I might have given you some back, but I always punish people who tell lies. If you are not kinder to my people, I will punish you even more severely the next time.'

Then Robin called for the Sheriff's pony, guided him back through the forest and sent him on his way to Nottingham. How Robin laughed at the trick he had played on the Sheriff!

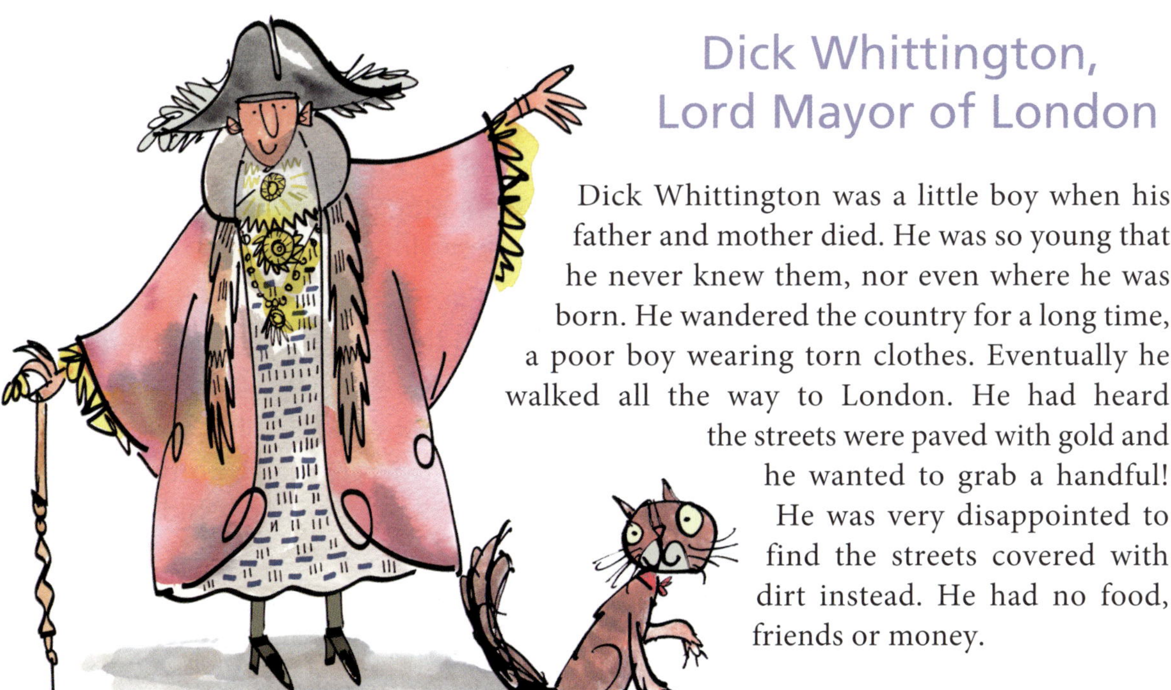

Dick Whittington, Lord Mayor of London

Dick Whittington was a little boy when his father and mother died. He was so young that he never knew them, nor even where he was born. He wandered the country for a long time, a poor boy wearing torn clothes. Eventually he walked all the way to London. He had heard the streets were paved with gold and he wanted to grab a handful! He was very disappointed to find the streets covered with dirt instead. He had no food, friends or money.

After a long time, half dead for want of food, he laid himself down at the door of the merchant named Alderman Fitzwarren. The merchant scolded the boy for blocking his doorway, and told him to go and find work. Whittington replied that he would work, if anyone would employ him. He tried to get up but was so weak that he fell down again. This made the merchant feel sorry for him. He took him in, gave him meat and drink and told him to help his cook to clean the kitchen.

Whittington would have lived there happily, if he had not been beaten so often by the cook. Then Miss Alice, the merchant's daughter, felt sorry for him and made the cook treat him more kindly. She put up a small bed in the attic for him, but there were so many rats and mice in that room that he could barely sleep. When a visiting gentleman gave Whittington a penny, he used it to buy a cat. The cat drove away all the mice and rats in his room.

One day, Mr Fitzwarren had a ship ready to sail. He asked all his servants if they would like to put anything on board the ship so that they could make some money by selling it abroad. 'I have nothing,' said Whittington, 'but my cat.'

'Then fetch the cat, my boy,' ordered the merchant, 'and send her.'

Whittington delivered the cat in tears. 'I shall now be eaten by the rats and mice,' he said, 'and this cat has been my best friend. I will miss her a lot.'

While the cat sailed the rough seas, Whittington was cruelly beaten at home by the cook, and the mice and rats returned to his attic bedroom. At last the poor boy became determined to run away. He left early in the morning of All Hallows' day. He got as far as Highgate Hill, but then he heard the sound of Bow Bells ringing. He had heard the bells of this famous church a hundred times, but this time they seemed to be speaking to him. 'Turn, turn again Whittington,' they seemed to peal. 'Turn again Whittington, Lord Mayor of London.'

'Now I can put up with some beatings, and even being eaten alive by rats and mice, if one day I can be Lord Mayor of London,' said Whittington to himself. So he ran back to Mr Fitzwarren's house. Fortunately he hadn't been gone long enough to be missed.

The ship that had borrowed his cat had nearly sunk at sea, but the sailors finally reached the Barbary Coast of Africa. The local people received them kindly. The captain showed them the ship's cargo, and the King of the country invited the captain and his crew to dine at his palace.

They were all seated on elegant chairs, and the floor was covered with thick carpets, edged with gold and silver. The King and Queen were seated at the upper end of the table. Their servants brought in a number of covered dishes but, the moment the covers were taken off, a pack of rats and mice jumped on the table, and ate all the food. The captain was shocked. He turned to the King and asked if the vermin were not offensive.

'Yes, very much so,' the King replied. 'Not only do they eat all our food, they even attack me in my chamber. I need a guard to keep watch for them even while I sleep.'

The captain thought of Whittington's cat and told their majesties that there was a small animal on board his ship that would get rid of the rats and mice very quickly.

'Bring the animal,' said the King. 'If she drives the pests from my court, I will load your ship with gold, and the richest jewels of my country.'

The captain fetched the cat and, as soon as she saw the vermin, she sprang out of his arms and killed or drove away every rat and mouse from the room. The King was astonished to see so small a creature drive away his old enemies, and the Queen took the cat in her lap, where the cat purred herself to sleep. The King bought all the goods the captain had in his ship, and then bought the cat, paying ten times as much money as he had given for the whole cargo.

The rats plaguing the King are just like those in the town of Hamelin before the Pied Piper led them away, which we read about in Year 2.

A year after the day on which Dick Whittington heard the Bow Bells telling him to go home, the captain brought the treasure back to Alderman Fitzwarren's house. The captain showed the Alderman the jewels for which his cargo had been sold. Then he showed the diamonds and rubies that he had received for Whittington's cat, which surprised the Alderman beyond words. He cried out:

'Go, call poor Dick. Let's tell him of his fame!
And Mr Whittington shall be his name.'

Whittington tried to excuse himself, saying the floor had just been cleaned and his shoes were dirty. The merchant, however, ordered a chair to be set for him, and showed him the treasure. He said: 'Mr Whittington, I congratulate you on the surprising success of your cat. She has made you more riches than I am worth. May you long enjoy them.' Mr Whittington thanked God and rewarded the captain and the ship's crew for the care they had taken of his cargo. He made presents to the servants, and even to his old enemy the cook.

Dick Whittington grew to become a great and successful man. He became Lord Mayor of London three times, just as the bells had foretold, and he even became Sir Richard Whittington. He married Alice Fitzwarren, the Alderman's daughter. They lived happily to an old age and had many children. Sir Whittington even paid for another ship to travel to the Barbary Coast to bring his beloved cat back to live with him in the Mansion House, which is a beautiful building where the Lord Mayor of London lives. (He sent the King of the Barbary Coast lots more cats to chase his rats and mice away, so the King didn't mind!)

The great City of London still has a Lord Mayor, who is elected each year. Every Lord Mayor knows of the adventures of Dick Whittington, which have been passed down from generation to generation by the people of London. Whittington taught us that we should never give up, no matter how bad things get. You never know what is just around the corner!

Dick Whittington's clever cat still sits on the Whittington Stone on Highgate Hill. This marks the spot where Whittington heard the sound of Bow Bells telling him: 'Turn again Whittington, Lord Mayor of London'.

Myths from Ancient Greece

Heroes and Monsters, Gods and Goddesses

Here are some stories that have been around for two thousand years or more. These stories come to us from ancient Greece.

We call these stories 'myths'. Many myths tell about brave heroes, great battles, terrible monsters, gods and goddesses. Some myths explain why we have seasons, or why there are volcanoes, or how come there are constellations in the sky. Of course today we know the real, scientific reasons that all these things happen. But long, long ago, many people believed the myths were true. Even though we no longer believe the old myths, we like to tell them because they're such wonderful stories.

Myths can also tell us important things about why people behave in the ways they do. The characters in myths are all make-believe, but the lessons about human nature are as true for us now as they were in ancient Greece.

Like the people in other ancient civilisations you've learned about, the ancient Greeks believed in many gods and goddesses. The Greeks built beautiful temples, like the Parthenon, to honour their gods. In the Greek myths, the gods and goddesses sometimes act like normal people – like you and me. They need to eat, drink and sleep. They can be happy one moment and angry the next. They fall in love and get married. They play tricks on each other. They argue and fight with each other.

Unlike people, however, the Greek gods had magical powers. Some gods could change into an animal, or hurl lightning bolts from the sky! Also, the Greeks believed the gods were immortal – which means that they never died, but lived forever.

The ancient Greeks believed the gods and goddesses lived on a mountain that rose high above the clouds, called Mount Olympus.

From there, they looked down on the earth, and they used their powers to help the people they liked or hurt the people they didn't like. Let's meet some of the main Greek gods and goddesses.

Zeus [zee-OOSE], the king of the gods, controlled the heavens and settled arguments among the gods. He could change his shape in an instant. If he wanted, he could come to earth as a swan or as a fierce bull. When he was angry, he had the power to throw lightning bolts down from the heavens! ▶

◀ **Hera [HERE-uh]**, the wife of Zeus, was queen of the gods and she was the goddess of marriage. She could be a very jealous person. But her husband, Zeus, had a habit of falling in love with many other goddesses and women, so Hera usually had a good reason to be jealous.

Poseidon [poz-IDE-on], the god of the sea, was an especially important god to the Greeks. Can you think why? (Look at the map on page 148 and see what's around Greece.) Poseidon could make the oceans as calm as a sleeping baby, or he could stir up high waves to crush a ship to pieces. In pictures, Poseidon often has a long beard and holds a trident, a kind of long pitchfork with three prongs. ▶

Apollo [ap-OLL-oh], a son of Zeus, was the god of the sun. He is sometimes called **Phoebus [FEE-bus]** Apollo. 'Phoebus' means 'brilliant' or 'shining'. He was also the god of poetry and music. No one could sing so beautifully or play so sweetly on the lyre (an instrument like a small harp). He was also the god of healing as well as the god of archery. ▶

◀ **Artemis [AR-ter-miss]**, the twin sister of Apollo, was the goddess of the moon and the goddess of hunting. She loved the woods and the wild creatures that lived there. Since she loved to be free and on her own, she asked her father, Zeus, to promise that he would never make her get married – which was a promise Zeus kept.

Aphrodite [af-roe-DIE-tee] was the goddess of love and beauty. When she was born, she rose out of the sea from the gentle waves on a cushion of soft foam. She had a son called **Eros [EAR-oss]**, though you may know him by a more familiar name, Cupid. Maybe you've seen a picture of him on Valentine's Day cards. The Greeks said that when Aphrodite wanted someone to fall in love, she ordered Eros to shoot that person with one of his magic arrows. If he hit you with an arrow, then you would fall in love with the first person you saw! No one could resist the power of his magic arrows, not even Zeus. ▶

Ares [AIR-eez] was the cruel and merciless god of war. Wherever he went, death and destruction followed. No one liked him, not even his parents, Zeus and Hera! ▶

◀ **Hermes [HER-meez]** was the messenger god. He carried commands from the gods to humans on earth. In pictures, he often has wings on his hat or sandals to show how fast he travelled.

Hephaestus [hef-AYE-stus] was the god of fire and the forge. He could stir up volcanoes, making the earth spit up hot flames and lava. (The word 'volcano' comes from the Roman name for this god, Vulcan.) But most of all he used fire to make things. He used it to heat metal and make armour, swords, spears, beautiful cups and shining jewellery. Hephaestus was lame, and he spent his time working at his fiery forge. ▶

◀ **Athena [a-THEE-ner]** was the goddess of wisdom. For the people of the Greek city called Athens, she was a special goddess, for they believed she protected their city. She had a most unusual birth. One day Zeus had a terrible headache. He complained to Hephaestus, who took his hammer and struck Zeus on the head. Out of Zeus's head jumped Athena, already grown-up and fully dressed in a suit of armour!

Hades [HAY-deez] was the grim god of the underworld, the dark and shadowy underground place where the Greeks believed people went when they died. The Greeks often called this place Hades, the same name as the god who ruled there over the dead. ▶

Same Gods, Different Names

The gods and goddesses of the ancient Greeks were later worshipped by the people of ancient Rome. If you look in your local library for books of myths, you may find that some books use the Greek names for the gods while others use the Roman names. Here's a chart to help you keep track of who's who. Are you familiar with some of the Roman names?

We learned about the Romans in Britain in Year 2 and will learn more about the Romans in the Year 4 book

Greek name	Roman name	Greek name	Roman name
Zeus	Jupiter (or Jove)	Ares	Mars
Hera	Juno	Hermes	Mercury
Poseidon	Neptune	Hephaestus	Vulcan
Apollo	Apollo	Athena	Minerva
Artemis	Diana	Hades	Pluto
Aphrodite	Venus		

Gods of Nature and Mythical Creatures

The Greeks believed in other gods and goddesses, too, who were connected to the earth and nature.

Dionysus [die-oh-NIE-sus] was the god of wine. Everywhere he went, he taught people how to grow grapes and make wine. But sometimes Dionysus and his helpers made people go mad and do outrageous things.

▶ **Demeter [dim-EATER]** was the goddess of grain and of the harvest. The Greeks believed that, because of her, trees grew tall, flowers bloomed and crops ripened in the fields. By the way, the Roman name for Demeter was **Ceres [SEER-eez]**. From that name we get our word for a food that you might often eat for breakfast – cereal!

In Greek myths you might meet some curious creatures. Some are beautiful, like the winged horse called **Pegasus [PEGG-a-suss]**. ▶

◀ Some are scary, like **Cerberus [SIR-burr-us]**, a dog that belonged to Hades, the god of the underworld. This dog was not man's best friend! He had three snarling heads. He guarded the gate to the underworld. He let in the spirits of the dead and then made sure they didn't get out.

Some mythical creatures are part human and part animal. The **centaur [SEN-torr]** was part human and part horse. ▶

◀ An odd-looking fellow named **Pan** had goat's horns on his head and hooves for his feet. He was a wild and frisky creature who loved to dance through the forests and mountains. He played lively music on a set of pipes that we now call 'panpipes'.

Prometheus Brings Fire, Pandora Brings Woe

Here is a myth about how a good thing happened, followed by a very bad thing.

Once, only the gods on Mount Olympus had fire. On earth, the people had nothing to give them light in the darkness, warm them on a cold night or cook their food.

A brave and powerful giant named **Prometheus [prom-EE-thee-us]** felt sorry for mankind. He stole fire from the gods and took it to the people on earth.

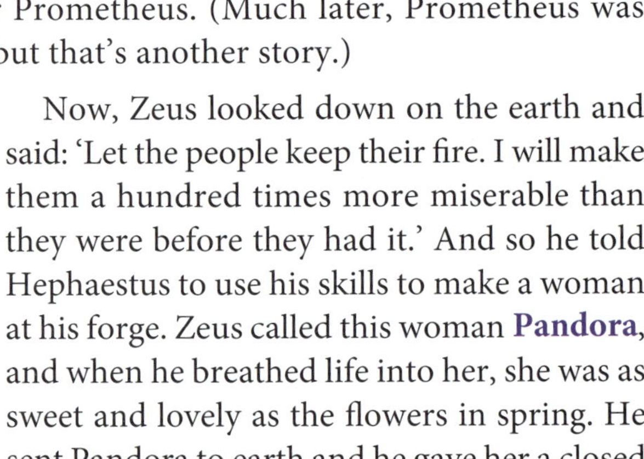

When Zeus, king of the gods, found out what Prometheus had done, he was furious. To punish him, he had Prometheus tied to a rock with unbreakable chains. Day after day, a fierce eagle flew down and ripped and clawed at the body of poor Prometheus. (Much later, Prometheus was finally set free by a hero named Hercules – but that's another story.)

Now, Zeus looked down on the earth and said: 'Let the people keep their fire. I will make them a hundred times more miserable than they were before they had it.' And so he told Hephaestus to use his skills to make a woman at his forge. Zeus called this woman **Pandora**, and when he breathed life into her, she was as sweet and lovely as the flowers in spring. He sent Pandora to earth and he gave her a closed box, which he told her she must never open.

But Pandora was very, very curious. Every time she looked at the box, she wanted to know what was in it. She knew very well that Zeus had told her not to open it. 'But,' she said to herself, 'what harm could it do to take just one little peek inside?' And so she lifted the lid. Out from the box flew all the bad things in the world – pain, disease, disaster, sorrow, jealousy and hatred. But some people say there was one more thing in Pandora's box – hope. Hope is what keeps people going despite all the bad things in the world.

Oedipus and the Sphinx

Long ago, near the Greek city of Thebes [theebs], there lived a terrible creature called the **Sphinx [sfinks]**. She had the face of a woman but the body of a lion with wings. When travellers came to the city, she would swoop down upon them. Then she would ask them a riddle. If they could answer the riddle, she would let them go. But if they couldn't, she would eat them! So far, no one could answer the riddle.

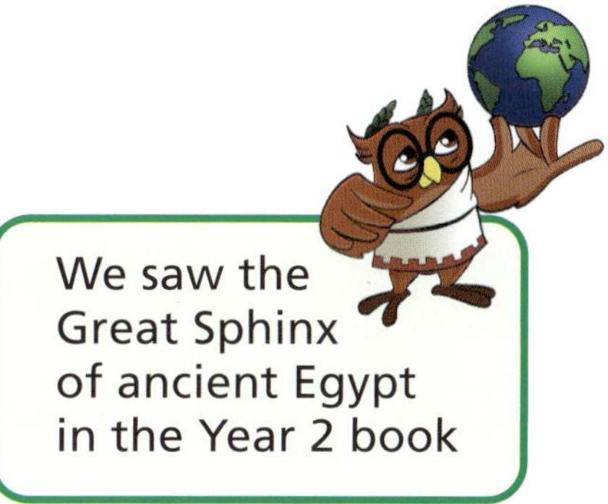

Everyone in Thebes lived in fear of the monster. Then one day a very smart and brave young man named **Oedipus [EED-ee-puss]** was on his way to Thebes. When the Sphinx saw him, she smiled, for she thought she would soon have a tasty lunch.

'Answer this riddle,' she said to Oedipus, 'or meet your doom. What creature goes on four feet in the morning, on two feet at noon and on three feet in the evening?'

Oedipus looked up at the Sphinx and said: 'Man. In childhood he crawls on his hands and knees, which is like four feet. In the middle of his life, when he is grown up, he walks on two feet. And in the evening of his life, when he is old, he uses a cane, which is like walking on three feet.'

The Sphinx was so angry that her riddle had been solved that she threw herself in the ocean and drowned. And the people of Thebes were so grateful to Oedipus that they made him their new king.

Theseus and the Minotaur

Once upon a time, not far from Greece on the island of Crete, there lived a king named **Minos [MY-noss]**. King Minos led a war against the Greek city of Athens. He burned the ships of the Athenians and destroyed their crops. Then he sent a cruel message to the ruler of Athens, **King Aegeus [ee-JEE-us]**. 'Every nine years,' said King Minos, 'when the springtime comes, you shall choose seven of your youths and seven of your maidens and send them to me in a ship. If you fail to do this, my soldiers will burn your city to the ground.'

'But,' the Athenians asked, 'what shall happen to the youths and maidens?'

'In Crete,' said King Minos, 'there is giant maze called the Labyrinth, designed by the master inventor, **Daedalus [DAY-da-luss]**. Whoever goes into the Labyrinth can never find his way out. Deep inside there lives a monster, half-man and half-bull, called the **Minotaur [MY-no-tor]**. I will put your youths and maidens into the Labyrinth, and there they will be eaten by the Minotaur.'

And so, when nine years had passed, and the flowers began to bloom in the spring, there was no joy in Athens, but only tears and sadness. Seven youths and seven maidens were put on board a black-sailed ship and sent to their terrible fate in the Labyrinth.

Now, another nine years had almost passed when a brave young man arrived in Athens. His name was **Theseus [THEE-see-us]** and he was a prince. In fact, he was the son of King Aegeus. He had been raised by his mother in a faraway town. Now that he had grown to manhood he had come to Athens to meet his father, the King. King Aegeus embraced his son with great joy.

Theseus arrived in Athens just a few days before seven youths and seven maidens were to be sent to the Minotaur. When Theseus learned of this, he said: 'I will take the place of one of the youths. I will kill the Minotaur and we shall all return safely.' King Aegeus begged his son not to go. But Theseus promised his father: 'When I return, I will change the sail of the ship from black to white, so you will know that I have succeeded.'

The ship sailed to the island of Crete. When they arrived, the young victims were marched through the streets on their way to the Labyrinth. And that is when **Ariadne [ar-ee-ADD-nee]**, the lovely daughter of King Minos, saw Theseus. She could not bear the thought of sending this young, handsome prince to his death. And so she went to Daedalus, the inventor of the Labyrinth. She asked him how anyone who entered the great maze could get out again. Daedalus gave her a clever idea, and she rushed to the prison where Theseus was locked up.

Ariadne whispered: 'Listen, Theseus. If you will promise to marry me and take me with you to Athens, I will help you.' Theseus gladly agreed. Then Ariadne gave him a ball of string and told him to tie one end to the gate of the Labyrinth and unwind the ball as he went along. That way, he could follow the string to find his way back out.

Theseus soon found himself deep in the dark, winding halls of the Labyrinth. He heard a rumbling, growling sound. It was the Minotaur, snoring in his sleep. Theseus leaped on the beast. He had never wrestled so strong or savage an opponent. With fierce roars, the Minotaur fought back. But Theseus had taken the beast by surprise, and in the end the Minotaur lay dead.

We read about Hansel and Gretel who were also clever enough to find their way out of the labyrinth of the forest in Year 2.

Theseus followed the string back out of the Labyrinth. With Ariadne's help, he freed the other Greek youths and maidens. Then they all boarded the ship and set sail for Athens.

But oh, what a sad mistake followed! In his rush, Theseus forgot to replace the ship's black sail with a white one. His father had been sitting for weeks on a cliff looking out over the sea, awaiting the return of his son. Now, when King Aegeus saw the black-sailed ship, he fainted and fell forward into the sea. And ever since then, the sea where he drowned has been called the Aegean Sea.

Daedalus and Icarus

As you know, the master inventor Daedalus designed the Labyrinth for King Minos. Daedalus also showed Ariadne how Theseus could escape from the Labyrinth. When King Minos found this out, he was so angry that he threw Daedalus in the Labyrinth, along with his young son, **Icarus [IK-ar-us]**.

Not even the man who invented the Labyrinth could find his way out of it. He had no ball of string to help him! Would the father and son die there? No – for when Daedalus saw the seagulls flying overhead, he got an idea.

Little by little, he gathered many feathers. He fastened them together with wax, and so made two pairs of wings like those of a bird. He put one pair on himself and the other pair on Icarus. He showed his son how to move his arms and catch the wind with his wings.

'Now, son,' he said, 'let us fly away from here. But listen carefully. Do not fly too high, or you will get too close to the sun and the wax on your wings will melt.'

Daedalus and Icarus flew up out of the Labyrinth, over the sea and away from the island of Crete. 'Oh,' cried Icarus, 'it's wonderful to be free and flying through the air!'

'Yes,' said Daedalus, 'but do not fly too close to the sun.'

A puff of wind lifted Icarus up. He was so excited that he forgot what his father told him. Higher and higher he flew, toward the highest heavens.

The warm sun began to melt the wax and, one by one, the feathers fell from his wings. Then down, down, down fell Icarus into the sea. Daedalus cried out in grief as he saw the waters close over his son far below.

Arachne the Weaver

In all of Athens, no one could spin such fine thread or weave such wonderful cloth as the young woman named **Arachne [ar-ACK-nee]**. People from miles around came to admire her cloth. Arachne grew so proud of her weaving that she began to boast: 'I am the most skilful weaver in the world!'

'Yes, of course,' said her friends, 'next to the great goddess Athena.'

'Athena? Ha!' said Arachne. 'Can she spin thread so fine, or weave it into cloth as beautiful as mine? Why, I could teach her a thing or two!'

An old woman in a dark cloak spoke to Arachne. 'Be careful, my dear,' she said. 'You must show respect for the gods. Your boasting may anger Athena.'

'I'm not afraid of Athena,' snapped Arachne. 'Let her come here and we'll see who is the better weaver.'

Then the old woman threw back her cloak. There was a flash of light, and there stood the grey-eyed goddess, Athena. 'I am ready,' said Athena quietly. 'Take me to a loom, and let us begin. When we are finished, if your work is best, then I will weave no more. But if my work is best, then you will never weave again. Do you agree?'

'I agree,' said Arachne. 'Let us begin.' She went to one loom and Athena to another. The people looked on in wonder as the goddess and the young woman wove brilliant designs into their cloth.

With threads of many colours, Arachne wove cloth as fine and light as a silken web. 'How beautiful!' said the people. 'It almost seems as if she could weave sunlight and rainbows into her cloth.'

Arachne stepped back from her loom and turned to look at Athena's work. Into her cloth the goddess had woven flowers that seemed to bloom, and a stream that seemed to ripple by, and clouds that seemed to float peacefully in a blue sky and, above them, the dazzling figures of the immortal gods themselves. When the people looked at it, they were so filled with wonder that they gasped. Arachne herself had to admit that Athena's work was more beautiful than her own. She hid her face in her hands and wept. 'Oh, how can I live if I must never spin or weave again?' she cried.

When Athena saw that Arachne would never have any joy unless she could spin and weave, she said: 'I cannot break the agreement we had, but I will change you so that you spin and weave forever.' And with a touch, she turned Arachne into a spider, which ran to a corner and quickly began to spin and weave a beautiful, shining web.

And that is why some people say that all spiders in the world are the children of Arachne.

There is a special name for the class of animals that spiders belong to. Spiders are not insects but arachnids. You can find out why on page 295. People who are afraid of spiders – is that you? – are said to suffer from arachnophobia. 'Phobia' is from a Greek word meaning fear of something.

Swift-Footed Atalanta

Atalanta [atta-LAN-ter] was a beautiful Greek maiden who could run faster than the winds. She loved nothing better than to run freely across the fields, through the woods and up and down the hills.

Atalanta's father thought that she should get married and settle down. But she cared nothing for the many young men who came daily to ask to marry her. So many men came, in fact, that one day she announced: 'If you wish to marry me, then hear this. I will marry the man who can beat me in a race.'

'Fine!' the men cried. 'Let's start now.'

'But there is one more thing,' said Atalanta. 'Whoever runs this race and loses to me shall also lose his life.' ('That should scare them away,' thought Atalanta, 'for they know that I can outrun the wind.')

And indeed, many of the men began to cough and feel a cold coming on, or suddenly remembered that they had forgotten some important business that they simply had to attend to at once.

But a few men stayed. Yes, they had heard about Atalanta's swiftness but, after all, could they be beaten by a girl? Nonsense! And so these men raced Atalanta. She even gave them a head start of a hundred paces. But for each, it was a race to his doom.

Then one day there arrived a young man named **Hippomenes [hip-POM-men-eez]**. Atalanta liked his fair features, his gentle eyes and his brave spirit, and she felt pity for him. 'Do not run against me,' she said, 'for I shall surely beat you, and that will be your end.'

'Let me try anyway,' said Hippomenes. Of course he knew that he did not have a chance to outrun her. But he had prayed to Aphrodite, the goddess of love, and asked for her help to win Atalanta as his wife. And Aphrodite had answered his prayers by giving him three golden apples and telling him what to do with them.

The race began. Even though Atalanta started a hundred paces behind Hippomenes, she quickly caught up with him. When he heard her breath close beside him, he took one of the golden apples and threw it over his shoulder.

When Atalanta saw the glittering apple, she left the path to pick it up. Hippomenes pulled ahead a little. But Atalanta easily caught up with him again. As she did, he threw the second golden apple even farther from the path. Again Atalanta left the path to get the apple, for she knew that she could still win. Again she caught up with Hippomenes, who was puffing and gasping. He took the third apple and threw it as far as he could. With an invisible nudge from Aphrodite, the apple rolled down a hill.

Atalanta could see that if she chased this apple, she might fall too far behind to win. But she dashed aside and grabbed the apple. Then she strained every muscle to catch up with Hippomenes. They were coming closer and closer to the finish line. She could see his face and hear his hard breathing. With one last burst of speed, she could pass him.

Suddenly, however, Atalanta felt something for Hippomenes that was not pity, but something warmer and more generous. And so she did not speed up, and the young man crossed the finish line first. With a laugh, Atalanta took his hand and led him to her father's house, where they were married that very day. And from above, Aphrodite looked down and smiled upon the happy couple.

Demeter and Persephone

Demeter [DIM-eater] was the goddess of all that grows from the ground. She made crops ripen, the orchards bear fruit and the flowers bloom.

More than anything else, Demeter loved her daughter, **Persephone [per-SEF-on-ee]**. Once, when Demeter was away looking after the crops in the fields, Persephone was playing in a field of flowers. As she stooped to pick a flower, she happened to pull the plant up by its roots, leaving a little hole in the ground. Then suddenly the hole grew wider and deeper, and Persephone heard a rumbling like thunder below her.

From the dark hole, four coal-black horses burst forth, pulling a golden chariot with a tall, sad-eyed driver wearing a golden crown. 'I am Hades, king of the underworld,' he said. 'Come with me and be my queen.' Then he snatched Persephone in his arms and carried her to his kingdom below.

When Demeter returned home, she could not find her daughter. She asked everyone, but no one had seen her. Then she asked the Sun, who sees all. And he told her that he had seen Hades take Persephone to the underworld to be his queen.

When Demeter heard this, she wept. She was so sad that the golden corn and waving wheat died, the trees dropped their leaves, and the grass turned brown. All the earth was cold and bare. And Demeter cried out: 'Nothing shall grow upon the earth until my daughter is returned to me.'

Then Zeus, king of the gods, saw that the people and animals were hungry, for they had no grain or fruit to eat. And so he sent Hermes, the messenger god, to tell Hades to let Persephone go back to her mother. 'You know the law, Hermes,' said Zeus. 'As long as the girl has not eaten any food of the underworld, she may leave. But anyone who eats down there must remain forever.'

Hermes flew from the heights of Olympus to the depths of the underworld. 'King of this dark place,' said Hermes to Hades, 'even you must obey the will of mighty Zeus. Bid farewell to your queen.'

Then Hermes turned to Persephone. 'Take my hand and let us go,' he said. 'But first, tell me, have you eaten anything while you were down here?'

'No,' said the girl, 'nothing but a few seeds from that bright red fruit, the pomegranate, which I plucked from a tree.'

Hades smiled. 'Then you must stay with me,' he said, thinking he had won his queen forever. But Zeus gave another command. He said that for each seed Persephone had eaten, she must spend one month of every year in the underworld with Hades. But she would be allowed to spend the other months with her mother.

And that is why every year, when Persephone must leave her mother and return to Hades, we have winter on earth. But while Demeter has Persephone with her, then she is happy, and brings forth the flowers and fruit and crops from the warm earth.

The Labours of Hercules

Most people know the Greek hero Heracles by the familiar Roman name **Hercules**, which we use here.

Hercules was the strongest man on earth. But he did not always use his strength wisely. Once, in a fit of anger, he struck and killed someone, though he did not mean to. He went to the temple of Apollo to ask what he could do to make up for his terrible mistake. He was told to go to the home of his cousin, a king named **Eurystheus [yur-iss-THEE-us]** and do whatever the king asked him to do.

King Eurystheus was a weak, mean man, and he was jealous of his big, strong cousin. So when Hercules came to serve him, he tried to think of the most difficult and dangerous tasks he could. 'Hercules,' said the king, 'for your first labour, go to the land of **Nemea [nem-EE-ah]**. A terrible lion has been killing both cattle and people there. He is so strong

that he can kill a man with one blow of his huge paw. His hide is so tough that no sword, spear or arrow can pierce it. You are to kill the Nemean lion, and bring its skin back to me.'

'Well,' thought the king to himself, 'that should be the end of Hercules.' But he did not know his cousin's strength. When Hercules found the lion, he jumped on the beast and grabbed him. Then he squeezed with all his might until, at last, the lion was dead. But how could he take off the lion's skin? When he tried to use his knife, the blade broke into pieces. Then Hercules got an idea: he used one of the lion's own sharp claws, and sure enough it cut the skin. After he had cleaned the skin, he wrapped it around him like a coat, with the head as a hood.

When Hercules returned, looking like a lion walking on two legs, the king was frightened. 'Stay outside the palace,' he said, 'and I will call out my orders to you.'

The king ordered Hercules to kill a fire-breathing, nine-headed monster called the **Hydra [HI-dra]**. Hercules used his huge club to knock off one of the monster's heads, but then two heads grew back in its place! So he grabbed a large stick and set one end on fire. Then, as he swung his club to knock off each head, he burned the stump of the neck to keep any other heads from growing back.

When King Eurystheus heard that Hercules had killed the Hydra, he thought: 'He kills beasts and monsters so easily that I must think of another kind of labour. Ah, I know! I will send him across the mountains to clean the stables of **King Augeas [aw-GEE-us]**. They are the biggest and dirtiest stables in the world, filled with the waste of thousands of oxen and cattle.'

When Hercules reached the Augean stables, he saw that it would take many years for a single man to clean them, even a man as strong as himself. But as he looked around he saw a river that ran nearby. 'Why not use that?' he thought. So he asked King Augeas to have all the animals taken out of the stable for a day. Then he dug a ditch from the river to the stable, and let the water run through the building. The water washed away all the filth in no time. Hercules filled the ditch and set the river back on its normal course.

'Very clever, Hercules,' said King Eurystheus. 'But now it's time for a real challenge. For your next labour, I order you to bring me the golden apples guarded by those three magical maidens, the **Hesperides [hess-PAIR-ee-deez]**.' The king chuckled because he knew that these apples belonged to Hera, queen of the gods, and were kept in a secret garden that no one had ever found. Hercules knew that he could not find the Hesperides. But he could find their father, Atlas, the great giant who carried the heavens and earth upon his shoulders.

'Mighty Atlas,' said Hercules, 'will you tell me where to find the golden apples of the Hesperides?'

'I cannot tell you such a secret,' said Atlas. 'But I could get the apples for you myself, if only I did not have to hold the heavens and earth on my shoulders.'

'Go and get the apples,' said Hercules, 'and I will hold the heavens and earth for you.'

'I would be glad to have someone else carry this load for a while,' said Atlas.

So Hercules took the heavens and earth upon his own shoulders. His knees shook and he gasped: 'Hurry, Atlas, for I do not know how long I can hold this.' In a short while Atlas came back with the golden apples, but he did not hand them over.

'Hercules,' he said, 'I will take these apples to King Eurystheus myself.'

Hercules could see that Atlas did not plan to come back. So he said: 'Thank you, Atlas, that is kind of you. But before you go, would you please hold the heavens and earth for just a moment? I'm not as strong as you so I need to put a pad on my shoulders to ease the pain.'

'All right,' said Atlas. He put down the apples and took the load from Hercules's shoulders.

'Thanks for the apples,' said Hercules, and he hurried off.

After Hercules completed these and other labours, the gods allowed him to leave King Eurystheus. He travelled all over Greece, doing many great deeds wherever he went.

In your classroom or library you may have a book full of maps called an atlas. The word 'atlas' comes from the name of the mythical character who held the heavens and earth on his shoulders.

Learning About Language

PARENTS: Written language has special characteristics that children need to learn in order to be able to talk about language and make progress in their writing. The section that follows introduces a number of terms and rules of written language, but children will need practice in school for these terms and conventions to sink in. In this book we introduce some terms and concepts that will be built on in later books. For example, in this book we introduce some parts of speech and, in later books, we will introduce other parts of speech, as well as explain more about the parts introduced here.

Sentences

When you read this, you are reading a sentence. Now you are reading another sentence. What is a sentence? It's a group of words that expresses a complete thought. Here are three groups of words. Are they all sentences?

1) Jennifer walks to the beach.
2) She takes her dog with her.
3) In the water.

Both (**1**) and (**2**) are sentences, but not (**3**) – it does not express a complete thought. It leaves you wondering, 'Who is in the water? Doing what?' But let's change (**3**) 'In the water' by adding some words.

Jennifer and her dog swim in the water.

Now, is that a sentence? Yes it is. It expresses a complete thought. Every sentence has a subject and a predicate. Here are some examples.

subject	predicate
Jennifer	walks to the beach.
She	takes her dog with her.
Jennifer and her dog	swim in the water.

Can you tell me which words make up the subject and which words make up the predicate in these sentences?

Our teacher baked cupcakes for a class party.

The alien spaceship landed in our garden.

Peter Piper picked a peck of pickled peppers.

Two Rules for Writing Sentences

Rule 1.

Every sentence must begin with a capital letter. Look at the sentences on this page. Notice that every sentence begins with a capital letter.

Rule 2.

You must end a sentence with a punctuation mark. You use a different mark for different kinds of sentences. Most often you use the little dot called a full stop. You use a full stop to end sentences that tell you something. The sentence you are reading here ends with a full stop. Some sentences ask a question. If you write a sentence that asks a question, you end it with a question mark. Is it raining today? To show excitement, you use an exclamation mark. We won! What an amazing shot!

Nouns Name a Person, Place or Thing

Look around you. What do you see? A book? A chair? A window? A garden or a street?

Book, chair, window, garden, street – all those words are nouns.

A noun names a person, place or thing. In the sentences at the top of the next page, the nouns are printed in purple.

The new **boy** from **Newcastle** brought his **rabbit** in a **cage** to **school**.

The **rabbit** got out. It ran to the **cafeteria** and ate a big **salad**.

Can you pick out the nouns in these sentences?

My sister likes slimy frogs.

The basketball swished through the net.

We saw amazing paintings and statues in the museum.

All these are nouns, too:

Oxford Street   Sheen Mount Primary School

Harry Potter   Queen Victoria

Did you notice that all those nouns just named began with a capital letter? That's because they don't name just any person, place or thing, like 'street', but a certain place, like Oxford Street, or a certain person, like Queen Victoria.

We call nouns that name a certain person, place or thing, proper nouns. You begin a proper noun with a capital letter. Remember that your own name is a proper noun, too.

Singular and Plural Nouns

A noun can name one thing or it can name more than one. Another word for just one of something is *singular*. All of these are singular nouns:

car   pencil   pig

Another word for more than one is *plural*. All of these are plural nouns:

cars   pencils   pigs

You can see that to change most singular nouns to plural, all you have to do is add the letter s. But for nouns that end in s, *ss*, *ch*, *sh* or *x*, you need to add es to show more than one, like this:

singular	plural
bus	buses
dress	dresses
lunch	lunches
wish	wishes
fox	foxes

For some plural nouns, you don't use *s* or *es*, but instead you spell the word in a new way, like this:

singular	**plural**
foot	feet
tooth	teeth
child	children
woman	women
man	men

Verbs: Action Words

sing	dance	eat	laugh
jump	shout	imagine	throw

All of those words are verbs. Verbs usually show actions. They show what someone or something does.

Jason **eats** a pizza.

Hannah **opens** a present.

Can you tell me which word is the verb in each of these sentences?

Lisa eats a banana.

The monkey slips on a banana skin.

The monkey chases Lisa.

Verbs: Past and Present

Verbs can tell about actions that happen now, or actions that happened before. We say that an action that happens now is in the present. We say that an action that happened before is in the past.

These verbs are in the present. (Notice how some end in *s* and some don't.)

Today I **dance**.   Ben **dances** with Alice.

Sherry **dances** with me.   We all **dance** together.

These verbs are in the past:

Yesterday I **danced**.

Ben **danced** with Alice.

Sherry **danced** with me.

We all **danced** together.

You can change many verbs from present to past by adding *ed*, like this:

present	**past**
Today I laugh.	Yesterday I laugh*ed*.
Juanita walks to town.	Last week she walk*ed* to school.
Today we watch a film.	Yesterday we watch*ed* a film.

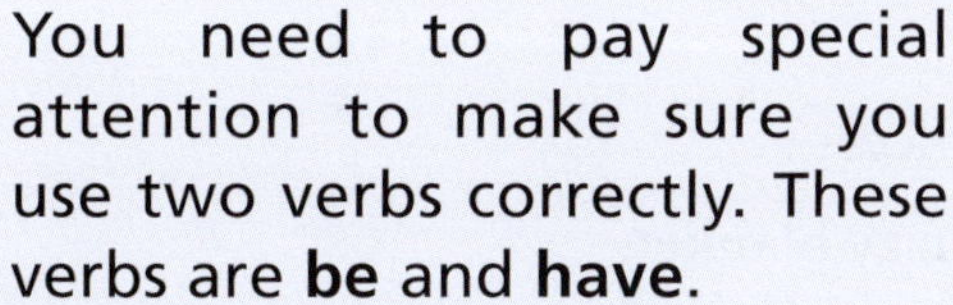

You need to pay special attention to make sure you use two verbs correctly. These verbs are **be** and **have**.

be

present	**past**
I am	I was
he, she, it is	he, she, it was
we are	we were
you are	you were
they are	they were

have

present	**past**
I have	I had
he, she, it has	he, she, it had
we have	we had
you have	you had
they have	they had

But some verbs are different. Here are some verbs to watch out for. Try making up some sentences using these verbs in the past and in the present.

verb in the present	**verb in the past**
I see, you see	I saw, you saw
he sees	he saw
I do, they do	I did, they did
she does	she did
I come, you come	I came, you came
he comes	he came
I run, we run	I ran, we ran
he runs	he ran
I go, you go	I went, you went
she goes	she went
we give, you give	we gave, you gave
he gives	he gave
you sing, they sing	you sang, they sang
she sings	she sang

Adjectives Describe Things

You know two kinds of words: nouns and verbs. Now let's find out about another kind, adjectives.

Adjectives are the words we use to describe nouns (people, places or things). Adjectives can tell how something looks or tastes or feels or sounds.

a **slippery** fish

a **loud** noise

a **cuddly** puppy with
brown fur and a **red** collar

Can you pick out the adjectives in these next sentences?

Sara loves her old, soft, fuzzy blanket.

The brown goat ate a large pizza.

Let's tell scary stories about massive ogres.

Sometimes adjectives tell how many. The words in **purple** in these sentences are adjectives that tell how many:

I have **many** pets.

I have **two** cats, **one** hamster and **some** goldfish.

I take good care of **every** pet.

You can use adjectives to compare. Often all you have to do is add *er* or *est*, like this:

Batman is **strong**.   Hercules is **stronger**.   Superman is the **strongest**.

My cat is **small**.   Olivia's cat is **smaller**.   Rajen's cat is the **smallest**.

More About Words: Antonyms and Synonyms

Let's play a word game. I'm going to tell you a word, then you tell me an antonym. Antonyms are words that mean the opposite of each other. What is the opposite of cold? Hot. So, cold and hot are antonyms. Tall and short are antonyms. Now, can you tell me an antonym for each of these words?

happy   tall   fast   win

Okay, let's change the game a little. This time I'm going to tell you a word and I want you to tell me a synonym. Synonyms are words that mean the same or almost the same thing. Pretty and beautiful are synonyms. Big and large are synonyms. Can you tell me a synonym for each of these words?

fast   angry   powerful   leap

Now, look at these pairs of words. Are they synonyms or antonyms?

love   hate

thin   skinny

begin   start

shout   whisper

loud   quiet

shiny   dull

calm   peaceful

wild   tame

*Are **wild** and **tame** synonyms or antonyms?*

Contractions

When you write, sometimes you combine two words into one short word called a contraction. To show that letters have been left out in a contraction, you use the punctuation mark called an **apostrophe [a-POSS-troe-fee]**, like this:

I am = I'm   do not = don't   can not = can't

you are = you're   is not = isn't   are not = aren't

Abbreviations

Have you ever looked at the address on a letter? You might see something like this:

The address uses many abbreviations. Abbreviations save time and space by making words shorter. Here are the words that match the abbreviations in that address:

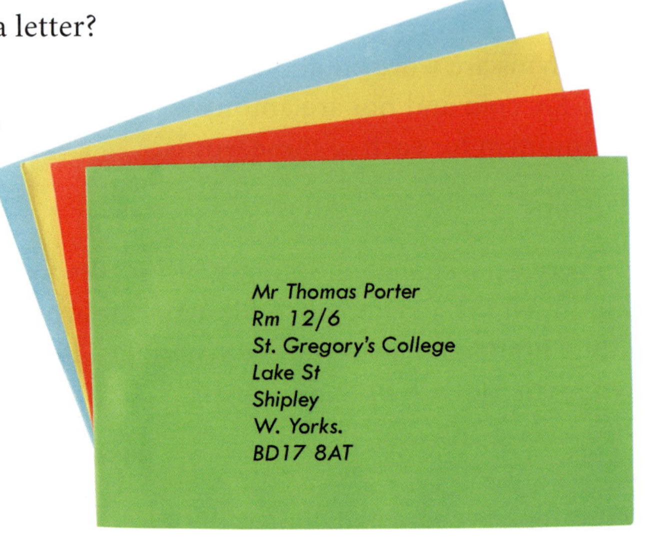

Mr	Mister
Rm	Room
St	Saint
St	Street
W.	West
Yorks.	Yorkshire

In addresses or on maps you may see other common abbreviations, such as Rd (Road), Ave. (Avenue), Pol. Sta. (Police Station). Sometimes two words can have the same abbreviation so you have to guess which makes better sense. 'Street Gregory's College in Lake Saint' would be too strange. The postcode is also like an abbreviation because the starting letters can mean a nearby big town. 'BD' here means Bradford. Do you know your postcode?

When you write to someone and you want to be polite, you might use an abbreviation, called a courtesy title, like this:

Dear Mrs Fletcher   Dear Ms Catt

Dear Prof. Saunders (Prof. stands for Professor)   Dear Dr Duffy (Dr stands for Doctor)

Abbreviations don't need a full stop when they end in the last letter of the word, like Mr for Mister or Dr for Doctor. You only need the full stop when they end with another letter, like Rev. for Reverend or Hon. for Honourable.

Using Capital Letters

You already know that you always use a capital letter when you start a sentence. When else do you use a capital letter? You use a capital letter when you write names of particular people, places or things, such as:

Martha Woodford   **W.S. Gilbert**

Pudsey   **Wembley Arena**

When you use initials in a name, you write them as capital letters followed by full stops. For example, in W.S. Gilbert the 'W.S.' stands for William Schwenk. How do you write your initials?

Here are some other rules for using capital letters when you write.

● When you refer to yourself, 'I' is always a capital.

● Use capitals for the months of the year and the days of the week.

January
August
Wednesday
Saturday

● Use capitals for the names of holidays.

New Year's Day
Christmas
Hanukkah
St Andrew's Day
Mother's Day

● Use capitals for the names of countries, cities, counties and landmarks.

Scotland
Boston, Lincolnshire
Beachy Head
Land's End

● Use capitals for the name of a team, major sporting event or band.

Tottenham Hotspur
Olympics
Rugby World Cup
Coldplay

● Use capitals for all the important words when you write the title of a book. You don't need them for little words like *a, the, at, in* or *of,* unless it's the first word of the title. You always give the first word a capital letter. Remember to underline the title of a book, like this:

<u>Paddington at Large</u>

<u>The Adventures of Mrs Pepperpot</u>

Familiar Sayings

PARENTS: Every culture has phrases and proverbs that make no sense when carried over literally into another culture. To say, for example, that someone has 'let the cat out of the bag' is not literally about freeing a trapped feline. Nor – thank goodness – does it ever literally 'rain cats and dogs'!

The sayings and phrases in this section may be familiar to many children, but the inclusion of these sayings and phrases in the Core Knowledge Sequence has been singled out and much appreciated by many parents and teachers who work with children from home cultures in which they may be unfamiliar with these sayings and phrases.

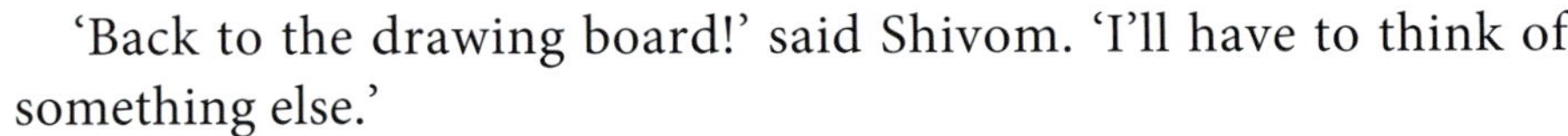

Back to the drawing board.

People use this saying when something they're doing doesn't work. Like someone drawing designs on a board, they need to start again and devise a new plan.

'Shivom, that was Natalie's father on the telephone,' said Deb. 'He says Natalie does have that joke book you wanted to buy for her birthday.'

'Back to the drawing board!' said Shivom. 'I'll have to think of something else.'

Better late than never.

People use this saying to mean that it's better that something happens late than not at all.

'Estevan, here's your birthday present. Sorry it's late. The shop was out of stock.'

'No worries, Dad. Better late than never!' said Estevan.

Cold Feet.

People say that someone who decides not to do something out of fear gets 'cold feet'.

'I want to jump off the diving board but, every time I try, I get cold feet. It feels like my feet are stuck in one place.'

It's no use crying over spilt milk.

People use this saying to mean that when something has gone wrong that cannot be mended, feeling sorry or worrying won't make it better.

'Hey, Greg, what's up? You aren't still upset about letting that goal in, are you? Come on, it's no use crying over spilt milk.'

Easier said than done.

People use this saying to mean that it's sometimes easy to say what should be done, but it's harder to do it.

Rachel and Tom found an old, bent bicycle frame in a rubbish skip. 'Let's take it home and mend it,' said Rachel.

'Easier said than done,' said Tom. 'Where are we going to get two wheels and a chain to fit it? And how are we going to straighten the frame?'

Eaten out of house and home.

People use this phrase, often humorously, to mean that a huge amount of food gets eaten, so much, in fact, that someone may have to sell the house to pay for all the food!

'Are you excited that your sister is getting married?' Aeryn asked Marie.

'I am. My Grandad and Granny are coming to the wedding, and my aunts and uncles and cousins, too. But my Dad seems a little worried. He says all Mum's relatives are going to eat us out of house and home.'

Get a taste of your own medicine.

People use this expression to mean that someone who has been bothering or mistreating others gets treated in the same way.

'So, did Graham hide anyone's football kit at school today?' asked Rosa's sister.

'No,' replied Rosa. 'And I don't think he will for a while. Before practice, we hid his socks and put some frilly pink ones in his sports bag so he had to wear those. He finally got a taste of his own medicine.'

Two heads are better than one.

People use this saying to mean that when one person is having trouble with a task or problem, a second person can often help out.

Pete was playing a geography game online. 'Rosie,' he asked his friend, 'what goes next to Devon?'

'Well,' said Rosie, 'try Dorset and Somerset. Or maybe Cornwall?'

'Dorset and Somerset both fit. You're a genius.'

'You could be right,' Rosie replied, 'but two heads are better than one.'

Get out of the bed on the wrong side.

People use this phrase to mean someone is in a bad temper, as if they had collided with a wall when trying to get up.

'My mum was in a bad mood all morning. I think she got out of bed on the wrong side.'

Practise what you preach.

People use this saying to mean that you should behave the way you tell others to behave.

'Mum! Mum! Help! Ben took my train. He's always snatching my toys,' Chris wailed. Then Chris snatched the train out of his little brother's hands.

'That's enough, boys,' said their mother. 'Ben, you shouldn't take the toy Chris is playing with. And, Chris, if you grab things back from him, he will think it's okay to grab things from you. You need to practise what you preach.'

In hot water.

People use this phrase to mean in deep trouble, as if they were being cooked for dinner.

'What was your favourite part of the film?' Ryan asked Josie.

'I liked the part when they fell into the snake pit and the snakes were slithering all over them, and then the bad guys found them and sealed the pit,' Josie said.

'Yeah,' Ryan agreed, 'they were really in hot water then.'

Turn over a new leaf.

To turn over a new leaf is to make a big change in the way you behave. A leaf is an old word for a page of a book and a new page could have a new story.

'I've been late for school nine times already this year. Today I'm going to turn over a new leaf. From now on, I'm always going to be on time.'

Where there's a will there's a way.

This saying means if you're determined to do something, you'll find a way to do it.

'The Guides need to raise so much for our new minibus,' said Hilary. 'How will we ever do it?'

'We've already started weeding gardens and washing car windscreens,' replied Tina. 'We desperately want that minibus, and where there's a will there's a way.'

Keep your fingers crossed.

People use this expression in several ways. They say it to ward off danger, and they say it to help make a wish come true.

'What do you want for your birthday, Carmen?' asked José.

'Well, I'd like to have a bicycle, but I'm really keeping my fingers crossed that my grandmother will be out of hospital by my birthday.'

You can't teach an old dog new tricks.

People use this saying to mean that as you get older you become more set in your ways. Once you are used to doing something in a certain way, it becomes very hard to learn a different way to do it.

'Grandfather, why are you going this way to the market?' asked Mei Jing. 'The new road is much quicker.'

'Oh,' laughed her grandfather, 'I always forget about that new road because I've gone this way all my life. I suppose you can't teach an old dog new tricks.'

Suggested Resources

Books

The Emperor's New Clothes by Hans Christian Andersen and translated by Naomi Lewis (Candlewick Press) 2000

Lighthouse Keeper series by Ronda and David Armitage (Scholastic) 2008

Something Else by Kathryn Cave (Puffin) 2011

Folk Tales of West Bengal by Swapna Dutta (Children's Book Trust) 2009

Green Bananas series, Red Bananas series and Blue Bananas series (Egmont) 2011

Billy's Bucket by Kes Gray and Garry Parsons (Red Fox) 2004

A Twist in the Tail: Animal Stories from Around the World by Mary Hoffman (Frances Lincoln) 2001

Pirican Pic and Pirican Mor by Hugh Lupton (Barefoot) 2003

Aesop's Fables by Beverley Naidoo and Piet Grobler (Frances Lincoln) 2011

The Adventures of Robin Hood by Marcia Williams (Walker) 2007

Greek Myths by Marcia Williams (Walker) 2006

The Iliad and the Odyssey by Marcia Williams (Walker) 2006

Poetry

Heard it in the Playground by Allan Ahlberg (Puffin) 1991

Please Mrs Butler: Verses by Allan Ahlberg (Puffin) 1984

The Oxford Book of Children's Poetry by Michael Harrison and Christopher Stuart-Clark (Oxford University Press) 2007

A Children's Treasury of Milligan: Classic Stories and Poems by Spike Milligan (Virgin) 2001

The Puffin Book of Utterly Brilliant Poetry by Brian Patten (Puffin) 1999

Mobile Apps

Greek God (Wuxi I Create Software) app for iPad or iPhone

Greek and Roman Gods and Goddesses Trivia (Swartz Enterprises) app for iPhone

Hangman Free HD (Optime) app for iPhone or iPad

Mad Libs (Penguin) app for iPhone [Stories to Practise Parts of Speech]

Paddington Bear (HarperCollins) app for iPad or iPhone

Sherwood Forest Archery HD (Revolution Games) app for iPad

SparkleFish (Joel Steinmetz) app for iPad or iPhone [for Parts of Speech]

Word Waggle Jr. (Kojoe Yirenkyi) app for iPhone or iPad

DVDs

A Christmas Carol (Boulevard Entertainments) 2010

Jason and the Argonauts (UCA) 1963

Miracle on 34th Street (Twentieth Century Fox) 2005 [colour version]

Miracle on 34th Street (Twentieth Century Fox) 1947, 2004 [original black and white version]

Paddington Bear - Please Look After This Bear (Abbey) 2006

Scrooge (Paramount Home Entertainment) 2004

Scrooge (Simply Media) 1951, 2012

Magazines

Carousel by the Federation of Children's Book Groups: www.carouselguide.co.uk

History and Geography

Introduction

For many years, British primary schools have taught history through topics, such as Florence Nightingale, Henry VIII and his six wives and the Great Fire of London. These topics are all interesting, and have an obvious appeal to children, but their popularity often results in children going over this material several times in the course of their school career, whilst not covering other very important areas. By treating history as a series of topic projects, there is a danger that children never learn the sequence of events in British history, which make it clear to them how one thing has led to another, and how each generation builds on the experiences of those who have gone before them.[1]

Learning history is not simply a matter of being able to recall names and dates, though the value of getting a firm mental grip on a few names and dates – such as 1066 and 1688 – should not be discounted. While Year 3 children have not developed a sophisticated sense of chronology, the development of a chronological sense is aided by having at least a few dates fixed in mind and associated with specific events, so that later, as children grow, they can begin to place these dates and events into a more fully developed sense of what happened when.

The thematic approach to history – looking at the development of toys or houses through the ages – is also appealing to children, and can be a useful means of conveying information about things with which the child is already familiar. However, with no chronological framework at all, it becomes difficult for the child to grasp even the development of these familiar concepts.

As anyone knows who has witnessed children's fascination with dinosaurs, knights in armour or kings and queens, young children are interested not just in themselves and their immediate surroundings but also in other people, places and times. In the Core Knowledge history and geography sequence, we seek to take advantage of children's natural curiosity and broaden their horizons. An early introduction to history and geography can foster an understanding of the wide world beyond each child's locality,

---

[1] For an explanation of the drawbacks of this approach see Chris McGovern's 'The New History Boys' in *The Corruption of the Curriculum* (Civitas) 2007.

and make children aware of people from the past they will never meet and places in the world they may one day visit. Our approach to history also seeks to develop our children's sense of their nation's past and its significance.

In the Year 2 book, we began to share with children, in a chronological sequence, the long and fascinating story of both the country they live in and the wider world beyond it. This process continues in Year 3, and each corresponding chapter in the Core Knowledge UK series of books is divided into sections including world history and geography and British history and geography. The extent to which children can appreciate the complexities of a given period will obviously increase with age. However, our aim is that children should have an overall grasp of the major outlines of both world history and British history by the time they finish their primary education.

While it's good to help children grasp a few important facts, for young children the best history teaching emphasises the story in history. By appealing to children's naturally active imaginations, we can ask them to 'visit' people and places in the past. For example, we take children to the Olympics in ancient Greece and to China with Marco Polo. They will learn how the barons forced King John to seal Magna Carta, how the little princes were murdered in the Tower of London and how Sir Francis Drake insisted on finishing his game of bowls as the Spanish Armada came over the horizon. We encourage parents and teachers to go beyond these pages to help children to learn about history through trips to museums, historic sites and buildings. There are also many excellent TV programmes on historical subjects, many of which are available on DVDs.

A Note on the History of the World Religions

In the World History and Geography section, we introduce children not only to ancient civilisations but also to topics in the history of world religions. As the many people who contributed to the development of the Core Knowledge Sequence agreed (see pages v–vi), religion is a shaping force in the history of civilisation, and thus should be part of what our children know about from a historical perspective. The pages on religion have benefited from the critiques of religious scholars and representatives of various faiths, whom we wish to thank for their advice and suggestions. In introducing children to the history of world religions, we focus on major symbols, figures and stories. Our goal is to be descriptive, not prescriptive, and to maintain a sense of respect and balance.

A Note on Geography

We encourage parents and teachers to place special emphasis on the geographical topics in the following pages. For some time now, geography has come to be regarded as a branch of environmentalism linked to political issues such as global governance. This has

---

[2] For an account of this process see Alex Standish's *Global Perspectives in the Geography Curriculum* (Routledge) 2008.

narrowed the focus of the subject in a way that has made it difficult for children to attain a reasonable grasp of the nature of the world around them.[2] The geography section of the Core Knowledge Sequence UK, on which this chapter is based, has been designed to restore the full range of topics to the disciplines of human and physical geography.

The primary school years are the best years for pupils to gain a lasting familiarity with the main features of world geography, such as the continents, the larger countries, the major rivers and mountains and the major cities of the world. These spatial forms and relationships, when connected with interesting stories, are not likely to be forgotten. Such knowledge may be reinforced by regular work with maps, which should include a lot of active drawing, colouring and identification of place names. Drawing maps, as well as associating shapes with names of places, is not only fun, but also an important step towards understanding the modern world.

Geography

A Quick Geography Review

Can you name the seven continents?* Trace the map below. Then locate each continent and write its name on the map.

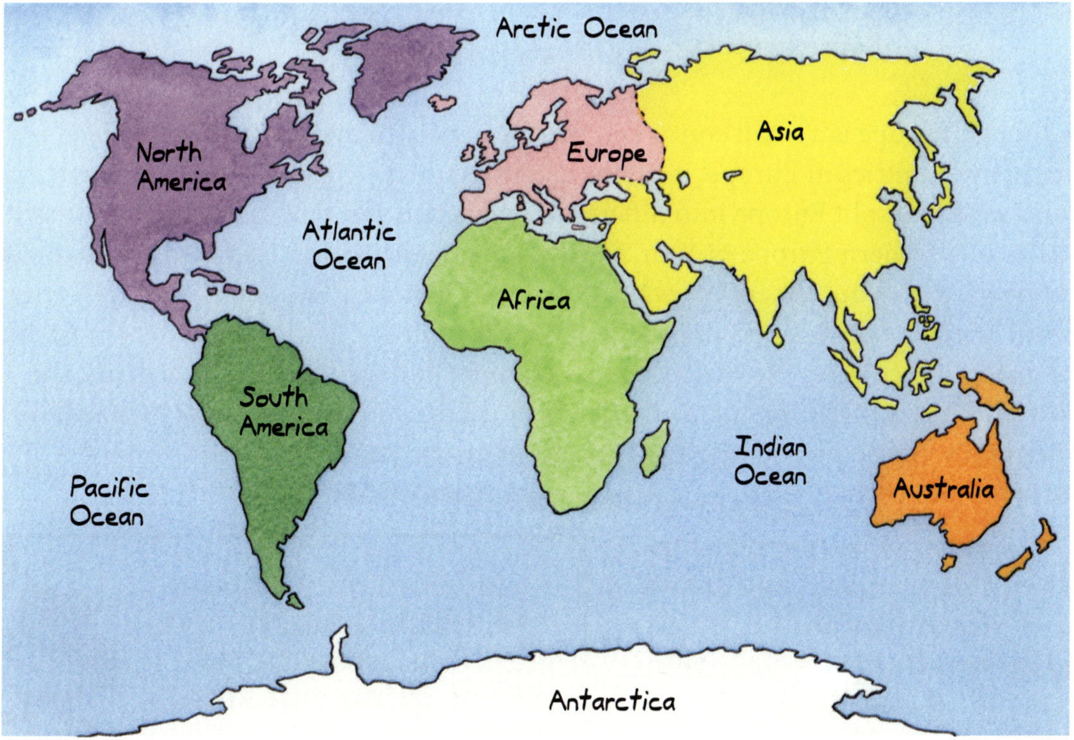

* They are, from biggest to smallest, Asia, Africa, North America, South America, Antarctica, Europe, Australia.

Visit your local library to see if you can find two books that will help you to read maps: *Mapping* (Investigate Geography) by Louise Spilsbury (Heinemann) 2010 and *Starting Geography: Maps* (Franklin Watts) 2009.

The next time you have a globe available, try this:

- Locate and name the seven continents.

- Locate the North Pole and the South Pole.

- Locate the imaginary line called the equator. The equator divides the globe into two equal parts. We call the part of the globe above the equator the Northern Hemisphere. The part of the globe below the equator is the Southern Hemisphere. ('Hemi' means half, so a hemisphere is half a sphere.) Is Australia in the Northern or Southern Hemisphere? Which hemisphere is Europe in – Northern or Southern?

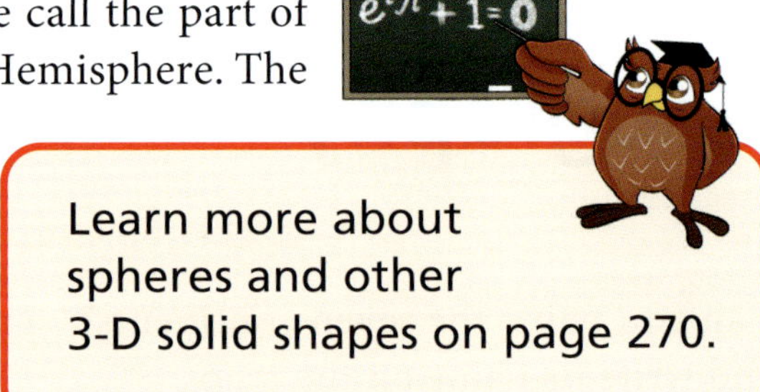

Learn more about spheres and other 3-D solid shapes on page 270.

Geography of Western Europe

Even though Europe is a small continent, there are many different countries. Because there are so many countries in Europe, it can be useful to use the compass points – north, south, east and west – to split Europe into different regions. Do you remember learning about the countries of Northern Europe in Year 2? They include the British Isles and the countries of Scandinavia. Can you remember what they are? (Norway, Sweden, Finland, Denmark, Iceland.) There are no exact boundaries for Western Europe. Location matters most, but so do language and culture. We shall describe Western Europe as France, Germany, the 'Low Countries' (that is, Belgium, the Netherlands and Luxembourg), Austria, Switzerland and northern Italy. Since the boundaries of Western Europe are unclear, sometimes the United Kingdom is also considered to be a Western European country.

Unlike much of Northern Europe, which can be very cold and snowy, most of Western Europe has what is called a *temperate climate*. This means it is not too hot and not too cold, and that it rains enough for lots of different

Read about how animals and people adapt to Northern Europe's cold climate in the Year 2 book.

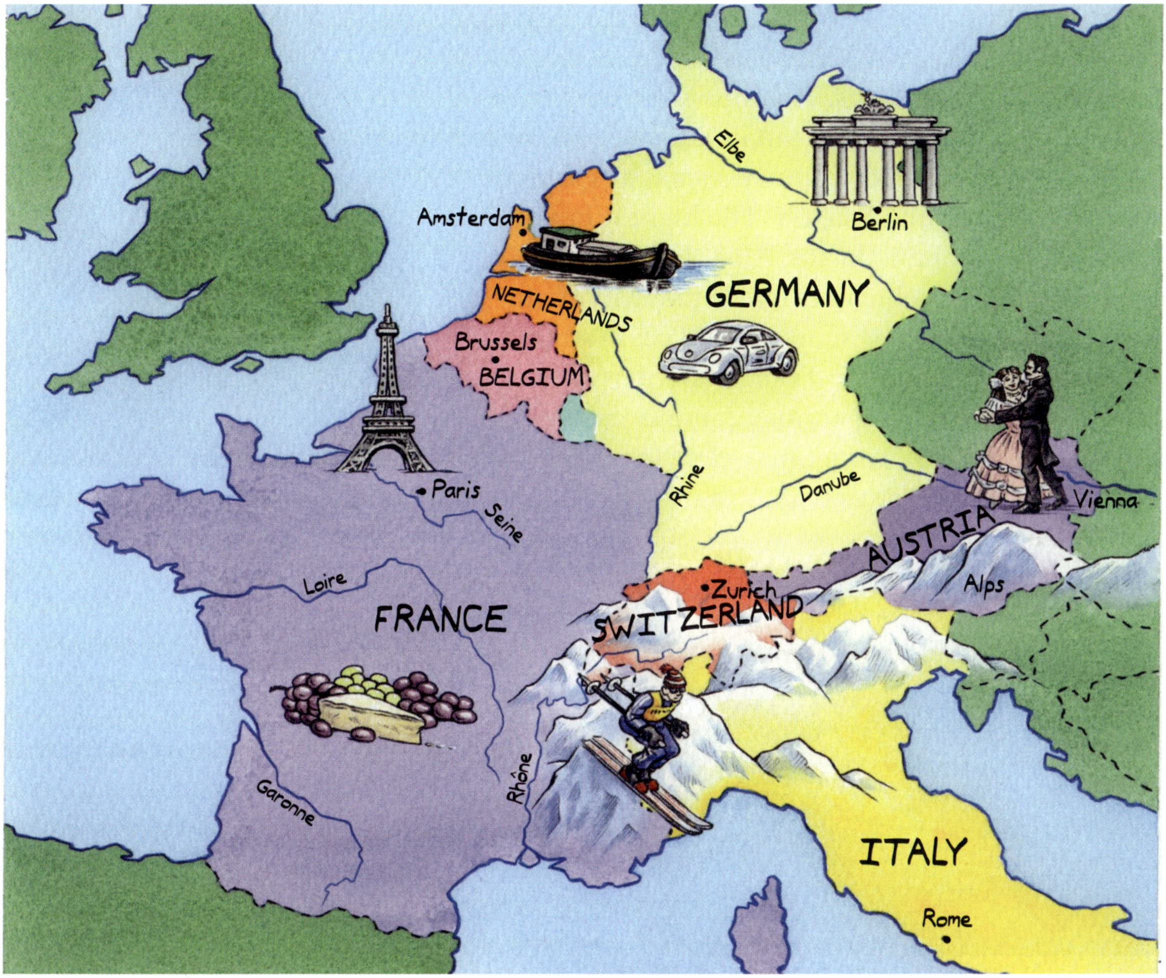

Western Europe

plants to grow. All parts of Western Europe are quite close to the sea. The sea keeps the land cool in summer and warm in winter. The climate means that much of the land of Western Europe is perfect for growing food and caring for farm animals. This is called *agriculture*. France is well known for growing lots of different foods, which are sold all around the world. France is famous for making good cheese (made from the milk of the cows, goats and sheep that live there) and wine (made from the grapes they grow), but lots of other things like fruit and vegetables are also grown there. On the higher ground and in the mountains the temperature is colder, and it is not as easy to grow food.

These dairy cows are grazing in France.

Western Europe has both flat land and really big, steep mountains, too. There is a huge range of mountains called the Alps. The Alps cover a large area. Some of these huge, snowy mountains are in France, but the Alps are also in countries such as Germany, Italy, Switzerland and Austria. The highest mountain in Western Europe is in the Alps. It is called *Mont Blanc* [mon blon] which means 'White Mountain' in French, because there is snow on it all year round. It is so big that part of it is in France and part of it is in Italy! The Matterhorn is another famous mountain in the Alps. It is on the border between Switzerland and Italy and, at 4,478 metres high, it is one of the highest mountains in the Alps.

The Matterhorn is known for its pyramid-like shape.

The climate is different in the Alps, and much colder than in the low-lying areas of Western Europe. The Alps have an *alpine climate*, which is more like the climate of Northern Europe. In Switzerland, where most of the country is covered by the Alps, some people live in the valleys created by these enormous mountains. It must be very different to living in the flat lands of the Netherlands. However, the largest city in Switzerland, Zurich, is not in the mountains. It is on flatter land where it is easier to build.

Zurich is built along a river and a lake. Can you spot the hills in the distance?

Do you remember learning about why people often live near water and how important rivers are to settlements? The river running through Zurich is fairly small, but there are quite a few large, important rivers in Western Europe, and lots of people live near them. In France, two of the biggest rivers are the Rhône [roan] and the Seine [senn]. The Seine flows through Paris, the capital city of France. Paris is the biggest city in Western Europe and the home of the famous Eiffel Tower. It is well known for art and culture.

The Eiffel Tower was built along the banks of the Seine.

The Rhine River passing through Basel in Switzerland.

As with London and the river Thames, the Seine helped Paris grow into the large city it is today. The Seine then flows north into the English Channel. In the south, the Rhône starts in mountains of the Swiss Alps. As it flows west then south, it gets bigger and joins other rivers as it flows towards the Mediterranean Sea. The French city of Lyon, the biggest in France after Paris, lies where the Rhône joins the Saône. Rivers are useful for transporting heavy things by boat. Rivers helped Lyon become an important industrial town in the 1800s (also called the nineteenth century), when it was well known for making silk. Lyon was also the home of the Lumière brothers, who were the first people ever to make films.

The Rhône and the Seine flow mainly through France, but some rivers in Western Europe are so long they flow through many countries. One of these is the Rhine, which flows through six countries, including Switzerland and Germany. The Rhine has been an important river in European history as far back as the time of the Romans. Because people have used the river to travel and to trade with people in other places for a long time, there are lots of cities near the Rhine. Where the river runs through Germany, the area nearby has plenty of factories and businesses. In

By the time the Rhine reaches Cologne in Germany, it is much larger because smaller rivers have fed into it.

fact, while France is famous for its agriculture, Germany is well known for making and building things. This is called *industry*, and there are lots of big companies from Germany that make all kinds of useful things, from cars to mobile phones.

In Germany, the capital city is Berlin. Berlin is in eastern Germany and its emblem is a big black bear standing on its hind legs. Another special symbol of Berlin is the Brandenburg Gate. For nearly 30 years, a high wall divided Berlin in two. The Gate, though much older than the wall, was one place where people could be allowed through.

The wall came down in 1989 and the Gate has become a popular tourist attraction.

Even though the Rhine is a big river, it is still smaller than the Danube, which flows through ten countries on its way east from Germany into Eastern Europe. The Danube is one of the most important rivers in Europe because it connects so many different places. Throughout history the river has helped people to travel east and west across Europe. There are even four different capital cities on the river. One of these is Vienna, the capital of Austria. Vienna is a centre for culture and music, and some great classical musicians have lived and worked there such as Franz Schubert [frants SHOO-burt], Johannes Brahms [yo-HANN-ez BRARMS] and Beethoven, whom you will find out about soon. Another composer who lived in Vienna, Johann Strauss [YO-hann str-OUSE], wrote a piece of dance music called a waltz with the title *On the Beautiful Blue Danube*.

In Western Europe, the two biggest countries by far are France and Germany. They each have their own culture and language. French is sometimes called a *Romance* language because it is a lot like Latin, the language of the *Romans*. People speak French in parts of Switzerland and Belgium, as well as in France. German, on the other hand, is called a *Germanic* language. German is not only spoken in Germany, but also in Austria and in parts of Switzerland, Belgium and alpine Italy.

The Danube River running through Vienna.

English is considered to be a Germanic language, but it has elements of both Romance and Germanic language. For example, the German word for grass is 'gras', which is very similar to our English word. The French word is 'herbe', close to our word for herbs. But language is not the only difference between the countries of France and Germany. The turbulent period called the Reformation was a time of huge change when Christians split into two groups (read more on page 172). Many in Germany became Protestant, preferring less decoration and ceremony, and they liked to read *scriptures*, religious texts, in their own language rather than Latin. Most French people remained Catholic, choosing to have educated priests to interpret the Latin scriptures for them. These are just two of the things that make each country special and different.

Each country in Western Europe has its own unique culture, but there are also things that they all have in common. There was a time when the Roman Empire stretched across most of Europe, and even today we can still see the influence of this, such as through language. Western Europe also has lots of shared history and culture. Some Western European artists and musicians have become known the world over.

If you look at the map of the Roman Empire in the Year 2 book or online at www.coreknowledge.org.uk/historygeography.php, can you point out the parts of Western Europe that the Roman Empire covered?

One of these musicians was Wolfgang Amadeus Mozart. He was born in the city of Salzburg in Austria in 1756 and is still remembered today. Mozart learnt how to play the piano when he was very young, and wrote his first piece of music when he was just five years old! He was called a *prodigy*, which means he could do things when he was very young that most grown-ups would struggle with. He went on to play to people all across Europe.

We read in Year 2 about the amazing talent of Mozart when he was a little boy. You can read about other European composers such as Vivaldi and Beethoven on pages 206–208.

We have already learnt how Vienna, the capital city of Austria, was an important city for music. Mozart moved there to find work, but so did many other musicians. One was Ludwig van Beethoven. He was born in the German city of Bonn, on the River Rhine. Beethoven could imagine music without having to hear it, so he could carry on composing even after he lost his hearing. Can you imagine how tragic that loss was for a musician?

There are also artists and painters from Western Europe whose work has become popular all across the world. One of these was Claude Monet [MON-ay]. Monet was from Paris. It was there that he showed his painting called *Impression, Sunrise* which gave its name to the style of painting he became famous for, *Impressionism*. This new way of painting was

Monet's painting Impression, Sunrise

different from traditional techniques and was criticised. Later on though, Monet's paintings became better liked and he sold more of them, and today his paintings are immensely valuable. You can see them in galleries in Cardiff, Birmingham, London, Edinburgh, Washington, Moscow, Canberra, Tokyo and many more besides.

One painter who really liked the way Monet painted was Vincent van Gogh [fan-HOCK]. Van Gogh was from the Netherlands, but moved to Paris then southern France to work as a painter. He developed the impressionist style and his paintings were even more different from traditional styles. He suffered an illness that affected how he viewed the world and, after an argument with his friend Paul Gauguin [GO-gan], he cut off part of his own earlobe. He only sold one picture in his lifetime, but people have grown to love the way he saw things. Today he is celebrated as a brilliant artist who was ahead of his time.

The borders of the 'Low Countries' have changed a lot in history. Now there are three small countries, on or near the North Sea and English Channel, that are north-east of France. They are 'low' because they have so few hills or mountains. Some, like the Netherlands, have parts that are even below sea level and need dykes to protect them from flooding. Today the biggest in this set of countries is the Netherlands, which actually means 'low countries'. The people there are called 'Dutch'. That is also the name of their language, which is a Germanic language. For example, 'red' and 'blue' are 'rood' and 'blauw' in Dutch and 'rot' and 'blau' in German.

Tulip flowers growing in the Netherlands

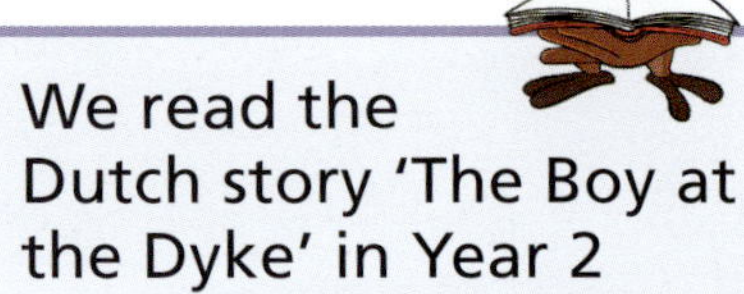

It is lovely cycling along the canals in the Netherlands.

The Netherlands is famous for being really, really flat. There is lots of agriculture and the Dutch people grow not only crops to eat but also lots of flowers. They are famous for their beautiful fields of flowers in springtime. In the capital of the Netherlands, Amsterdam, many people travel on bicycles because it is so flat. Amsterdam is also full of canals. These are man-made rivers, used for transport. They are like roads of water, and people travel along the canals in boats. The Dutch people have always been good at sailing, and Amsterdam used to be one of the busiest ports in the world. Now the port of Rotterdam is bigger.

Sometimes people say 'Holland' to mean all of the Netherlands, especially when they are following football, because Holland is the largest part of the Netherlands and it includes the country's biggest cities, like the ports of Amsterdam and Rotterdam. We have read about the painters Vermeer and Rembrandt in Year 2, and the scientist van Leeuwenhoek on page 320 of this book. They all came from Holland. Van Gogh came from a part of the Netherlands outside Holland.

Belgium became a separate country around 200 years ago. They speak two languages: French and Dutch. Their version of Dutch is called Flemish, after the province of Flanders. Made rich by trading cloth in the Middle Ages, Flanders has many beautiful towns, like Bruges, Ghent and Mechelen. Beethoven's grandfather came from Mechelen before he moved to Germany, which is why the German composer had a Dutch-sounding name. People today love Belgium for its chocolate, but Flanders was also home to skilled artists, such as Jan van Eyck [yan fan ayk] and Rogier van der Weyden [ROJ-i-a fan duh VAY-duhn]. In the twentieth century (the 1900s),

Bruges has many beautiful buildings and is also known for making lace.

Flanders was the scene of serious fighting during the First World War. The capital of Belgium is Brussels, and it is known for its good food including waffles, chips, mussels and, again, chocolate!

Belgian chocolates and… oops! I already took a bite of the waffle.

The smallest of the 'Low Countries', one that does have a few hills, is Luxembourg. Together with Belgium and the Netherlands, it was one of the six countries that began what is now the European Union. Luxembourg is located between Germany, France and Belgium and, as such, it is trilingual ('tri' means three and 'lingual' refers to language): the three official languages are German, French and Luxembourgish. Like the languages they speak, the people from Luxembourg – called the Luxembourgers – have a culture that is a mix of Romance Europe, Germanic Europe and their own unique traditions. The name of Luxembourg's capital city is easy to remember – it's also called Luxembourg.

We have learnt about many cities in Western Europe like Luxembourg, Berlin, Vienna, Paris and Amsterdam. These and many other cities are exciting and interesting places to visit. Many people in these cities work in hotels, restaurants and museums, looking after their visitors. Have you ever visited any of these cities?

Not surprisingly, a river runs through the city of Luxembourg.

By now you know that there are lots of different countries and cities in Europe, with people who speak many different languages, but it is still important for everyone to be able to work together. Sometimes this can be difficult or confusing, so many of the different countries in Europe decided to make some decisions together. As we mentioned earlier, it all started with just six countries. The leaders thought that if the countries of Europe could trade more easily with each other, and exchange the things that each country made well, then they would not fight wars against each other. They came together to form what eventually became the European Union (or the EU for short). There are now 27 countries in it, agreeing not to charge extra taxes on trade between them. People are also free to move to any other country in the EU to live and work there. In Western Europe the countries of France, Germany, the Netherlands, Belgium, Austria and Luxembourg are all members, just like the United Kingdom, but Switzerland is not.

The European Union has its own parliament where the representatives picked by each member country make decisions together. It can be complicated working together to make decisions because the EU has 23 official languages! The motto of the European Union is 'United in Diversity'. This means that, even though all the countries are very different and have their own unique cultures, they can still work together. The EU even has its own flag; it has 12 golden stars on a blue background. You earlier read about composer Ludwig van Beethoven. His music for *Ode to Joy* is the European Union's anthem.

Where You Live

Post boxes are some of the helpful things you find in a settlement.

When you come to school every morning, what sort of things do you see on your way? Maybe you pass by lots of different types of houses, or can you see parks with lots of trees and grass? Are there other kinds of buildings like shops, factories or maybe even a train station? You probably see lots of really useful things that people use, like Post Offices and post boxes for people to send letters, or maybe buses and bus stops to help take people where they need to go. Do you live in a city, with lots of other people, or maybe a smaller town? If you live in the countryside, what kinds of things do you need to go into a town or city for?

People often live close together in towns or cities because it is useful to be near shops and services. What kind of things do you think you might need from other people?

Fire engines help us stay safe. Do you hear many where you live?

Most towns and cities have important things like hospitals for people who become ill, fire stations in case things catch fire and police to keep everyone safe. If you wanted to go somewhere else, you might want to take a train. So it is handy if you have a train station near where you live, too. People need shops as well to buy food and other things they might need, or banks where they can put their money. Can you think of other useful shops or services you might find in a town or city? There are lots of examples.

People live in settlements of different sizes. Farmers, for example, might live in a house in the countryside, far away from other people. When there are just a few houses together, it is known as a hamlet. Slightly bigger in size is a village, which would have quite a few houses as well as shops and other useful things, but villages are still usually in the countryside near to fields, forests and hills – and sometimes by the sea.

Towns are bigger still. Towns have lots of people living in them, with lots of shops and other services. They usually have a train station as well. Cities are next up in size and are some of the biggest settlements. They have even more shops and services than a town. People often live very close together in a city. This is a called a dense population. Can you name some of the cities in the UK? Did you think of London, Edinburgh, Glasgow, Cardiff, Swansea, Belfast, Liverpool or others?

Places like hamlets and villages are in the countryside where there are fewer people and open spaces with lots of plants and animals. This is called a *rural* area. Towns and cities, where there are lots of people in a small space, all living close together, are known as *urban* areas. An urban area is a place with lots of buildings and streets and where there are lots of things built by humans. When you

A small hamlet in the English countryside

Staithes is a seaside village in North Yorkshire. Which type of clouds do you see? See page 290 to find out.

Oban is a port town in western Scotland with ferries bringing people to and from small island villages.

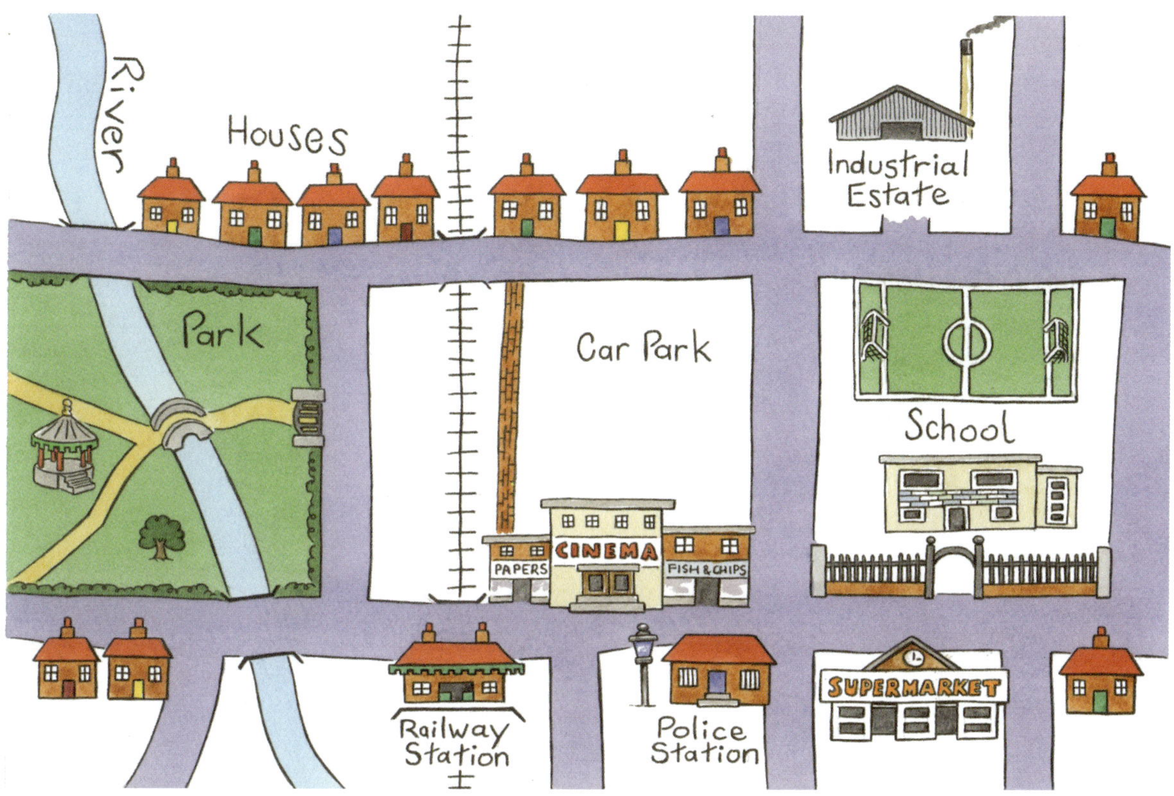

look outside, can you see fields and hills, or do you see streets and houses? This is a clue to know whether you are in a rural or urban area. Could you draw a map of your school and the area around it, showing whether you are in a town or the countryside? If you are in a town, you could show your nearest open spaces like parks. Include things that are useful, like shops and places where you go to have fun, like the cinema.

A really big urban area is called a *conurbation*. A conurbation is when a city gets so big that it connects with other nearby towns and cities to form a huge urban area. This is because lots of people need to live in or near to cities, so they get bigger and bigger as more houses are built for people. But because the countryside is really important too, there are rules to stop people building too many new roads and houses in rural areas. This is to protect the plants and animals that live in the countryside, as well as to make sure we have land to farm and grow food on.

In towns and cities, there are also lots of different types of houses. Some people live in flats, which are homes in big buildings where lots of other people also live. Some houses are connected to the ones next to them all along the street. These are called terraced houses. Houses on their own are called detached houses. Next time you go out, have a look and see what different kinds of houses you can spot.

Rivers and Basins

Whether you live in an urban area (in a town) or a rural area (in the countryside) it is quite likely that you live near a river. Through the ages, people have often built their houses near to a river, because it can be useful in lots of ways.

In Year 2 we read about how important the Nile was in ancient Egypt because its fertile flood plains made it easy to grow wheat.

People can travel on rivers, bathe in rivers (if they're clean enough!) and use river water in their fields and orchards. Do you remember in Year 2 Science we learned about how water in the sea is salt water, which people can't use to drink or water crops. Water in rivers is fresh water. Also, when rivers flood and recede, they leave behind rich soil which is good for growing crops.

Providing water and rich soil, rivers help people grow lots of food. Where plenty of food can grow, civilisation develops. Many of the world's great civilisations – ancient Egypt, ancient Mesopotamia, India and China – started near a river.

Before there were any trains, buses or cars, travelling by boat on a river – and canals connecting to rivers – used to be one of the best ways to get around. This was really important to people who made a living by buying and selling things to other people. We call this 'trade' and these people 'traders' or 'merchants'. Being close to a river or to the sea was really important if you wanted to send and receive goods.

Marco Polo's father and uncle were merchants who travelled by sea and by land. Read more on page 140.

Today we don't have to worry about any of these things when we are thinking about where we want to live, but a long time ago they would have been very important. This is why so many cities and towns are near big rivers. London is on the River Thames, and other cities, like Liverpool on the River Mersey or Newcastle on the River Tyne, have grown up on the banks of big rivers. This is because they were so useful.

The Aysgarth Falls on the River Ure in Yorkshire

Rivers change a lot as they carry water all the way down to the sea. It could be a journey of hundreds of miles. The Rhine River grows much larger on its journey through Western Europe between Basel and Cologne.

Imagine travelling all the way along a river. Every river begins as a little stream, at a starting point called the river's *source*. This might be on a mountain where the stream would be very narrow but flow very quickly down the steep mountainside. You might come across a waterfall where the river goes off the edge of a cliff or down a set of natural 'steps' – such as with the Aysgarth Falls – and falls down into a pool below before continuing its journey.

As you followed the river, it would get wider and deeper as it collected more and more water on its way to the sea. Next, the river might flow down a valley, with mountains or hills on either side. When it rains, the water drains down the sides of the valley and into the river. So the river gets bigger and bigger.

There might be farms that you would see in this valley as you went past. The river would mean that the land is fertile and perfect for growing food because there is a source of water. As the river drew nearer the sea, it would usually be very wide and deep, and the water would be flowing more slowly. At this point there might be boats on the river as it is wide and deep enough.

By the time the river reaches the sea, it is usually very wide. This point is called an *estuary*. It is quite a journey, and there are lots of changes on the way.

The River Ure passes many farms and towns, such as Boroughbridge.

Several streams, called tributaries, flow together and join to make a river. A really big river might have a tributary that is also big enough to be considered a river. For example, the Humber estuary is the notch in the coastline of north-east England where several rivers – including the River Ure – have joined together and the water is low and wide enough to let the sea in and out at every tide. The Rivers Ure, Swale, Wharfe and others form in the hills of the Yorkshire Dales, which are beautiful steep valleys on either side of those rivers. They meet and turn into the River Ouse [ooze]. The Ouse flows through the flat landscape around York and passes through the city, carrying water from its tributary rivers all the way to the Humber.

The River Ure turns into the River Ouse, which is quite large by the time it passes through York.

Many other tributary rivers also drain into the Humber estuary. The high ground on the North York Moors feeds some rivers that flow south first into the Derwent and then into the Ouse. The Don flows in from Sheffield, and the River Hull emerges at Kingston upon Hull. Further south, the Trent winds through Stoke and Nottingham, and is joined by tributaries from Derby, Leicester, Birmingham and elsewhere. They all flow eventually into the Humber.

The drainage basin from the whole system of rivers is extensive, serving most of the Midlands and much of the north of England.

The area of land from which the water has drained into a river is called the *drainage basin* or, for short, a basin. Like the basin where you wash, a drainage basin holds water and only lets it out at the bottom. When it rains or snows, some water soaks into the ground, but some runs into rivers and helps to drain the land. Anywhere that the water has no easier path down to the sea becomes part of the drainage basin, because the water eventually drains into one main, big river before it flows into an estuary and reaches the sea. That is why sometimes a drainage basin is also called a river basin.

The Humber Bridge helps people travel over the large Humber estuary. Does it look like it is high tide or low tide?

The edge of the basin, called the *watershed*, follows the highest passes and ridges between the hills and mountains. On our map of the Humber it is the line where the pale green area touches the darker green. Outside the watershed, the rainwater can flow down the other way to find the sea. Rain falling in Dentdale, just west of the River Ure, seeps into the River Dee and off westwards towards the Irish Sea. Inside the watershed, the rainwater is funnelled along the rivers towards the Humber. The lowest point of the basin, like a plughole, is where it empties into the estuary.

See more about the tides in the Year 2 book

Great Rivers of the World

Let's visit the great rivers of the world. Rivers flow through every continent of the world, and we'll learn about some of the world's greatest rivers.

Use the maps here to locate each river, but also look on a big world map or globe.

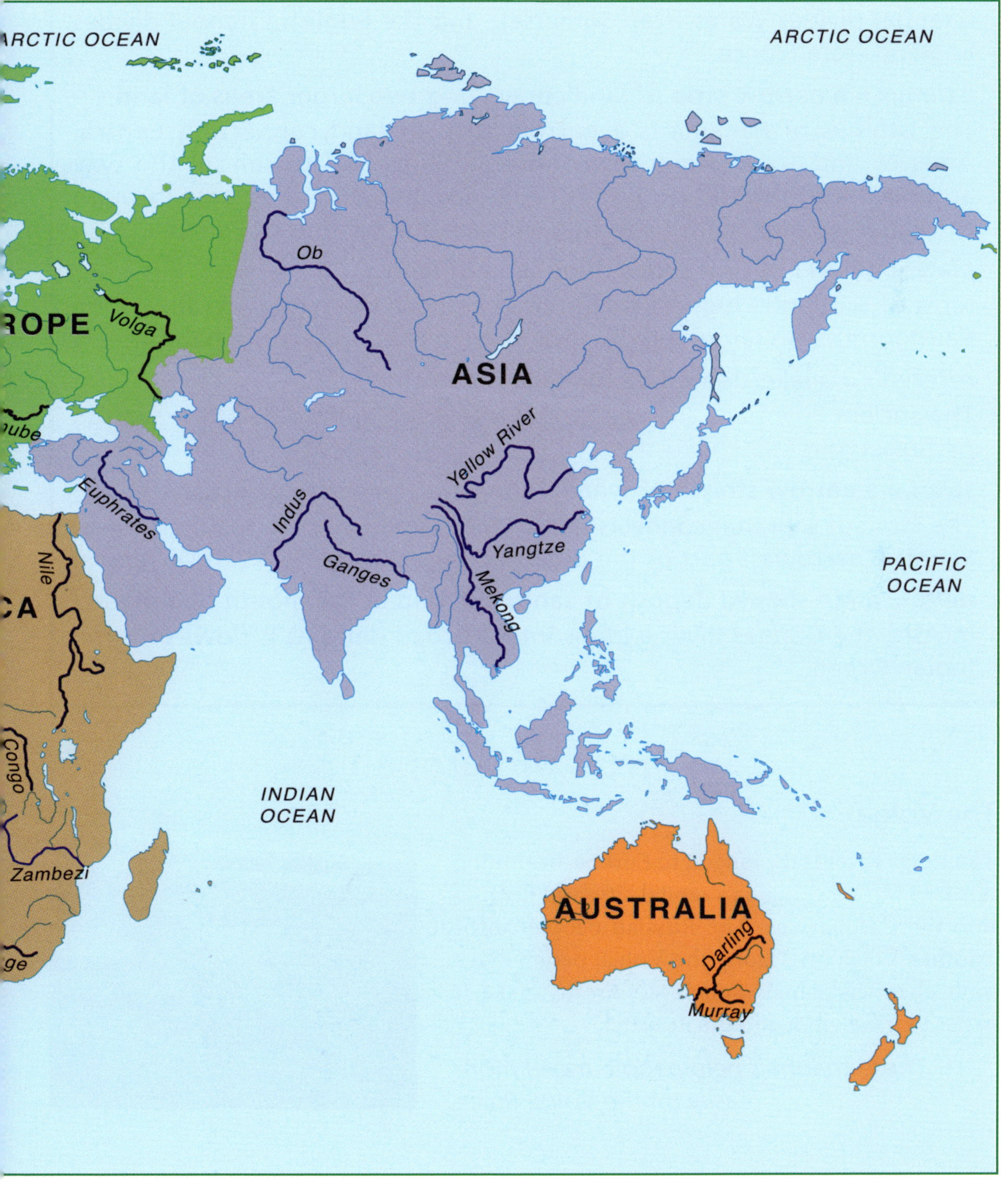

Some Geography Words

channel = a thin expanse of sea separating two areas of land

St George's Channel separates South Wales and Ireland. The Bristol Channel divides Wales from Somerset, and the English Channel divides England from France.

isthmus = a narrow strip of land connecting two larger areas of land

The Isthmus of Panama is a narrow strip of land connecting Central America and South America. Long ago, ships had to sail all the way around the southern tip of South America, but now they pass through the Panama Canal, which was dug through the Isthmus of Panama.

plateau [PLATT-oe] = a broad, high area of land

Most of Scotland's highest mountains rise from the high plateaux of the Cairngorms. This large, remote area is an important wildlife habitat.

reservoir = a lake created by humans for storing water

The ancient Egyptians, living near the Nile River, built some of the world's first reservoirs.

strait = a narrow stretch of water connecting two seas or oceans

The Strait of Gibraltar connects the Atlantic Ocean and the Mediterranean Sea. The narrowest part of the English Channel is the Strait of Dover.

delta = a fan-shaped deposit of sand and mud at the mouth of a river

In Asia, the Ganges River widens into a broad delta as it flows into the Indian Ocean.

Rivers of Europe

The Volga

The Volga River is the longest in Europe, beginning north of Moscow, Russia's capital city, and flowing into the Caspian Sea. The Russian people call it 'Mother Volga'. All along the Volga, people have built channels, canals and reservoirs to make it easier to travel on it and use its water.

These channels help people travel more easily on the Volga River.

The Danube

We learned how the Danube River flows from Germany into Austria – past Vienna – then through Eastern Europe and, eventually, to the Black Sea. Can you see the couple waltzing on page 103? Try listening to Johann Strauss' lovely waltz called *On the Beautiful Blue Danube*.

The Rhine

The Rhine River starts high in the Alps in Switzerland, then flows north through or along the borders of Liechtenstein and Austria. It flows through Basel and then passes through France on its way to Cologne in Germany. From the Netherlands, it empties into the North Sea. Parts of the Rhine have been dug wide and deep to make canals for big barges that carry timber, iron, coal and grain.

Rivers of Africa

The Nile

What is the longest river in the world? It's the Nile. The Nile flows north through Egypt and empties into the Mediterranean Sea. Egypt is so hot

and dry that most Egyptians live close to the Nile. In southern Egypt, the huge Aswan High Dam creates a reservoir and controls the flow of the Nile.

The Congo

Imagine travelling on the Congo River through the rainforest of central Africa. You could not travel on some stretches of the river because of dangerous waterfalls. The path of the Congo makes a big loop. It empties into the Atlantic Ocean.

The Niger

The Niger River travels through four countries in western Africa: Guinea, Mali, Niger and Nigeria. Some of Africa's great, ancient kingdoms developed near the Niger.

Fishermen are already at work on the Niger River at sunrise near Bamako in Mali.

Rivers of Asia

The Yellow and the Yangtze

In China, where these two rivers flow, people call them by different names. The Yellow River is called the Huang He. The Yangtze River is called the Chang Jiang, which means 'long river'. The Yangtze is more than three thousand miles long, flowing from the high mountains of Tibet all the way across China into the East China Sea.

A bright bridge connects the steep hills on either side of the Yangtze River along Three Gorges in China.

The Ob

If you go to Siberia in northern Russia in wintertime, you will find the Ob River frozen solid. If you go in springtime, you might see the Ob overflowing its banks. As the snow and ice melt, the water from the drainage basin fills the river.

The Ganges

The Ganges River flows through India and Bangladesh. The source of the Ganges is in an icy cave, high in the Himalaya Mountains.

The Ganges River passes through the busy Indian city of Varanasi.

The Indus

Thousands of years ago, the great civilisation of ancient India started along the Indus River. The Indus is still an important river, but the country through which it flows is now called Pakistan because India's borders have since changed. Along the Indus River valley, people grow corn, rice and dates.

Rivers of Australia

Let's go 'down under' and visit the continent of Australia.

The Darling and the Murray

In the south-eastern part of the country, the Darling River joins the Murray River. The Murray then flows south into the Indian Ocean. The people in south-eastern Australia use the Murray's water for irrigation – watering their crops – and for use in thousands of homes. Several dams along the river produce electricity from the water passing through them. Elsewhere, Australians and tourists alike enjoy water sports on the Murray River.

The Murray River passes rocky, red cliffs.

Rivers of South America

The Amazon

The world's second longest river, the Amazon, starts in the Andes Mountains in Peru and flows through the rainforest in Brazil. It has the largest drainage basin in the world: 2,700,000 square miles of land drain into the Amazon!

Look who's waiting for his lunch in the Amazon River!

The Paraná

If we go to Buenos Aires, the capital of Argentina, we find ourselves at the mouth of the Paraná River. The Paraná is so wide and deep that ocean freighters can travel four hundred miles up the river. The Paraná begins high up in the mountains and spreads into a wide delta as it empties into the Atlantic Ocean.

The Orinoco

The Orinoco River flows through Venezuela into the Caribbean Sea. The explorer Christopher Columbus, who is thought to be the first European to sail to the Americas, probably sailed into the mouth of the Orinoco in 1498. Today you can travel up one of the tributaries of the Orinoco and visit Angel Falls, the world's highest waterfall.

Do you see how Angel Falls towers over the trees below?

Rivers of North America

The Mississippi

Climb aboard this big paddleboat. The paddle wheel turns to make the boat move. We're going to ride down the Mississippi, the most important river in the United States. Big tributary rivers flow into the Mississippi, including the Missouri River from the northwest and the Ohio River from the northeast. The Mississippi River spreads into a wide delta in the state of Louisiana.

The Mississippi River has been given many names. Native Americans called it 'gathering of waters', since so many tributaries flowed into it. That is probably the original meaning of the name we now use.

Natchez, *a paddleboat on the Mississippi River*

The Mackenzie

Canada's Mackenzie River flows north into the Arctic Ocean. It was named after Sir Alexander Mackenzie, the first explorer to travel from its source to its mouth.

Boats are taken out of the Mackenzie River before the snowy winter arrives.

The Yukon

The Yukon River begins in the Canadian Rocky Mountains, just as the Mackenzie does, but it flows west through Alaska. The entire river stays frozen from October to June. Salmon like to swim through its cold, fresh water.

Civilisations in Asia

Long Ago in Asia: Civilisation in the Indus Valley

In the Year 2 book in this series, you learned about King Tut and the civilisation of ancient Egypt. Thousands of years ago, while the pharaohs in Egypt built pyramids along the banks of the Nile, another civilisation was growing in another part of the world. Let's go there now.

Look at the map on page 119. Can you find the Indus River in India? The Indus River, like the Nile in Africa, overflowed its banks every year. These yearly floods made the land around the river very fertile ('fertile' land is land that's good for growing many big, healthy plants). So, like the people in ancient Egypt and Mesopotamia, the people in the Indus Valley could grow lots of food because of the flooding river, fertile soil and warm weather.

After they learned how to farm, what do you think the people in the Indus Valley did next? If you said, 'Settle down and build cities,' you're right.

Not long ago, archaeologists discovered the ancient cities of the Indus Valley. The archaeologists were amazed to see how the old cities, like Mohenjo-Daro, were laid out in a very neat and organised way. The streets were as straight as a ruler. The houses were like boxes with flat roofs made of sun-baked brick. If you had lived back then, you might have taken a woven mat up to the roof and spread it out for a nap in the warm breeze and sunshine.

Although the complete buildings of Mohenjo-Daro are no longer standing, you can see how the city was organised, and how hot and dry it looks!

Civilisation Along the Ganges

Historians – the people who study history – know that long, long ago the people of ancient India began to leave their cities along the Indus River. But why did they leave? Was there some great disaster, such as a terrible flood or earthquakes? That is something we just don't know.

But we do know that after the people left the cities along the Indus River, a new civilisation developed in another part of India. This civilisation grew along the banks of yet another flooding river, called the Ganges [GAN-jeez]. Can you find the Ganges River on the map on page 119?

The Ganges is the longest river in India. In ancient India, many people made their home near the Ganges. But then new people came to this region, and they did not come as friends. These new people, who came from the northwest, were called Aryans (AIR-ee-uns]. The Aryans had large and powerful armies. They conquered and ruled over the Indian people living along the Ganges. They changed the way the Indian people lived. Let's look at some of the biggest changes, starting with their religion.

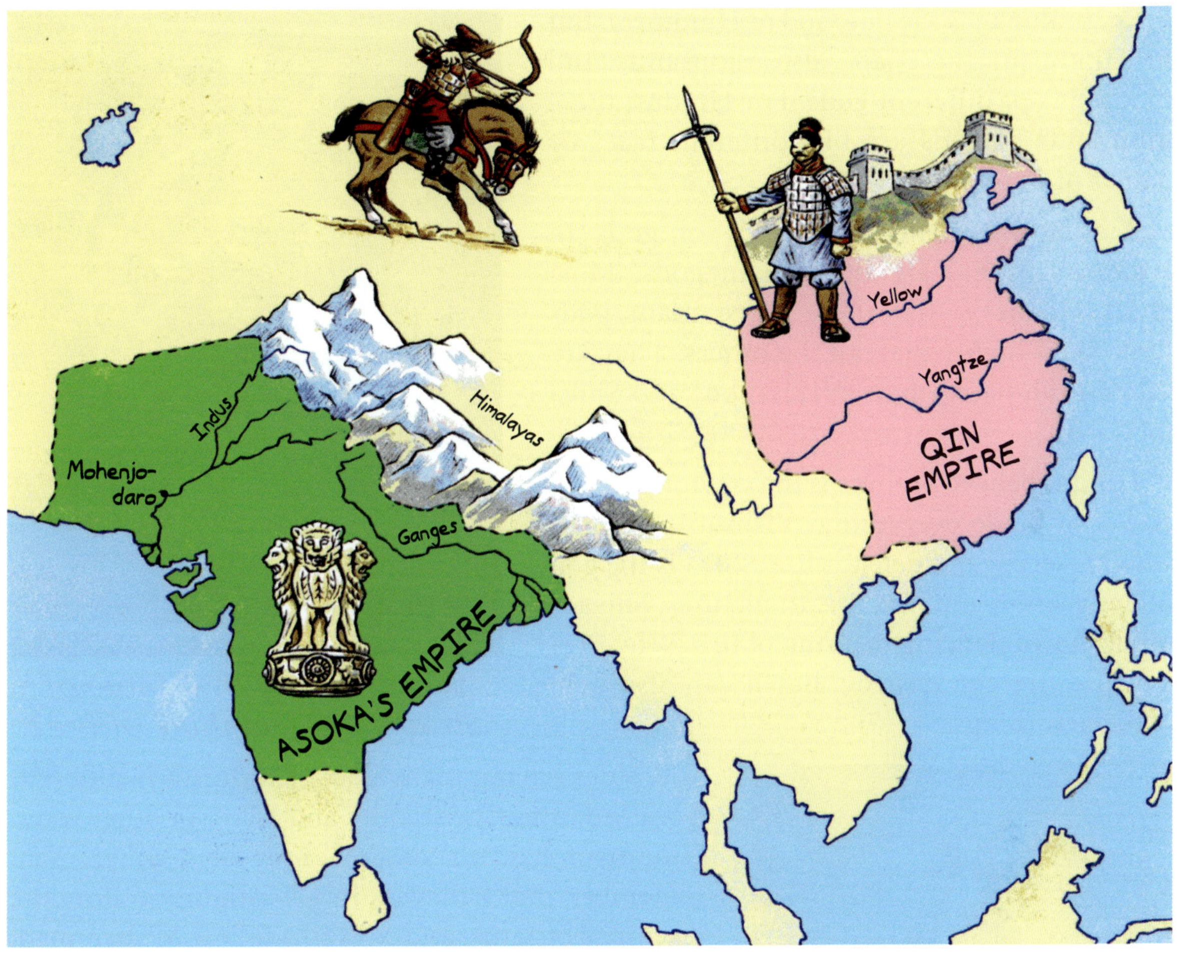

Asia

Hinduism

The Aryans changed the religion of the Indian people. Over many years, the gods of the Aryans combined with the gods worshipped by the Indian people. This was the beginning of Hinduism.

Hinduism is the oldest major religion still practised in the world today. Before we learn more about Hinduism, think back to the religions you've already learned about (in the Year 2 book in this series). Do you remember learning that Judaism, Christianity and Islam all teach about one God, and that the ancient Egyptians believed in many gods?

Well, Hinduism is different, and may seem a little confusing at first. That's because most Hindus believe in one God *and* in many gods. For Hindus, the one God is called Brahman. Hindus believe Brahman is a spirit in everything in the universe – in people, animals, trees, water, the ground, the stars, everything.

So, Brahman is the one God of Hinduism. But in Hinduism there are also thousands and thousands of different gods. For Hindus, these thousands of gods are like different faces or names of Brahman.

Among the many thousands of gods in Hinduism, there are three main gods. Most Hindus believe that these three main gods rank more highly than all the others. They are called Brahma, Vishnu [VISH-noo] and Shiva [SHE-vah].

Hindus believe Brahma is the creator god, the god who made everything. Vishnu is the god who preserves and defends life. Shiva is the god of destruction and new life. In pictures, Shiva is often shown dancing in a ring of fire. Why fire? Because fire can destroy, but it can also help make new things.

What parts of this statue of Shiva make you think of fire?

This man is washing in the Ganges.

Besides having many gods, Hinduism is different from Judaism, Christianity and Islam in other ways. Hinduism has no single leader or teacher. You remember that believers in Christianity follow the teachings of Jesus, and Muslims follow Muhammad. But Hinduism has no one leader or teacher that every Hindu is expected to follow.

Some animals are sacred to Hindus. For Hindus, the cow is the most sacred animal. Hindus are strictly forbidden to kill a cow or eat its meat. Many Hindus are vegetarians – they do not eat any meat.

For Hindus, the Ganges is a holy river. Many Hindus try to make a trip to the Ganges and wash themselves in the water.

A Story from the Holy Books of Hinduism

You've learned about religions that have a book of sacred writings. For Jews, the holy book is the Hebrew Bible, the first part of which is called the Torah. The holy book of Christians is the Bible, and the holy book of Muslims is the Qu'ran. Hinduism does not have one holy book – instead, it has several sacred books.

One of the oldest sacred books of Hinduism is the Rig Veda [RIG VAY-da]. It is filled with beautiful poems, and it tells Hindus how to celebrate weddings, funerals and holy days. If you lived in India today, you could still hear many people saying hymns from the Rig Veda at important times in their lives.

Another important holy book for Hindus is the Ramayana [RAHM-ah-YAHN-ah]. It is full of stories of great deeds and adventures. Many stories in the Ramayana tell about the hero, Prince Rama [RAHM-ah]. In some of these stories, the Hindu god Vishnu assumes different forms: sometimes he takes the form of the human hero, Rama,

or sometimes that of Parasurama [pah-rah-soo-RAH-mah]. Here is a story about Rama and his wife Sita [SEE-tah]. It shows the importance of being courageous, and reminds people that evil can be very tricky, but good can win in the end.

In this painting, the seventeenth century Indian painter named Manohar combines three scenes from the Ramayana. Can you spot Rama and his brothers in the chariots, their father (King Dasaratha) on the white horse and the large form of Parasurama?

Rama and Sita: A Tale from the Ramayana

Once long ago in India, in the kingdom of Ayodha [ah-YOD-ha], there lived a king called Dasaratha [DAHS-ah-RAH-tha]. He was growing old and tired, and he decided that it was time to pass on the kingdom to his favourite son, Prince Rama. But King

Dasaratha's wife, who was Rama's stepmother, wanted her own son, Prince Bharat [bah-RAHT], to be king. She knew that Dasaratha loved her so much that he would give her anything she desired. So she went to him and asked him to send Rama to the forest of Dandak for fourteen years and make Bharat king. Dasaratha was both angry and upset, but he did exactly as she asked.

The next day, Rama left his father's palace with his wife, Sita, and his brother, Lakshman, and went into the dark forest of Dandak. On their journey they met an old wise priest who warned them that demons hid within the shadows of the trees. He gave Rama a quiver of magic arrows to protect himself from the evil in the forest.

After many days travelling, Rama, Sita and Lakshman came to a place where the old man had told them they would be safe. They built themselves a house from hardened earth and bamboo. And so they lived happily for many years.

Then one day a little fawn came running out of the forest. It was the most beautiful animal Sita had ever seen and she begged Rama to catch it for her. Leaving Lakshman to look after his wife, Rama chased the little fawn deeper and deeper into the forest. It led him down winding paths, through tangles of branches and into darkened thickets until he was completely lost. No matter how fast he ran, he could never quite catch it.

Suddenly Sita thought she heard Rama's voice crying from the forest: 'Help me, Lakshman, help me!'

Lakshman ran off into the forest to try to find his brother. No sooner was he out of sight than an ugly little old man appeared as if from nowhere. As Sita watched, the little old man grew, his face changed and there stood Ravana [ra-VAH-na], the king of the demons!

Sita screamed but there was no one to hear her. Rama and Lakshman were now both lost in the heart of the forest. Ravana had sent the little deer to draw Rama away and then tricked Lakshman with false cries for help. Now, with a wave of his hand, Ravana summoned his magic chariot and he swept Sita up and away into the sky, over the forest and across the plains and mountains beyond, until at last they crossed the sea and landed on the demon island of Lanka.

Rama and Lakshman finally found their way home. They realised that they had been tricked and that Sita had been taken away by demons. Picking up his quiver of magic arrows and his bow, Rama set out with Lakshman in search of his wife. They travelled for many miles through the forests and across the plains and mountains, but they found no sign of her.

Then one day, as they were crossing a wooded mountain pass, an enormous monkey jumped down from a rock onto the path in front of them. 'I am Hanuman,' he said, 'the captain of the Vanar tribe of monkeys.' He told them how he had seen Ravana's chariot flying through the sky with Sita aboard, and he promised Rama that he and his army would help in the search for Sita. He clapped his paws together and suddenly, down from the rocks, came hundreds and hundreds of monkeys.

Rama and his new army travelled on across the mountains until they reached the seashore, where the angry waves grew higher and higher, beating wildly against the rocks. Rama could not see how he would ever reach the demon island of Lanka. Then Hanuman said: 'We must build a bridge to the island from trees and rocks and anything else we can find.'

All the monkeys set to work. They broke off boulders from the cliffs and hurled them into the sea. When the bridge was finally finished, Rama led his army across the sea.

With a roar, Ravana and his hordes of demons came to meet them. There was a bloody battle in Lanka between Rama's army of men and monkeys and Ravana's army of demons. In the end, Rama took a magic arrow from his quiver and let it fly. The arrow struck Ravana and the demon sank to the ground. A great cheer went up – Ravana was dead and Rama had won.

The British Museum's painting from the Ramayana, showing Rama going into battle in Lanka. Can you spot Rama, Lakshman and Hanuman?

What do you see happening during the Battle at Lanka?
This painting is at the British Library.

Rama and Sita were together again at last, and the streets of Lanka were filled with the sounds of laughter and singing as the celebrations began.

Fourteen years had passed since Rama had left his father's palace and now it was time for him to return to Ayodha. In a magic chariot drawn by swans, Rama and Sita flew up into the clouds to begin their last journey home.

> In the autumn in India, many Hindus celebrate Rama's victory over Ravana, and the homecoming of Rama and Sita, in a festival called Diwali [dih-VAH-lee]. As part of the festival, the people light many lamps and candles, and sometimes they put on plays telling the story of Rama and Sita.

Buddha: The Enlightened One

You've just learned about one great religion that began in India – Hinduism. Now let's learn about another, called Buddhism [BOO-dhiz-um]. Buddhism is the religion of millions of people, but most of them are not in India. Today many Buddhists live in

Southeast Asia, China and Japan. But Buddhism began in India, and it grew out of Hinduism. It began a long time ago, with a young prince named Siddhartha Gautama [sid-DART-tuh GOW-tuh-muh].

Siddhartha was born the son of a very rich king and queen. His father ruled a kingdom in the foothills of the high Himalayan mountains. Siddhartha wore soft, beautiful clothes made of the finest silk. Colourful flowers, soft music and sweet smells surrounded him. When he walked, servants held umbrellas over him to keep off the sun or rain. When he grew to be 16 years old, he married a beautiful princess.

What a life! All pleasure, and no pain. Siddhartha's father, the king, tried to make sure that his son was always happy. He even ordered that no one who was sick, old or poor should ever come near the prince. That way, thought the king, the prince would live in a world without suffering, a world filled with beautiful things and happy people.

But one day, when Siddhartha was riding in his chariot outside the palace walls, he saw an old, grey-haired man, bent over and wrinkled, leaning on a stick. Soon after, he saw a sick man lying along the side of the road, and heard his pained cries for help. Later, for the first time in his life, he saw a dead person. Finally, he saw a holy man with a shaved head and a peaceful expression on his face.

Now Siddhartha knew what his father had tried so hard to hide from him. He saw that there is pain in the world, and that people grow old and die. He was troubled by what he had seen, and he thought for a long time. Was it right that just because he was born rich, he should be comfortable and happy while other people were unhappy and miserable?

Then he made a hard decision. He made up his mind to leave his family and his home, and his easy, comfortable life. He set off to try to understand why there was suffering and what to do about it. He cut off his long hair. He gave his soft, silk gowns to a poor man and put on the poor man's old, ragged clothes. He wandered for years and years, looking for answers to his questions.

Then one night he sat down under a tree to be quiet and think. He sat and thought for a long time, and in the morning when the sun rose, he felt that now he understood. He had become 'enlightened', which means wise and aware. And so he was called Buddha, which means 'the enlightened one, the one who knows'.

This is one of the first statues of Buddha: it is over 1,800 years old.

Buddha's Teachings

What did Buddha know? He said that he now understood that suffering and death are part of life. He said that life is like a great wheel in which birth, suffering and death come round and round again. And he said that the most important thing is to live a life of goodness. Buddha taught people how to be good and many people, including his wife and his father, began to follow his teachings. He said, for example, that people should harm no living thing. He told his followers to be kind and merciful to humans and animals alike.

The core of the Buddha's teaching is the Four Noble Truths:

1. All life, from birth to death, is filled with suffering.

2. This suffering is caused by a craving for worldly things.

3. Suffering will stop when one learns to overcome desire.

4. We can learn to overcome desire by following the eightfold path.

The eightfold path is a list of eight things Buddhists must to do to escape from desire and suffering. Among other things, Buddhists are expected to practise right speech, which means never lying or using bad language; right behaviour, which means never doing anything one might later regret; and right effort, which means always working for the good. By following the eightfold path, Buddhists believe that, like Buddha, they will become enlightened.

King Asoka: From War to Peace

Many people still visit this giant statue of the Great Buddha in Kamakura in Japan. This Buddha is 11 metres high!

About two hundred years after Buddha died, a king helped spread Buddha's teachings. King Asoka didn't believe in Buddha's teachings at first. You remember that Buddha said people should harm no living thing. But King Asoka was a warrior. He led his soldiers in fierce battles, in which many men were hurt or killed. Through these wars he brought the northern and southern parts of India together under his rule.

But after one fierce and bloody battle, King Asoka looked around and saw the death and hardship caused by war. He remembered

King Asoka had the top of a column (called a capital) carved with lions and put up where Buddha first explained his beliefs about peace. This capital has become a symbol for India.

that Buddha had said: 'Harm no living thing,' and he felt ashamed. He decided to stop making war and instead to devote himself to spreading Buddha's teachings throughout his kingdom. All over India he built hospitals for both people and animals. He told his workers to plant trees and dig wells for fresh water. He even set up houses along the road for travellers who were tired from walking great distances.

King Asoka wanted the people of India to learn more about Buddha's teachings, so he had Buddha's words carved on tall pillars and put them in places where many people would see them. Even though Asoka strongly believed in Buddha's teachings, he also believed that kings should let their people worship as they wanted to. So, many Indian people felt they could worship their different gods and also listen to Buddha's words.

King Asoka sent Buddhist priests across Asia to tell people in other lands about Buddha's teachings. So Buddha's ideas spread all over Asia, and Buddhism remains one of the largest religions in the world today.

A Wise Teacher in China: Confucius

Look at the map on page 127. Can you see India with the lion capital? Now look north and east of India and find the big country called China.

Long, long ago, about the same time that Buddha lived in India, another wise man was teaching in China. His name was Confucius. Confucius was a very peaceful man. But during his life, China was not a peaceful country. Instead, many groups were fighting each other. They rode around the countryside and robbed and hurt the people in the villages.

Confucius, who was wise, gentle and thoughtful, grew tired of all this fighting. He said that the fighting should stop and that all the people should come together under a single,

A statue of Confucius in Shanghai, one of China's largest cities

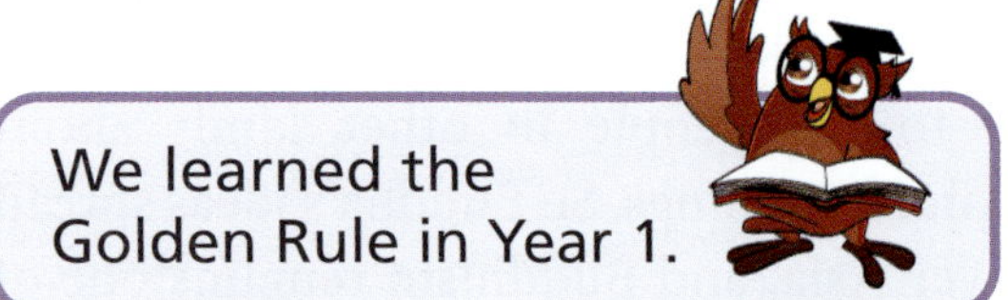

wise ruler. The people, he said, should obey a good ruler, while a good ruler should take care of the people. He said to the rulers: 'You are there to rule, not to kill. If you desire what is good, the people will be good.'

Confucius said many other things about how people should live and treat each other. For example, he said that you should respect your parents and teachers, and honour your ancestors.

You know the Golden Rule, don't you? It says: 'Do unto others as you would have them do unto you.' Confucius was the first person we know of who taught the Golden Rule, although he put it this way: 'What you do not wish for yourself, do not do to others.'

Many people in China began to listen to his teachings, which became known as 'Confucianism'. Confucianism is not a religion, like Islam or Christianity, because Confucius did not have anything to say about God or the gods. Confucianism is a way of thinking about how to live a good life and how to treat others.

China: Great Rivers and a Great Wall

If you look at the map on page 127, you can see that China is separated from India by the high Himalaya Mountains. Where did civilisation begin in China? You can probably guess – yes, by a river! Just as in ancient India, Egypt and Mesopotamia, the first cities in China were built near rivers that regularly flooded and left rich soil, good for growing grains like millet and rice. Look again at the map on page 127 and find these two important rivers in China: the Yellow River and the Yangtze River. (In China, the Yellow River is called the Huang He, and the Yangtze is called the Chang Jiang.)

Between these rivers, the people in China long ago built their first cities. Some of the people built large houses, created art, made fine clothes and sent their children to schools.

But many of the people were poor, because their rulers kept fighting one another to try to become the one all-powerful ruler.

Finally, one strong and very strict ruler brought China together under his leadership. He was China's first emperor, and he was called Qin Shihuangdi [CHIN shih-hwahng-DEE]. The name 'China' comes from his family name, 'Qin' (which you pronounce 'chin').

Qin stopped the rulers from fighting among themselves. But he still had to worry about fighting against people who were attacking China from the north. These people were rough warriors called Mongols.

Qin decided that one way he could protect the Chinese people would be to build a wall big enough and strong enough to keep out the Mongols. There were already some big walls made of packed earth, and Qin ordered many people to do the hard work of connecting these walls, as well as building new walls.

Over 8,000 life-sized terracotta warriors protect Qin's tomb.

But this was too big a job to finish in one lifetime. Many years after Qin, later emperors of China ordered many workmen to keep making the wall longer and longer. The work was very hard, since the wall went on for 5,500 miles! It went up mountains, down valleys and along the curving paths of rivers. The workmen built towers so that guards could look out for invaders from the north. Much of the Great Wall of China is still standing today. It is so long that, if you laid out just the remaining sections of the wall in a single line, they would take you from London, across Europe and Turkey and as far as ancient Babylon.

The Great Wall of China

Papermaking

An Important Invention

Long ago, the Chinese came up with some important inventions. You can see a Chinese invention right in front of you. The Chinese invented paper! They made paper from the bark of mulberry trees, rags and sometimes even old fishing nets. Chinese travellers showed people in other countries how to make paper. As the years went on, more and more people, in Asia and even in faraway Europe, learned how to make paper. Think about this: why was paper such an important invention?

Smooth as Silk

A traditional silk loom in China

Here is an old legend from China. Once upon a time, an empress was having tea in her garden under the shade of some mulberry trees when… plunk! Something splashed into her teacup. She looked in and saw a small, white, fuzzy thing. It was a cocoon! It had fallen from the mulberry trees above, where little worms lived and ate the leaves.

Now, you might expect the empress to say 'Yuck!' and throw out her tea, but she was a calm and curious person. She noticed something coming off the cocoon. When she looked closer, she saw it was a thread. When she touched the thread, it felt smooth and strong. She thought: 'If we had a lot of this thread, and if we could weave it, we could make a very special cloth.'

Soon the empress and her servants were caring for all the worms in the mulberry trees and gathering many cocoons. From the thread, they wove a new kind of cloth. It was like no cloth that anyone had ever felt before – so smooth, soft, shiny and cool. The empress, the emperor and all the noble people began wearing clothes made of this new cloth, called silk. Visitors from other countries saw these fine silk clothes and said: 'We want silk, too.'

This girl is wearing a silk dress, which is red to bring her good luck in the Chinese New Year.

That's the legend, and parts of it are really true. Silkworm caterpillars do eat mulberry leaves. When they make their cocoons, they do produce a thread that can be made into silk cloth. And, many people did want silk from China.

The Chinese people made a lot of silk and traded it with people from other countries. Merchants from as far away as Europe and Arabia travelled to China to buy silk and then took it back home to sell.

> Silk feels so fine and smooth that even today, if things are going very well, people say that everything is 'smooth as silk'.

New Year in Hong Kong

Chinese New Year

From as long ago as the time of Confucius up to the present day, the Chinese people have enjoyed celebrating the New Year Festival. On New Year's Day, Chinese families gather together – grandparents, parents and children. They decorate their homes and shops with bright colours, especially red, and often wear red outfits, because in China red means good luck and happiness.

The Chinese New Year does not happen on the first day of January, because the date of the Chinese New Year is based on a special calendar that follows the cycles of the moon. Usually, the Chinese New Year happens on a day somewhere between the middle of January and the middle of February. It starts on the first day of lunar new year. The Chinese New Year Festival lasts for 15 days with fireworks and parades in which people dress up in dragon costumes and dance in the streets. It ends on the day that there is a full moon.

In the Chinese lunar calendar ('lunar' means 'of the moon'), each year is under the protection of one of twelve different animals. Find out what animal goes with the year you were born in – maybe a donkey, dragon, rabbit, tiger or dog – by visiting your library for books on the Chinese New Year, such as *The Great Race: The Story of the Chinese Zodiac* by Dawn Casey (Barefoot Books) 2006; *Lin Yi's Lantern: A Moon Festival Tale* by Brenda Williams (Barefoot Books) 2009; *We Love Festivals: Chinese New Year* by Saviour Pirotta (Wayland) 2009.

Great Explorers: Marco Polo

Marco Polo was born in 1254 to a well-to-do family in Venice, which was an important Italian city where many people would come to buy and sell things. Marco's father, Niccolò, and his uncle, Maffeo, were merchants who often went on long journeys for their work. When Marco was six years old, Niccolò and Maffeo left on a trip that lasted nine years and took them on travels throughout Asia.

By chance, Niccolò and Maffeo Polo met a representative of the court of Kublai Khan, who was also known as the Great Khan and was the Mongol ruler of China at that time. The representative invited Niccolò and Maffeo to Khan's court, and they decided to visit him in China. This was a very long journey indeed! When they arrived at Khan's court in Beijing, they became great

The Polos and several European scholars leave Venice and begin their journey to Khan's court in China.

friends and stayed with him for a year. When they left on their long, three-year journey home, they promised Khan that they would return with scholars who would teach Khan about Christianity and the scientific discoveries of Western Europe.

Niccolò and Maffeo returned home when Marco was 15 and, two years later, they set off again for Khan's court. This time, Marco was able to join them, as well as several scholars. The Polos left home for 24 years as they travelled and lived all around Asia!

Khan favoured Marco and sent him on many trips around China to meet with important nobles, which Marco enjoyed as he met many different people and had the opportunity to see many different parts of Asia. He learned about the history, culture and folktales of China and made observations about animals and plants. Marco was impressed to see China's size, wealth and power, and he was also very interested in the daily lifestyles of the different people he visited. For example, he was used to using gold and silver for money as was common in Europe at that time, and he was surprised to see people using paper money in China, because the Chinese were the first to invent paper!

Compare this drawing from Marco Polo's book, The Travels of Marco Polo, *with the illustration of the Polos leaving Venice. What are some things from Marco's travels that may have surprised the readers of his book?*

Although Marco left home when he was a teenager, he finally returned when he was 41 years old. He had lived a life of great adventure and everyone was eager to hear his many tales from his travels. Helped by a friend, he published a book called *The Travels of Marco Polo* that captured many of his adventures. He told of the Mongol empire's power and the exotic customs of the different cultures he encountered in Asia, India and Africa.

The Travels of Marco Polo became one of most popular books in Europe at the time although many people didn't believe Marco's stories because they told of things that were so different from what most Europeans knew. Marco insisted: 'I have only told the half of what I saw!' and this was written on his gravestone when he died at the age of 70.

Marco Polo is recognised as a great explorer. He provided us with the most important written account of what life was like outside Europe almost eight hundred years ago.

Let's Visit Japan: The Land of the Rising Sun

You've been learning about the long-ago times in India and China. Now, let's look at another important Asian country, Japan.

Japan is the easternmost country in Asia. Since the sun rises in the east, Japan has long been called 'the land of the rising sun'. A rising sun is pictured on the flag of Japan, which has a red circle on a white background.

Compared to China, Japan is a very small country in its size. Japan is a densely populated country made up of many islands that are actually the tops of a great mountain range. There are four major islands. Honshu is the largest – and the home of both the modern capital city of Tokyo and the country's tallest mountain, Mount Fuji. The island of Hokkaido lies to the north, and Shikoku and Kyushu are to the south. There are many volcanoes in Japan, and there are frequent earthquakes.

Mount Fuji

China
Korea
Sea of
Japan
Japan
Tokyo
Mount
Fuji
Pacific
Ocean

Japanese weather is influenced by monsoons, wind systems that bring heavy rains in summer and winter. The summer monsoons bring rain, crucial for growing rice and other crops, to southern and central Japan. The winter monsoons blow cold air from northern China and from Siberia, which is even further north. This cold air blows across the Sea of Japan and leaves lots of snow on Hokkaido and Honshu.

In late summer, storms called typhoons also strike the eastern coast of Japan. Typhoons bring very strong, swirling winds. Tsunamis [soo-NAH-meez], gigantic waves caused by earthquakes beneath the ocean floor, also can cause a lot of damage in Japan.

Feudal Japan

We have already learned about China's first emperor, Qin Shihuangdi. Japan also had emperors and, by the 1500s, there had already been a long line of emperors in Japan. The emperors were mainly religious and cultural leaders. Real political power was in the hands of major landholders called *daimyos* [DIME-yos] who fought each other for more power. The most powerful daimyos would press the emperor to name them *shogun*, which means 'great general'.

Because warfare was so important to this way of life, a special class of swordsmen arose – the *samurai*. They followed a strict code called *bushido* [bush-EE-do], which required bravery, self-control and loyalty to their daimyo.

A samurai warrior on horseback. When the samurai went into battle, the hundreds of tiny wooden and leather plates that made up his armour clattered against each other, making an alarming sound.

Feudal Japan had a very rigid class system. The samurai class – from which the daimyos and shoguns came – was on top. Then came peasants, followed by artisans and then merchants. Peasants were ranked higher than artisans because they fed people. Merchants were on the lowest rung of the social ladder because they did not produce anything; they only traded.

The Japanese did not always welcome foreigners. For a few decades in the 1500s, the Japanese welcomed some European traders and even a few Christian missionaries. However, in the early 1600s, the shogun closed all Japanese ports to Europeans, except near one city, Nagasaki, where the Dutch were allowed to land on a small island in the bay and trade. Japan continued its policy of isolation and excluding European traders for more than 250 years.

Japanese Religions

A Japanese garden

In Japan, different religions managed to co-exist. One of the most important religions in Japan is Buddhism, which you learned about earlier in this chapter.

Shintoism, or just Shinto, is a religion that began in Japan. Its followers worship nature spirits called kami [KAH-mee] who are believed to live all around – in rocks, trees, lakes, even in blades of grass. The Japanese also honour their ancestors, emperors and great heroes.

The Japanese people have built elaborate gardens on the grounds of their Buddhist temples and Shinto shrines.

Modern Japan

In Japan you'll find one of the largest cities in the world, called Tokyo. Tokyo is a busy, crowded, modern city that has many banks, shops, restaurants and museums.

If you were to visit a Japanese family living in a flat in Tokyo, the first thing you would do when you entered their home would be to take off your shoes. You would wear socks or special slippers to show respect, but you would never wear your outside shoes indoors!

If your Japanese friends invited you to stay for dinner, you might not sit in a chair but instead kneel on a cushion around a low table.

Modern Toyko

To pick up your food, you would not use a fork – and no, you wouldn't use your fingers – you would use two slender pieces of wood about the size of pencils, called chopsticks.

In many ways, Japan is a very modern country with lots of modern business and industry. Japanese people also care about their old ways and customs. For example, children in Japan learn a very old art form called *origami*. To make *origami*, you fold paper in special ways, without cutting or sticking it, to make lovely figures such as this crane, which is a type of bird.

On special holidays, many Japanese people – men and women, boys and girls – wear a *kimono*, a beautiful robe that is tied at the waist. *Shogatsu*, New Year's Day, is a special holiday. The Japanese also celebrate two holidays that we don't have in Britain: one is called Girls' Day (in March), and the other is Boys' Day (in May). On these days, children may dress in bright kimonos, play games and often receive presents.

This Japanese girl is dressed in a kimono for a special holiday.

Read the Japanese folktale called 'The Tongue-Cut Sparrow' on page 38.

Ancient Greece

Birthplace of the Olympics and More

Have you ever watched the Olympics on television or been lucky enough to see the games live? If you have, then you know how exciting it is to see some of the best athletes from all around the world come together to compete in many sports, such as running and swimming in the Summer Olympics, or skiing and skating in the Winter Olympics. London has been very lucky to host the Summer Olympics three times: in 1908, 1948 and 2012. In 1948, for the first time, sporting events were organised for people with disabilities. The Paralympic Games, in which sportsmen and women with various disabilities compete, are now part of every Olympic Games.

Do you know where the Olympics first started? In a land that is now the country called Greece. Did you know that the first Olympics were held in Greece more than 2,500 years ago?

In the men's 5,000m athletics event, popular Team GB athlete Mo Farah pulled ahead to win the gold medal.

These Olympic athletes were painted on a vase in ancient Greece.

The ancient Greeks loved athletics. Every four years, they would hold a week of games at a place called Olympia. The best athletes would gather to run, jump, wrestle, throw weapons and race chariots and horses.

The Olympics of the ancient Greeks were in some ways different from our Olympics today. The ancient Greeks held contests in music and poetry, which are not part of our modern games. In ancient Greece, only men were allowed to compete, and they did not wear uniforms – in fact, they didn't wear anything! Today, the winners receive medals, but in ancient Greece winners were crowned with a wreath made of wild olive leaves.

The ancient Greeks gave us the Olympics, but they also gave us much more. Ancient Greece is the birthplace of many of the ideas and beliefs that are still important to us today. Let's find out more about the civilisation of the ancient Greeks.

A Civilisation of City-States

In ancient Greece, did civilisation begin by a big, flooding river? Not this time! Greece is different. Greece has no flooding river like the Nile in Egypt. Greece is mostly a rocky, dry land, broken by many hills and mountains. The hills and mountains kept groups of people apart. Each group didn't have much to do with its neighbours, because its neighbours were so far away. Some of these groups of people grew into large communities, which were called city-states. Look at the map to find some of the most important city-states: Athens, Sparta and Thebes.

Ancient Greece and nearby regions

The people in these separate city-states all spoke the Greek language. They told many of the same stories, and worshipped many of the same gods. Like people in other ancient civilisations you've learned about, the Greeks believed in many gods, whom you can read about in the Language and Literature chapter. But the Greeks did not have a single ruler. In fact, the city-states often argued and sometimes fought against each other, although they always stopped fighting when the Olympics were held every four years.

There's a famous, old story about a fierce monster that lived on the island of Crete. You can read the story of 'Theseus and the Minotaur', as well as many other Greek myths, on pages 65–85.

Most people in ancient Greece lived near the sea. Look at the map and find the Mediterranean Sea and the Aegean [ih-JEE-un] Sea. Can you also find the island in the Mediterranean called Crete [rhymes with 'street']?

When you look at Greece on the map, you can see that it is a peninsula. A peninsula is almost an island – it is land surrounded by water on most sides, but not all sides. The British coastline has many peninsulas, like the Gower in South Wales and the Lizard off Cornwall, which is itself a larger peninsula. There is also a splendid example of an isthmus (see page 120 to review what this means) at Corinth.

Athens: Birthplace of Democracy

As you know, many things important to us today got started in the ancient civilisations – things like agriculture (growing crops for food), cities and writing. The ancient Greeks gave us many new ideas, including a very important idea from the city of Athens: democracy. Let's learn more about it.

For hundreds of years, the Athenians had tried different ways of governing their city. They argued a lot about the best way. Some Athenians were tired of being ruled by a small group of powerful and strict leaders. Leaders who make bad laws and are cruel to the people are called 'tyrants'. Many Athenians were tired of being ruled by a few tyrants, so they spoke up and said: 'Why should just a few people make laws for everyone else, especially when they make bad laws? Let's get rid of the tyrants and rule ourselves!'

This sculpture from ancient Greece was made 2,500 years ago. Both the young man and the older man are citizens who can vote.

And that is what the Athenians did. They invented a new kind of government in which the people chose their leaders. If those leaders began to act like tyrants, then the people had the power to choose new leaders. This new kind of government is still with us today and is used by many countries around the world, including here in the UK. It is called 'democracy', which means 'rule by the people' or 'power from the people'.

In Athens, democracy was not perfect. Not all the people had power. Not all the people were allowed to take part in the government. Only citizens were allowed to vote, and not every adult was a citizen. Women and slaves were not citizens, so they could not vote. It would take many more years for human beings to consider that all people are created equal and should have equal rights, not just grown men who own a lot of property.

Still, even though democracy in Athens left out women and slaves, it was the beginning of an idea that is very important today in our own country – the idea that ordinary people can help make the laws and choose their own leaders. This idea of democracy made ancient Athens different from most other places on earth at that time, where the laws were made by a king, an emperor or a small group of warriors or priests. Where would you rather live? In a place where you help make the laws and choose the leaders, or where you never had any say?

The United Kingdom is a democracy. Our government rules in the name of the Queen (or King), but to make decisions it needs the approval of Members of Parliament (MPs). There is one MP for each area of the UK, chosen every few years in an election according to who receives the most votes. Adults from the UK are allowed to vote, as are people from the European Union and the Commonwealth while they live here.

Rough, Tough Sparta

Not far from Athens there was another Greek city-state called Sparta. The Spartans were tough. They were great warriors. When Spartan boys were only seven years old, they were taken from their families and trained to be soldiers. Their heads were shaved and they were given only rough clothing, no shoes and very little food to eat. They slept on hard beds with no covers. Why? To make them tough and ready for war.

The Spartan girls were also trained to compete in sporting events. The Athenians thought this was shocking because they believed that young girls should learn to take care of the home and children, and should grow up to be quiet and gentle. But not the Spartans. They wanted the girls to grow up to be tough, and they wanted these strong women to raise good Spartan soldiers. Although the Spartan women weren't allowed to participate in the Olympics, women like the one in this statue were allowed to compete in the Heraia, an athletic festival for the goddess Hera. Still, like the Athenians, the Spartans did not let women vote or take part in the government of the city-state.

This statue at the British Museum shows an athletic Spartan girl running.

Today, people use the word 'Spartan' to describe something that is very plain and basic, with nothing fancy about it. To live a 'Spartan' life means to live a life with very few comforts. For example, if you lived a Spartan life, you might wake up very early, take only a cold shower, wear plain clothes and never eat any sweets.

The Persian Wars

While the city-states of ancient Greece, such as Athens and Sparta, were growing bigger and stronger, another civilisation was growing to the east. These people were the Persians. The Persians had conquered the people in both Babylon and Egypt.

This 2,400-year-old coin shows a Persian king holding a spear and a bow.

When a country conquers and takes charge of other lands, it makes those lands part of its 'empire'. About 2,500 years ago, the Persian empire was the mightiest in the world. The Persians ruled over most of the lands between the Indus River and the Mediterranean Sea. Wherever the Persians went, they spread their civilisation. They gave the different peoples they conquered one government, one kind of money to use and even one single postal system.

This painting, Scythian Emissaries Meeting with Darius, *shows King Darius meeting with people from Scythia after invading their land.*

As the Persians pushed farther west, their empire came closer and closer to Greece. The Persians came first to some Greek cities in the area called Ionia [eye-OH-nee-uh]. Look at the map on page 148 and you'll see that Ionia was not far to the east of Athens and Sparta. The Persian armies conquered Ionia. But then the Ionian people surprised the Persians: they didn't just act sad and defeated. The Ionians wanted to be free, so they fought back. The Ionians asked Athens for help, and the Athenians sent ships and soldiers. The Persian king named Darius I [duh-RYE-us the first], called Darius the Great, was furious: 'How dare these Greeks fight back!' he thought. King Darius gave orders for many soldiers and a large fleet of ships to prepare to attack the mainland of Greece.

And so the Greeks and Persians were at war. King Darius believed that he would easily defeat the Greeks because, after all, the Greek city-states were always fighting each other. But, as you will see, Darius was wrong.

Battles That Live in Memory

Even though the Greeks and Persians fought more than two thousand years ago, people still remember and tell the stories of some famous battles.

Marathon

King Darius sent six hundred ships with thousands of soldiers to conquer Athens. The Athenians knew they needed help. So they turned to the city-state that had sometimes been their enemy, Sparta.

Back then, there were of course no telephones, emails or other ways of quickly getting a message to someone far away. The fastest way to get a message to Sparta was to send a runner. The Athenians chose a runner named Pheidippides [fie-DIH-pih-deez]. For two days and nights, he ran, swam, climbed and ran some more until he reached Sparta.

When Pheidippides asked the Spartans for help, they said: 'We will send two thousand men to help you, but they cannot come until the next full moon, when they are finished with our religious festival.' Pheidippides ran back to Athens with the news. The Athenians said: 'We cannot wait. The Persians are close! Get ready for battle.'

This statue of Pheidippides, called The Soldier of Marathon announcing the Victory *is at the Louvre museum in Paris.*

Meanwhile, the Persian soldiers of King Darius had sailed their ships to a place called Marathon. From there they planned to march to the city of Athens. (Find Marathon and Athens on the map on page 148.) The Greek general knew that the Persians had many more soldiers, so he came up with a daring plan. At Marathon, he ordered the Greek soldiers to attack the Persians! The Greeks ran furiously right into the Persian lines. The Persians were surprised, and many of them ran back to their ships. By the end of the battle, many more Persians lay dead than Greeks.

The Greek general then turned to Pheidippides, who was already weary from the battle, and said: 'Run to Athens with the news of our victory.' From the battlefield to Athens, Pheidippides ran and ran about 26 miles as fast as he could. He reached the city and managed to gasp out the good news – 'We are victorious!' – then the poor man dropped dead.

Today, people still run in long-distance races called 'marathons'. A marathon is about 26 miles.

Thermopylae

King Leonidas, who led the Spartans in great battles

'The Greeks have won for now,' said King Darius, 'but I promise, we will crush them all!'

Before he could keep his promise, however, Darius died. His son, named Xerxes [ZURK-seez], became king. 'I will keep my father's promise,' he said, and he prepared a great army. Hundreds of thousands of Persian soldiers attacked Greece from the north. They marched southward, toward Athens and Sparta. Could anything stop them?

The Persians came to a narrow strip of land between the mountains and the sea. At this place, called Thermopylae [ther-MOP-ih-lee], a group of about three hundred Spartan soldiers, with some other Greeks to help them, waited for the Persians. How could a handful of soldiers hope to stand against so many thousands?

Bravely the Spartans faced their foes. To the Spartans, there was no such thing as fear. The Persians came forward, only to meet death at the points of the Spartan spears. But there were so many more Persians than Spartans that, one by one, the Spartans fell. At last the Spartans' spears were broken. Yet still they stood side by side, fighting to the last. Some fought with swords, some with daggers and some with only their fists. All day long they fought and held back the Persians. But when the sun went down, not one Spartan was left alive. Each and every one had died for his country.

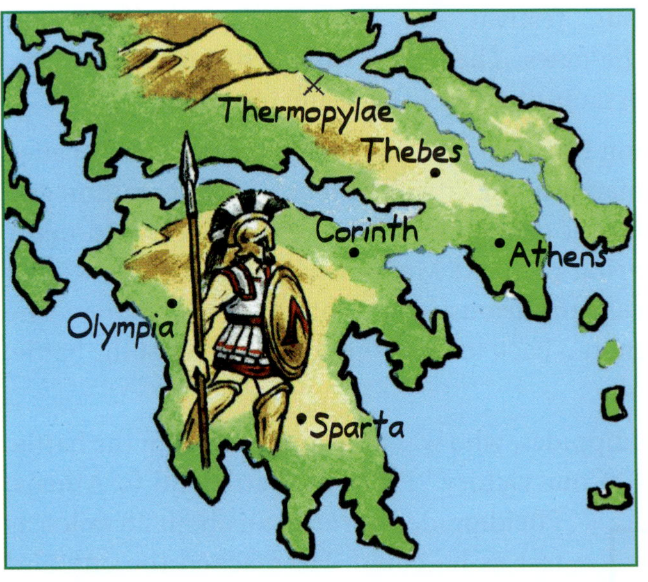

To reach southern Greece, the Persian army had to march through the narrow pass at Thermopylae.

Great Thinkers in Athens

After the Persian wars the people of Athens enjoyed some years of peace, and they worked hard to rebuild their city. During the leadership of a wise man named Pericles [PER-ih-cleez] they built a big new temple and dedicated it to Athena, the goddess they believed watched over their city. They built this temple out of marble and filled it with beautiful statues. It was called the Parthenon.

Many great thinkers lived in Athens. These thinkers were called philosophers, which means 'lovers of wisdom'. The philosophers asked big questions, such as: 'How should we live? What are our duties? What is the best form of government?'

Learn more about the Parthenon starting on page 192.

Part of Pericles' Funeral Oration

We do not imitate other people in the way in which we govern ourselves. Instead, we set an example to others. Our system favours the many rather than the few: that is why it is called a democracy. We are all equal in the eyes of the law. We choose people to manage our affairs according to their abilities, not who their parents are. Even if people are poor, they can still play a part in the life of the community.

Pericles is giving a speech to honour soldiers who have died and speaks about the importance of democracy as he points towards the Parthenon.

Let's meet three of the most important Greek philosophers: Socrates [SOCK-ruh-teez], Plato [PLAY-toe] and Aristotle [ARR-ih-stot-ul].

Young men from all over Greece came to learn from Socrates. Socrates once said: 'There is only one good, knowledge, and one evil, ignorance.' What do you think he means? Socrates loved to ask questions. He made his students think by asking lots of questions and then questioning their answers! Some people felt that Socrates asked too many questions, and they felt angry at him and threatened him. But Socrates did not stop asking questions. He wanted to know the truth.

Plato was a student of Socrates, and he wrote down much of what he learned from his wise teacher. Plato believed in the importance of education. Near Athens, he started a school called the Academy. Plato said: 'The direction in which education starts a man will determine his future life.'

Plato's best student was Aristotle. Aristotle was interested in everything around him. He loved to look closely at plants and animals, and to think about how things work. He thought a lot about people as well. He asked: 'What makes a person a good ruler? What are the best ways for people to live so that they get along with each other?'

Read more about Aristotle's important scientific work on page 318.

The School of Athens is a famous painting by Raffaello Santi, who is also known simply as Raphael. Can you spot Plato and Aristotle walking together in the centre? Plato is wearing pink robes and Aristotle is in blue. Socrates, wearing dark green robes, is deep in conversation with three men, standing to the left of Plato and Aristotle.

The ancient Greeks wrote a lot about philosophy and history. They also wrote many poems and plays. The ancient Greeks used an alphabet which is still used in Greece today. Here are its first four letters.

A	B	Γ	Δ
alpha	beta	gamma	delta

The first two letters are called 'alpha' and 'beta'. Do you see where our word 'alphabet' comes from?

Can you spot Plato, Aristotle and Socrates in The School of Athens?

Alexander the Great

Aristotle had a student named Alexander. When he grew up, Alexander became so powerful and famous that he was called 'Alexander the Great'.

From the time that he was very young, Alexander's mother told him that he would do wonderful things. From his teacher, Aristotle, Alexander learned much about the world, about people and about how a good king should rule. From others, Alexander learned how to fight well.

Alexander was the son of King Philip, the ruler of Macedonia [mass-ih-DOE-nee-uh] in the northern part of Greece (see the map on page 148). By the time Alexander was a young man, his father had already led his armies to the south and conquered many Greek city-states, including Athens. There is a story that, one day, King Philip took the twelve-year-old Alexander to a sale of horses. One horse kept snorting and bucking furiously.

Alexander turning Bucephalus away from his shadow

'No one can ride so wild and savage a beast,' the men said. King Philip ordered the servants to take the horse away, but Alexander spoke up. 'Those men do not know how to treat him,' he said.

'Perhaps you can do better,' said his father doubtfully.

'Yes,' said Alexander confidently. He ran to the horse and quickly turned his head toward the sun, because he had noticed that the horse was afraid of his own shadow. He then spoke gently to the horse and patted him with his hand. When he had quieted him a little, he quickly leapt on the horse's back.

Everybody expected to see the boy tossed to his death. But Alexander held on tight and let the horse run as fast as he could. By and by, the horse became tired, and Alexander rode him back to where his father was standing.

'My son,' said King Philip, 'Macedonia is too small a place for you. You must seek a larger kingdom that will be worthy of you.'

A few years later, after his father died, that is just what Alexander did. When he was only 22 years old, Alexander set off on his horse, which he named Bucephalus [byoo-SEF-ah-lus], to conquer the world.

The Gordian Knot

Alexander was a strong, intelligent ruler, but he could also be hot-tempered and cruel. Not long after he became king, the Greek city-state of Thebes decided that it no longer wanted to be ruled by Alexander. The young king moved quickly to show his strength: he burned the city to the ground and ordered that the citizens be sold as slaves.

Alexander and his army could not be stopped. With Greece under his control, he marched eastward.

There is a famous legend about Alexander. The legend says that, hundreds of years before Alexander, a king named Gordius made a knot with so many twists and turns that

Alexander the Great cutting the Gordian Knot

nobody could untie it, a knot more tangled than the worst knot you've ever had in your shoelaces. This famous knot, called 'the Gordian knot', was tied in a rope on an oxcart. People said that anyone who could release the knot would have the world for his kingdom.

When Alexander heard about the Gordian knot, he said: 'Take me to it.' The people took him to a little temple. There stood the oxcart, with the famous knot tied to it.

'Tell me again,' said Alexander, 'what you believe about this knot.'

'It is said,' the people replied, 'that the person who can release it shall have the world for his kingdom.'

Alexander looked carefully at the knot. He could not find the ends of the rope because they were tucked away inside the knot. He raised his sharp sword and, with one stroke, sliced through the knot. The rope fell to the ground, and the people cheered.

'The world is my kingdom,' said Alexander.

What Lies Beyond?

Over the next few years, Alexander conquered a huge empire. He led his armies into Egypt. There, near the Nile River, he built a splendid new city which he named after himself,

Alexandria. He then attacked the heart of the once mighty Persian empire, near the Tigris River. Alexander won a great victory during a battle at Issus in Persia and he also conquered Persepolis, but only after burning the palace and destroying the city.

Alexander now ruled over most of the ancient world. (See the map below.) But that was not enough for Alexander. Always, as soon as he had conquered one land, he would ask: 'What lies beyond?' He pushed his army forward into battle after battle. The soldiers were sometimes tired of fighting, and they grumbled and argued. However, Alexander's soldiers were generally very loyal to him throughout thirteen years of near-constant battles and fighting.

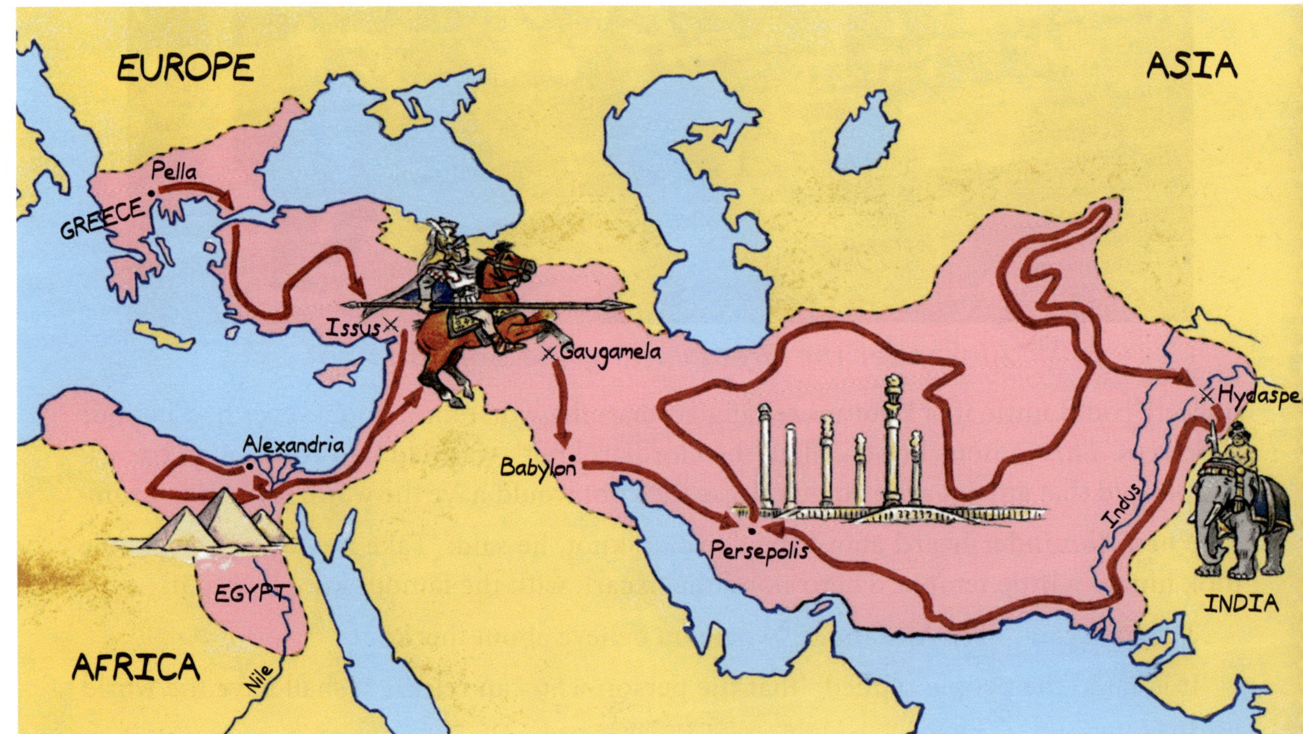

Alexander's Empire

We will never know whether Alexander would have been a good ruler of his empire, because he soon fell ill and died. He was only 33 years old.

In just ten years, Alexander had conquered the largest empire ever known at that time. But soon after his death, his empire fell apart. Other leaders got into fights about who should rule, and none of these leaders was as strong as Alexander. Still, even though his empire did not last, Alexander had a lasting effect on the world because, everywhere he went, he spread Greek ideas and learning that are still important today.

British History

A Quick Look Back

If you've read the Year 1 and Year 2 books in this series, then put on your thinking-cap and let's see what you remember.

Let's take a quick look back to the times long, long ago, all the way back to prehistoric times. In those days, the British Isles didn't exist, because they weren't islands! The land that is now Ireland, England, Wales and Scotland was all joined to the rest of the continent of Europe, so you could have walked across them all. Then an ice age came, when it was so cold no humans could live in those conditions, and hardly any plants or animals. But eventually the climate became warmer and the ice melted. The melted ice ran into the sea and the sea level started to rise, until Great Britain and Ireland were cut off from each other and from the rest of Europe by water, as we still are today.

When the weather became warmer, people could live in the British Isles again. They lived in a very simple way, without many possessions or proper houses, and they had to hunt for their food, or eat whatever fruit and other things they could find. We call this time the Stone Age because people used stone tools.

Then people discovered how to make bronze, a very hard metal that is useful for things like cooking vessels and swords. We call that period the Bronze Age. The Bronze Age was followed by the Iron Age. Do you know why? Yes, because people discovered how to make iron, which is even more useful because it is stronger than bronze.

The Iron Age came to an end when the Romans arrived in Britain and made it a part of their empire. The Romans could read and write, so the history of Britain began to be written down. We have to use other ways to find out what happened before that, like examining the objects that have survived from the period, which is called archaeology [arr-kee-OLL-oh-gee].

In Year 2 we read about how the Romans built cities and roads across Britain, and even built a great wall called Hadrian's Wall to keep the tribes in the north from invading. When the Romans left, other groups of people called

Anglo-Saxons invaded Britain and conquered it. They set up several kingdoms, and spent a lot of time fighting each other, until a warlike people from Scandinavia called Vikings started to invade and build their own settlements. Then the Anglo-Saxons fought together under King Alfred the Great, who was king of Wessex. Alfred drove the Vikings away and the different Anglo-Saxon kingdoms were at last united as England.

Then, in 1066, Duke William of Normandy in France arrived, saying that he was the rightful king of England. He defeated the English army in a great battle at Hastings and became William I of England. He has been known ever since as William the Conqueror.

William the Conqueror was so powerful that he was able to make sure that his son became king after him, and for hundreds of years his descendants – relatives in his line of ancestry – ruled England. William's great-grandson Henry became king of England in 1154. He was Henry II because his grandfather, who was king before him, was also called Henry.

William the Conqueror greets English leaders.

Norman Monarchs

William I reigned for 21 years, from 1066 to 1087
William II reigned for 13 years, from 1087 to 1100
Henry I reigned for 35 years, from 1100 to 1135
Stephen reigned for 19 years, from 1135 to 1154

The Rule of Law and Murder in the Cathedral

One of the main reasons why Henry II is remembered is because of the changes he made to the legal system in England. Have you ever thought about how important the law is in a country? The law helps to make sure that everyone knows what is right and wrong. It makes sure that people treat each other fairly and don't do things to hurt other people. It also lets people get on with their lives without worrying about something bad happening to them. Sharing and living by the same laws is an important part of being a country, and Henry II's changes were important for England when it was still a new country.

Henry II gained influence in England.

In Year 2, we read about the Code of Hammurabi in which King Hammurabi first set down laws for the people of ancient Babylon.

Henry II knew that it was important that people felt they were protected from bad things happening to them, and that they could receive justice if somebody treated them unfairly. Henry sent judges all over the country to make sure that the law was the same everywhere. These royal judges travelled around making legal decisions in local matters. Earlier, the local barons had a lot of influence over disputes in their areas, but now the king had more influence. This meant that Henry had greater control over the country than earlier kings, and he limited the control of local barons.

Today, we think that our legal system is fair because we have juries. Juries are groups of ordinary people who have no connection with either side in a dispute. Henry II was the first king to use juries widely in settling disputes fairly.

> One of the reasons that trial by jury became popular was that it was so much better than what it replaced – trial by ordeal. Trial by ordeal made people who were accused of crimes do terrible things, like hold onto red hot iron bars or put their arms into boiling water. Their wounds were examined after three days and, if they were festering, the person was considered guilty. Does that seem fair to you?

One of the most famous stories from Henry II's reign is the murder of Thomas à Becket. It is a tale of two friends who were torn apart by events, and it has a very sad end. As part of Henry's attempts to have more control over the country, he appointed his friend Thomas à Becket to be Archbishop of Canterbury, the most important person in the Church in England. But it did not work out as Henry had planned.

When his friend Thomas à Becket started making his own decisions rather than doing what he was told, Henry was not happy. Do you remember how Henry was trying to gain more control by requiring the same laws throughout the country? Well, a part of that was saying that priests and religious leaders should be subject to the King's courts when they broke the law. He didn't like that fact that the Catholic Church, which was led by the Pope in Rome, had so much power in England.

Thomas à Becket disagreed; he thought that priests should only be tried by the Church itself and, because both Thomas and Henry were stubborn, neither would back down. The argument became very bitter. Henry became fed up with Thomas and one day he said: 'Will no one rid me of this troublesome priest?' Four of his knights, who were standing by, heard this and thought that Henry was saying he wanted Thomas à Becket to be killed. They travelled to Canterbury where they murdered Thomas in the Cathedral.

This shocked everyone and the King was very upset. He said he hadn't meant his words to be acted on like that, but nobody has ever really been sure. People were very angry that an Archbishop had been killed in his own Cathedral, and they started visiting his tomb to say their prayers.

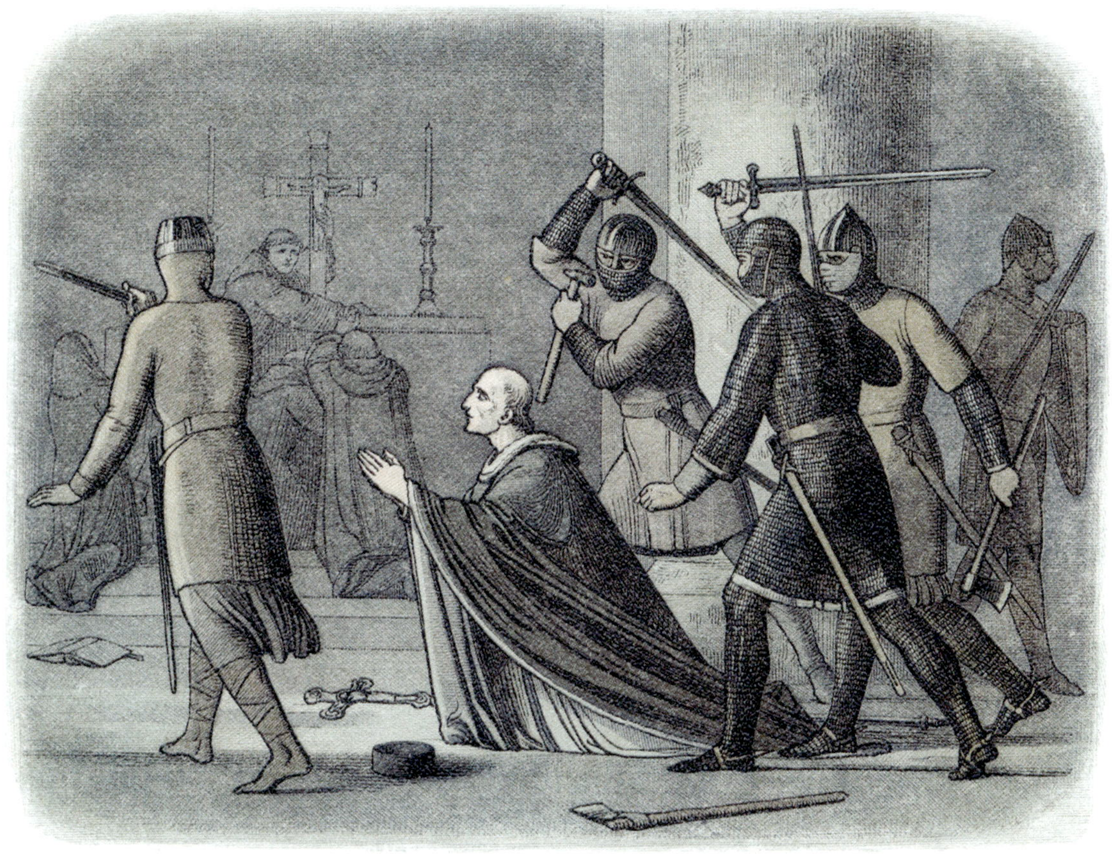

Thomas à Becket is praying in the Canterbury Cathedral as the knights surround him.

The Crusades

King Henry II wanted to show how sorry he was about Thomas à Becket's murder, so he went to Canterbury to pray at Thomas's tomb. As Henry approached the city, he took off his shoes and walked the last few miles barefoot. However, the Pope told Henry that, to show that he was really sorry, he had to go on a Crusade. This meant travelling to the Holy Land to fight a religious war.

The Holy Land was located in what is now Israel, Palestine and parts of other countries. It is still an important place for Jews, Christians and Muslims today. There are lots of historic religious buildings there and it is the place where many of the Bible stories took place. Back in Henry's time, the Holy Land was controlled by Saracens, who were Muslims. The Pope in Rome decided that Christians should drive the Saracens out of the Holy Land.

Even though Henry never actually went, his son Richard I and lots of other kings and knights from around Europe did. Richard led the Third Crusade, which took place between 1187 and

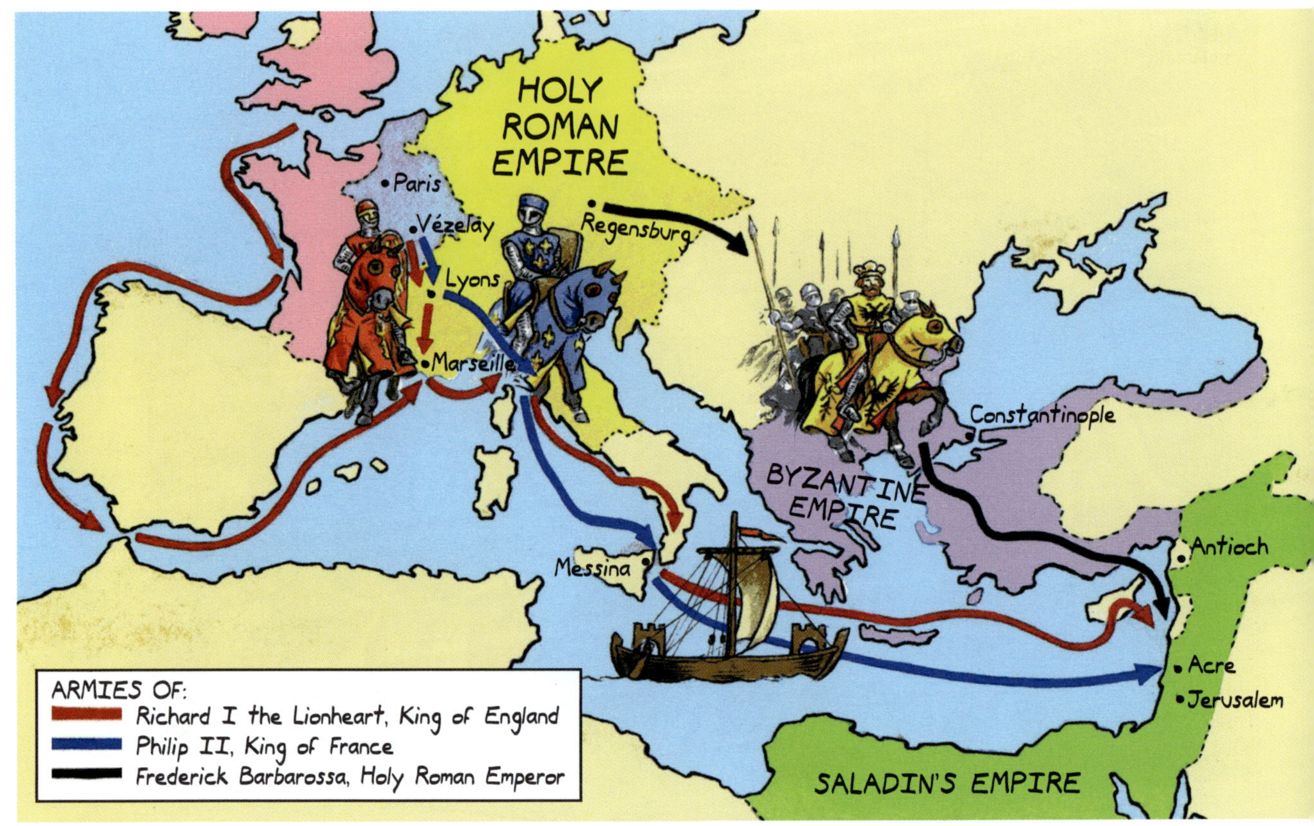

1192. After great military successes, the Islamic ruler Saladin had united the Muslims in the Holy Land into a strong force and re-conquered much of the land that the earlier Crusaders had invaded. So Richard set out with a strong army to regain control of these lands. Because of his successes and bravery on crusade, Richard became known as Richard the Lionheart.

Even though Richard won many battles, he was not able to defeat Saladin completely or control Jerusalem, the centre of the Holy Land. However, the reason that the Third Crusade is so well remembered is because of the battles between Richard the Lionheart and Saladin. Both men were powerful and successful leaders of their armies. Even though they fought many times in bloody conflicts, they had great respect for each other. In Western Europe, Saladin was remembered as a strong and noble opponent and, in the Islamic world, Richard won respect for his military abilities. They also trusted each other enough to be able to agree to stop fighting.

The two leaders agreed on a peace treaty called the Treaty of Ramla. The treaty was supposed to last for three years, three months, three weeks, three days and three hours exactly and it marked the end of the Third Crusade. Although it made sure that Jerusalem was open to Christians again, it meant that Richard had to return home without achieving

Richard I leaves on the Third Crusade

what he set out to do, which was taking control of the holy city of Jerusalem.

But Richard's success as a soldier caused some big problems. As he spent most of his time away from England fighting in the Crusades, he left his brother Prince John in charge at home. But John was not popular: people thought he was a bad man. So whilst Richard was doing well on Crusade, there were problems in store for England and English kings over the next few years.

You can read about Richard the Lionheart – Richard Coeur de Lion in French – on page 55, and learn why Prince John was unpopular and why Robin Hood stole from the rich to give to the poor.

Restraints on Royal Power: Magna Carta

When Richard the Lionheart died in 1199, the English Crown was seized by his brother John. Many of the important barons were not happy about this, because John wanted to gain more control over the barons. Instead of asking the barons for help and advice about ruling the country, he brought in his own friends from France and gave them important positions. As you can imagine, this made many of the barons angry. The barons were very powerful men, but John was their King. What could they do about it? Early in 1215, the barons decided to try and restrict what John could and couldn't do as King. They drew up a list of things they wanted to change.

The barons demanded lots of big changes. Among lots of other things, they tried to stop the King taking money from the barons whenever he wanted and to make sure that he could not punish anyone without a fair trial. They said that if the King broke the new laws then the barons had the right to overrule the King and take his property. They also said that these new laws had to last forever and not just for King John. Altogether, it meant that the King did not have the power to do whatever he wanted, and that there were certain rules that even a king had to obey.

King John putting his seal to the Magna Carta

King John didn't like these new ideas at all, but he realised that he couldn't fight all of the barons and win, so he met them at a place called Runnymede on 15 June 1215. He gave in to the barons by putting his seal to the list that became known as the Magna Carta, which is Latin for the Great Charter.

But it didn't end there. Even though the King had agreed to have limits on what he could do, he quickly went back on his word. He didn't believe that a king had to answer to anyone. This caused a big fight with the barons, and it looked as though all the things agreed in the Magna Carta had been lost. But then something changed: King John became ill and died. His son, Henry III, was only nine years old when he became the next king. When he was young, Henry had people to rule the country for him, and they did so by the rules laid down in the Magna Carta. In time, many of the ideas in it came to be accepted. It was the first step towards controlling the power of the king and giving the people more of a say in how the country was run.

How the crown jewels were lost in the Wash

Wherever King John travelled, he carried all of his valuable things with him in wagons, including the crown jewels. A year after putting his seal to Magna Carta, he was travelling in a part of East Anglia called the Wash when he began to feel ill. He decided to take the shortest possible route to get out of the fens – a very cold and windswept stretch of land – to go to a more comfortable place. His wagons were moving across a stretch of treacherous sands when the tide started to come in. The wheels of the wagons and the hooves of the horses were getting stuck in quicksand, and many people ran away to escape drowning. Many of the King's most precious possessions were lost, including the crown jewels.

Restraints on Royal Power: de Montfort's Parliament

Henry III was the King of England for over 50 years and, just like his father King John, he had problems with the barons over how he ran the country. One particular fight with the barons led to what became known as 'de Montfort's Parliament'.

Simon de Montfort was a French baron who also owned land in England. He was the same age as Henry III and they were both friends. De Montfort even married Henry's sister Eleanor. Despite being brothers-in-law, they fell out with each other. In England, the barons were not happy with Henry. They didn't like the fact that he took money from them to fight wars in Europe, and they thought he favoured his family and friends in France over the English barons – just like his father. The barons tried to control Henry, but the King refused to agree to their demands.

The barons finally decided to rebel. They raised an army and asked Simon de Montfort to lead it. He was a very good soldier, and he was able to capture the King at the Battle of Lewes in 1264. With the King locked up, de Montfort had to decide what to do, and how he was going to run the country. There had only ever been kings in charge before. What would you have done? Well, de Montfort decided to ask every county in England to send two people to his Parliament to represent them. It was the first time in English history that the people in charge were 'elected'. Elected means that they were chosen by others, rather than being born into power like a king or queen.

This democratic government was new for Britain, just as democracy was a new way of governing ancient Athens. Today all adults can elect members of parliament, which means that everyone has a small say in how the country is run, rather than having a king or queen who can do whatever he or she wants. De Montfort's parliament was the first time something like this had happened in Britain.

Henry III meets with Simon de Montfort's parliament.

The Wars of the Roses

For 30 years in the fifteenth century, two families fought each other for the English crown. On one side was the House of Lancaster, whose emblem was a red rose, and on the other side was the House of York, whose rose was white. This is why the struggle became known as the 'Wars of the Roses'.

King Henry VI sits while the Duke of York and the Duke of Somerset argue.

The King, Henry VI, was weak and ill, and some people saw this as a chance to get power for themselves. King Henry was part of the House of Lancaster, and Richard, the Duke of York, fought against the Lancastrians in the first battle of the Wars of the Roses, which was the Battle of St Albans. Richard and the Yorkists won that battle, and even though Henry and the Lancastrians then forced Richard to flee abroad, eventually Richard's son Edward became King. Edward IV, as he became, was a Yorkist King.

These battles between the two sides continued for years and years.

The little princes were locked in the Tower of London.

Normally when a king died, his son would become the next king. But when Edward IV died in 1483, his son, who was also called Edward, was only 12 years old. This meant that the young King's uncle, who was called Richard of Gloucester, was able to steal the crown and become King Richard III. But Richard III had a big problem: Edward was the rightful king and he and his brother were growing up. Soon they would be old enough to fight for the crown. Richard locked the two little boys away in the Tower of London. He told people that it was for their own safety and that he was protecting them. The two young princes were last seen playing in the gardens of the Tower of London in the summer of 1483, and nobody really knows to this day what happened to them. It is one of the biggest historical mysteries. Who could have killed such innocent little boys? The main suspect is their uncle, King Richard III, but we cannot know for sure. The story of the Princes in the Tower is famous because it is so sad, and because it is a real-life mystery. If you ever visit the Tower of London, you will be asked what you think!

One thing we do know is that Richard was not king for very long. Henry Tudor, a Lancastrian from Wales, claimed that he should be king. He was related to Edward III, who had been the King of England over 100 years earlier. Henry fought Richard at the one of the most famous battles in English history, the Battle of Bosworth Field in 1485. Henry won the battle and became king.

Richard III fighting during the Battle of Bosworth

The Tudor rose

Even though he was a Lancastrian, Henry ended the Wars of the Roses by marrying Princess Elizabeth from the House of York and uniting the two families. That is why the Tudors – Henry VII and the kings and queens who followed him – took as their emblem a white rose inside a red rose. It meant that the fighting had come to an end. England had peace, and people could get on with their lives knowing that there would be no more battles over who should be king.

Plantagenet Monarchs

Henry II reigned 35 years, from 1154 to 1189

Richard I reigned 10 years, from 1189 to 1199

John reigned 17 years, from 1199 to 1216

Henry III reigned 56 years, from 1216 to 1272

Edward I reigned 35 years, from 1272 to 1307

Edward II reigned 20 years, from 1307 to 1327

Edward III reigned 50 years, from 1327 to 1377

Richard II reigned 22 years, from 1377 to 1399

Henry IV reigned 14 years, from 1399 to 1413

Henry V reigned 9 years, from 1413 to 1422

Henry VI reigned 39 years, from 1422 to 1461

Edward IV reigned 22 years, from 1461 to 1483

Edward V, one of the little princes in the Tower, reigned a little more than two months, from April 6th to June 26th, 1483

Richard III reigned 2 years, from 1483 to 1485

The Reformation

We have already learnt how important Christianity was to people in Europe. Do you remember the Crusades? We also saw how powerful the Pope and the Church were, too. By the 1500s this had not changed much. The Pope, who lived in Rome, had a huge influence over all the kings in Europe, including the kings of England.

In Europe, some people were beginning to think that the Church had too much power. They said it was corrupt, and they were not happy with how some people were using religion to make money. One man in particular was not happy. His name was Martin Luther, and in 1517 he nailed a list of his complaints about the Church to the door of a church in his hometown of Wittenberg in Germany. In those days, people used to do this if they thought something needed to be talked about.

This was the start of the Reformation. Lots of people agreed with Martin Luther, and soon he had many followers. Luther thought that God's word in the Bible was more important than the Pope. He translated the Bible into German so that more people could understand it. People, he taught, could be saved just by believing in God. Because his followers were protesting against some things the Church did, they were called *Protestants*.

Martin Luther is nailing his list of complaints to the church door

In the part of Europe that we now call Germany, there were lots of separate places ruled by different princes. Many of these princes liked this new 'Protestant' Christianity because it meant that they didn't have to be told what to do by the Pope any longer. Arguments over these two types of Christianity led to lots of long and fierce wars during the next 200 years all around Europe. One of the results of the Protestant Reformation was that people were expected to read the Bible in their own language (rather than Latin), so it encouraged people to learn to read. At about this time, the printing press was invented, which meant that more people were able to read lots of different things. This helped new ideas to spread faster than before.

The English Reformation

There were some people in England who agreed with Martin Luther and were not happy with the Church as it was. William Tyndale was one of them: he translated the Bible into English so that people could read it themselves. But the King was not a Protestant. Henry VIII didn't like these reforms at first, although he soon found his own reason for quarrelling with the Pope and the Catholic Church.

Henry had a serious problem. Like all kings, he wanted to make sure that he had a son who could become king after him. This was really important because England had been torn apart by fighting over the crown for so long during the Wars of the Roses, and Henry didn't want those arguments to start all over again.

Henry wasn't happy because his wife, Catherine of Aragon, could not give him a son. Henry thought that only a boy could grow up to rule the country, so he tried to end his marriage to Catherine. The Pope would not agree to this, so Henry decided to break from Rome. In 1534, Parliament declared him head of the Church in England in what was called the Act of Supremacy. This meant that Henry didn't have to listen to what the Pope said any more.

Henry VIII divorced Catherine of Aragon and married Anne Boleyn. Unfortunately for Henry, that wasn't the end of his problems. Anne did not give birth to a son either, but instead gave birth to another daughter, Elizabeth. Henry was angry about this and cut off Anne Boleyn's head. Henry married again, and this time his new wife, Jane Seymour, gave birth to a baby boy. Henry was overjoyed that he finally had a son. Sadly, Jane died soon afterwards and Henry went on marry again… and again… and again! He had a grand total of six wives!

So now the Church in England was separate from Rome and, to keep it that way, Henry destroyed all the monasteries in England and sold the land. This is known as the 'Dissolution of the Monasteries'. It made the King very rich as he was able to seize all the land and all the precious things that had been given to the church over hundreds of years. It was very unpopular with the people, though, and led to a great protest known as 'The Pilgrimage of Grace'. Tens of thousands of people joined in an uprising to protest against the religious

Byland Abbey in North Yorkshire was dissolved in 1538, and you can still see its ruins today.

changes and the seizure of church property. There were so many protestors that Henry was worried. He sent the Duke of Norfolk to promise them all a free pardon if they would lay down their arms, and that he would consider their requests. As soon as the men had gone back to their homes, the leaders were arrested and executed, and none of the promises were kept.

However, even though Henry had broken from Rome, he still wanted to keep the Church just the same in most ways. He made sure that no big changes were made to the way people worshipped. The main difference was that now the king was in charge of the Church.

Religious Conflicts:
From Protestant to Catholic and Back Again

Gerlach Flicke's painting of Thomas Cranmer is in London's National Portrait Gallery.

When Henry's only son Edward became King in 1547, at the age of nine, he also inherited the position of head of the Church in England. Unlike his father, Edward had been raised a Protestant, and he believed that England should be a Protestant country.

Some strict Protestants thought that religion should be as simple as possible, and so Edward decided to remove all the pictures, ornaments and altars from churches across England. He even ordered beautiful wall paintings to be covered by whitewash. As well as this, the Archbishop of Canterbury, Thomas Cranmer, wrote a book designed to tell local ministers how church services should be carried out. It was called *The Book of Common Prayer*. For the first time there were real changes to the church that people could see and, instead of listening to services in Latin that most couldn't understand, the people heard them being said in English.

Edward was not king for long, though. He died when he was 15, only six years after he had first become king, so his older sister Mary was given the crown and became Queen Mary I. Do you remember Henry VIII's first marriage? He was married to the Spanish Catholic princess, Catherine of Aragon. Mary was their daughter, and unlike Edward, she was raised a Catholic. Edward had not wanted her to become queen because he was scared that she would try to make England Catholic again, and he was right.

Mary I reversed all of Edward's religious changes and joined England with the Pope and the Catholic Church in Rome again. She put to death so many people who wanted to remain Protestant that she became known as 'Bloody Mary'. She married the King of Spain, who was a Catholic, but they didn't have any children. This meant that, when Mary died, her sister Elizabeth became queen, and England became a Protestant country again.

This portrait shows that Elizabeth I was proud of her Navy.

The Elizabethan Era

Elizabeth I was queen for a very long time. During her 44-year reign, Elizabeth saw huge changes across the British Isles, and it was much more peaceful than in the years before.

Elizabeth wanted to find a middle ground between Catholicism and Protestantism. This middle ground is sometimes called the Elizabethan Religious Settlement because she tried to settle some of the arguments over religion.

Elizabeth was a Protestant, but she wanted to have a religion that as many people as possible would accept and follow. Elizabeth was the daughter of Henry's second marriage to Anne Boleyn, which the Pope had refused to accept, so she didn't want England to be loyal to the Pope. But also she did not want to upset people by removing all the familiar bits of churches and church services that people had been used to. Elizabeth's answer to these problems was a kind of Protestantism that looked a bit like Catholicism. Priests were expected to wear *vestments*, which were special robes for church services, and Elizabeth had a *crucifix*, which is a small model of Jesus on the cross. In the Act of Supremacy she confirmed that the Church of England was separate from the power of the Pope in Rome, just as her father Henry VIII had done years earlier. Then the process was completed with the Act of Uniformity, which made sure that everyone had to attend these new church services and use the new *Book of Common Prayer* that told people how to worship.

The compromise worked because Elizabeth was less extreme in her views than either her Protestant brother Edward or her Catholic sister Mary. The Elizabethan Religious Settlement formed the basis for the Church of England today.

In Scotland, things happened differently and a stricter form of Protestantism became the official religion. John Knox was a religious thinker and preacher who led the Scottish Reformation. He had worked for Edward VI in England when he was enforcing strict Protestantism, and then escaped to Switzerland when Queen Mary tried to turn England Catholic. He didn't like Catholics at all, and in 1560 he helped to organise an uprising in Scotland against the Roman Catholic Church. This led to the Scottish Parliament giving up Catholicism and eventually becoming a much stricter Protestant country than Elizabethan England.

It was not just in religion that Elizabeth tried to continue the efforts started by her father, Henry VIII. Henry had organised and expanded the English Navy, building many new ships such as the famous Mary Rose.

Unlike Edward and Mary, Elizabeth spent a lot of money on the English Navy, which built more modern ships. Not only did the Navy grow during Elizabeth's reign, but it

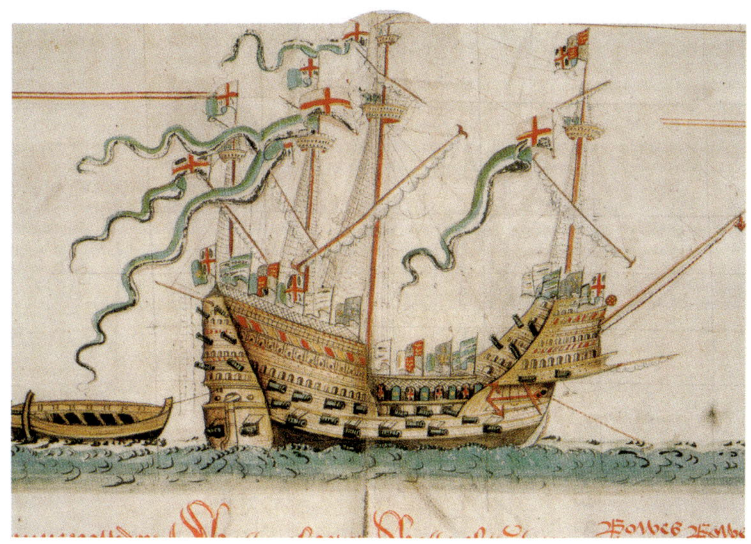

The Mary Rose

was also a good time for private sailors and explorers. The seas around Europe were full of 'privateers'. Privateers were like pirates, but they wereloyal to one country. Sailors like Sir Francis Drake would attack ships from other countries, especially countries England was at war with, and would get to keep whatever treasure they found on board – after giving some to the Queen! This was great for Elizabeth because it meant that they didn't have to be paid. Privateers from lots of different European countries made European waters and the Atlantic Ocean very dangerous places for merchant ships that were trading with different countries.

It was not just merchants, pirates, privateers and navies that were helped by the new, bigger and faster ships. This was a great time for explorers. Sir Francis Drake managed to circumnavigate the globe; this means he sailed all the way around the world. Walter Raleigh was another explorer and he sailed to America, known then as the New World. He started the first English settlement there, called Roanoke. Years later, European

Do you notice similarities between this portrait of Sir Francis Drake and the portrait of Elizabeth I?

settlements in America would eventually lead to the creation of the United States of America, but Roanoke was a mysterious failure. The governor of the Roanoke colony, John White, went back to England for supplies, but when he returned to Roanoke all the people had gone and the small town was empty. No one who had lived there was ever found, and nobody knows what happened to them. The mystery of Roanoke has never been solved.

You can read a story which explains why the British people were so successful at building a navy to 'rule the waves' on page 50.

England's Navy and the skill of England's privateers were tested by the Spanish Armada. In 1588, King Philip II of Spain, who had been married to Mary I, launched a large fleet of ships to invade England and overthrow Queen Elizabeth I. It was called the Spanish Armada. The Spanish ships planned to collect many soldiers in the Netherlands and then cross the channel to invade England. They never managed this because, while they were taking on supplies in Calais in France, the English Navy sent some burning ships into the port where the Spanish ships were at anchor. These 'fireships' meant the Spanish had to leave in a hurry. They were chased into the North Sea and around the British Isles. The Armada tried to sail back to Spain, but there were storms when they passed the west coast of Ireland, and many of their ships were wrecked on the rocky shores there. The defeat of the Spanish Armada was one of the first important victories for the growing English Navy.

Elizabeth's reign was quite stable, so people were able to spend time doing things that they enjoyed, like going to the theatre. There were lots of successful playwrights and actors, but the most famous of them was William Shakespeare. Shakespeare's plays survive today and are still very popular, even though they were written more than 400 years ago.

Sir Francis Drake was one of the captains commanding the English fleet when the Spanish Armada was expected. He was playing a game of bowls on Plymouth Hoe – a stretch of flat, grassy land overlooking the English Channel – with his fellow captains when the Spanish Armada came into sight. The other captains stopped their game and made haste towards their ships, but they were called back by Sir Francis Drake saying: 'Plenty of time to finish the game and beat the Spaniards too!' He was right!

Shakespeare wrote different types of plays: funny plays called comedies, sad plays called tragedies and plays about the past called histories. He also wrote poems called sonnets. Shakespeare's plays were performed by actors at the Globe Theatre in Southwark, London, where you can still see them being performed today in a replica of his theatre.

A replica of the Globe Theatre

Tudor Monarchs

Henry VII reigned 24 years, from 1485 to 1509

Henry VIII reigned 38 years, from 1509 to 1547

Edward VI reigned 6 years, from 1547 to 1553

Mary I reigned 5 years, from 1553 to 1558

Elizabeth I reigned 45 years, from 1558 to 1603

Suggested Resources

Athens is Saved! The First Marathon by Stewart Ross (Evans Brothers) 2006

Avoid Exploring with Marco Polo by Jacqueline Morley (Book House) 2009

Britannia: 100 Great Stories From British History by Geraldine McCaughrean and Richard Brassey (Orion Childrens) 2004.

Discover the Tudors: Elizabeth I by Moira Butterfield (Franklin Watts) 2010

Lin Yi's Lantern: a Moon Festival Tale by Brenda Williams (Barefoot Books) 2009

Mapping (Investigate Geography) by Louise Spilsbury (Heinemann) 2010

Our Island Story by H.E. Marshall (Civitas/Galore Park) [1905] 2005

Starting Geography: Maps (Franklin Watts) 2009

The Great Race: The Story of the Chinese Zodiac by Dawn Casey (Barefoot Books) 2006

We Love Chinese New Year by Saviour Pirotta (Wayland) 2009

Where You Live: Around the School by Paul Humphrey (Franklin Watts) 2007

Your Local Area: Rivers by Ruth Thomson (Wayland) 2010

Visual Arts

Introduction

The Pleasure of Art

The best way to bring art to life is to experience it first-hand. For the child in Year 3, this means seeing the wonderful surfaces, sizes and details of paintings (or sculptures, prints and drawings!) in a gallery or museum; then it means going home afterwards and exploring art materials on the kitchen table and trying out the techniques, styles and colours you both liked. Reading about art in a book like this one with your child is an important way to increase their knowledge and understanding of great art and artists, but it cannot replace the experience – and pleasure – of physically engaging with art.

You don't need special or expensive materials to experience the pleasure of art at home; simply tracing over a gallery postcard or reproduction then colouring your tracing, or cutting it and collaging it into a new creation, would be a rewarding, creative and educational art experience. Throughout this chapter we suggest other activities your child can do which will extend and embed their understanding of the works of art written about here. To explore art further still, we suggest you dip into some of the books suggested in the resources section at the end of this chapter, and that you make use of the free, family-oriented events that galleries and museums offer at weekends and during school holidays.

Taking a Line for a Walk

The Swiss-German artist Paul Klee [clay] described drawing as 'a line going for a walk'. Next time you set out to draw something, think about your pencil making a journey – going for a walk – and see if holding that thought while you draw helps the lines you create come to life. Drawing is such an important part of being a practising artist; in the past young people learning to be artists were not allowed to use paint or other materials until their teacher felt they could draw well enough. When it came to painting or sculpting, first they had to use drawing to make their plans.

It is thought that when the Dutch artist Rembrandt taught young artists, one of the first things he would make them do was draw something with a continuous line – in other words the students could not lift their hand until the drawing was finished! It might be easy to draw a ball, but can you imagine how hard it would be to draw a face, for example, without lifting your pencil off the page at all? How would you do it? You could make your line zig-zag or curve, you could press hard at times to darken it and press lightly at others to make it soft, but how would your line travel between the different features without breaking?

Here is a continuous line drawing by Paul Klee. What a walk he has taken this line for! It travels from an eye to a nose, through a brow to an arm, a leg and back again. He called this drawing *Was Fehlt Ihm?* which is German for 'What's Wrong with Him?' Take a close look at the drawing, perhaps tracing over it with your finger. Notice how cleverly Klee has defined different parts of the face and body but managed to keep everything connected.

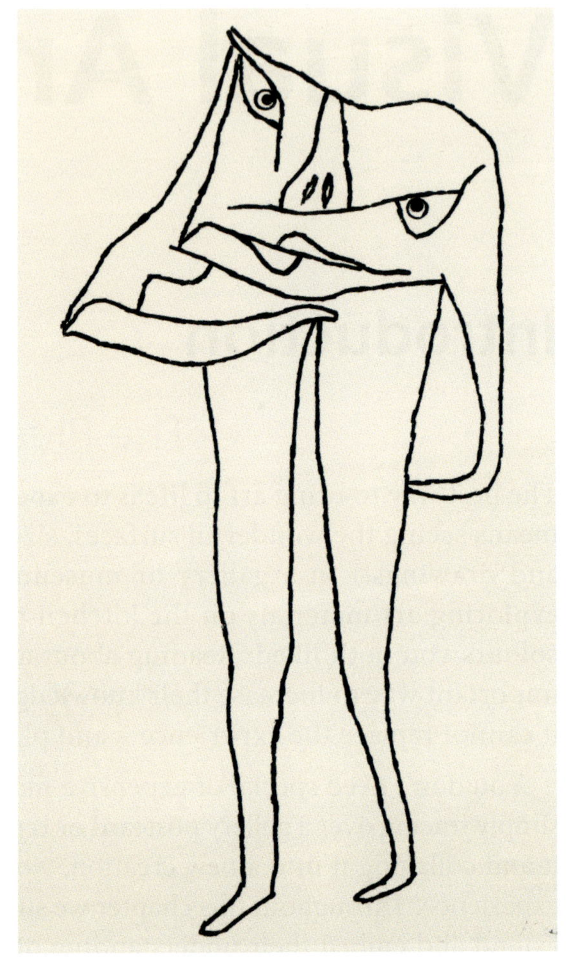

Was Fehlt Ihm?
(What's Wrong with Him?)

There are names for different kinds of lines, and it can be useful when you are talking or writing about art to use them. A line that goes straight up and down is called a *vertical* line. A line that travels from side to side is known as *horizontal* (after the horizon), and a line that leans is *diagonal*.

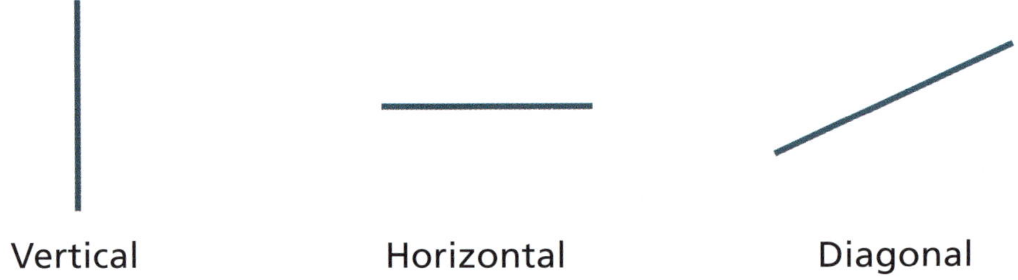

Vertical   Horizontal   Diagonal

You probably know the names for other kinds of lines, too. Can you picture a zig-zag line, a curved one or a wavy one?

The kinds of lines an artist chooses to work with are important because they can help him or her create depth or distance in their pictures (properly known as *perspective*). They also help to create movement, and even mood. Let's look at the line choices three very different artists have made and consider how they affect the resulting pictures.

Mother and Child

Lines and Form

In *Mother and Child* by the Spanish artist Pablo Picasso [pee-KHAS-o] do you see more straight or curved lines? Use your finger to help you decide, or perhaps make a tracing using a pencil. The many curving lines add to the gentle atmosphere of this picture. Picasso has used another element of art, called *form*, to emphasise the feeling of softness the lines create. Form is a word to describe how three-dimensional shapes are shown in art. Picasso's lines in *Mother and Child* build up to make rounded 'forms', and these rounded forms almost curve inwards on one another, so that we no longer see just a collection of lines: they are transformed into an image of a relaxed hug. Can you also see how Picasso has used the short, diagonal line of the mother's nose to direct where we look in the picture? The line from her nose follows the direction of her gaze: down towards her son's head and onwards to the bottom right corner of the painting. This is an example of how, sometimes, an artist can suggest a line, without needing to draw or paint it. The short (drawn) diagonal line, which is the mother's nose, seems to extend invisibly through her head and along the child's body, on out to the knee on which he is supported. By organising the figures along this invisible diagonal, Picasso has reinforced their closeness. Can you see other things that Picasso has done to show how close they feel? What about the colours he has used, and the gestures?

Lines and Movement

In his picture of an enormous wave, the Japanese artist Katsushika Hokusai [cat-sue-SHE-car HOCK-ew-sigh] shows us other ways that lines can be used.

This picture is actually a coloured woodblock print, called *The Great Wave off Kanagawa*. It was very popular among artists, and Picasso and van Gogh (we looked at his self-portrait in Year 2) were among the important

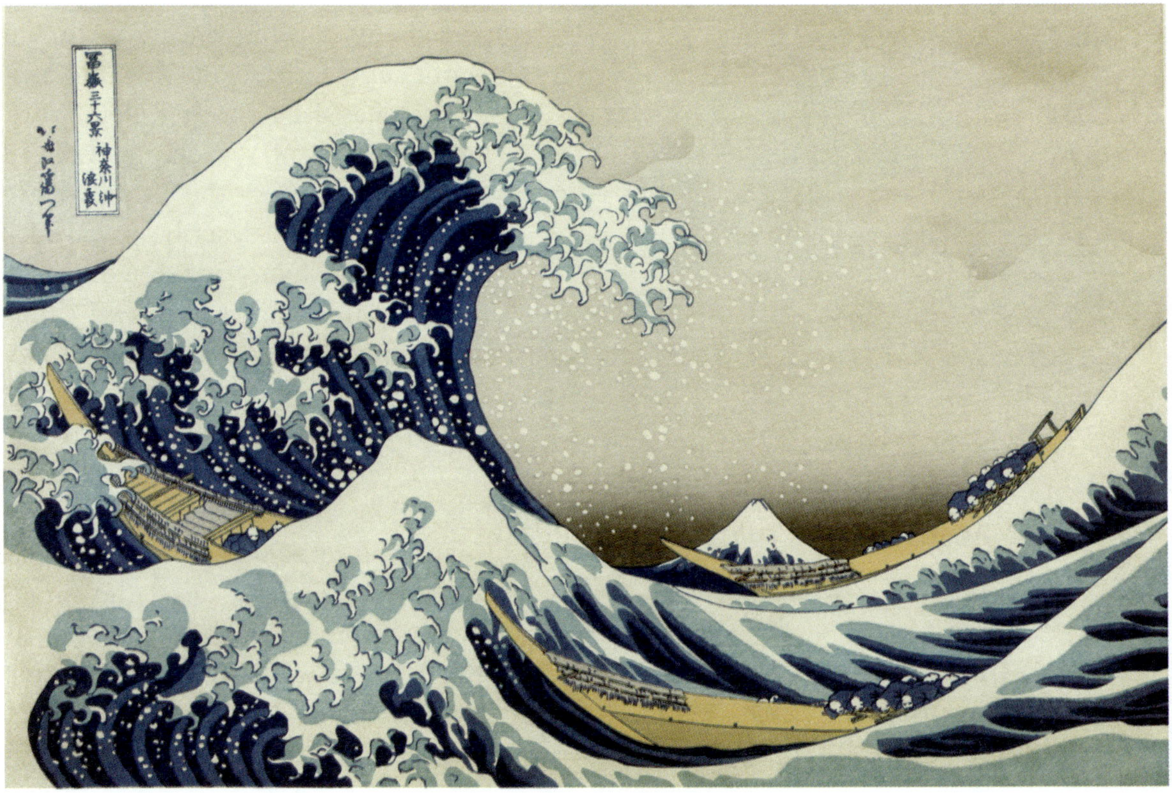

The Great Wave off Kanagawa

European artists who owned copies of Hokusai's work. What do you think they liked about it? Perhaps it was the way the various types of lines combine to create a sense of motion. Where is the wave moving to; what shape will it make as it travels on? Hokusai's curving lines makes us curious about that. Can you spot the tiny fishermen huddled together in their wooden boats? The long parallel lines of their boats contrast with the tiny, curled lines used for the frothy breaking tips of the wave; these are gnarled like grabbing fingers, threatening the boats!

Lines and Symmetry

The Italian artist and inventor Leonardo da Vinci [leo-NAR-do da-VIN-chi] shows us yet another way that line can create powerful works of art. In his *Last Supper*, which was painted on the wall of the refectory, or dining room, for the holy men at Santa Maria della Grazie in Milan, Leonardo has used a combination of vertical, horizontal and diagonal lines to arrange the scene. Jesus and his disciples, designed with mostly rounded lines, are seated at the table in a room with windows, all composed from straight and diagonal lines. One of the things Leonardo uses his lines here to do, particularly the diagonal ones, is direct where we look. The lines all point to the centre of the picture where the oval face of Jesus is framed by a window.

Do you think the form of the *Mona Lisa* from the Year 2 book is similar to those in the *Last Supper*? Both were made by Leonardo da Vinci.

Last Supper

The lines work to make sure we know who is the most important character in this story. Leonardo's lines also balance the painting, so that the setting on the right-hand side of Jesus is echoed on the left, even though the figures and faces are different. The painting,

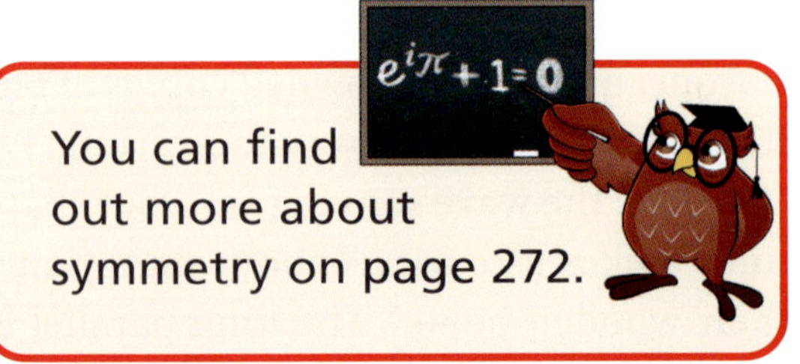

we say, is *symmetrical*, and the boundaries you can see or imagine that equally divide balanced or reflecting forms are known as lines of symmetry.

Activity 2: From half to whole!

Create a symmetrical work of art using lines, like Leonardo. Fold a piece of paper exactly in half, press the crease to mark it, then open the page out again and flatten it. Taking a soft pencil, a piece of charcoal or chalk, draw a scene made up of lines on one side of the fold line only. It must only be half a drawing, and it must touch the folded line. You could draw half a house or, inspired by Leonardo's *Last Supper*, compose half a room with windows, a table and a floor or walls made from lines. Fold the paper in half again and rub over the outside so that your drawn lines transfer on to the plain half of the page. Open up once more and admire your linear, symmetrical drawing.

Looking at Landscapes

If you've read the Year 2 book in this series, then you'll have learned about two of the many kinds of pictures there are: portraits and self-portraits. In Year 3 we are going to learn about other kinds of pictures: landscapes, still lifes and mythologies. Landscapes are works of art showing mostly countryside or coastlines. You can think of landscapes as being a bit like painted plays: in a landscape the ground is the stage, the sky is the set and the trees and weather are the characters! People, animals, buildings and boats may feature in landscapes but they are usually there to provide realistic details or to give us the idea that we are looking at a large, open space; these details are not usually the main focus of landscapes.

In the Netherlands in the seventeenth century, landscape paintings were extremely popular. In fact, Dutch artists at this time were the first to specialise in creating landscapes.

Before this, landscape was usually just the background for paintings from history, the Bible or mythology. In some Dutch towns almost every house had at least one landscape painting inside it and, most often, they were hung in the main family room. It may be that these landscape paintings were used as a kind of entertainment – remember there were no televisions then and even books were quite expensive. When we might relax by watching a film, the Dutch people of those

Bentheim Castle

days seem to have enjoyed using their imaginations to explore their paintings. An adult might imagine a walk in the tranquil countryside while a child might embark on a great adventure. An example of this kind of landscape painting is *Bentheim Castle* by Dutch artist Jacob van Ruisdael [RICE-dale]. The painting creates a very realistic scene, with the castle perching dramatically, on a craggy outcrop, above a dense, green forest. Can you imagine a princess trapped inside, a knight struggling through the thickets to reach her, or do you sense something else?

Does this remind you of the story of the Sleeping Beauty that we read in Year 2?

We can tell that the painter van Ruisdael was feeling imaginative when he designed *Bentheim Castle* because in real life the castle is not perched on a mountain; it is set on a low hill! Van Ruisdael has raised up the castle in his painting and added craggy rocks to increase the drama. The castle is still there today, on the border between the Netherlands and Germany, so you could go and see it for yourself one day.

In landscape paintings, artists generally leave clues to let us work out the time of year, what the weather is like and even what time of day has been shown. Be an art detective and follow the clues in *Salisbury Cathedral from the Meadows* (next page), by English artist John Constable so that you can read the season, the weather and time of day. What have you decided? I expect the bright rainbow that arcs across the middle of the painting quickly caught your attention. What did it tell you about the weather? What about the sky on either side of the rainbow. Why are there grey, choppy-looking clouds on the cathedral side of the rainbow but fluffy, white clouds and brighter blue sky to the other side? Is a storm coming towards us or moving away? What season is shown and how can you tell? Are you looking at the colour and number of leaves on the large tree, or did you notice the clothes of the men in the carts? The time of day is harder to work out – did you spot any clues Constable painted for that? Maybe you could try seeing where the light comes from, and look at any shadows to work out whether this is a morning, midday or early evening scene.

Landscapes don't have to be of real places. They can also be of imaginary ones. The French artist Henri Rousseau [on-REE ROO-sew]

Salisbury Cathedral from the Meadows

never actually visited a tropical jungle, but he did many paintings set in lush, green jungles. We looked at one of them in Year 1. It was called *Surprised!* and showed a tiger frightened by lightning in a forest. Rousseau could have seen a tiger, caged at an exhibition in Paris. For the jungle plants, however, Rousseau had to use the ordinary plants he saw at home, and his imagination. He made them look tropical by enlarging the leaves and mixing up a lot of different greens to paint them.

Still Life

As the name suggests, still-lifes do not contain things which move. There are no people in them, but there could be flowers, fruit, china, silverware, glass, books, furniture, fabrics and even pencils. The only living creatures permitted in still life pictures are insects! To paint a still life, first an artist must decide which objects to depict, and then she has to arrange them in a pleasing or interesting way. Which shapes and colours go well next to one another? Where is the light casting shadows or adding highlights?

How much background will be shown? What about the textures? Will different surfaces be faithfully recorded, using rough and smooth strokes, heavy and light paint, or will all the objects be reduced to their basic shapes and colours? What a lot of decisions to make!

Have a look at *Still Life with Apples* by French artist Paul Cézanne [say-ZAN]. What can you say about the decisions he made when he designed this scene? Notice how the apples look as if they have been outlined in a dark tone, which emphasises their circular shapes. Cézanne's apples don't look like flat shapes, however, because their roundness pops out from their outlines. To show that they are three-dimensional forms, Cézanne has combined a range of colours and applied them in a rough painting style. Focus on one apple in particular. How many patches of colour and areas of texture can you pick out? I can see yellows, reds, browns, oranges and even off-whites.

Still Life with Apples

For more on two- and three-dimensional figures, see page 268.

Activity 3: Multi-colour still life

Choose a single fruit from the fruit bowl or fridge at home. Then choose some sort of coloured material: it could be crayons, coloured pencils or paint. Draw the outline shape of your fruit, so that you have a basic, two-dimensional – or flat – shape on your page. Using colour only, see if you can turn the basic shape into a three-dimensional form, as Cézanne did. How many different colours did you need to use to turn your outline shape into a still life artwork?

Mythology

Mythological pictures couldn't be more different from still-lifes. People are the most important element in mythological paintings, as they re-tell – in visual form – the dramatic adventures of gods and goddesses of the ancient past. You will know, from the Language and Literature section of this book, about the extraordinary events and characters who fill Greek myths; the half-man half-beast creatures like the Minotaur, terrible monsters like Cerberus, not to mention the passionate and vengeful gods and goddesses, like Jupiter and Venus. For thousands of years, and in all media, artists have enjoyed capturing these characters and their stories.

Although the subject of the next painting we are going to look at dates back to ancient Greece, the picture is comparatively young; it was made in fifteenth century by one of two Italian painter brothers, probably Antonio del Pollaiuolo [pol-eye-YOU-oh-low]. There are only two figures in del Pollaiuolo's painting, but without using any words these two tell a powerful story. See if you can work it out, just from looking... the male character, Apollo, chases after the woman, Daphne, and reaches out to catch her with his arms. He is mid-stride, feet not quite on the ground, scarf flying and hair blown behind him. What a rush he is in to catch her! Daphne does not seem happy that Apollo has caught her, though, does she? She won't look at him and she is not smiling. It is also as if she is floating up away from the ground. Although Apollo tries his best to hold on to her, we can see, from his stretched-looking arms and parted hands, that he cannot manage it.

Read more about the mythology of Ancient Greece starting on page 65.

Apollo loves Daphne, having been shot with a love arrow by Cupid, but Daphne rejects him; she is cursed never to love. She prays to her father, a river god, to rescue her from Apollo's pursuit. Her wish is granted, but by transforming her into a natural form: a tree! Can you see now how the artist has painted Daphne's arms like bark-encrusted branches? I am sure you noticed her bushy, leaf-laden arms. The heartbroken Apollo was powerless to stop Daphne's transformation – all he could do was keep her immortal by making the laurel tree she became evergreen.

Apollo and Daphne

Activity 4: Words for pictures

Cut some 'post-it' notes into speech bubble shapes. Stick them on to the image of Apollo and Daphne on this page and imagine what the characters are thinking, or what they would be saying if they could talk. Would Daphne be praying to her father? Would she be expressing sadness at losing her mortal body? Adopting the poses the characters hold in the paintings, and trying to copy their expressions, might help you understand them better.

The Art of Designing Buildings: Architecture

Our word 'architect', the name we use for a person who designs buildings, comes from the combination of two ancient Greek words, the first meaning 'chief' and the second, 'builder'. One of the most famous buildings of ancient Greece, so well designed and built it is still standing today, is the Parthenon [parth-er-NON]. Its architects were Ictinos and Callicrates, and they worked together with a famous Greek sculptor, Phidias. Set on the Acropolis hill overlooking the centre of the capital city of Athens, it was designed as a temple (a place of worship) for the goddess Athena in 440 BC. Since it was built for this purpose and in such a prominent place, it shows us that mythology was important and very real to the ancient Greeks, although it can be just a set of great stories to us. Now you know that a temple for Athena stood at the heart of Athens, you can see where the city's name came from.

Discover more about the ancient Greeks in the World History section starting on page 147.

The Parthenon today

Replica of the Greek Parthenon in Nashville in the United States

A Building of Lines

When the Parthenon was first built, it would probably have looked like the replica (real-life copy) that was built in Nashville in the United States. As the replica shows, not all of the building would have been plain white stone as it is today: the pale marble would have been painted in bright colours in places, such as the background of the frieze, so that the sculpted figures would be easier to see from below and from far away.

Activity 5: Soap stone

Carve your own section of a frieze (decoration in architecture) to enhance an imaginary building, like the frieze that once decorated the Parthenon and is now in the British Museum. Find a fresh, white bar of soap – a square shape would be ideal. Use a strong and sharp instrument, like a tooth-pick, to scratch the outline of a design into the soap's surface on the largest side. Something simple, like a heart shape, might be easiest for your first attempt. Then use something like a metal nail file, or knife that is not sharp enough to cut you, and carve away the soap surface from around the outside of your shape. Once you have lowered the surface of the remainder of the soap square by a few millimetres, so that your design is now higher than the background, start to refine it by adding form, texture and detail, as Phidias did on the Parthenon frieze. You could carve your shape so that it becomes higher in the centre than it is at the sides, and you could add stripes or spots. Now that you have some experience of 'relief sculpture', see if you can carve a face into the other long side of the bar of soap, or take another bar if you prefer. For some ideas on how to create a face in low-relief, take a look at how the Queen's face is moulded on coins. If your finished carvings are successful, wrap them in tissue paper and give them to your friends as small gifts!

The Parthenon frieze is now in the British Museum.

Does the replica also help you see how important line was to the architects who designed the Parthenon? Use some of the names to describe kinds of lines, as we talked about earlier in this chapter, to describe this building. It is easy to spot the long, horizontal lines of the roof and the vertical lines of the columns that support it. What about curving or diagonal lines – can you find some? They are there if you look carefully! Here's a clue: think about the columns, and take a look at ends of the roof.

The language of line is useful for appreciating the architects' design of the Parthenon. In the illustration here, we have added a dotted vertical line. It runs from the highest point on the roof down to the steps. How many columns are there on each

The British Museum's recreation of the Parthenon frieze's original colouring

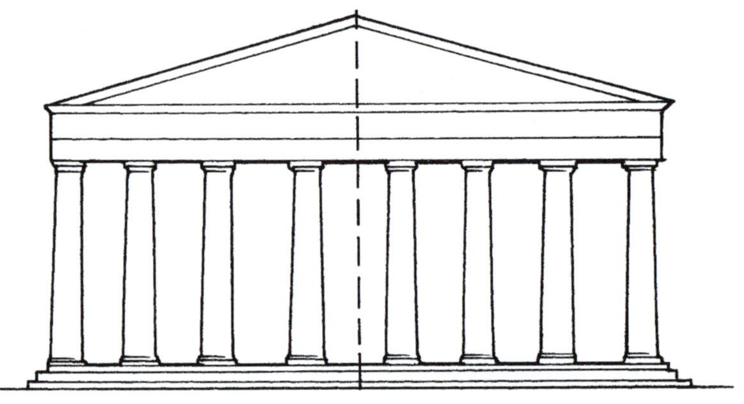

The Parthenon, with a line of symmetry

side of this dotted line? Can you remember, from when we talked about Leonardo's *Last Supper*, what we call an imaginary line that shows where equal forms are reflected? It is a line of symmetry. Can you think of something else that's symmetrical? Take a look in a mirror – your face is basically symmetrical, isn't it? The ancient Greeks thought that everything in nature was balanced or symmetrical in some way. Many architects designed buildings to copy the proportions and lines of symmetry they saw in the world around them. It could be, then, that the symmetry in the short side of the Parthenon reflects the symmetry of a human face. Even the columns could reflect the line of the human body. Ancient Greek architectural writers stated that columns were designed to echo the balance between the legs, body and head in the human form. Could this be one of the reasons why we still find the Parthenon such an appealing building to look at after all this time?

St Paul's Cathedral in London

The balanced and symmetrical buildings of the ancient Greeks continue to influence modern architects. In most cities you will be able to find at least one building influenced by a Greek model. Next time you are in a city, see if you can find one. A famous example in London is St Paul's Cathedral. The architect who designed it was an Englishman, Christopher Wren, who was honoured with the title 'Sir' for his achievements as an architect. Although he was active in the seventeenth century, he was very interested in the masterpieces designed by architects of the past. Can you see which design details Wren has borrowed from classical buildings like the Parthenon? What has he done differently?

Learn about the beginning of the religion of Buddhism on page 132.

A Building of Curves

On the other side of the ancient world, in India, King Asoka wanted a monument to Buddha. His architect decided to use curved lines and circles as the basis of the design.

The Great Stupa

The building is known as the Great Stupa, which could come from a Sanskrit word for 'measure' or a Hindi word for 'moulded stone'. It is the oldest stone building in India, and is at Sanchi in Madhyah Pradesh.

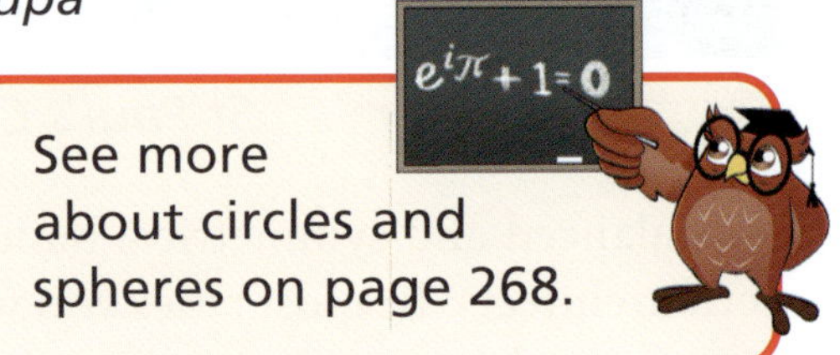

See more about circles and spheres on page 268.

If you walked around the outside of the Parthenon, what would you have to do to follow the perimeter (outside) of the building? You'd have to keep turning each time you reached a corner, wouldn't you? What about if you walked around the Great Stupa? If your footprints left impressions in the ground, they could be joined up to form the line of a circle. In fact, curved pathways around the main building form part of the original design. A line running from one side of the Stupa across the top to the other side would also be curved. The profile of the Stupa is actually half of a sphere, known as a *hemisphere* (similar to a halved globe or ball). In architecture there is a special name for a hemisphere in buildings: *dome*. Depending on how high up the dome is, it may remind you of different natural forms. The dome of St Paul's Cathedral makes some people think of a giant sunrise; until the twentieth century it was the tallest structure in London, visible for miles. The dome of the Great Stupa is set much closer to the ground, making it look more like a hill. People in India say that when you walk around the Great Stupa you are walking 'the Path of Life around the World Mountain'.

Taking a Different Line: A Modern Museum

Architects working today often strive to design buildings in new ways; not just re-working the best designs of the past but adding to them and even questioning them. The Canadian-American architect Frank Gehry [GAIR-ree], for example, rarely works with straight or continuous lines like the architects of the Parthenon, St Paul's and the Great Stupa. Gehry seems to start his design thinking not about line, but about surfaces, materials and how light will play across them.

The Guggenheim Museum in Bilbao, Spain

Have you ever been to a museum? They are among our favourite places to visit and, in Britain, many are free. Museums often contain beautiful and interesting works of art. When Gehry was asked to design a new museum, he decided to create a building that not only housed great art, but that was a work of art itself.

His Guggenheim Museum for modern art is in Bilbao in Spain. It sits beside the Nervion River and many people think it looks like a giant version of one of the many cargo ships that pass nearby. Others, however, don't see it as a ship. The irregular surfaces and form of Gehry's building, combined with its glittering metal skin, can give the impression of shiny, splashing fish! It is said that Gehry's grandmother used to keep live fish in a bath before she prepared them for special meals. The young Gehry was fascinated by how the solid forms of the fish changed as the light played across their metallic scales. What do you think of when you look at the Bilbao Guggenheim: a ship, a glinting fish or something else?

New Lines for Breaking New Ground

After not having their own parliament for almost 300 years, the Scottish people voted in 1997 to establish a new Scottish Parliament. First, a site was chosen for the new building: it would be at the lower end of the historic Royal Mile, nestled near Carlton Hill with its architecture inspired by the ancient Greeks (can you spot it?), across from the Queen's Palace of Holyroodhouse and with lovely views of its natural surroundings.

The Scottish Parliament

There was a competition to choose the right architect for this project, and the Scottish people were invited to view and comment on the proposed designs. In the end, Enric Miralles was chosen to develop a parliament building that was both practical and artistic, representing tradition and new ways forward. What do you think of the lines and curves in his work?

The Members of the Scottish Parliament (also known as MSPs) each have offices where they conduct research, have meetings and think about how best to represent the Scottish people. Their offices are designed with 'think pods' – including window seats and built-in bookshelves – to inspire the MSPs in their work.

The MSPs' seats in the debating chamber, unlike those of the Houses of Parliament in London, are designed in a semi-circle to help them work together and come to agreements. You can watch and listen to their debates in person and, even if the public is not there, the designs of people on the wall help the MSPs remember whom they represent.

The windows of the MSPs' 'think pods'

The debating chamber

You can go on a free tour of the Scottish Parliament building to learn much more about this modern building and its symbolism. See how many St Andrew's crosses you can count in the architecture!

Suggested Resources

Art activity books

Make This Model Greek Temple by Iain Ashman (Usborne) 1998

The Usborne Introduction to Art by Rosie Dickins and Mari Griffith (Usborne) 2010

Looking at and talking about art books

Explore the Parthenon: An Ancient Greek Temple by Ian Jenkins and Kate Morton (British Museum Press) 2009

Paul Klee for Children by Silke Vry (Prestel) 2011

Look! Zoom in on Art! by Gillian Wolfe (Frances Lincoln) 2008

Art story books (including artists or works in this chapter)

Cézanne and the Apple Boy by Laurence Anholt (Frances Lincoln) 2009

Leonardo and the Flying Boy by Laurence Anholt (Frances Lincoln) 2003

Philip and the Magic Castanets: An Amazing Journey into the Parthenon Frieze by Mania Douka (Mpiri-Nees Selides Books) 2000

Katie and the British Artists by James Mayhew (Orchard) 2009

Colouring/complete the masterpiece books

Colour Your Own John Constable by Marty Noble (Dover) 2007

Colour Your Own Still Life Paintings by Marty Noble (Dover) 2005

Paul Klee Colouring Book by Annette Roeder (Prestel) 2008

Where to find the works of art in this chapter

Paul Klee, *'Was fehlt ihm?' (What's wrong with him?)*, 1930 (Fondation Beyeler) Basel, Switzerland

Pablo Picasso, *Mother and Child*, 1922 (Baltimore Museum of Art) Baltimore, USA

Katsushika Hokusai, *The Great Wave off Kanagawa*, 1829-33 (British Museum, Print Room) London, UK

Leonardo da Vinci, *The Last Supper*, 1498 (Refectory of Santa Maria della Grazie) Milan, Italy

Jacob van Ruisdael, *Landscape with Bentheim Castle*, 1653 (National Gallery of Ireland) Dublin, Ireland

John Constable, *Salisbury Cathedral from the Meadows*, 1831 (National Gallery) London, UK

Paul Cézanne, *Still Life with Apples*, c. 1878 (Fitzwilliam Museum) Cambridge, UK

Antonio del Pollaiuolo, *Apollo and Daphne*, c. 1470-80 (National Gallery) London, UK

Ictinus and Callicrates with Phidias, The Parthenon, 440 BC, Acropolis, Athens, Greece

Great Stupa, 3rd Century BC, Sanchi, near Bhopal, Madhya Pradesh, India

Sir Christopher Wren, St Paul's Cathedral, 1710, London, UK

Frank Gehry, Guggenheim Museum, 1997, Bilbao, Spain

Eric Miralles, Scottish Parliament Building, 2004, Edinburgh, UK.

Music

Introduction

A book alone cannot adequately convey the experience of music or the impact of visual art. While this book can hope to provide some basic knowledge about art and music, nothing can replace visiting museums; attending performances; listening to recordings; and encouraging children to sing, dance, paint, sculpt and play-act for themselves.

When it comes to music, one of the best activities – and one of the easiest – is singing with your child. We suggest some familiar children's favourites in this section. The more you sing with your child, the more you'll enjoy music together.

We also encourage you to listen to recordings with your child and attend musical performances to help build his or her love of different kinds of music. In the Year 2 book in this series, we introduced jazz, classical music and opera, as well as different kinds of dance. In this book we build on that earlier knowledge by introducing patriotic music and folk music, and by extending the discussion of classical music to include more composers. We also build on the Year 2 introduction to melody, harmony and rhythm by exploring a few of the basics about how music is written down.

While some families will choose to provide lessons that will lift children to a level of musical competence beyond what we describe in the following pages, it is important for everyone to enjoy music. We hope this chapter will help increase that enjoyment.

Many Kinds of Music

People around the world love to sing and play music. Here in the United Kingdom, where we have many different kinds of people, we have many different kinds of music. If you turn on a radio, you might hear reggae, jazz, classical, songs from musicals or bhangra.

Let's find out more now about three kinds of music: patriotic music, folk music and classical music. Whenever you can, sing the songs that we give the words for, and try to listen to recordings of all these kinds of music.

Patriotic Music

When an athlete receives an Olympic gold medal, the national anthem of his or her country is played. The national anthem is the country's official song. The National Anthem of the United Kingdom is 'God Save the Queen'. It is played and sung at other occasions too, such as ceremonies to honour people who have died in war. Here are the words:

God save our gracious Queen,
Long live our noble Queen,
God save the Queen.
Send her victorious,
Happy and glorious,
Long to reign over us,
God save the Queen.

Thy choicest gifts in store
On her be pleased to pour.
Long may she reign.
May she defend our laws
And ever give us cause
To sing with heart and voice
God save the Queen.

Songs and music that honour a country are called patriotic music. Just about every country has its own patriotic music. Patriotic music makes people feel proud of their country. Do you know any other patriotic songs about Britain?

A patriotic song for Italy, not their national anthem, is from an opera, *Nabucco*, by Giuseppe Verdi. It is sung by Hebrew people, who have been taken as captives to Babylon. You can see from the words how some people care even more for their home country when they are away from it.

Above middle: *'God Save the Queen' is played at the remembrance ceremony at the cenotaph in London.*

Above right: *The National Anthem was played for Jessica Ennis after she won a gold medal in the Heptathalon of the London 2012 Olympics.*

See the Year 2 book for more on opera.

Chorus of the Hebrew Slaves

Fly, my thoughts, fly on gilded wings, go swiftly.
Fly, and on those slopes come to earth,
Where the soft, scented breeze blows so sweetly,
Through the warm, gentle hills, the land of my birth.

Greet the banks of the Jordan with affection,
Greet the wrecked towers of Sion lying in dust,
Oh remembrance, so dear yet ill-destined,
Oh my country, so beautiful and lost!

Do you remember the beautiful Gate of Ishtar in Babylon and the exodus of the Hebrew slaves from Egypt, which we learned about in Year 2? These are the same Hebrew slaves.

A happier patriotic song has been the national anthem for at least five countries. Once the unofficial anthem just of the black people of South Africa, it now starts the anthem for the whole nation, with lyrics in several languages. If you can, sing it in Xhosa, the language it was written in first.

Nkosi, sikelel' iAfrika
Maluphakamis'upondo lwayo
Yizwa imithandazo yethu
Nkosi Sikelela
Thina lusapho lwayo.

Chorus:
Yehla Moya, Yehla Moya,
Yehla Moya Oyingcwele

In English:

Lord, bless Africa;
May her horn rise high up;
Hear Thou our prayers
And bless us.

Chorus:
Descend, O Spirit,
Descend, O Holy Spirit.

Folk Music

Do you know the song called 'The Lincolnshire Poacher'? Here are the words. Let's sing it.

When I was bound apprentice, in famous Lincolnshire,
Full well I served my master for more than seven year,
Till I took up to poaching, as you shall quickly hear;
Oh, 'tis my delight of a shiny night in the season of the year.
Yes, 'tis my delight of a shiny night in the season of the year.

We took a hare alive my boys and then we trudged home
We took him to a neighbour's house and sold him for a crown,
We sold him for a crown, my boys, but I did not tell you where,
Oh, 'tis my delight of a shiny night in the season of the year.
Yes, 'tis my delight of a shiny night in the season of the year.

Success to every gentleman that lives in Lincolnshire,
Success to every poacher that wants to sell a hare,
Bad luck to every gamekeeper that will not sell his deer,
Oh, 'tis my delight of a shiny night in the season of the year.
Yes, 'tis my delight of a shiny night in the season of the year.

Who wrote 'The Lincolnshire Poacher'? No one knows. It's a song that has been passed down from parents to children for many years. We call this kind of song a folk song. Another word for 'folk' is 'people'. Folk songs have been sung and enjoyed by people for so long that, most of the time, we don't know who made them up. Many of the lyrics of our favourite folk songs come from regions where English is spoken with a dialect. A dialect is like a local language. Phrases like 'seven year' would be wrong in standard English but can be normal in dialect. Another example is 'He's my ain for ever mair' from the song 'Bobby Shaftoe' on page 220. We can all imagine ourselves as part of the story. People who would never dream of poaching can still sing 'The Lincolnshire Poacher'.

'The Lincolnshire Poacher' and other songs and tunes are on the album *Folk Music of England* recorded by the Yetties on the Grasmere label.

Just about every country has its own folk music. In France, people enjoy singing a folk song about 'Frère Jacques' (Brother John). You probably know the English words for this song: 'Are you sleeping, Brother John?'

Classical Music

We read about Wolfgang Amadeus Mozart in the Year 2 book in this series, and perhaps you've heard some of his music. He was a great composer, and he began composing music when he was only five years old!

We call the kind of music Mozart wrote *classical music*. Some classical music is played by a large group, called an orchestra. An orchestra is made up of many musicians who play many different instruments:

A portrait of the Mozart family

violins, clarinets, trumpets, drums and a lot more. Do you remember what the person who directs the orchestra is called? (The conductor.) A long piece of music played by an orchestra is called a *symphony*. Although Mozart did not live to be very old, he wrote forty-one symphonies!

The Dublin Philharmonic Orchestra is performing a symphony composed by Tchaikovsky.

Meet Some Great Composers

You've met Mozart, and I hope you've heard some of his music. Now let's meet some other great composers of classical music. Try to hear their music, too.

Vivaldi, born in Italy in 1678

When he was a boy growing up in Italy, Antonio Vivaldi [vi-VAL-dee] learned to play the violin from his father. When Vivaldi grew up, he became a priest. He was nicknamed the Red Priest, because of his curly red hair (in the painting he is wearing a wig!). He worked at an orphanage for girls. He taught the girls to play the violin. Many people came to the concerts given by the orchestra of orphan girls, and everyone said they played beautifully.

Vivaldi composed hundreds of pieces of music. His most famous work is called *The Four Seasons*. For each season, Vivaldi wrote a *concerto* [con-SHER-toe]. A concerto is played by an orchestra, and usually one instrument or a group of instruments gets to show off a bit.

Bach was born in Germany in 1685

The organ in the Saint-Mihiel Church

Beethoven was born in Germany in 1770

When one instrument receives the most attention, the person who plays this instrument is called the *soloist*. In Vivaldi's *The Four Seasons*, the soloist plays a violin, and he or she gets to make sounds that make you think of birds singing in the spring, or others like lightning flashing in a summer storm.

Johann Sebastian Bach [the 'ch' sounds as in 'Loch Ness'] came from a family filled with music. When Bach grew up, he became a great organist. He composed lots and lots of music, including organ music, concertos and a lot of choral music for the church. Bach had many children – twenty in all! Four of them grew up to be composers.

Ludwig van Beethoven [BAY-toe-vun] did not have a happy childhood. When the boy was four years old, his father started to give him piano lessons. He made the boy practise for hours, sometimes late into the night. If young Ludwig made a mistake, his father would shout or hit the boy's knuckles.

You might think that Beethoven would grow up hating music, but music was his whole life. He became famous as the greatest pianist in Europe, and as a great composer.

Beethoven wrote nine symphonies. Try to listen to his Sixth Symphony. It's also known as the 'Pastoral' Symphony, because the music is full of peaceful feelings about Beethoven's love of nature and the countryside. But Beethoven was not a peaceful man. He was often moody and he had a fiery temper. By the time he wrote his great Ninth Symphony, a very sad thing had happened. Beethoven had become deaf. He could not hear the orchestra play his wonderful music.

Beethoven did not live long enough to complete another symphony. Almost his last words were to thank the whole people of England because the Philharmonic Society had shown him kindness in performing the Ninth and in supporting him in his final illness.

Do you remember the name of the European Union's anthem (see page 111)? It is the 'Ode to Joy', which is part of Beethoven's Ninth Symphony.

Composers and their Music

Try to hear some performances of composers' music. A good place to start is the BBC Radio 3 series (90 – 92 FM or digital radio), *Composer of the Week*, which combines stories and music. They have programmes on Bach, Beethoven and Vivaldi that are available as podcasts at http://www.bbc.co.uk/podcasts/series/cotw/all. The series covers many more composers besides. Presenter Donald Macleod guides you through an aspect of a composer's life, with illustrations from their music. New broadcasts are every weekday at noon and 6:30 p.m.

Music is at its best live, with the performers and the audience in the same room. Bach's music is popular with many church organists, so you can often hear his works played as 'voluntaries' at the end of church services. For Beethoven and Vivaldi, the concert hall is a more usual place to hear their music. Several Beethoven symphonies are broadcast as part of the BBC Proms every summer, normally on Radio 3 and BBC 4 television. There are usually special family Proms as part of the season.

A performance during the BBC Proms in the Albert Hall, London

If you prefer listening to recordings, try the Naxos label. They offer CDs, double CDs and downloads in their 'Best of' and 'Very Best of' series for each composer in this chapter. There is also the Sony Classics 'Greatest Hits' series on CD. Remember that there is a lot of beautiful music beside the most famous bits. If you like a track, look up the whole work that it is taken from and try listening to it all. You may like the less famous bits even better.

Families of Instruments: A Closer Look

You may remember from Year 2 that an orchestra is made up of different families of instruments. Can you name an instrument in the *brass* family? How about an instrument in the *woodwind* family? In the *percussion* family? In the *string* family?

Let's take a closer look now at the string family and the percussion family.

The String Family

You may know some stringed instruments: the guitar and the bass guitar. You play them by using the fingers of one hand to press on the strings that run up the long neck of the instrument, while you use your other hand to strum or pick the strings.

The guitar and bass are popular stringed instruments, especially for rock music, where they are usually electric, but you won't find them often in an orchestra. The main stringed

This boy is learning to play the guitar

instruments in an orchestra are the violin, viola, cello and double bass. The violin is the smallest; the others look like bigger and bigger violins.

Each of these instruments has four strings. You can pluck the strings to make a sound, but most of the time you play them by sliding a bow back and forth over the strings. When you play the violin or viola, the instrument rests between your shoulder and chin. But the cello is much bigger: you sit and hold the instrument between your legs. To play the big double bass, you either have to stand beside it or sit on a tall stool. To change note, you press a string against the fingerboard with a left-hand finger. The further up the fingerboard, the higher the note.

This girl is playing the violin

Of these four stringed instruments, the violin makes the highest sounds. The viola can make slightly lower sounds. The cello's sounds are even lower, while the double bass plays the lowest pitches of these four instruments. For many notes with pitches around the middle, composers choose whether to write them as low notes for the violin or high notes for the cello.

The French composer Camille Saint-Saëns [san-sonss] wrote a work for orchestra called *The Carnival of the Animals*, in which he used the sounds of different instruments to make us think of different animals. He used a cello to make us think of a lovely swan floating gracefully on the water. And what stringed instrument do you think he used to make us think of big, heavy elephants? The double bass!

This girl is playing the cello

The Percussion Family

The instruments in the string family look like each other, but the instruments in the percussion family are as different as can be. The percussion family includes tiny clicking castanets, a triangle that goes *ding-a-ling-a-ling* and a big bass drum that goes *boom-boom-boom*.

They are all percussion instruments because you *hit* them. You play most percussion instruments by hitting them with your hand or with a stick. You shake some percussion instruments, like the maracas.

Some percussion instruments can add excitement to music. When the French composer Georges Bizet [BEE-zay] wrote the overture to his opera *Carmen*, he used cymbals to give a big, bright splash of sound.

Smaller percussion instruments can add a kind of decoration to music. For example, when you shake sleigh bells or hit a wooden block, you can make sounds that are just right for Christmas music, since they make you think of a horse pulling a sleigh down a snowy path.

The main job of percussion instruments is to beat out the rhythm. In a marching band, the big bass drum helps keep a steady beat. In flamenco music, castanets click out the beat of the music.

Some percussion instruments can also play melodies. You can play songs on the xylophone or marimba, which have keys that you strike with mallets.

To hear percussion as part of the orchestra, listen to *Belshazzar's Feast*, by William Walton, especially the fourth movement 'Praise Ye the God of Gold'. To hear what percussion alone can achieve, listen to O Duo, who perform remarkable feats with tuned and untuned percussion instruments (Sony Classical). Carlos Chavez, a Mexican composer, wrote some more music just for percussion instruments. His *Toccata for Percussion* (Dorian label) is exciting to hear.

An orchestral kettle drum

This woman dances flamenco while playing the castanets

Keyboard Instruments

Is there a piano at your school? On a piano you can play many different kinds of music: classical, jazz, rock, as well as melodies to go along with songs you might sing at home or school.

A modern piano has eighty-eight keys. When you push the keys, it causes little wooden hammers covered with hard felt to strike the strings inside the piano, and that's what makes the sound. In a sense, a piano is also a percussion instrument and a stringed instrument, too. You can push one key with a single finger, or you can play many notes at the same time.

A piano is a keyboard instrument. Another keyboard instrument is the organ (see a photo of an organ on page 207). Some organs have two, three or even four keyboards. That keeps the organist's hands very busy! But that's not all: really big organs have many pedals that the organist plays with his or her feet. In some churches or auditoriums, you might see a big organ called a pipe organ. When you press a key, it allows air to be sent through a pipe. So an organ is a wind instrument as well as a keyboard instrument.

This girl is taking piano lessons

Mr Bach at the Keyboard

A lot of wonderful music for the organ was composed by Johann Sebastian Bach, who was himself a great organist. Did Bach also play the piano? No – but that's because the piano had barely been invented in Bach's time (about three hundred years ago). Bach played other keyboard instruments that were the ancestors of the piano, such as the harpsichord. The harpsichord looks like a piano, but it makes a more plucky, jangly sound.

When Johann Sebastian Bach was only ten years old, both his parents died, so he went to live with his older brother, Johann Christoph. The whole Bach family was very musical: Johann Christoph was the church organist in the town where he lived. He gave his younger brother music lessons, but he was a very hard, strict teacher. He would not let his brother study a very valuable book of organ music that he kept locked in a bookcase. But Johann

Sebastian wanted so much to learn and play the music in that book! So, at night, while his brother was asleep, Johann Sebastian would creep downstairs in the dim moonlight, squeeze his hand between the bars of the bookcase door, take out the valuable book and then copy the music note by note! He did this every night until he had copied the whole book. But then his stern brother found the copies, and he took them away as a punishment.

But do you know what? Even without the copies, young Johann Sebastian could play much of the music, because it was in his head! He had memorised the music – it was now stored in his memory.

This painting, A Young Woman playing a Harpsichord to a Young Man, *by Jan Steen is in London's National Gallery.*

There is so much wonderful music written for the piano or organ that it's hard to say where to begin! For starters, try listening to these:

'Minuet in G major' from J. S. Bach's *Anna Magdalena Notebook*

Rondo 'Alla turca' from *Piano Sonata No. 11, K. 331* by Mozart

'Für Elise' by Beethoven

'Spring Song' from *Songs Without Words* by Felix Mendelssohn

'Toccata and Fugue in D minor' (for organ) by J. S. Bach

Writing Music Down

You've read about some famous composers, such as Bach and Mozart. Now, imagine that you are a composer. You have written a song. How can you get other people to play it as you want it to sound? Well, you could play the song for them and they could follow along. But what about people far away, who can't be right there with you to hear your song? If you want them to play the song just right, then you have to write it down.

When composers write down music, they use special marks and follow rules that they all agree on. Music that is written down is like directions that tell you what to do. Here is how part of a song you probably know looks when it's written down.

Twin-kle, twin-kle, lit-tle star, how I won-der what you are.

Sing aloud the first words: 'Twinkle, twinkle, little star.' Now, sing it again, but clap along with the strong sounds, like this:

Twin	**kle**	**twin**	**kle**	**lit**	**tle**	**star**
clap		*clap*		*clap*		*clap*

When you clap at the strong sounds, you get the beat.

Now sing the words again, but this time clap on each sound, like this:

Twin	**kle**	**twin**	**kle**	**lit**	**tle**	**star**
clap	*clap*	*clap*	*clap*	*clap*	*clap*	*clap*

When you clap on each sound, you get the rhythm. Now hum the tune, but don't say the words, like this:

him hum him hum him hum himmm

When you hum the sounds, you get the melody. When you sing the song, then you get it all: the beat, the rhythm, the melody and the words, all at once.

Follow the Notes

When composers write music down, they use special marks called notes. Here are some musical notes:

crotchet minim semibreve

The notes tell us the rhythm. They tell us how the music moves. That's because each note has a different length. Another way of saying that is, each note stands for a sound that lasts for a different amount of time. On the crotchet, you count one. On the minim, you count to two. On the semibreve, you count to four. You might also hear people say that a crotchet gets one beat, a minim gets two beats and a semibreve gets four beats.

Try this: find a clock with a second hand, the kind that goes 'tick-tick-tick' loud enough for you to hear. Now, say 'ahh' for four ticks. You've just made a sound that lasts as long as a semibreve. Really, in different songs, notes can last for different times, but we can use the seconds of a clock as an example of how long notes can last. A second for each beat is quite slow music. If a semibreve lasts for four ticks of the clock, then how long would a minim last? Say 'ahh' for two ticks – that's how long a minim lasts. Now, say 'ah' four times, in time with the ticking of the clock like this: 'ah-ah-ah-ah.' You've just made the sound of four crotchets.

A minim lasts twice as long as a crotchet. It takes two minims to make up a semibreve. How many crotchets do you think it takes to make up a semibreve? (Four.)

Look again at this music from 'Twinkle, Twinkle Little Star'. Can you put your finger on the crotchets? On the minims?

Twin-kle, twin-kle, lit-tle star, how I won-der what you are.

Pitch: High and Low

Let's think of some high sounds and low sounds. What are some high sounds? How about a bird chirping, or the brakes on a car squeaking? Can you think of some low sounds? How about thunder rumbling, or a big dog growling?

When we talk about how high or low a sound is, we are talking about pitch. Pitch is how high or low the sounds are.

When you sing a song, your voice goes higher and lower. Listen to yourself as you sing just the first two words of 'Twinkle, Twinkle Little Star'. Do you hear how your voice goes higher on the second 'twinkle'?

When composers write music, they tell us how high or low the notes should be by placing the notes in different positions on a stave. A stave looks like a wide ladder. See one on the next page.

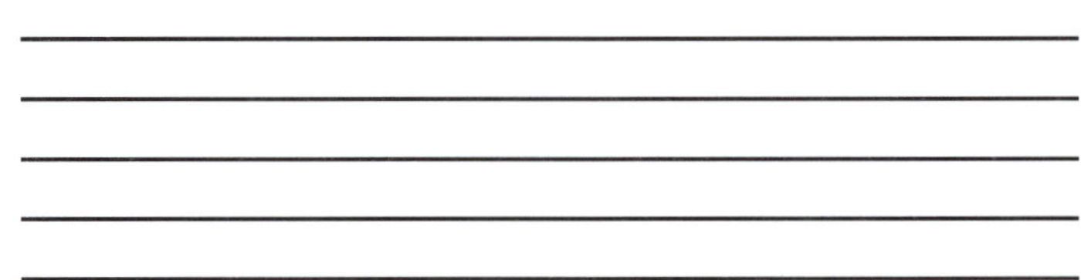

When you follow the notes as they go up and down on the stave, you get the melody. When you put notes near the top of a stave, they are high notes. The notes near the bottom of the stave are lower notes.

Often at the beginning of a stave you will see a special mark called a treble clef. When a stave has a treble clef at the beginning of it, then the lines and spaces of the stave have special names. These names tell musicians how high or low the notes are. The names for the pitches are taken from the alphabet. The music alphabet is A B C D E F G. Can you say the music alphabet forwards and backwards?

We use the music alphabet to name the lines and spaces of the stave. Count how many lines are in the stave. Now count the number of spaces between the lines. Did you count five lines and four spaces? Here are their names:

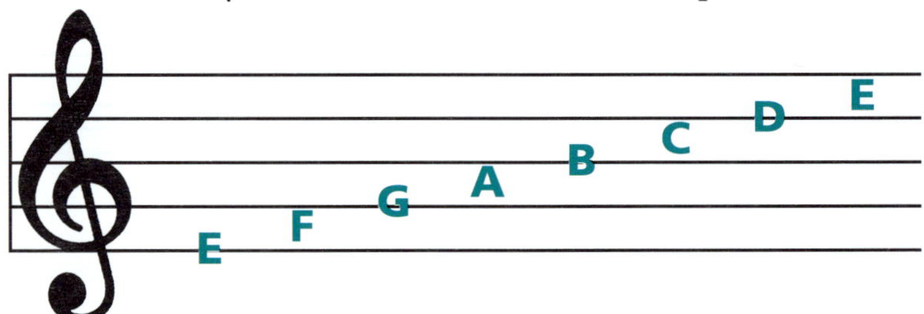

Do you see how the music alphabet is repeated? Look at the bottom line of the stave, which is an E. You go up to F, then G. What comes next? Not H. Instead, you start again with A.

Sometimes a composer wants silence as part of the music. Then he or she writes a mark called a rest. A crotchet rest lasts as long as a crotchet. A minim rest lasts as long as a minim. A semibreve rest lasts as long as a semibreve. It says to the musician: 'Stay quiet for this many counts.'

semibreve	semibreve rest	minim	minim rest	crotchet	crotchet rest

A Musical Scale

You've seen that musical notes have letter names: A B C D E F G. When you sing or play these notes in a row, one after the other, you are singing or playing a musical scale.

On a piano or electric keyboard, you can play a scale called the C major scale. It begins and ends with C, but the first C is a lower pitch than the last one. Begin with a white key just below two black keys, and play only the white keys. (Later books in this series will tell you what the black keys do.)

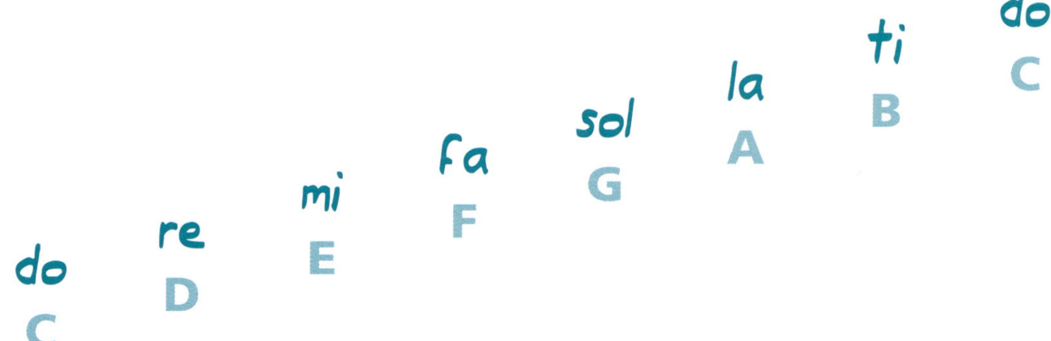

You can use letters to name the notes of the C major scale, or you can use some special sounds. Here are the sounds that go with each letter:

do C
re D
mi E
fa F
sol G
la A
ti B
do C

Here are the words to a song written by Richard Rodgers and Oscar Hammerstein II for the musical *The Sound of Music* that you can sing to help you learn the special names of the notes.

Do-Re-Mi

Doe – a deer, a female deer,
Ray – a drop of golden sun,
Me – a name I call myself,
Far – a long, long way to run,
Sew – a needle pulling thread,
La – a note to follow sew,
Tea – a drink with jam and bread,
That will bring us back to <u>do</u>!
Do-re-mi-fa-sol-la-ti-do!

Some Songs for Year 3

PARENTS: Here we present the words to some favourite children's songs. For more suggestions, try:

- The Usborne *Children's Songbook*, edited by Anthony Marks (2004). This comes with simple accompaniments and links for hearing the tunes online.

- *The National Songbook: Fifty Great Songs for Children to Sing!* (2008). Accompaniments are printed in the book but can also be played on the companion CD.

> You can find more songs for Year 3 children elsewhere in this chapter, including:
>
> God Save the Queen
>
> Chorus of the Hebrew Slaves
>
> Nkosi Sikelel' iAfrika
>
> The Lincolnshire Poacher
>
> Do-Re-Mi

Clementine

In a cavern, in a canyon,

Excavating for a mine,

Dwelt a miner, forty-niner,

And his daughter, Clementine.

[chorus]

Oh my darling, oh my darling,

Oh my darling, Clementine,

Thou art lost and gone forever,

Dreadful sorry, Clementine.

Light she was and like a fairy,
And her shoes were number nine,
Herring boxes without topses,
Sandals were for Clementine.
[repeat chorus]

Drove she ducklings to the water,
Every morning just at nine,
Hit her foot against a splinter,
Fell into the foaming brine.
[repeat chorus]

Ruby lips above the water,
Blowing bubbles soft and fine,
But, alas, I was no swimmer,
So I lost my Clementine.
[repeat chorus]

Bobby Shaftoe

Bobby Shaftoe's gone to sea,
Silver buckles on his knee;
He'll come back and marry me,
Bonny Bobby Shaftoe.

[chorus]
Bobby Shaftoe's bright and fair,
Combing down his yellow hair,
He's my ain for ever mair,
Bonny Bobby Shaftoe.

Bobby Shaftoe's tall and slim,
He's always dressed so neat and trim,
The lassies they all keek at him,
Bonny Bobby Shaftoe.
[repeat chorus]

Bobby Shaftoe's gett'n' a bairn
For to dangle on his airm,
On his airm and on his knee,
Bonny Bobby Shaftoe.
[repeat chorus]

Bobby Shaftoe's been to sea,
Silver buckles on his knee,
He's come back and married me,
Bonny Bobby Shaftoe.

My Grandfather's Clock

My grandfather's clock
Was too large for the shelf,
So it stood ninety years on the floor;
It was taller by half
Than the old man himself,
Though it weighed not a pennyweight more.
It was bought on the morn
Of the day that he was born,
And was always his treasure and pride;
But it stopped short
Never to go again,
When the old man died.

[chorus]
Ninety years without slumbering,
Tick, tock, tick, tock,
His life seconds numbering,
Tick, tock, tick, tock,
It stopped short
Never to go again,
When the old man died.

The Hippopotamus Song

A bold hippopotamus was standing one day
On the banks of the cool Shalimar.
He gazed at the bottom as it peacefully lay
By the light of the evening star.
Away on the hilltop sat combing her hair
His fair hippopotamine maid.
The hippopotamus was no ignoramus
And sang her this sweet serenade.

[chorus]
Mud, mud, glorious mud,
Nothing quite like it for cooling the blood.
So follow me, follow, down to the hollow,
And there let us wallow in glorious mud.

Oranges and Lemons

'Oranges and lemons,'
Say the bells of St. Clement's.

'You owe me five farthings,'
Say the bells of St. Martin's.

'When will you pay me?'
Say the bells of Old Bailey.

'When I grow rich,'
Say the bells of Shoreditch.

'When will that be?'
Say the bells of Stepney.

'I do not know,'
Says the great bell of Bow.

Here comes a candle to light you to bed,
And here comes a chopper to chop off your head!

Who Killed Cock Robin?

Who killed Cock Robin?
'I,' said the sparrow,
'With my bow and arrow,
I killed Cock Robin.'

Who saw him die?
'I,' said the fly,

'With my little eye,

I saw him die.'

Who caught his blood?

'I,' said the fish,

'In my little dish,

I caught his blood.'

All the birds of the air fell a-sighing and a-sobbing

When they heard of the death of poor Cock Robin,

When they heard of the death of poor Cock Robin.

Who'll make his shroud?

'I,' said the beetle,

'Can bring thread and needle.

I'll make his shroud.'

Who'll dig his grave?

'I,' said the owl,

'With my spade and shovel,

I'll dig his grave.'

Who'll toll the bell?

'I,' said the bull,

'Because I can pull.

I'll toll the bell.'

All the birds of the air fell a-sighing and a-sobbing

When they heard of the death of poor Cock Robin,

When they heard of the death of poor Cock Robin.

The Happy Wanderer

I love to go a-wandering,
Along the mountain track,
And as I go, I love to sing,
My knapsack on my back.

[chorus]
Val-deri, Val-dera,
Val-dera,
Valde-ha-ha-ha-ha-ha-ha
Val-deri, Val-dera.

My knapsack on my back.

I love to wander by the stream
That dances in the sun,
So joyously it calls to me,
'Come! Join my happy song!'

[repeat chorus]
'Come! Join my happy song!'

I wave my hat to all I meet,
And they wave back to me,
And blackbirds call so loud and sweet
From ev'ry greenwood tree.

[repeat chorus]
From ev'ry greenwood tree.

Oh, may I go a-wandering
Until the day I die!
Oh, may I always laugh and sing,
Beneath the clear blue sky!

[repeat chorus]
Beneath the clear blue sky!

Suggested Resources

Books

Make and Use Musical Instruments by Anna-Marie D'Cruz (Wayland) 2010

Musical Instruments Around the World by Godfrey Hall (Hodder Wayland) 1999

Why Beethoven Threw the Stew: And Lots More Stories About the Lives of Great Composers by Steven Isserlis (Faber and Faber) 2001

Kickstart Music 2: Music Activities Made Simple – 7–9 Year-Olds by Anice Paterson and David Wheway (A & C Black) 2010

Bach: First Discovery Music by Yann Walcker (Oxford University Press) 2002 – book and CD

Beethoven: First Discovery Music by Yann Walcker (Oxford University Press) 2001 – book and CD

Mozart: First Discovery Music by Yann Walcker (Oxford University Press) 2001 – book and CD

Vivaldi: First Discovery Music by Yann Walcker (Oxford University Press) 2002 – book and CD

Audio Recordings

The Best of Beethoven, performed by Balazs Szokolay and others (Naxos) 2005

'Carnival of the Animals' in *My First Classical Music Album*, performed by the Slovak Radio Symphony Orchestra (Naxos) 2011

'Chorus of the Hebrew Slaves' (in English) in *Italian Opera Choruses*, conducted by Oliver Dohnanyi and performed by the Slovak Philharmonic Chorus and Slovak Radio Symphony Orchestra (Naxos) 1997

'Chorus of the Hebrew Slaves' (in Italian) in *Verdi Opera Choruses, Preludes and Ballet Music,* conducted by Riccardo Muti and performed by the Orchestra and Chorus of La Scala, Milan (EMI Classics) 2011

Für Elise – My First Recital, performed by Maria João Pires (Deutsche Grammophon) 2002

'God Save the Queen' in *The Last Night of the Proms Collection*, conducted by Barry Wordsworth and performed by the BBC Concert Orchestra (Philips) 1996

'The Lincolnshire Poacher' in *Folk Music of England*, performed by the Yetties (Grasmere)

Mozart Piano Sonatas and Fantasia in D Minor, performed by Mitsuko Uchida (Universal Classics) 2005

Mozart: Symphonies 35–41, conducted by Sir Neville Marriner and performed by the Academy of St Martin-in-the-Fields (EMI Classics)

'Nkosi Sikelel' iAfrika' in *Blessed*, performed by the Soweto Gospel Choir (Abc Music) 2005

O Duo, performed by Owen Gunnell and Oliver Cox (Sony Classical) 2007

'Praise Ye the Gods' in *William Walton – Belshazzar's Feast*, conducted by Andrew Davis and performed by Bryn Terfel, BBC Singers, BBC Symphony Chorus & Orchestra (Warner Classics International) 2001

'Symphony No 6 (Pastoral)' in *Beethoven Symphonies 1 and 6*, conducted by Günter Wand and performed by the North German Radio Symphony Orchestra (Red Seal) 2002

'Toccata for Percussion' in *Carlos Chavez*, conducted by Eduardo Mata and performed by La Camerata and Tambuco Percussion Ensemble (Dorian) 2005

The Very Best of Bach, performed by Wolfgang Rubsam (organ), Janos Sebestyen and Eteri Andjaparidze (piano) (Naxos) 2005

Vivaldi: The Four Seasons, directed by Christopher Hogwood and performed by the Academy of Ancient Music (Decca) 2007

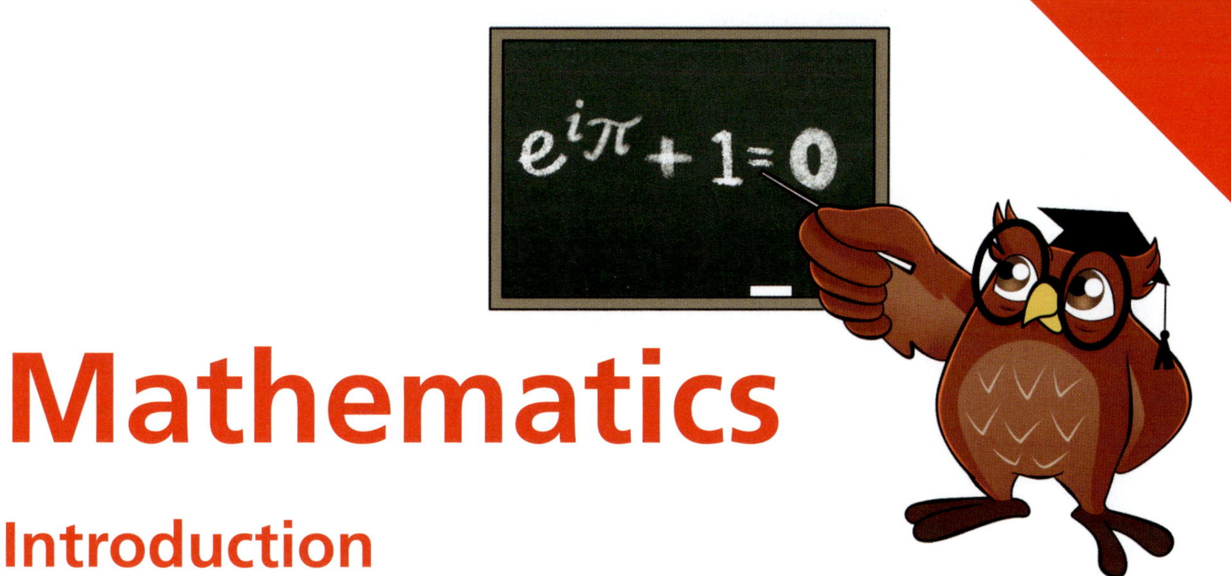

Mathematics

Introduction

In school, any successful programme for teaching maths to young children follows these three cardinal rules: 1) practise, 2) practise and 3) practise. Not mindless repetition, of course, but thoughtful and varied practice in which children are given opportunities to approach problems from a variety of angles, and in which, as they proceed to learn new facts and operations, they consistently review and reinforce their earlier learning. Psychologists who specialise in the subject explain that gaining ability through practice is not opposed to mathematical understanding, but in fact is the prerequisite to thoughtful problem solving. Those who take extreme positions that polarise practice and problem solving are greatly oversimplifying the issues.

Some well-meaning people fear that practice in mathematics – for example, memorising the addition and subtraction facts, or doing timed multiplication worksheets – leads to joyless, soul-killing drudgery. However, the destroyer of joy in learning mathematics is not practice but anxiety – the anxiety that comes from feeling that one is mathematically stupid or lacks any 'special talent' for maths.

The most effective school maths programmes that we know of incorporate the principle of incremental review. By incremental review, psychologists mean that, once a concept or skill is introduced, it is consciously and regularly presented in later exercises, gradually increasing in depth and difficulty. This feature in mathematics materials helps to cultivate a child's automatic understanding of what is to be done. When children reach the point that they automatically know the basic facts – when, for example, they can instantly tell you what 9 + 8 equals – then and only then are their minds left free to tackle more challenging problems that ask them to apply or extend the skills and concepts they have learnt. School maths programmes that offer both incremental review and varied opportunities for problem solving tend to get the best results.

In the pages that follow we present a brief explanatory outline of maths skills and concepts that should form part of a good Year 3 education. However, we must emphasise that this outline *is not meant to constitute a complete maths programme*. These pages can provide a useful supplement for review at home, but in school children need more extensive and regular opportunities for practice and review than these pages can offer.

In addition to the activities found in this section, your Year 3 child may benefit from revising the money section, as well as the multiplication and division facts for the 2, 5 and 10 times tables from *What Your Year 2 Child Needs to Know*.

Working with Numbers to 100

Skip-Counting

Mario: Can you count to a hundred really fast?

Dana: Yes. One, two, skip a few, a hundred!

Dana's way is sneaky, but you know better ways to count to one hundred, like counting in fives or in tens. Try it now. Count out loud in fives to one hundred. Then count out loud in tens to one hundred.

When you count in fives and tens, you are 'skip-counting', because you skip over some numbers. You should also learn to skip-count in twos and threes. Practise now by reading only the numbers in red in the lines below. Keep practising until you can do it without looking at the numbers.

Counting in twos:

1, 2, 3, 4, 5, 6, 7, 8, 9, 10, 11, 12, 13, 14, 15, 16, 17, 18, 19, 20

Counting in threes:

1, 2, 3, 4, 5, 6, 7, 8, 9, 10, 11, 12, 13, 14, 15, 16, 17, 18, 19, 20

Some Special Maths Words

When you add numbers together, the numbers you add are called the *addends*. The answer you get is called the *sum*.

$$\left.\begin{array}{r} 5 \\ + \ 3 \end{array}\right\} \text{addends}$$
$$\overline{8} \ \text{sum}$$

You can have more than two addends. What are the addends here?

$$2 + 3 + 5 = 10$$

When you subtract, the number left over is called the *difference*. In $9 - 7 = 2$, the difference is 2. What is the difference here?

$$\begin{array}{r} 7 \\ - \ 4 \\ \hline 3 \end{array}$$

Between, One More and One Less

When a number comes in the middle of two other numbers, we say it is *between* them. For example, 7 is between 6 and 8. What number is between 11 and 13? (12) What numbers are between 5 and 9? (6, 7 and 8)

You know that 9 comes just before 10. Another way of saying that is: 9 is one less than 10. You can say that 11 comes just after 10, or that 11 is one more than 10. If I give you a number, can you tell me what is one less and one more than the number? Let's try it. The number is 7. What is one less than 7? What is one more than 7? Practise telling what is one less and one more than any number up to 100. Try these:

5   19   30   43

Counting with a Tally

Imagine you're at a cricket match. You want to keep track of how many runs your team makes, so you use a *tally*. You mark down a small straight line for each run they make. After a batsman hits a ball all the way to the boundary, which is worth four runs, you make four lines, like this:

If the bowler bowls a wide, then the batting team is awarded 1 run. How many runs does that make in all? Five, so far. When you get to five in a tally, you make a line through the first four lines, like this:

As the game goes on, continue your tally with one mark for each run, and on each fifth run your tally mark should again show a mark through the first four lines in that set.

Later, when the match is over, you can quickly skip count in fives to see how many runs your team scored. Can you tell from this tally how many runs they scored?

Well, 52 runs – not a bad innings!

Using Graphs

In Year 2, we started learning about graphs. Now look at these ones.

The children in Mrs Chen's class chose their favourite kind of fruit. They put their choices on a graph, like this:

Our Favourite Fruits							
Bananas							
Peaches							
Apples							
Grapes							
	0	1	2	3	4	5	6	7

What is the most popular favourite fruit of the children in Mrs Chen's class? The largest number of children (6) liked apples. Which two fruits had equal numbers of votes? We call this kind of graph a 'bar graph', because it shows information in the form of bars. A bar graph can also look like this one on the right.

This graph shows the favourite pets of the children in Mr Levy's class. Just by looking quickly at the graph, without reading any numbers, can you tell what pet is the favourite of most children? Now, read the graph and tell how many children like dogs best, how many like cats best, how many like rabbits best and how many like birds best.

Writing Numbers as Words

Can you write all the words for the numbers from 1 to 30, just as we did in Year 2? Practise writing those words until you can do it easily. Also, practise writing the words for the tens up to one hundred:

10	ten	60	sixty
20	twenty	70	seventy
30	thirty	80	eighty
40	forty	90	ninety
50	fifty	100	one hundred

Be careful with 'forty'. It doesn't have a 'u' in it, as 'four' and 'fourteen' do.

Once you know these words, you can write the words for any number up to 100. Here are some examples:

21 twenty-one   **45 forty-five**   **83 eighty-three**

Can you write the words for these numbers?

18   **33**   **42**   **59**   **76**

Reading a Number Line

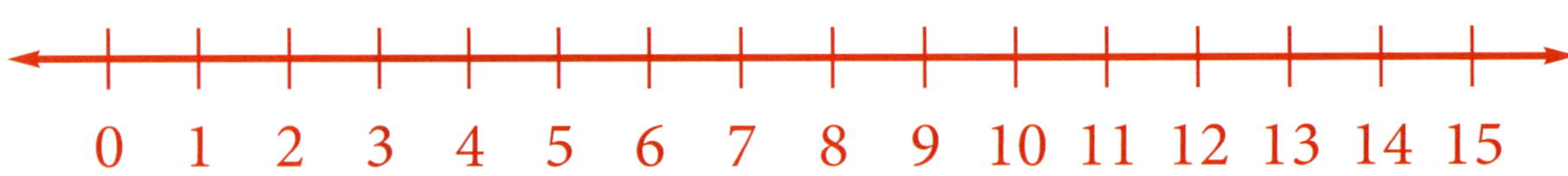

This is a number line. It shows the numbers in order. A number line has arrows because the numbers keep on going forever. All the numbers you've learnt, and a whole lot more, can be shown on a number line.

You can use a number line to practise addition and subtraction. For example, to find the sum of 7 + 4 on a number line, first go forwards to 7. Then go forwards four more numbers. Where do you end? On 11. So, 7 + 4 = 11.

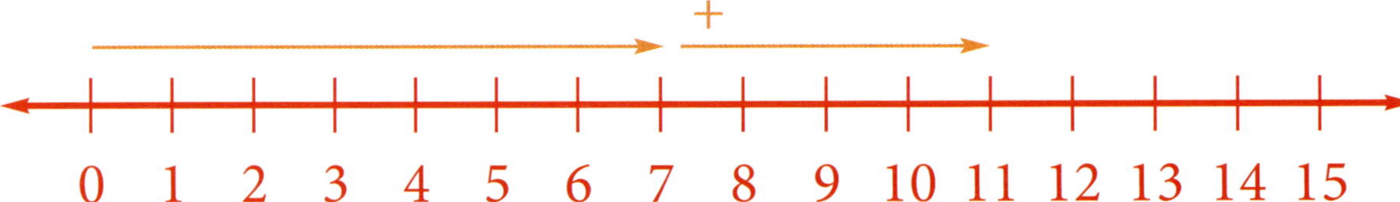

You can also use a number line to practise subtraction. For example, to find the difference of 32 − 7, first go forwards on the number line to 32.

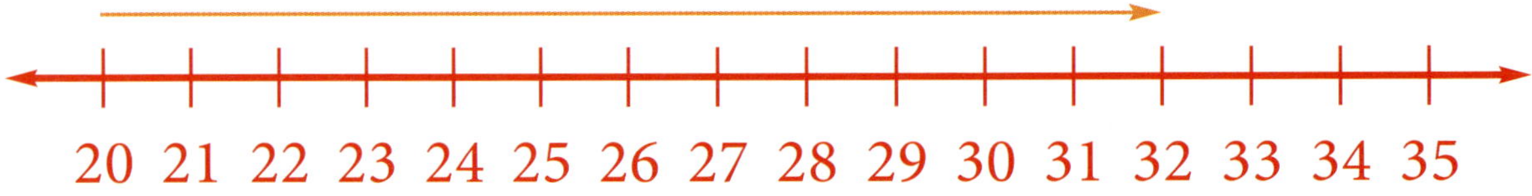

Then go backwards 7 numbers.

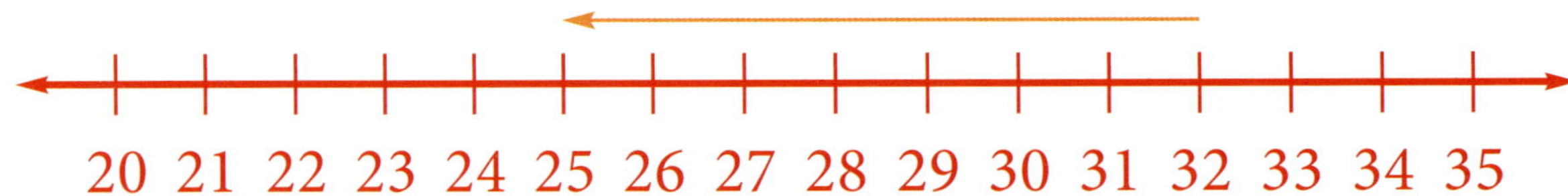

Where do you end? At 25. So, with the help of a number line, you can work out that 32 − 7 = 25.

Review: Addition and Subtraction Facts to 20

In Year 2 we learnt the addition facts to 20 and the subtraction facts from 20. Use *What Your Year 2 Child Needs to Know* to review these addition and subtraction facts. Practise until you know them without having to stop to count.

Quick, now! What are the addition facts for the sum of 9? What are the subtraction facts from 18? Write them out and even decorate your work for your family to see.

Review: Adding in Any Order, and Adding Three Numbers

We learnt in Year 2 that it does not matter what order you add numbers in, because the sum is still the same. Complete these sums to make sure:

$$9 + 4 = \underline{} \text{ and } 4 + 9 = \underline{}$$
$$7 + 12 = \underline{} \text{ and } 12 + 7 = \underline{}$$

Great work! So you *can* check your work by adding the numbers in a different order. Do you remember how we can also do this by adding three numbers? What is the sum of the first two numbers? Now write down that number and add the third number, like this:

Then check by adding up, like this:

Either way, no matter what order you add in, you get the same sum.

Review: Checking Addition and Subtraction

You know that addition is the opposite of subtraction. So, you can always check a subtraction problem by doing addition, like this:

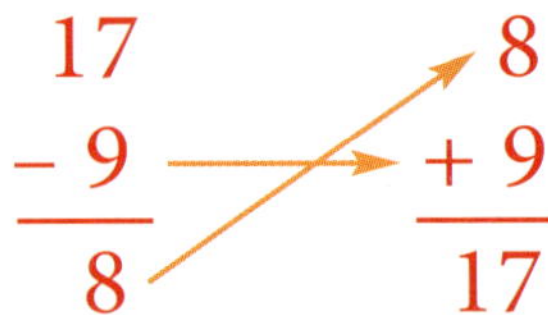

When you check, you should end up with the same number you began with. You began by subtracting from 17. When you check, you add 8 and 9 and you get 17, so you know you have the right answer.

You can also check addition by doing subtraction, like this:

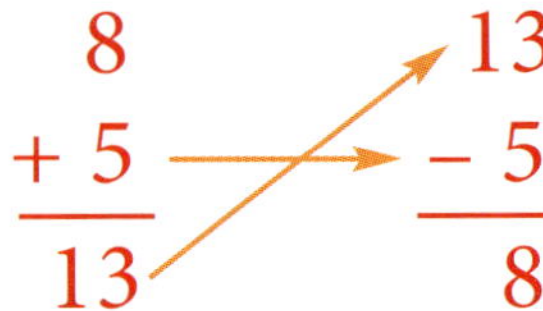

Review: Fact Families

A fact family brings together addition facts with their opposite subtraction facts. Here is a fact family you know:

$$5 + 2 = 7 \qquad\qquad 2 + 5 = 7$$
$$7 - 2 = 5 \qquad\qquad 7 - 5 = 2$$

Practise forming fact families with the addition and subtraction facts you've learnt, using numbers up to 20. For example:

$$9 + 4 = \underline{\quad} \qquad\qquad 4 + \underline{\quad} = 13$$
$$13 - 4 = \underline{\quad} \qquad\qquad \underline{\quad} - 9 = 4$$

Do you see how making fact families is just like checking addition by subtraction and checking subtraction by addition?

Here are two more addition facts. Can you give the rest of the facts in each fact family?

$$9 + 7 = 16 \quad\underline{\qquad\qquad} \qquad\qquad 6 + 9 = 15 \quad\underline{\qquad\qquad}$$

$$\underline{\qquad\qquad}\quad\underline{\qquad\qquad} \qquad\qquad \underline{\qquad\qquad}\quad\underline{\qquad\qquad}$$

Doubles and Halves

When you add a number to itself, you are *doubling* the number, or multiplying by two. When you add 3 and 3, you double 3. $3 + 3 = 6$, or $3 \times 2 = 6$. So double 3 is 6. Another way to say that is 'twice 3 is 6'. Practise doubling the numbers from 1 to 9 until you know them by heart.

$$
\begin{array}{ccccccccc}
1 & 2 & 3 & 4 & 5 & 6 & 7 & 8 & 9 \\
+\,1 & +\,2 & +\,3 & +\,4 & +\,5 & +\,6 & +\,7 & +\,8 & +\,9 \\
\hline
2 & 4 & 6 & 8 & 10 & 12 & 14 & 16 & 18
\end{array}
$$

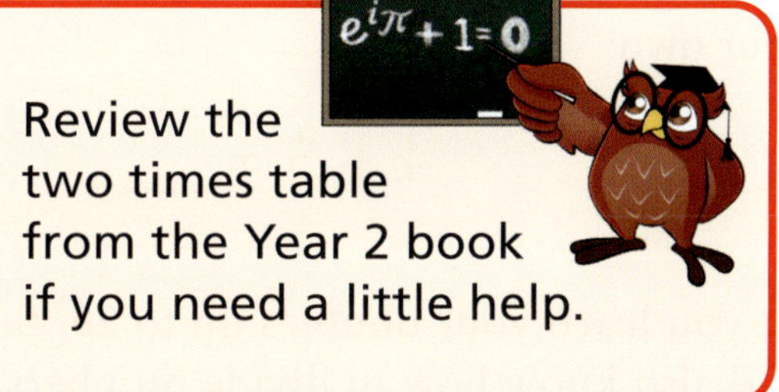

Look at the sums of the doubles above, and the products of each number multiplied by two below. Do you see a pattern? Do you see how the answers go up by twos? Did you also notice that when you double any number, the result is always an even number?

$$
\begin{array}{ccccccccc}
1 & 2 & 3 & 4 & 5 & 6 & 7 & 8 & 9 \\
\times\,2 & \times\,2 & \times\,2 & \times\,2 & \times\,2 & \times\,2 & \times\,2 & \times\,2 & \times\,2 \\
\hline
2 & 4 & 6 & 8 & 10 & 12 & 14 & 16 & 18
\end{array}
$$

Even if you double an odd number, the double turns out even. Try it: double 3 marbles, and you get 6 marbles. Double 5 and you get 10. So, all even numbers are a number doubled. What number is doubled to get 2? What number is doubled to get 18?

Doubles can help you when you're adding. If you know that $7 + 7 = 14$, then you can quickly work out the sum of $8 + 7$. You know that 8 is one more than 7. So, $8 + 7$ must be one more than $7 + 7$. See the next page to work this out.

$7 + 8$ is the same as $7 + 7 + 1$, or $(7 \times 2) + 1$

$7 + 8 = 14 + 1$

$7 + 8 = 15$

Try to work out some more of these 'doubles-plus-one' problems. What is $6 + 7$?

$6 + 7$ is the same as $6 + 6 + 1$, or $(6 \times 2) + 1$

$6 + 7 = \underline{\quad} + 1$

$6 + 7 = \underline{\quad}$

Now try these doubles-plus-one problems on your own:

$5 + 6 = \underline{\quad}$ $\qquad\qquad$ $8 + 9 = \underline{\quad}$ $\qquad\qquad$ $4 + 5 = \underline{\quad}$

If you learn your doubles up to 20, then you'll also know how to divide numbers *in half*. If you cut a piece of toast into two equal parts, then each part is a half. When a number is divided into two equal parts, each part is a half.

What is half of 8? You know the answer if you know what number you double to make 8. You double 4 to make 8. So, 4 is half of 8.

What number do you double to get 4? To get 4, you double 2. So, half of 4 is 2. What number do you double to make 12? To get 12, you double 6. So, half of 12 is 6. Can you tell me what half of 6 is? Now, how many bags would you have if you took home half of these bags?

Sum of 10

All of the problems below have a sum of 10. See if you can give the missing number in each problem.

$$\begin{array}{ccccccccc} 5 & 6 & 1 & 3 & 2 & 7 & 4 & 8 & 9 \\ +\underline{} & +\underline{} & +\underline{} & +\underline{} & +\underline{} & +\underline{} & +\underline{} & +\underline{} & +\underline{} \\ 10 & 10 & 10 & 10 & 10 & 10 & 10 & 10 & 10 \end{array}$$

Practise your sums of 10, because you will be able to do lots of maths problems more easily if you know by heart the numbers that add up to 10.

Find the Missing Number

Practise finding the answers to problems with a missing number, like this:

$$7 + \underline{} = 12 \ \text{(The missing number is 5.)}$$

$$\underline{} - 6 = 7 \ \text{(The missing number is 13.)}$$

When you know your addition and subtraction facts by heart, then you can quickly solve a problem with a missing number. Just by looking at this problem, can you tell me the missing number?

$$3 + \underline{} = 9$$

Sometimes you might need to work out the missing number. You can do that by thinking about what you've learnt from fact families, and by checking addition with subtraction, as well as checking subtraction with addition. You know that addition and subtraction are opposites. So, look at this problem:

$$9 + \underline{} = 17$$

If you don't know the missing number instantly, you can work it out by turning the addition problem into a subtraction problem.

$$17 - 9 = 8$$

So the missing number is 8:

$$9 + 8 = 17$$

To work out the missing number in a subtraction problem, you can turn it into an addition problem. For example:

$$\underline{\quad} - 8 = 5$$

You can find the missing number by adding 5 and 8.

$$5 + 8 = 13$$

So, the missing number is 13.

$$13 - 8 = 5$$

Practise doing problems with missing numbers. Here are some to get you started.

$$8 + \underline{\quad} = 14 \qquad 9 + \underline{\quad} = 18 \qquad \underline{\quad} - 6 = 6 \qquad \underline{\quad} - 6 = 9$$

$$3 + \underline{\quad} = 15 \qquad 8 + \underline{\quad} = 17 \qquad \underline{\quad} - 7 = 8 \qquad \underline{\quad} - 7 = 9$$

Missing Number Problems with Greater Than and Less Than

Do you remember the signs for greater than and less than? The sign > means 'greater than'. The sign < means 'less than'. When you see $10 > 8$, you read that as '10 is greater than 8'. Try reading the following out loud:

$$9 > 7 \qquad 7 + 6 > 5 + 6 \qquad 23 < 72 \qquad 15 - 8 < 11$$

You can solve missing number problems with the greater than and less than signs. With these problems, there may be more than one right answer, like this:

$$15 - \underline{\quad} > 11$$

You could fill in that blank with 0, 1, 2 or 3. They're all correct.

Try these problems:

$$7 + \underline{\quad} < 12 \qquad 13 - \underline{\quad} > 8 \qquad 19 - \underline{\quad} > 16$$

Working with Equations

When you write $7 - 4 = 3$, or $5 + 3 = 8$, you are writing an *equation*. An equation compares numbers using an equals sign: =. As you know, the equals sign means 'is the same as'. All of these are equations:

$$7 + 7 = 14 \qquad 36 = 36 \qquad 4 + 1 = 9 - 4$$

Whenever you change one side of an equation, you have to make the same change to the other side so the two sides stay equal.

For example, you have a basket of six oranges plus a bowl of three oranges. I have two oranges in one basket and another basket that is spilling seven oranges. We each have nine oranges.

$$6 + 3 = 2 + 7$$

Now we decide to make orange juice. In an equation, when we decide to take away from one side, we have to take away from the other side as well. So, we each take five oranges to squeeze into orange juice.

$$6 + 3 - 5 = 2 + 7 - 5$$

We each have four oranges left, and a glass of fresh orange juice to drink!

Now, let's say that we're adding footballs. Look at the groups of footballs below:

How would we write an equation with numbers to stand for our groups of footballs?

$$\underline{} + \underline{} = \underline{}$$

Yes, $3 + 5 = 8$. Now, if I add 2 footballs to the side with 3 and 5 footballs, then what do I have to do to the side with 8 footballs, if I want the two sides to stay equal? I have to add 2 footballs to the 8 footballs as well. How would I write that?

$$2 + 3 + 5 = 2 + 8$$

Tens and Ones

You know that 1 ten is the same as 10 ones.

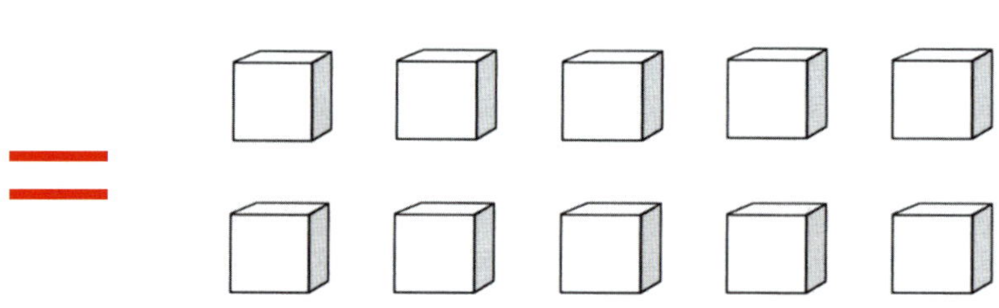

When you have 27 of something, you have 2 tens and 7 ones. You can write 27 as a sum of tens and ones:

$$27 = 10 + 10 + 7 \quad \text{or} \quad 27 = 20 + 7$$

How many tens are in 44? How many ones? So, you can write 44 as a sum of four tens and four ones:

44 is the same as 40 + 4

Practise writing some numbers as a sum of tens and ones. For example, you can write 46 as 40 + 6. Following that pattern, how would you write 77? How about 32, 56 and 98?

Adding Numbers with Two Digits

Another word for any of the numbers from 0 to 9 is a *digit*. The number 43 has two digits, a 4 and a 3. As you know, 43 is 4 tens and 3 ones. When we look at the digits in the number 43, we say that the 4 is in the tens place and the 3 is in the ones place.

You learnt in Year 2 that, when you add two-digit numbers, first you add the ones, then you add the tens. When we write an addition problem with two-digit numbers, we say that the numbers in the ones place are in the ones column, and the numbers in the tens place are in the tens column. Let's work out this sum:

tens   23   ones

+ 35
___

First we add the numbers in the ones column. Add 3 and 5, and you get 8. Then add the numbers in the tens column. Add 2 and 3 and you get 5. But you're really adding 2 tens and 3 tens, which makes 5 tens, or 50. So the sum is 5 tens plus 8 ones, or 50 + 8, which equals 58:

tens   23   ones   tens   23   ones

+ 35   + 35
___   ___
8   58

Now we'll tackle some more difficult problems with two digits. Sometimes when you add two-digit numbers, you have to 'regroup'. For example, look at this problem:

48
+ 26
___

You begin by adding the numbers in the ones column. When you add 8 + 6, you get 14 ones. You know that 14 is the same as 10 + 4. So, you need to 'regroup' 14 into 1 ten and 4 ones. You write the 4, which means 4 ones, at the bottom of the ones column.

Then you write the 1, which means 1 ten, at the top of the tens column, and add it to the other tens:

Add the ones and regroup:

tens   48   ones

$+\ 26$

4

Now add the tens:

tens   48   ones

$+\ 26$

74

Altogether you have 7 tens and 4 ones, which makes a sum of 74.

Writing a new ten at the top of the tens column is also called 'carrying'. In the problem above, when you added the numbers in the ones column, you got 14. You wrote the 4 at the bottom of the ones column. Then you wrote a 1 (for 1 ten) at the top of the tens column, which is the same as saying that you 'carried the 1' (for 1 ten) to the tens column.

Checking Addition by Changing the Order of Addends

You know that it does not matter what order you add numbers in, because the sum is still the same: $7 + 3 = 10$ and $3 + 7 = 10$. So, you can check your answer to an addition problem by writing the addends in a different order and then adding again. You should get the same sum both times. For example:

Change the order of the addends.

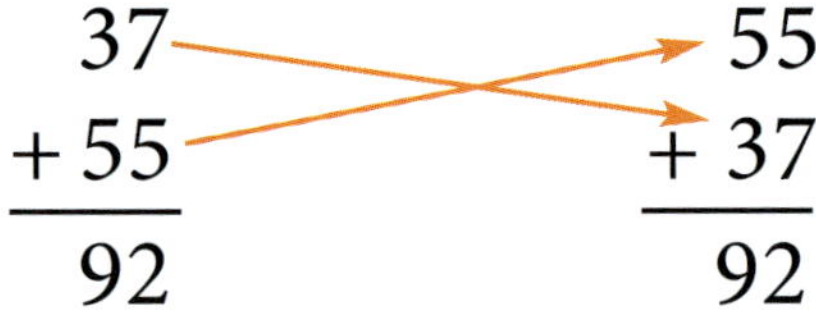

$$37 \qquad\qquad 55$$
$$+\ 55 \qquad\qquad +\ 37$$
$$92 \qquad\qquad 92$$

Adding Three Numbers

Let's try adding three numbers. First you add the numbers in the ones column. If they add up to more than 10, you need to regroup and carry.

tens   43   ones

28

$+\ 14$

When you add 3 + 8 + 4, you get 15. So, you need to regroup. Write the 5 at the bottom of the ones column, then carry the 1 (for 1 ten) to the top of the tens column. Add the numbers in the tens column (don't forget to add the 1 you carried), and you'll get the sum.

Add the ones and regroup:

$$\begin{array}{r} 1 \\ \text{tens} \quad 43 \quad \text{ones} \\ 28 \\ + 14 \\ \hline 5 \end{array}$$

Now add the tens:

$$\begin{array}{r} 1 \\ \text{tens} \quad 43 \quad \text{ones} \\ 28 \\ + 14 \\ \hline 85 \end{array}$$

Subtracting Numbers with Two Digits

When you subtract from a two-digit number, first you subtract the numbers in the ones column. Here's an example:

$$\begin{array}{r} 97 \\ - 55 \\ \hline \end{array}$$

You start by subtracting the ones: 7 − 5 leaves 2. You write 2 at the bottom of the ones column. Then you subtract the tens. When you take 5 tens away from 9 tens, the difference is 4 tens. So you write 4 at the bottom of the tens column.

Subtract the ones

$$\begin{array}{r} \text{tens} \quad 97 \quad \text{ones} \\ + 55 \\ \hline 2 \end{array}$$

Subtract the tens

$$\begin{array}{r} \text{tens} \quad 97 \quad \text{ones} \\ + 55 \\ \hline 42 \end{array}$$

Sometimes when you subtract you will need to regroup. But instead of changing 10 ones to 1 ten, you will regroup 1 ten into 10 ones. Let's see how it works.

Pretend you have 27 pencils. You want to take away 9 pencils. How many will you have left? Let's write that as a subtraction problem.

$$\begin{array}{r} 27 \\ - 9 \\ \hline \end{array}$$

Look at the numbers in the ones column. You want to take away 9. But you only have 7 ones. Remember, however, that 27 is the same as 2 tens and 7 ones.

There are 27 pencils above. Take 1 of those tens and regroup it with the ones. That will leave you with 1 ten and 17 ones.

You have regrouped 2 tens and 7 ones into 1 ten and 17 ones. Some people say that you have 'borrowed' 1 ten from the tens column and put it in the ones column. You still have 27 pencils in total right now. Now, you know how to take away 9 from 17. That leaves you with 8 ones. But don't forget you still have 1 ten left. So, 27 – 9 = 18.

Let's do some more subtraction problems with regrouping, and learn a way to write the problems to keep each step clear as you go along. Look at the ones column in this problem:

$$\text{tens} \quad \begin{array}{r} 65 \\ -\ 48 \\ \hline \end{array} \quad \text{ones}$$

8 is greater than 5, so you can't take away 8 from 5. You need to regroup. You know that 65 is the same as 60 + 5, or 6 tens and 5 ones. Take 1 ten and add it to the 5 ones.

What does that leave you with? 5 tens and 15 ones. Cross out the 6 in the tens place and write 5 above it. Cross out the 5 in the ones place and write 15 above it. Now you can subtract easily. Remember, start with the ones.

Subtract the ones and regroup

$$\text{tens} \quad \begin{array}{cc} 5 & 15 \\ \cancel{6} & \cancel{5} \\ -\ 4 & 8 \\ \hline & 7 \end{array} \quad \text{ones}$$

Subtract the tens

$$\text{tens} \quad \begin{array}{cc} 5 & 15 \\ \cancel{6} & \cancel{5} \\ -\ 4 & 8 \\ \hline 1 & 7 \end{array} \quad \text{ones}$$

Checking Two-Digit Subtraction

Remember that addition is the opposite of subtraction, so you can check subtraction by addition. Here's a subtraction problem.

$$\begin{array}{r} 62 \\ -\ 35 \\ \hline 27 \end{array}$$

You can check this by going from bottom to top and turning it into an addition problem. The sum should be the same as the number you first subtracted from, which is 62. Try it. Does it check?

$$\begin{array}{r} 27 \\ +\ 35 \\ \hline \end{array}$$

Adding and Subtracting Horizontally, Vertically and in Your Head

You know that addition and subtraction problems can be written in two ways: across or up and down. We also say that a problem written across is written *horizontally*. A problem written up and down is written *vertically*. Either way, the answer comes out the same.

Horizontal $11 + 17 = 28$ is the same as

$$\begin{array}{r} 11 \\ +\ 17 \\ \hline 28 \end{array}$$ Vertical

Horizontal $23 - 12 = 11$ is the same as

$$\begin{array}{r} 23 \\ -\ 12 \\ \hline 11 \end{array}$$

Vertical

When you see a two-digit addition problem written horizontally, it is sometimes easier to solve it by writing it out vertically. For example, what is the sum of 12 + 39? Rewrite the problem vertically, and make sure you keep all the ones in the ones column and the tens in the tens column.

Rewrite the problem vertically

tens   ones

$$\begin{array}{r} 1\ 2 \\ +\ 3\ 9 \\ \hline \end{array}$$

Add the ones and regroup

tens   1   ones

$$\begin{array}{r} 1\ 2 \\ +\ 3\ 9 \\ \hline 1 \end{array}$$

Add the tens

tens   1   ones

$$\begin{array}{r} 1\ 2 \\ +\ 3\ 9 \\ \hline 5\ 1 \end{array}$$

Here is a way to solve a horizontal two-digit addition problem in your head. Try this problem: find the sum of 57 + 32. First, you break the numbers into tens and ones: 57 is the same as 50 + 7. 32 is the same as 30 + 2. In your head, add the ones: 7 + 2 is 9.

Now add the tens: 50 + 30 is 80. So the sum is 80 + 9, or 89.

If you need to solve a subtraction problem written horizontally, you can rewrite it vertically.

$65 - 43 =$ _____   rewrite vertically as

$$\begin{array}{r} 65 \\ -\ 43 \\ \hline \end{array}$$

You can also look at the problem as it's written horizontally and try to solve it in your head. Try to find the difference of 65 − 43. Break the numbers into tens and ones: 65 is the same as 60 + 5, and 43 is the same as 40 + 3. 5 − 3 = 2, and 60 − 40 = 20. So the difference is 22. It's not as easy to add and subtract in your head when you have to regroup. When you have to regroup, you will probably want to rewrite the problem vertically. But, even when you need to regroup, you can learn to add and subtract in your head if you think of a maths fact you already know. For example, think first of what you know to solve this problem:

$$28 + 6 = \ \underline{\quad\quad}$$

You know that $8 + 6 = 14$

So in your head regroup 28 as $20 + 8$, and think of the problem like this:

$$20 + (8 + 6) = \underline{\qquad}$$

Now add $8 + 6$, which you know is 14: $\quad 20 + 14 = \underline{\qquad}$

Now you can work out the sum in your head: $\quad 20 + 14 = 34$

Let's try a subtraction problem in our heads:

$$35 - 8 = \underline{\qquad}$$

You know that $15 - 8 = 7$

In your head, regroup 35 as $20 + 15$ and think of the problem like this:

$$20 + (15 - 8) = \underline{\qquad}$$

Now subtract 8 from 15, which you know is 7 $\quad 20 + 7 = \underline{\qquad}$

Now you can work out the sum in your head: $\quad 20 + 7 = 27$

So $35 - 8 = 27$

It may be tough at first to do problems like these in your head, but keep trying. With practice, it will get easier, and then you'll be ready to tackle even harder and more interesting maths problems. When you're ready for a challenge, try doing these problems in your head:

$$38 + 7 = \underline{\qquad} \qquad 43 - 8 = \underline{\qquad} \qquad 25 + 8 = \underline{\qquad} \qquad 65 - 6 = \underline{\qquad}$$

Adding and Subtracting 9 in Your Head

You can use a little trick to solve problems that ask you to add or subtract 9. For example: $25 + 9 = \_$. Change the 9 to 10, and in your head you can quickly work out that $25 + 10 = 35$. Now, just subtract 1 from 35 (because 10 is 1 more than 9) and you get the answer, 34. So, to add 9 in your head, a short cut is to add 10 then take away 1.

Now let's try subtracting 9. Here's the problem: $53 - 9 = \_$. Change the 9 to 10, and in your head you can quickly work out that $53 - 10 = 43$. Now, because you're subtracting, and you've taken away 1 more than 9, you need to add that 1 back. Add 1 to 43 and you get the answer, 44. So, to subtract 9 in your head, a shortcut is to subtract 10 then add 1.

Try doing these in your head:

$$37 + 9 = \underline{\qquad} \qquad 76 - 9 = \underline{\qquad} \qquad 45 + 9 = \underline{\qquad} \qquad 58 - 9 = \underline{\qquad}$$

Estimating and Rounding to the Nearest Ten

Tim likes to collect Lego bricks. When you visit him, he opens a box and pours out a pile of Lego bricks. 'Fantastic! How many do you have?' you ask. 'About 300,' says Tim.

Sometimes it's easier to say *about* how many you have instead of *exactly* how many. When you say about how many, you are *estimating*.

Sometimes, when you are adding and subtracting, you only need to know *about* what the answer is. When you don't need to know the exact answer, then you can estimate the answer – you can work out roughly what it is. For example, how would you estimate the sum of 23 + 45? To begin, you turn the numbers into numbers that are easier to work with in your head. It's easier to work with numbers like 10, 20, 30, 40, 50 and so on. So, you need to 'round' the numbers to the nearest ten.

Let's see what it means to round 23 to the nearest ten. Look at this number line.

You can see that 23 is between 20 and 30. But it's closer to 20. So, 23 rounded to the nearest 10 is 20.

What is 45 rounded to the nearest ten? To answer that, you need to know a special rule: When a number is exactly between two numbers, you round up to the greater number.

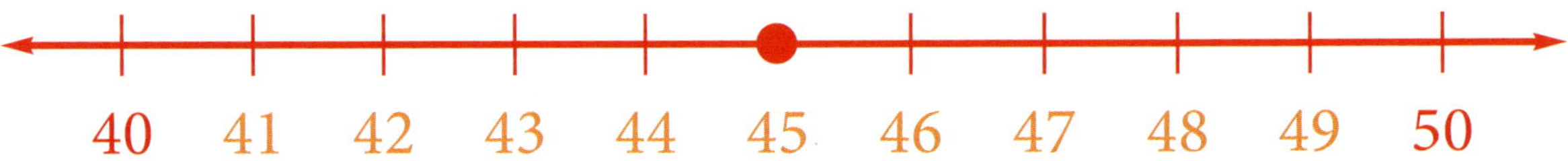

You can see on the number line that 45 is exactly between 40 and 50. So you round it up to 50.

Let's go back to our addition problem: how would you estimate the sum of 23 + 45?

$$
\begin{array}{lll}
23 & \textit{rounds to} & 20 \\
+\ 45 & \textit{rounds to} & +\ 50 \\
\hline
& & 70 \\
\end{array}
$$

So 23 + 45 = is **about** 70

You can also use estimation when you subtract two-digit numbers and only need to know about what the difference is. For example:

$$\begin{array}{r} 87 \\ -\ 41 \\ \hline \end{array} \quad \textit{rounds to} \quad \begin{array}{r} 90 \\ -\ 40 \\ \hline 50 \end{array}$$

So $87 - 41 =$ is **about** 50

Fractions

A fraction is a part of something. In Year 2 you learnt these fractions:

¼	½	¾
one quarter	*one half*	*three quarters*

A fraction has a top number and a bottom number. The bottom number tells how many equal parts there are. The top number tells how many equal parts you are talking about. For example, in the first circle above, one part is orange. How many equal parts are there? 4. How many parts are orange? 1.

So this fraction shows ¼ (one quarter).

If something is divided into three equal parts, each part is one third, which in numbers is written as ⅓. This pizza is divided into three equal slices.

Each slice is ⅓.

If you were very hungry and ate two large slices, what fraction of a whole pizza did you eat? You ate ⅔ (two thirds).

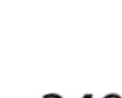

Here is a rectangle divided into five equal parts. Each part is ⅕ (one fifth). Four parts of the rectangle are orange. What fraction is orange? ⅘ (four fifths) of the rectangle is orange.

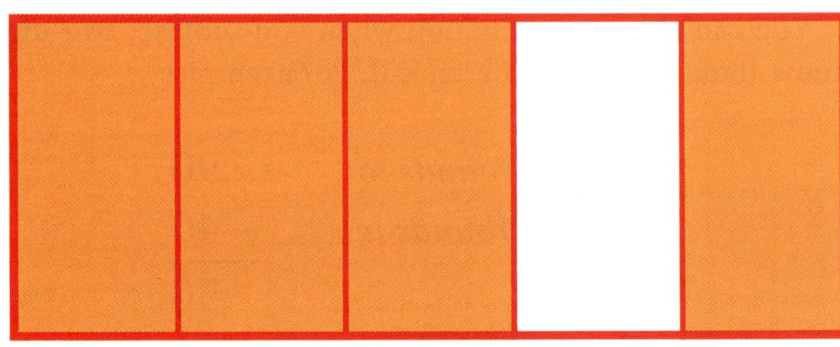

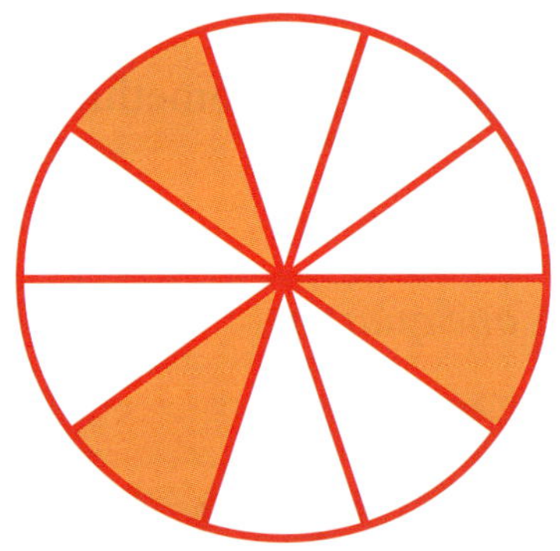

I have baked an apple pie, and Josie has already eaten a slice of it! How many equal slices are there in this pie? 6. What fraction of the pie has Josie eaten? ⅙ (one sixth).

This circle has ten equal parts. What do you think each equal part is called? Each part is ¹⁄₁₀ (one tenth). Count how many parts are orange. What fraction of the circle is orange?

Now you know these fractions:

½	⅓	¼	⅕	⅙	¹⁄₁₀
one half	*one third*	*one quarter*	*one fifth*	*one sixth*	*one tenth*

 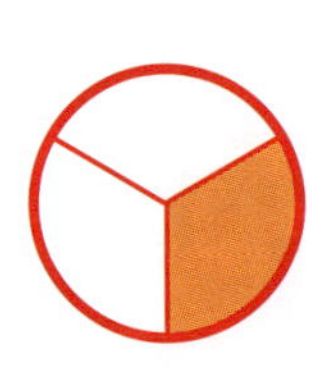    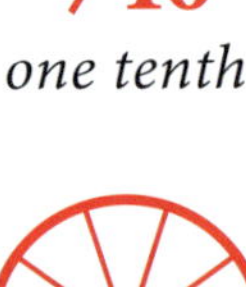

You can also use fractions to talk about parts of a group. For example, there are ten girls in the class. Seven of them are in the football team. What fraction of the girls in the class are in the football team? ⁷⁄₁₀ (seven tenths) of the girls in the class are in the football team.

Working with Numbers to 1,000

The Hundreds

Count out loud in tens from 10 to 100. How many tens are in one hundred?

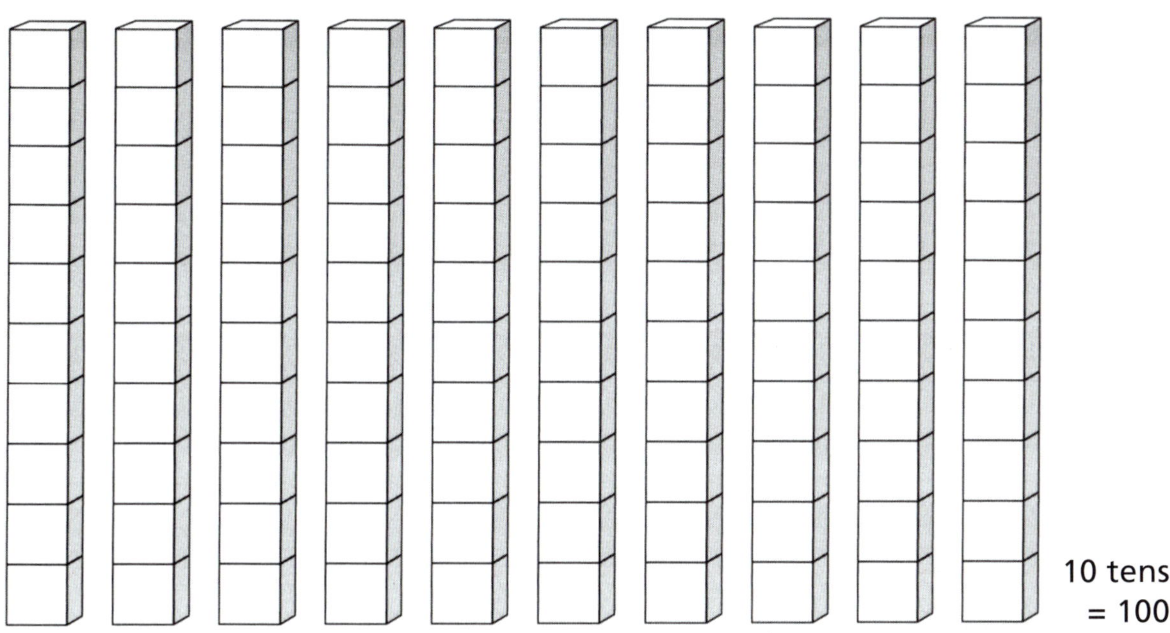

100 is the same as 10 tens. 100 is written in words as one hundred. Here are the numbers and words for the hundreds. Learn to write the numbers and words, and practise counting the hundreds out loud. Let's count them out in hundreds:

100   one hundred
200   two hundred
300   three hundred
400   four hundred
500   five hundred
600   six hundred
700   seven hundred
800   eight hundred
900   nine hundred

How many hundreds are there in 200? 2. How many hundreds are there in 800? 8. Do you notice a pattern?

Counting Between Hundreds

Let's count out loud in ones, starting with 100. After 100 comes:

101, 102, 103, 104, 105, 106, 107, 108, 109, 110, 111, 112...

All right, you can stop for now. When you read those numbers, you say: 'one hundred and one', 'one hundred and two', 'one hundred and three', 'one hundred and four', 'one hundred and five', and so on.

Now, let's start at 189 and keep on counting.

189, 190, 191, 192, 193, 194, 195, 196, 197, 198, 199...

What comes after 199? A new hundred, which is 200. After 200, you can keep counting in the same way:

200, 201, 202, 203, 204, 205, 206, 207, 208, 209, 210, 211, 212...

What comes after 299? 300. You can keep counting till you get to 999 (nine hundred and ninety-nine). What's the number after that? It's ten hundreds, or to use its proper name:

1,000 *one thousand*

> Do you notice the comma after the 1 in 1,000? It doesn't change the value and you don't always need to write it. One thousand is still ten hundreds. The comma goes between the thousands and the hundreds and helps you see quickly where you are.

Count On!

Practise counting in hundreds from 100 to 1,000, like this:

100, 200, 300, 400, 500, 600, 700, 800, 900, 1,000

Now try counting in fifties to 1,000. We'll get you started, and you finish:

50, 100, 150, 200, 250, 300, 350...

Practise counting in tens and in fives from any hundred to the next hundred. For example:

in tens (from 400): 400, 410, 420, 430, 440, 450, 460, 470, 480, 490, 500 *in fives (from 525):* 525, 530, 535, 540, 545, 550, 555, 560... (on to 600)

Now try this: count in tens from any odd number. For example, start with 37. We'll get you started, then you go on a bit longer:

37, 47, 57, 67, 77, 87, 97, 107, 117, 127... (go on to 227)

Count in tens from an even number like 176. Again, we'll get you started.

176, 186, 196, 206, 216, 226... (go on to 326)

Practise until you can count easily in tens from any number. Also, practise counting backwards in tens from any number. For example:

235, 225, 215, 205, 195, 185, 175... (Can you keep going backwards in tens to 25?)

Practise writing the words for three-digit numbers. For example: 843 is eight hundred and forty-three, 607 is six hundred and seven.

Now try writing the words for 156, 403 and 987.

Place Value

Remember that we call numbers like 21 and 73 'two-digit' numbers. Notice that 100 has one more digit. It is a three-digit number. We say that the first digit is in the hundreds place. You know where the next digits are – in the tens place and the ones place.

Let's look at the number 245 (two hundred and forty-five). The 2 in the hundreds place means there are 2 hundreds. The 4 in the tens place means there are 4 tens. And what does the 5 in the ones place mean?

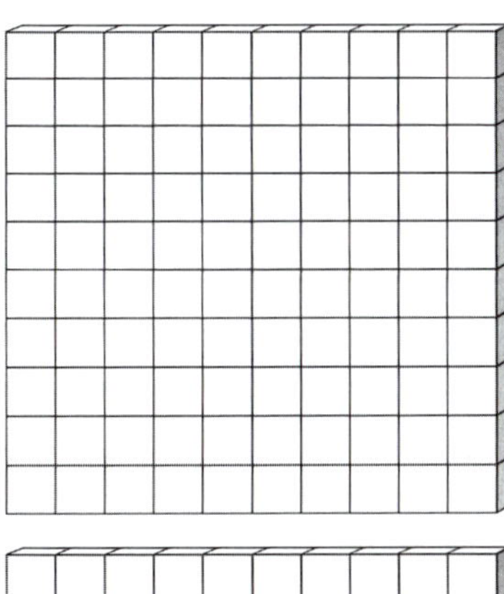

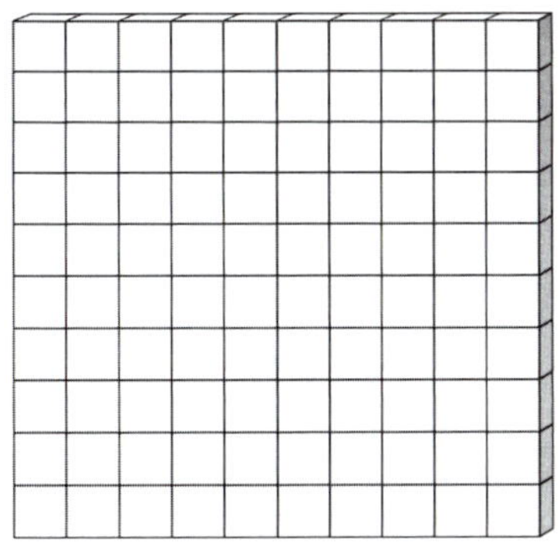

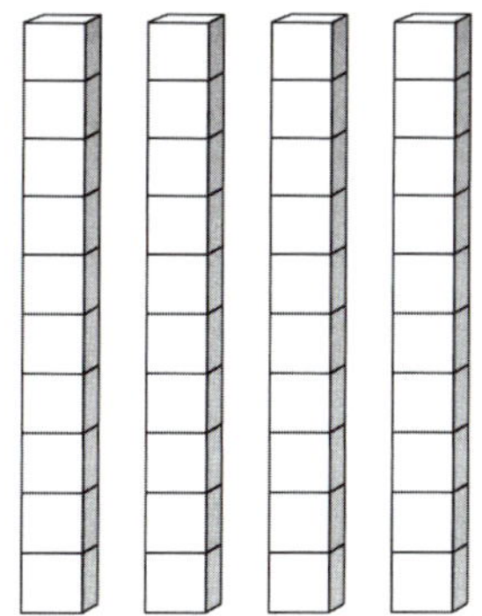

hundreds	tens	ones
2	4	5

You can use place-value blocks to help you understand what each digit in a three-digit number means, like this:

259

hundreds	tens	ones
2	5	9

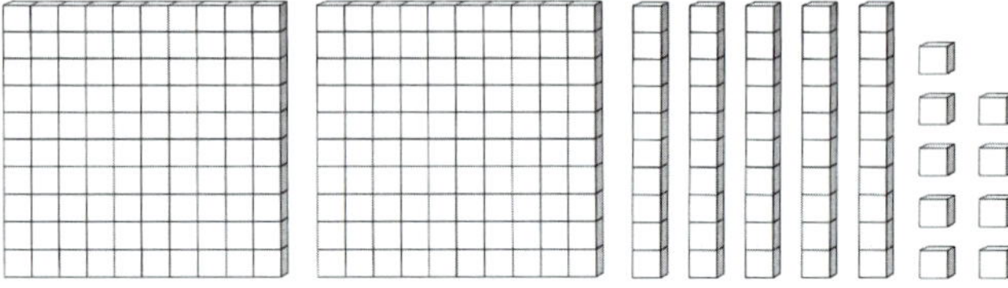

504

hundreds	tens	ones
5	0	4

Only one of the following numbers has 8 tens and 4 hundreds. Can you tell which one? (You might find it helpful to write the numbers in a place-value block.)

418   884   814   148   481   448

Expanded Form

You know that 73 is 7 tens and 3 ones. You know that another way to write 73 is 70 + 3. When you write 73 as 70 + 3, you are writing the number in '*expanded form*'. ('Expanded' means stretched out.)

You can also write three-digit numbers in expanded form. For example, in expanded form, 273 is 200 + 70 + 3. Here are other examples:

359 = 300 + 50 + 9

603 = 600 + 3 (There are no tens in this number.)

740 = 700 + 40 (There are no ones in this number.)

Try writing these numbers in expanded form:

394   571   805   630   912

Comparing Three-Digit Numbers

Which number is greater: 689 or 869? When you compare a three-digit number, look at the hundreds place first. If you look at the hundreds place in 689 and 869, you'll see that 8 is greater than 6. So you can quickly say that 869 > 689.

If the number in the hundreds place is the same, then you need to look at the tens place. For example, 371 > 359. If the numbers in both the hundreds place and the tens place are the same, then look at the ones place. For example, 863 < 867.

Put the correct sign between the following pairs of numbers.

>	<	=
greater than	less than	equal to

876___599   348___384   765___769   116___116   252___225

Adding Three-Digit Numbers

To find the sum of three-digit numbers, first add the ones. Then add the tens, and then add the hundreds.

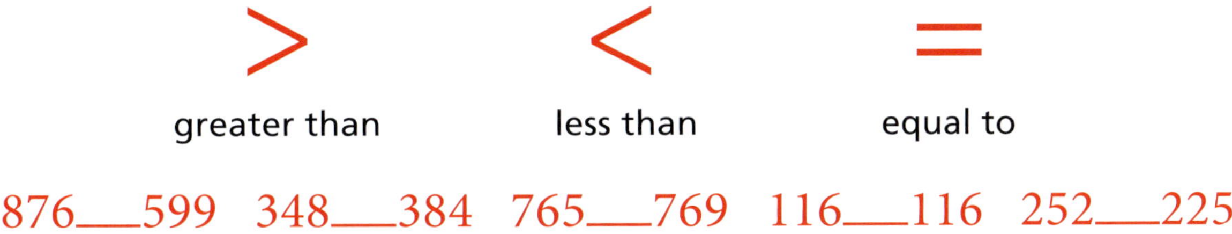

Find the sum.

$$\begin{array}{r} 253 \\ +\ 338 \\ \hline \end{array}$$

*Add the **ones**. Regroup if necessary.*

$$\begin{array}{r} 1 \\ 253 \\ +\ 338 \\ \hline 1 \end{array}$$

*Add the **tens**.*

$$\begin{array}{r} 1 \\ 253 \\ +\ 338 \\ \hline 91 \end{array}$$

*Add the **hundreds**.*

$$\begin{array}{r} 1 \\ 253 \\ +\ 338 \\ \hline 591 \end{array}$$

Regrouping Tens as Hundreds

In the addition example above, you needed to regroup ones as tens. Sometimes when you add you need to regroup tens as hundreds. It's not much different from regrouping ones as tens. Let's see by finding the sum of 80 + 40. How many tens are in 80? Yes, 8. And 40 is 4 tens.

$$8 \text{ tens} + 4 \text{ tens} = 12 \text{ tens}$$

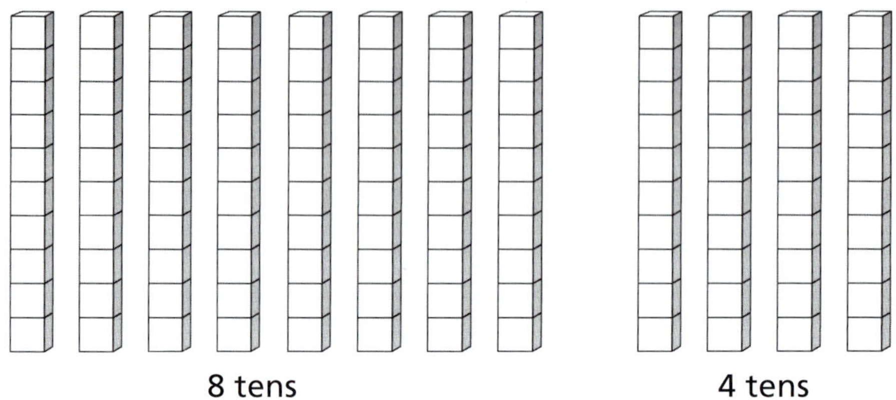

So, now you have 12 tens. You can take 10 of the tens and group them together to make 1 hundred, with 2 tens left over. So, 12 tens is the same as 1 hundred and 2 tens.

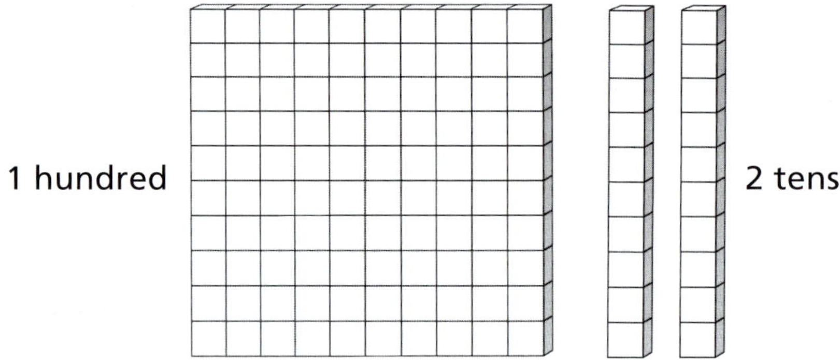

In an addition problem, when you have 10 or more tens, you need to regroup them as hundreds. Here is an example:

Find the sum. *Add the **ones**.* *Add the **tens**. Regroup if necessary.* *Add the **hundreds**.*

$$276 + 663$$

$$276 + 663 = 9$$

$$\overset{1}{276} + 663 = 39$$

$$\overset{1}{276} + 663 = 939$$

When you add the tens in this problem, you add 7 tens plus 6 tens. That makes 13 tens. 13 tens is the same as 1 hundred and 3 tens. So you write 3 at the bottom of the tens column, then you 'carry the 1' (which stands for 1 hundred in this problem) to the top of the hundreds column.

Now let's try a harder problem in which you have to regroup both tens and ones.

Find the sum.	*Add the **ones**.* *Regroup.*	*Add the **tens**.* *Regroup.*	*Add the **hundreds**.*
	1	11	11
638	638	638	638
+ 265	+ 265	+ 265	+ 265
	3	03	903

> Practise doing many three-digit addition problems until you can do them easily. Check your addition. Remember, you can check yourself by changing the order of the addends then adding again to see if you get the same answer.

Subtracting from a Three-Digit Number

To subtract from a three-digit number, first subtract the ones. Then subtract the tens. Then subtract the hundreds.

Find the difference.	*Subtract the **ones**.* *Regroup.*	*Subtract the **tens**.*	*Subtract the* ***hundreds**.*
	712	712	712
582	582	582	582
− 269	− 269	− 269	− 269
	3	13	313

Remember, you can check subtraction by adding, like this:

$$
\begin{array}{ccc}
582 & 313 & \quad\;1 \\
-269 \longrightarrow +269 & & 313 \\
\overline{313} & \overline{} & +269 \\
& & \overline{582}
\end{array}
$$

Subtraction and Regrouping Hundreds

As you know, sometimes when you subtract you need to regroup 1 ten as 10 ones. For example, you would need to regroup a ten as 10 ones in this problem:

$$\begin{array}{r} 82 \\ -\ 57 \\ \hline \end{array}$$

In some problems, you may also need to regroup 1 hundred as 10 tens. Say you have 230 pencils. They are bundled together in 2 hundreds and 3 tens.

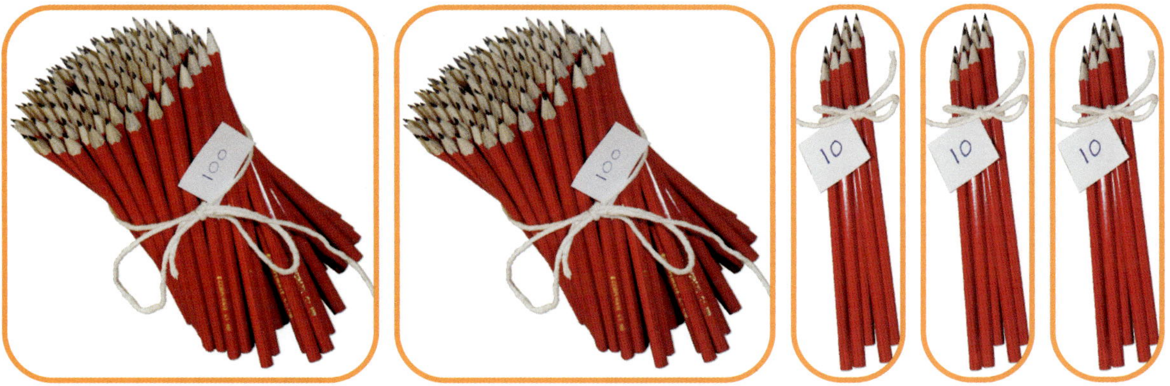

You want to give away 60 pencils. How can you do this? You only have 3 tens, but you need 6 tens to make up 60. So, you need to regroup one of the hundreds into tens.

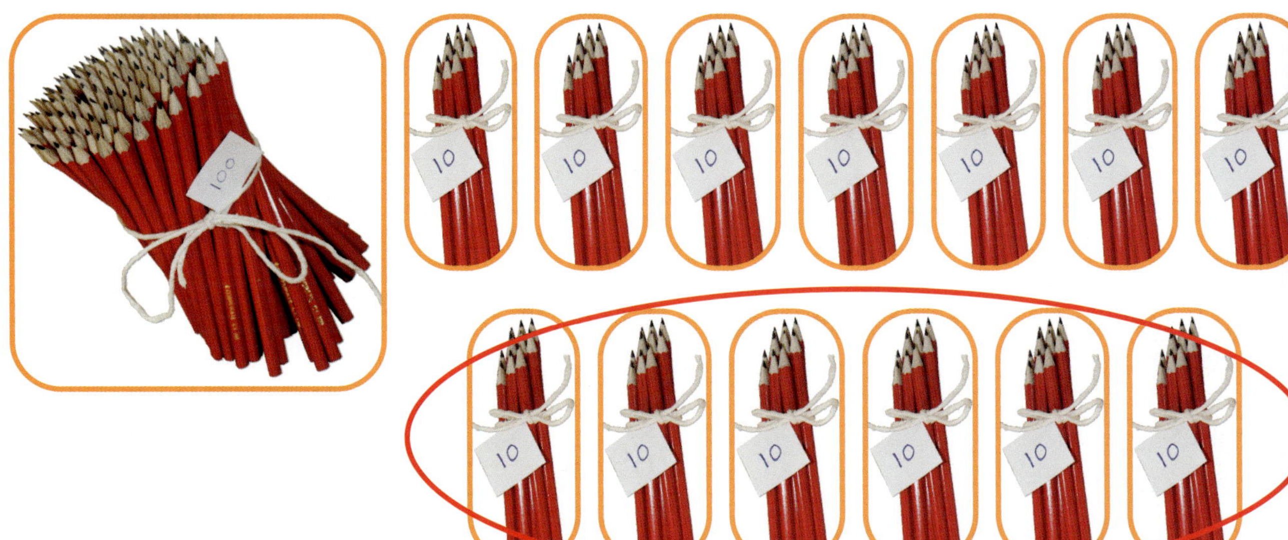

You can regroup 2 hundreds and 3 tens as 1 hundred and 13 tens. Take away 6 tens (the pencils circled in the picture), and that leaves you with 1 hundred and 7 tens, or 170 pencils. So, 230 – 60 = 170.

Now let's try another subtraction problem in which you need to regroup 1 hundred as 10 tens.

Find the difference.	*Subtract the ones.*	*Subtract the tens. Regroup.*	*Subtract the hundreds.*
556 − 372	556 − 372 ——— 4	4 15 5̶5̶6 − 372 ——— 84	4 15 5̶5̶6 − 372 ——— 184

> **Practise doing many three-digit subtraction problems until you can do them easily. Remember, you can check your subtraction by adding.**

Word Problems

As you practise maths, you will do many word problems. The trick is working out what the word problem is asking you to do. Is it asking you to add? Or maybe to subtract?

What is this word problem asking you to do?

The third-year classes at St Matthew's Primary School collected cans for recycling. Ms Johnson's class collected 345 cans. Mr Franklin's class collected 275 cans. How many cans did they collect in all?

This is an addition problem. To solve it:

You write:	*You add:*	*You check:*
345 + 275	11 345 + 275 ——— 620	11 275 + 345 ——— 620

The third-year classes collected 620 cans in all. Now, try another word problem:

Margaret brings £9.25 to the cinema. The ticket for the film costs £5.75. After she buys her ticket, how much money does she have left?

This is a subtraction problem. To solve it:

You write:	You subtract:	You check:
	8 12	1
9.25	9.25	3.50
− 5.75	−5.75	+ 5.75
	£3.50	£9.25

How would you solve this problem? At the museum gift shop, Tricia bought animal figurines for £6.47. Her friend, Harry, bought a dinosaur poster for £4.29. How much more did Tricia spend than Harry?

When a word problem asks you 'how much more', you need to subtract, like this:

You write:	You subtract:	You check:
	3 1 7	1
6.47	6.47	2.18
− 4.29	− 4.29	+ 4.29
	£2.18	£6.47

So, Tricia spent £2.18 more than Harry.

Measurement

Measuring Length

When you measure how long something is, you measure its *length*. Length can be measured in different units, such as centimetres and metres. Practise measuring different objects in centimetres, using tools like a ruler or a tape measure.

Most things are not an exact number of centimetres long. Sometimes you just need to estimate about how long something is. For example, rounding to the nearest centimetre, the pencil below is about 14cm long.

At home, you may have a tape measure that is 100 centimetres long. 100 centimetres is also called a metre. At school, you may have a ruler that is 100 centimetres long, called a 'metre rule'. Now why is it called that?

100 cm = 1 metre

Practise measuring in metres and centimetres. You might start by measuring how tall you or your friends are. Would it be easiest to use a metre rule, a tape measure or a ruler? What tool should you use to measure the width of this book?

Do you see that this ruler has numbers on the top that are closer together than the numbers on the bottom? The numbers on the top, that you used to measure the pencil, measure centimetres. In the UK, we use centimetres and metres to  measure a lot of things. But we can also use another set of measurements, called inches and feet, to measure length. A centimetre is shorter than an inch; it's not quite half an inch.

Inches are shown on the bottom of the ruler. They are upside down because you should turn the ruler (or this book!) the other way around to measure things in inches. There are 12 inches in 1 foot.

The toy taxi is along the side of the ruler that measures in inches. How long is the toy taxi in inches? It is about 3 inches long.

If you have a ruler or tape measure, check to see if it has centimetres and inches, then practise measuring some objects in both types of measurement.

When we write measurements, we often use abbreviations, like this:

centimetres = cm   metres = m

inches = in   feet = ft

Measuring Weight

When you measure how heavy something is, you are measuring *weight*. We often measure weight in grams. The abbreviation for grams is g. This pasta weighs 26g. How much does the tomato weigh?

A gram is quite light so for heavier things we might measure their weight in kilograms (abbreviated as kg).

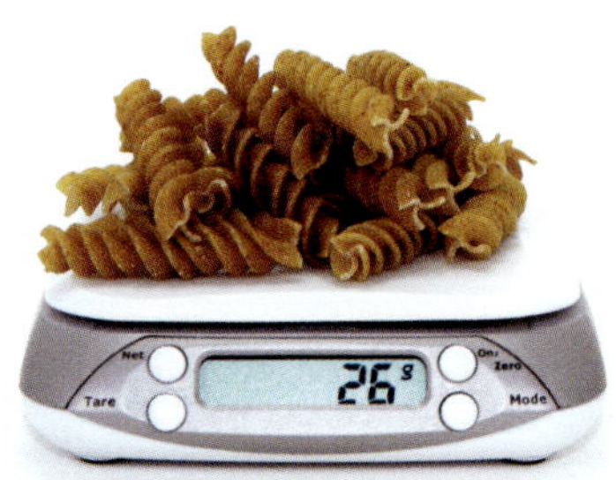

1 kilogram = 1000 grams

These vegetables weigh 1000 grams, or 1 kilogram. ▶

One tool for weighing is called a balance. When the balance is level, both sides weigh the same. This scale is level, so that means that the tomatoes weigh 1kg. ▼

When one side of the balance is lower than the other, the lower side weighs more. Look at the balances in the pictures here. Does the bread weigh more or less than one kilogram? Do the cherries weigh more or less than one kilogram?

Look again at the pictures of the balances with the tomatoes, the cherries and the bread. Now list the objects in order from the lightest to the heaviest. Since the bread weighs less than 1kg, the tomatoes weigh about 1kg and the cherries weigh more than 1kg, then from lightest to heaviest they are: the bread, the tomatoes, the cherries.

OCTOBER

SUNDAY	MONDAY	TUESDAY	WEDNESDAY	THURSDAY	FRIDAY	SATURDAY
		1	2	3	4	5
6	7	8	9	10	11	12
13	14	15	16	17	18	19
20	21	22	23	24	25	26
27	28	29	30	31		

Measuring Time:
The Calendar

We measure time in many units, including years, months and days. You probably know what year it is now, and what month, too: can you tell me? Sometimes you need to refer to a calendar to tell what day of the month it is. Practise reading a calendar to identify what day it is, as well as what day of the week it is.

On this calendar, the day marked in a blue square is the fifteenth of October. What day of the week is it?

You know it's a Tuesday, because the number is in the column under Tuesday. One day on this calendar is circled. Can you say the date that's circled, and what day of the week it is? (The circled day is the twenty-fifth of October, and it's a Friday.)

The months of the year have anywhere from 28 to 31 days. Practise saying and writing the ordinal numbers up to thirty-first. Here they are, written as numbers and words.

1st	first	11th	eleventh	21st	twenty-first
2nd	second	12th	twelfth	22nd	twenty-second
3rd	third	13th	thirteenth	23rd	twenty-third
4th	fourth	14th	fourteenth	24th	twenty-fourth
5th	fifth	15th	fifteenth	25th	twenty-fifth
6th	sixth	16th	sixteenth	26th	twenty-sixth
7th	seventh	17th	seventeenth	27th	twenty-seventh
8th	eighth	18th	eighteenth	28th	twenty-eighth
9th	ninth	19th	nineteenth	29th	twenty-ninth
10th	tenth	20th	twentieth	30th	thirtieth
				31st	thirty-first

Can you say and write the names of the twelve months of the year in order, starting with January? Do you know how many days are in each month? Can you write the names of the days of the week?

Do you remember the poem that begins 'Thirty days hath September', which we read in Year 2? It can help you remember the number of days in each month.

Measuring Time: Clock Time to 5 Minutes

How many minutes does it take for the minute hand to go once all the way around the clock? Another way of asking that question is: 'How many minutes are in an hour?'

There are 60 minutes in 1 hour. One hour (or 60 minutes) is how long it takes for the hour hand on a clock to move from one large number to the next on the clock face. (The hour hand is the short hand.)

On a clock, when the minute hand (the long hand) moves from one number to the next, 5 minutes have passed. For example, the time on this clock is 5 minutes past 4.

When the minute hand moves from the 1 to the 2, that means 5 more minutes have gone by. What time will it be then? It will be 10 minutes past 4.

The numbers on the clock face tell you the hours, and you have to work out the minutes. You can count in fives for each new number on a clock face to find out how many minutes have passed since the hour. For example, look at this clock. The minute hand is on the 7. How many minutes have passed since the hour? Count in fives, starting with the 1 on the clock (touch each number on the clock face as you count aloud): 5, 10, 15, 20, 25, 30, 35. When you know your five times tables, you can use multiplication to make this quicker because you know that $5 \times 7 = 35$.

So, when the minute hand is on the 7, 35 minutes have passed since the hour on the clock on the last page. Now look at the hour hand (the short hand). It is between the 5 and the 6. That means the time is after 5 o'clock, but it is not yet 6 o'clock. It is 35 minutes past 5.

There's a short way to write 35 minutes past 5. It looks like this:

5:35

The two little dots are called a *colon*. The number to the left of the colon tells the hour. The number to the right of the colon tells the minutes. The quick way to say this time is just to say 'five thirty-five' instead of '35 minutes past 5'.

Measuring Time: Half and Quarter Hours

There are 30 minutes in half an hour. On this clock, the time is 30 minutes past 2, which is also called 'half past two', or 2:30.

When it is more than 30 minutes past the hour, we sometimes count backwards around the clock and say how many minutes it is until the next hour. For example, look at this clock: ▶

What time does the clock show? If you count in fives, you'll see that it's 40 minutes past 5. You can also say that it's 20 minutes before 6. This makes sense because, as you know, there are 60 minutes in an hour, and 20 + 40 = 60. For 20 minutes before 6, people also say:

'It's twenty to six.'

Can you tell the time on this clock by saying how many minutes before the hour it is?

When you learnt about fractions, you learnt about ¼ which is one quarter. Fifteen minutes is one quarter of an hour. That is why, when the time is 2:45, people often say it is 'quarter to three'. Now, what time is it on this clock? It is 4:15, and people often say that it's 'quarter past four'.

So, 'quarter past' means 15 minutes after the hour, and 'quarter to' means 15 minutes before the hour.

Do you remember what AM and PM mean? The time before noon is called AM. The AM hours are between 12 midnight and 12 noon. Time after noon is called PM, and the PM hours are between 12 noon and 12 midnight.

So, in each day there are 12 AM hours and 12 PM hours, which make how many hours in a whole day? (12 + 12 = 24 hours in a day.)

Do you go to bed closer to 9:00 AM, or 9:00 PM?

Does the sun rise closer to 6:00 AM or 6:00 PM?

Measuring Time: How Much Time Has Passed?

Sometimes we need to know how much time has passed. Rajen leaves his house at 2:00 to play with John. Rajen's mother tells him to be back home in 3 hours. So, when does Rajen have to be back home? At 5:00. From 2:00 to 5:00 is 3 hours.

At 10:00 in the morning, Andrea's stomach starts to growl. She knows that she must wait until 1:00 in the afternoon before lunch will be served in the school canteen. How many hours will pass before she can eat lunch? To work this out, you can't just subtract 10 from 1. Instead, first you think that from 10:00 to 12:00 is 2 hours, and from 12:00 to 1:00 is 1 hour. So, 1 + 2 = 3 hours before Andrea can eat lunch. Poor Andrea!

Christie gets out of school at 2:45. She goes to the library and then to gymnastics training. When she gets home, it is 5:45. How many hours have passed since she got out of school? To help you work that out, look at the two clocks on the next page.

When Christie left school.

When she got home.

You can see that the minutes are the same on both clocks. When the minutes are the same, the change in hours tells you how much time has gone by. Three hours passed between the time Christie left school and the time she got home.

Geometry

Plane Figures

You know the names of these flat shapes:

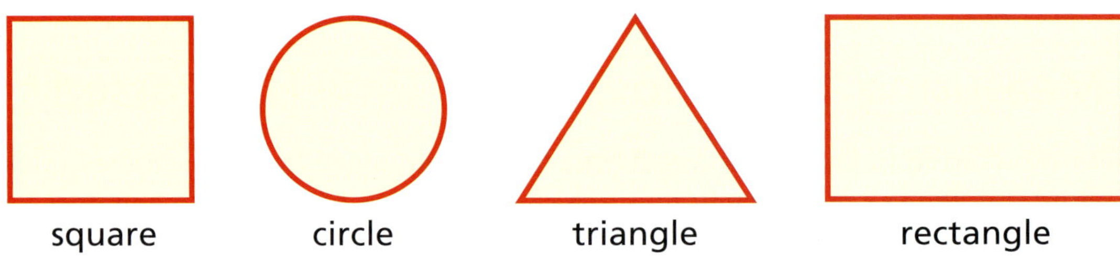

Flat shapes are also called *plane shapes* or *plane figures*. Can you answer these questions about some plane shapes?

- All rectangles and squares have the same number of sides – how many? (All rectangles and squares have four sides.)

- What's the difference between a rectangle and a square? (All the sides of a square are the same length.)

- How many sides does a triangle have? (A triangle has three sides.)

● What do we call figures that are the same size and shape? (Figures that are the same size and shape are called 'congruent'.)

These two squares have the same shape and the same size. They are congruent.

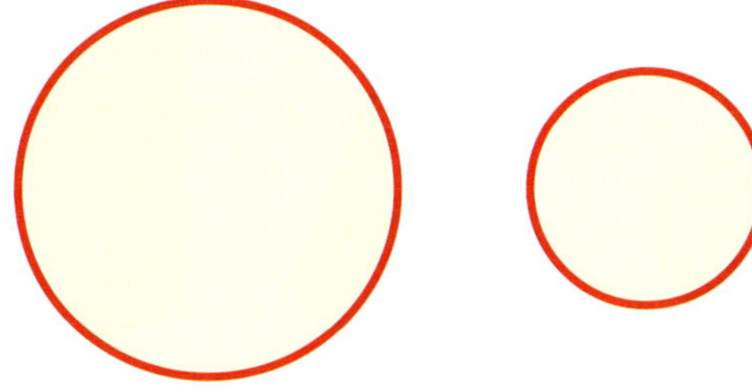

These two circles have the same shape but not the same size. They are *not* congruent.

interior

exterior

The inside of a shape is called the **interior**. The outside of a shape is called the **exterior**.

You can measure the length of the sides of a square or rectangle. When you add up the length of all four sides of a square or rectangle, you get the *perimeter*, which is the distance around a plane figure. Look at this rectangle. Add the length of each side: 2cm + 2cm + 4cm + 4cm = 12 cm. The perimeter is 12 centimetres.

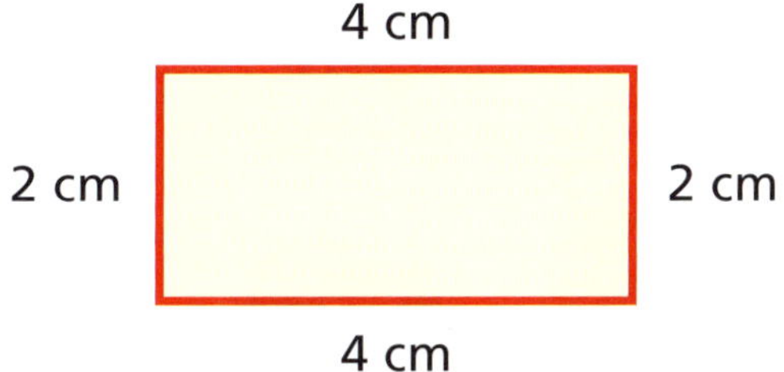

Solid Figures

Trace this pattern on a piece of paper. Cut it out, then fold at the dotted lines and tape the edges.

You have made a solid figure called a cube.

Do you see how each side of the cube is a square?

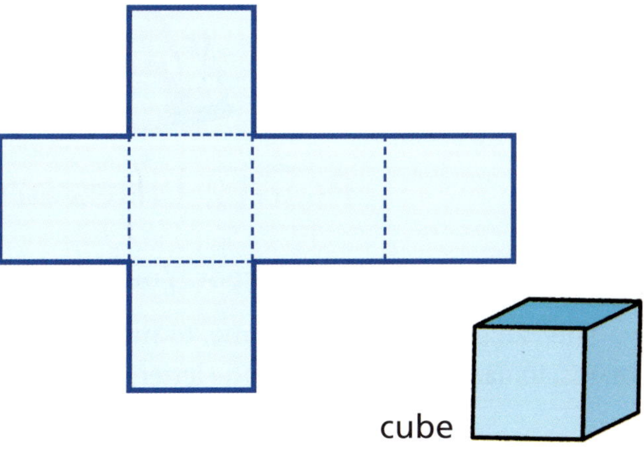

cube

Here are the names and shapes of other solid figures:

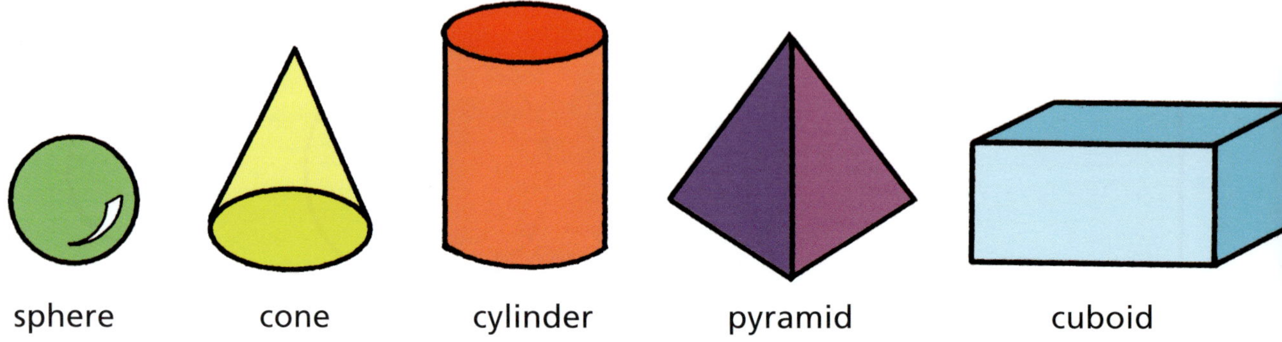

| sphere | cone | cylinder | pyramid | cuboid |

What plane shape is each side of the pyramid? Each upper side of a pyramid is a triangle. The base can be a different shape, like a square.

Imagine that you were to cut a spherical object, like a grapefruit, down the middle. What plane shape would you see? A circle!

Here are some things you might see at home or school. Each one has the shape of a solid figure. Can you name the solid figure for each object?

Points, Lines and Segments

In maths, a *point* is an exact spot. You show a point with a dot like this: ●

You can give the point a name, to make sure that we can tell it from other points. In maths, to name a point we use the letters of the alphabet. So, we'll call it point A, like this: 

If you put two points on a piece of paper and then connect them, you will have a *line*. Here is a line going through point A and point B:

In geometry, a line is straight and goes on forever. The arrows show that the line continues forever in both directions. The line goes through points A and B, so we call it line AB or line BA. A short way to write line AB is

$$\overleftrightarrow{AB}$$

A segment is a part of something. A *line segment* is a part of a line. A line goes on forever, but a line segment has two endpoints.

We name a line segment by its endpoints. What do you think this line segment is called? It can be called either line segment CD or line segment DC. A short way to write line segment DC is

$$\overline{DC}$$

Which way does a vertical line go? Does it go side to side or up and down? What about a horizontal line? A diagonal line?

Check your answers and learn more about how lines are used in art on page 182.

Have you ever watched gymnastics competitions during the Olympics and seen gymnasts use the piece of equipment called the parallel bars? If lines run side by side and never meet, they are called parallel lines. Here are some pairs of parallel lines:

Parallel lines always stay the same distance apart, so that means they never cross each other.

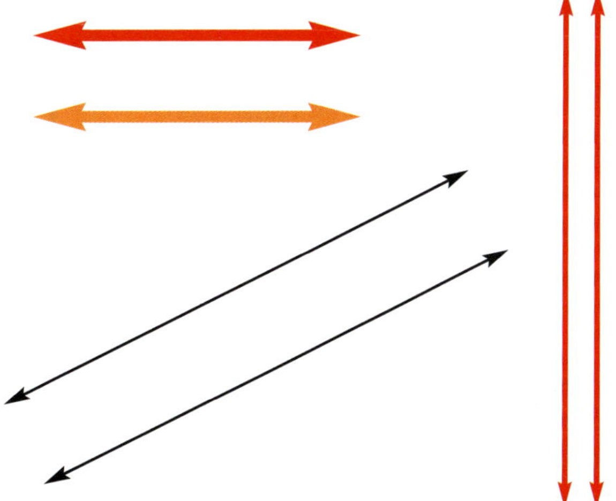

When two lines meet and form an exact L (either a forward, backward or upside down L), then those lines are called *perpendicular* lines. Here are two pairs of perpendicular lines:

These two lines meet but they are not perpendicular:

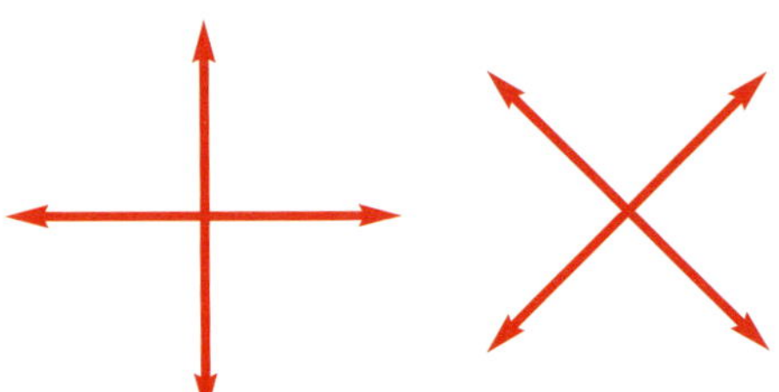

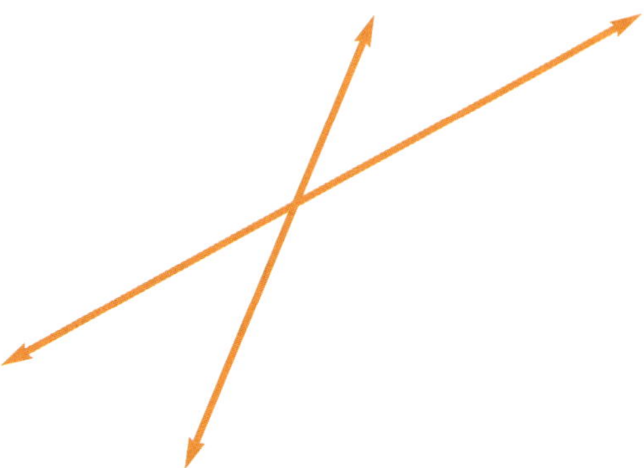

You can find segments of perpendicular lines in any square or rectangle. Use your finger to trace the perpendicular lines in these figures:

Lines of Symmetry

Take a piece of blank paper and fold it exactly in half so the two parts match. Now open the paper. Do you see the line down the middle, formed by the crease where you folded the paper? That is called a line of symmetry. A line of symmetry divides a shape into two parts that match.

If a shape can be divided into two parts that match, we say it is *symmetrical*. These two figures are symmetrical:

See how the painting *The Last Supper* is symmetrical on page 185, and the Parthenon on page 194.

These two figures are not symmetrical:

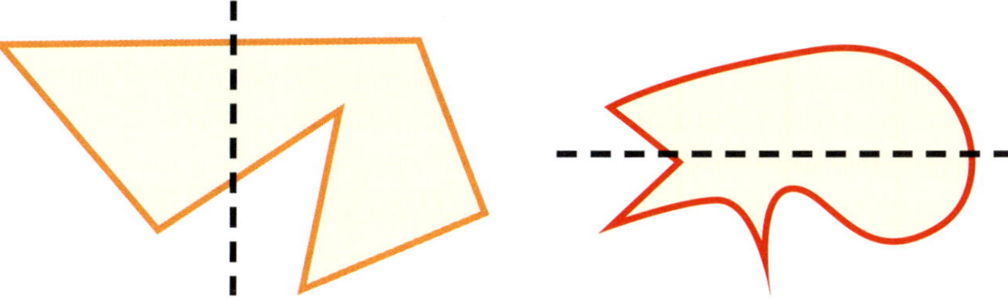

Multiplication and Division

Multiplication

Multiplication Words

In Year 2 we learnt that, in the equation $2 \times 5 = 10$, 2 and 5 are factors and 10 is the product. You can multiply factors in any order without changing the product.

$$2 \times 5 = 10 \qquad 5 \times 2 = 10$$

Multiplying Vertically

$$4 \times 5 = 20 \quad \text{can also be written} \quad \begin{array}{r} 5 \\ \times\, 4 \\ \hline 20 \end{array}$$

You read both as 'four times five equals twenty'. Notice that when you read a vertical multiplication problem, you begin with the number next to the multiplication sign and read up.

Showing Multiplication

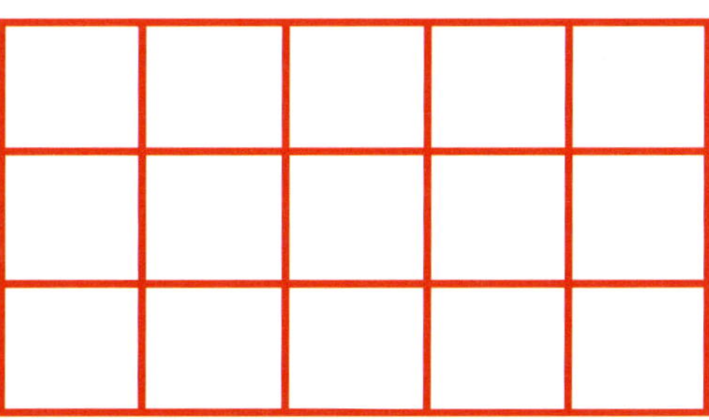

You can make a 'picture' of a multiplication problem using graph paper. For example, you can show 3×5 by a rectangle with 3 rows and 5 columns, like this ▶

If you count the squares by the rows, you have $5 + 5 + 5$, which is 3×5. How many is that?

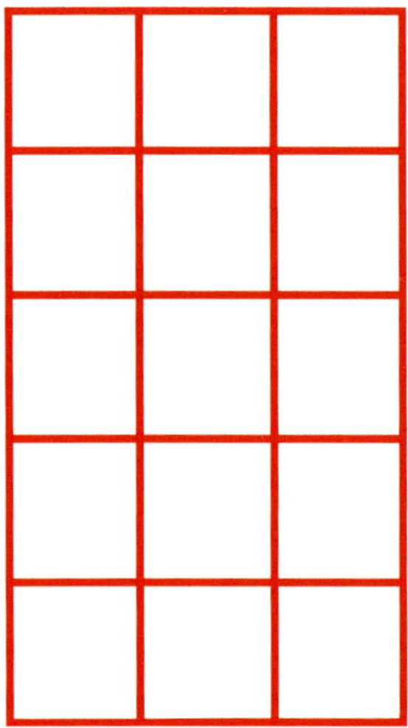

If you count the squares by the rows on the left, you have:

3 + 3 + 3 + 3 + 3, which is 5 × 3

Either way, there are 15 squares in all.

> **Now have some fun making at least three other multiplication facts into graph-paper pictures just like we did for 5 × 3 and 3 × 5. Try 3 × 4, or 4 × 5. What about 8 × 3?**

Multiplication is a quick way of doing repeated addition. It's good to practise writing multiplication as repeated addition, and repeated addition as multiplication. For example, 4 × 5 can also be written 5 + 5 + 5 + 5. And 3 + 3 + 3 + 3 + 3 + 3 can also be written 6 × 3. How would you write these?

$$8 + 8 + 8 + 8 = \underline{\qquad} \qquad\qquad 4 \times 6 = \underline{\qquad}$$

The Multiplication Table

In Year 2, you learnt the multiplication rules and tables for 0, 1, 2, 5 and 10. Here are the multiplication tables for some more factors: 3, 4 and 8.

3 as a factor	4 as a factor	8 as a factor
0 × 3 = 0	0 × 4 = 0	0 × 8 = 0
1 × 3 = 3	1 × 4 = 4	1 × 8 = 8
2 × 3 = 6	2 × 4 = 8	2 × 8 = 16
3 × 3 = 9	3 × 4 = 12	3 × 8 = 24
4 × 3 = 12	4 × 4 = 16	4 × 8 = 32
5 × 3 = 15	5 × 4 = 20	5 × 8 = 40
6 × 3 = 18	6 × 4 = 24	6 × 8 = 48
7 × 3 = 21	7 × 4 = 28	7 × 8 = 56
8 × 3 = 24	8 × 4 = 32	8 × 8 = 64
9 × 3 = 27	9 × 4 = 36	9 × 8 = 72
10 × 3 = 30	10 × 4 = 40	10 × 8 = 80

Only the multiplication facts in red are actually new. The others you already know. For example, if you know that $5 \times 8 = 40$, then you know that $8 \times 5 = 40$. Learn these facts so that you can say them easily. Also be able to give any product quickly, without making any mistakes. Remember that you can skip-count to get to the next fact in a table. $8 \times 3 = 24$, so 9×3 is 3 more, or 27. $8 \times 8 = 64$, so 9×8 is 8 more, or 72.

When you know all the multiplication facts well, practise filling in this table with factors from 1–8. What patterns do you see in the table? You will learn the times tables for 6 and 7 in Year 4, or you can try to work them out now.

x	1	2	3	4	5	6	7	8
1								
2								
3				15				
4								
5							35	
6							42	
7								
8								

Brackets, Multiplying Three Numbers

The symbols ( ) are brackets. In maths, you do what is inside brackets first.

You add $(2 + 3) + 5$ like this:

$$(2 + 3) + 5 = 5 + 5 = 10$$

You add $2 + (3 + 5)$ like this:

$$2 + (3 + 5) = 2 + 8 = 10$$

Notice that whether you put $2 + 3$ in the brackets or $3 + 5$ in the brackets, the sum is the same. No matter how you group the numbers you are adding, the sum stays the same.

You can also multiply three or more numbers using brackets. Try these problems:

$$(3 \times 2) \times 4 = \underline{\quad} \times 4 = \underline{\quad}$$

$$3 \times (2 \times 4) = 3 \times \underline{\quad} = \underline{\quad}$$

Notice that the product is the same both times. No matter how you group factors, the product is the same.

However, the brackets are very important when you are solving multiplication and addition in one problem because, if you don't solve the part in the brackets first, your answer will come out differently. Let's see why.

If the problem were $7 + 3 \times 4$ then you wouldn't know which part of the problem to solve first. Would it be $(7 + 3) \times 4$ or $7 + (3 \times 4)$?

$$(7 + 3) \times 4 = 10 \times 4 = 40 \quad \text{OR} \quad 7 + (3 \times 4) = 7 + 12 = 19$$

Do you see why the brackets are important here? They show you which part of the problem to solve first so you know whether the answer should be 40 or 19. There's a big difference between those two answers!

Division

In Year 2, we learnt the division rules and facts with 0, 1, 2, 5 and 10 as divisors. Now we can learn the division facts with 3, 4 and 8 as the divisors.

3 as a divisor	4 as a divisor	8 as a divisor
$0 \div 3 = 0$	$0 \div 4 = 0$	$0 \div 8 = 0$
$3 \div 3 = 1$	$4 \div 4 = 1$	$8 \div 8 = 1$
$6 \div 3 = 2$	$8 \div 4 = 2$	$16 \div 8 = 2$
$9 \div 3 = 3$	$12 \div 4 = 3$	$24 \div 8 = 3$
$12 \div 3 = 4$	$16 \div 4 = 4$	$32 \div 8 = 4$
$15 \div 3 = 5$	$20 \div 4 = 5$	$40 \div 8 = 5$
$18 \div 3 = 6$	$24 \div 4 = 6$	$48 \div 8 = 6$
$21 \div 3 = 7$	$28 \div 4 = 7$	$56 \div 8 = 7$
$24 \div 3 = 8$	$32 \div 4 = 8$	$64 \div 8 = 8$
$27 \div 3 = 9$	$36 \div 4 = 9$	$72 \div 8 = 9$
$30 \div 3 = 10$	$40 \div 4 = 10$	$80 \div 8 = 10$

Division Word Problems

There are 56 books on the teacher's table and she asks Alex to stack them in 8 equal piles for each of the eight small groups of Year 3 pupils. How many piles will there be on the teacher's desk? How would you write that? 56 ÷ _ = _.

Sue selects 18 seashells and decides to sell them in silk sachets on the seashore. She has 3 silk sachets. If Sue puts the same number of seashells in each sachet, how many seashells will she sell in each silk sachet on the seashore? Are you sure?

Mum asks Felix to divide 64 cubes of sugar so there are 8 cubes in each bowl for her party. How many bowls will Felix need?

If Serena has 36 cards and there are 4 players, how many cards must she give each player if each player has the same number of cards?

Remainders

Mrs Hughes wants to divide 47 sheets of craft paper among 10 students, so that each student has the same number of sheets. If she gave each student 4 sheets, she would use 40 sheets (4 × 10 = 40). If she gave each student 5 sheets, she would use 50 sheets (5 × 10 = 50). She only has 47 sheets: she has enough to give 4 sheets to each student, but not enough to give 5 sheets to everyone. Since 47 − 40 = 7, there will be 7 sheets left over if she gives 4 to each student. Here is how you write this division problem if Mrs Hughes wants to divide 47 sheets of craft paper among her 10 students:

$$10 \overline{) 47}$$

What is 47 divided by 10? 10 doesn't go into 47 evenly. The closest we can come is 4 × 10 = 40. So we write 4 in the ones place for the quotient. Then we put 40 below the 47 (the dividend) and subtract it, to show how many we have left over: 7. Our remainder is 7. So we write R7 next to the quotient, 4, like this:

$$
\begin{array}{r}
4 \quad \text{R7} \quad \longleftarrow \quad \text{quotient (with remainder)} \\
\text{divisor} \quad 10\,\overline{)\,47} \quad \longleftarrow \quad \text{dividend} \\
-\,40 \quad \longleftarrow \quad \text{product of } 4 \times 10 \\
\overline{7} \quad \longleftarrow \quad \text{remainder}
\end{array}
$$

Notice how you multiply the divisor (10) and the quotient (4), then subtract this product (40) from the dividend (47) to find the remainder (7).

When you do a division problem like this, the quotient needs to be as big as possible. If the problem is 23 divided by 5, what would your quotient be? 3 or 4? It would be 4, because 3 × 5 = 15 and 23 − 15 gives you 8 left over. Since you can subtract 5 from 8, you know that your quotient can be 1 greater. 4 × 5 = 20 which leaves you 3 left over. Because you can't take 5 away from 3, you know you've found the largest possible quotient.

When you find the largest quotient for this problem that is a whole number (4), multiply it by the divisor (5) to find their product (20), then subtract this product (23 − 20). The result is the remainder (3). You can always check your work by making sure that the remainder is less than the divisor. If the remainder is not less, you need to try again, with a larger quotient. Here is an example.

$$
\begin{array}{llr}
 & & 3 \quad \text{R12} \\
 & & 7\,\overline{)\,33} \\
\text{Subtract} & 7 \times 3 & -\,21 \\
 & & \overline{12} \\
12 < 7? & & \\
\text{NO} & &
\end{array}
\qquad\qquad
\begin{array}{llr}
 & & 4 \quad \text{R5} \\
 & & 7\,\overline{)\,33} \\
\text{Subtract} & 7 \times 4 & -\,28 \\
 & & \overline{5} \\
5 < 7 & & \\
\text{YES} & &
\end{array}
$$

Practise doing problems like 29 ÷ 3 or 49 ÷ 8, finding the quotients and the remainders. Remember that 3 $\overline{)29}$ and 29 ÷ 3 are the same problem.

The remainder shows us how many things are left over when we can't divide them evenly. We can say the number of remainders, like 16 apples ÷ 3 children = 5 R1, or we could use a fraction. On top is the remainder and on the bottom is the divisor.

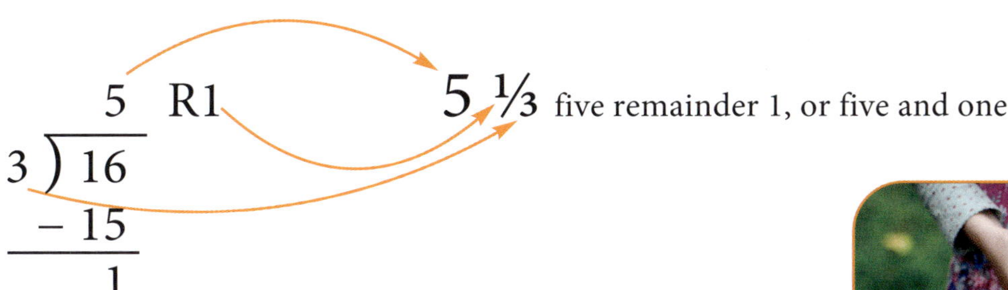

$$3\overline{)16}$$

5 R1   5 ⅓ five remainder 1, or five and one third.

     5 R1
  3) 16
   − 15
      1

Each child will have five whole apples. There is one apple remaining and, to be fair, they would like to divide the last apple into three parts so each child can have one part. If the one remaining apple is divided into three, each part would be one third. The 16 apples are divided evenly amongst the children so each receives 5 ⅓ apples. We'll see more about fractions in Year 4.

Now try these:

        R ___
  6) 25   or   _____ ⁻⁄₆
    −
  ______

        R ___
  4) 35   or   _____ ⁻⁄₄
    −
  ______

        R ___
  5) 47   or   _____ ⁻⁄_
    −
  ______

Suggested Resources

Books

A Parent's Survival Guide to Maths Homework by Andrew Brodie (Andrew Brodie) 2010

Oxford Primary Maths Dictionary by Peter Patilla (Oxford University Press) 2008

The Butterfly Arithmetic by Irina Tyk (Civitas) 2012

Mobile Apps

Arithmemouse Addition Subtraction Game (Galen Tingle) app for iPad or iPhone [free].

Arithmetic Wiz (The Rocket Studio) app for iPad or iPhone [free].

Division Wiz (The Rocket Studio) app for iPad or iPhone [free].

Multiplication + (The App Gate Inc.) app for iPad or iPhone [free].

Pizza Fractions: Beginning with Simple Fractions (Brian West) app for iPad or iPhone [free].

Science

Introduction

Children gain knowledge about the world around them in part from observation and experience. To understand magnetism, insect life cycles or human body systems, children need opportunities to observe and experiment. In the words of the Association for Science Education, science education is important for 'the development of children's natural curiosity; appreciation of the importance of science for understanding the world; and active participation in the acquisition of scientific knowledge, understanding, skills and language'.[1]

While experience counts for much, book learning is also important, for it helps bring coherence and order to a child's scientific knowledge. Only when topics are presented systematically and clearly can children make steady and secure progress in their scientific learning. The child's development of scientific knowledge and understanding is in some ways a very complex process, different for each child. But a systematic approach to the exploration of science, one that combines experience with book learning, can help provide essential building blocks for deeper understanding at a later time. It can also provide the kind of knowledge that one is not likely to gain from observation: consider, for example, how people long believed that the earth stood still while the sun orbited around it, a misconception that 'direct experience' presented as fact.

In this section we introduce Year 3 children to a variety of topics consistent with the early study of science in countries that have had outstanding results in teaching science at the primary level. Let us repeat that whilst book learning is essential, children also need imaginative help from teachers and parents in providing opportunities for observation and hands-on experience of the natural world.

---

[1] Association for Science Education Primary Science Committee, 2010: 'ASE Primary and Early Years Science Education Vision Statement'. Available at: http://www.ase.org.uk/documents/primary-vision-statement

The Cycle of Life and the Seasons

The Life Cycle

Do you know the word 'cycle', or a word with 'cycle' in it? How about words like 'bicycle' or 'tricycle'?

Think about a bicycle's wheel: can you tell where it begins or ends? You can't really find a beginning or end, can you? It's a circle that goes around and around.

That's the way it is with cycles in nature, too. In nature, all living things are part of the cycle of life, a process that keeps going around and around. All living things are born, grow and eventually die. To keep life going, living things need to *reproduce,* which means to make young like themselves.

Imagine a farmyard with lots of chickens. A chicken lays an egg. Out of the egg hatches a little baby chick. The chick grows up to be a hen. The hen mates with a cockerel, then soon the hen lays an egg. Out of the egg hatches a chick. That chick grows up and the cycle continues.

This kitten looks like its mother.

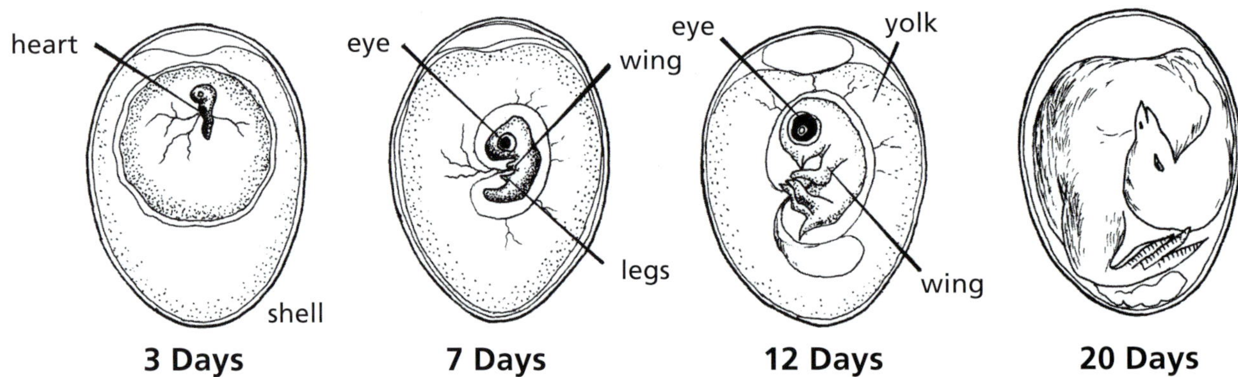

A baby chicken grows inside an egg.

Look at the picture of the life cycle of a chicken. Here's an old question that no one has ever answered: which came first, the chicken or the egg? You can't tell. It's a cycle – with no beginning or end – that keeps going around and around.

The life cycle of a chicken

The cycle of life has four parts: birth, growth, reproduction and death. Let's look at the life cycles of some different living things.

From Seed to Seed: A Plant's Life Cycle

When you plant a seed in the ground, what happens? With the right combination of soil, water and temperature, the seed sprouts and a plant starts growing. Roots grow down and leaves grow up. The plant grows bigger, until it is mature enough to make flowers.

Flowers help the plant reproduce. How? Often it happens like this. Part of the flower, the *anther,* makes male *pollen.* Then the wind blows, or maybe a bee lands on the flower and carries the male pollen to the female part of the flower, called the *ovule.* ('Ovule' means 'little egg'.) When this happens, we say that the ovule has been 'fertilised', and now it can grow until it becomes a seed.

If you plant that seed in the ground, what happens? The seed sprouts, and a new plant grows. It makes new seeds, and the plant's life cycle goes on.

Can you see the many seeds in these sunflowers?

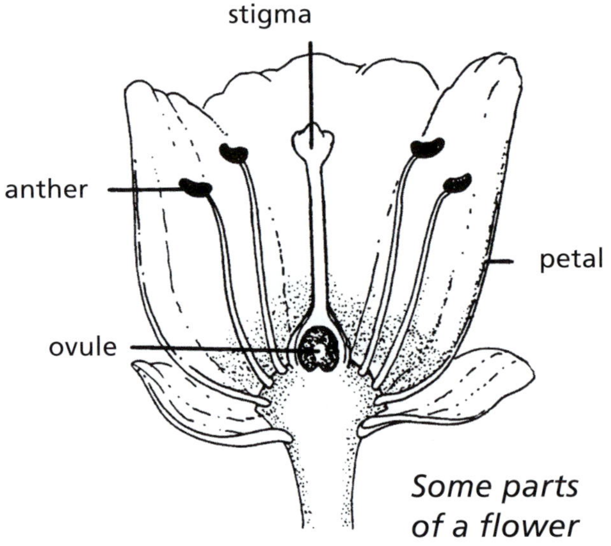

Some parts of a flower

From Frog to Frog: An Amphibian's Life Cycle

Animals go through the same life cycle as plants: birth, growth, reproduction, death and everything all over again. You can see this in the life cycle of a frog.

Imagine a little pond. At the edge of the pond you see something floating on the greenish-brown water. It's a bunch of frog eggs, called frogspawn. It looks like little balls of almost clear jelly, all clumped together.

If you look closely, you see a dark speck inside each little ball. The speck grows bigger and begins to take shape. When it hatches it has a broad face and a long, flat tail. This baby frog is called a tadpole. It lives in water, and swims around in the pond.

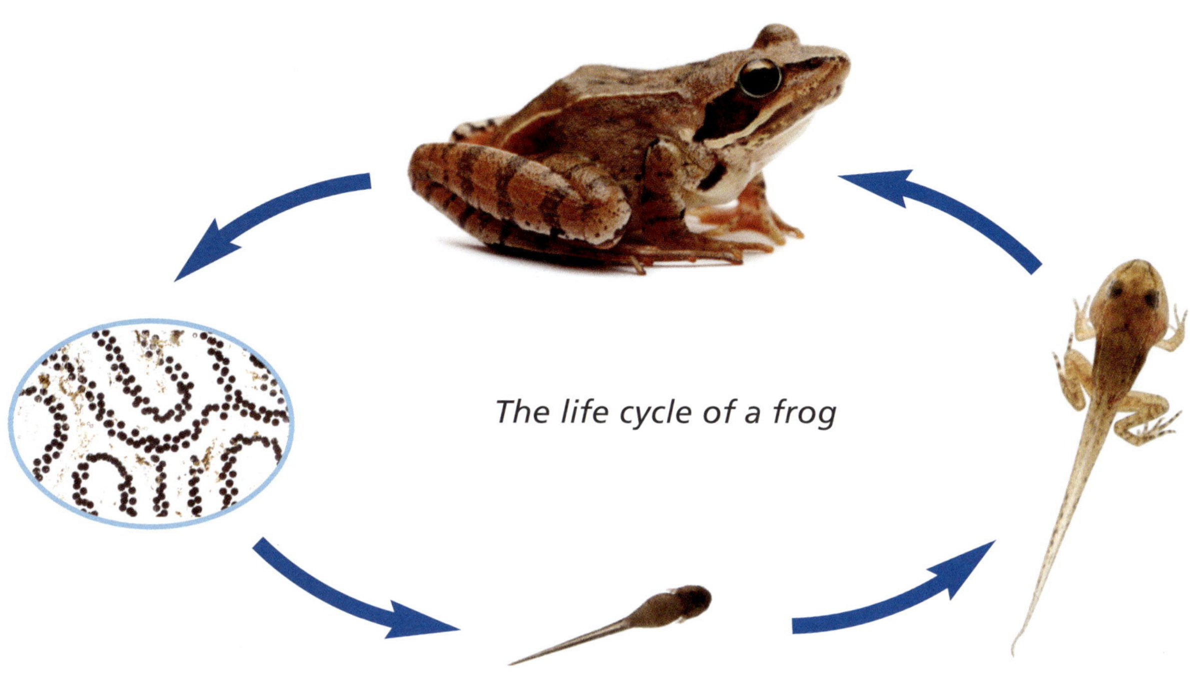

The life cycle of a frog

As the tadpole grows, two little legs begin to sprout from the back of its body. Soon, two more little legs begin to grow in front. At the same time, the tadpole's body grows bigger and its tail then shrinks. It looks more and more like a frog.

The frog grows and matures until it is ready to reproduce. A female frog lays about one thousand eggs at a time! But not many of these eggs will hatch into tadpoles because so many other creatures in the pond, such as fish, like to eat frog eggs. After the female frog lays the eggs, and a male frog fertilises them, then the fertilised eggs float in the water like a blob of little jelly balls with dark specks inside. The specks grow bigger and begin to take shape, and the life cycle of the frog keeps on going.

The Cycle of the Seasons

You know that the life cycle has four parts: birth, growth, reproduction and death. For many living things, the cycle of life follows the cycle of the four seasons of the year: spring, summer, autumn and winter. For example, a sunflower seed sprouts from the ground in the spring. The plant grows in the summer. The seeds of this adult plant ripen in the autumn, and some of the ripe seeds fall on the ground. The plant dies in the winter. But next spring, some of the seeds that fell on the ground sprout, and new sunflower plants begin to grow. Just as the life cycle repeats itself, the cycle of the four seasons also happens over and over again every year.

Let's look at how the lives of some plants and animals in the UK change with the different seasons.

Spring

After the cold winter, nature seems to wake up and come alive. In spring, as the earth grows warmer, the seeds of plants begin to sprout. A sunflower seedling will become a new sunflower plant. It sends a root down from the seed into the warm soil and a little green shoot up into the air. Maple and oak trees that were bare and leafless during winter begin to send sap up to their branches to help new leaves sprout and grow. (Sap is a sugary liquid that carries nutrients. You can eat the sap of some maple trees – it's where maple syrup comes from!)

A nest of cygnets

In spring, many baby animals are born or become active. Squirrels scurry about, and young badgers born during the winter now have grown so that they can see, hear and start exploring outside of their badger sett. Birds that had flown south for the winter (why do you think they went south?) now return and build nests where they will lay their eggs. Other birds like swans also lay eggs and their babies – called cygnets – hatch. Insect eggs that lay quietly all winter now begin to hatch. From some eggs, out come tiny grasshoppers that feed on the just-budding leaves of the plants.

The cygnets are growing larger and more adventurous.

Summer

In summer, when the weather is warm and there's plenty of sunshine, many plants and animals grow larger. The little sunflower seedling grows into a mature, adult plant and begins to make seeds. Fruits like strawberries and vegetables like onions grow bigger and begin to ripen. Trees add inches to their branches. In summer, the baby animals that were born in the spring grow bigger and stronger. The baby birds that hatched out of their eggs in the spring grow up and learn to find their own food, and stray further from their parents. Tadpoles grow into adult frogs. Young insects like grasshoppers become adults.

Autumn

In the autumn, many plants become mature, which means fully grown. On an apple tree, the apples grow heavy on the branches and, if you don't pick them first, they fall to the ground. Acorns fall from the oak trees. Courgettes swell and turn into huge marrows. In the fields, stalks of wheat turn brown and bend over, weighed down by plump heads of grain. On many trees, the leaves turn from green to red, gold, yellow or brown, and then fall to the ground.

These migrating greylag geese are passing through the Wildfowl & Wetlands Trust in Gloucestershire.

As the weather gets cooler in the autumn, many animals prepare for the coming changes. Squirrels scurry about gathering nuts and storing them for the cold months ahead. Otters eat as much as they can to build up extra fat, and they look for a den to protect them from the cold. Some birds like willow warblers and greylag geese make a long journey, or *migrate*, by flying south to warmer weather. In the oceans, big whales also migrate to warmer waters. Some grey whales swim for thousands of miles to find warmer water.

Hedgehogs build special nests and curl up in them during their long winter sleep.

Winter

In winter, the world of living things grows more quiet and still. Many small, green plants have shrivelled up and died, leaving their seeds in the ground. The seeds will sit quietly through the winter, ready to sprout when warm weather arrives again. Trees that have dropped their leaves may look dead although they're really alive. They're just *dormant*, not actively growing but, in a way, sleeping though the winter.

Some animals sleep through the winter, too, which is called *hibernation*. For example, hedgehogs curl up into spiky balls and dormice sleep in their little nests through most of the winter, living off fat they built up during summer and autumn. Frogs hibernate too: they burrow into the cold mud at the bottom of a pond and wait for spring to come again.

Birds that migrated south in the autumn spend the winter resting and eating. They need to build up their strength for the long trip back north in the spring.

And then, as surely as the earth moves along in its orbit around the sun, spring comes again. The weather warms up, sap rises, seeds sprout, animals wake from hibernation, baby animals are born and the cycle of life on earth begins again.

The Water Cycle

You've been learning about different cycles in nature, such as the cycle of the seasons and the life cycles of plants and animals. Well, here's another cycle. It's called the water cycle, and it has a lot to do with the weather.

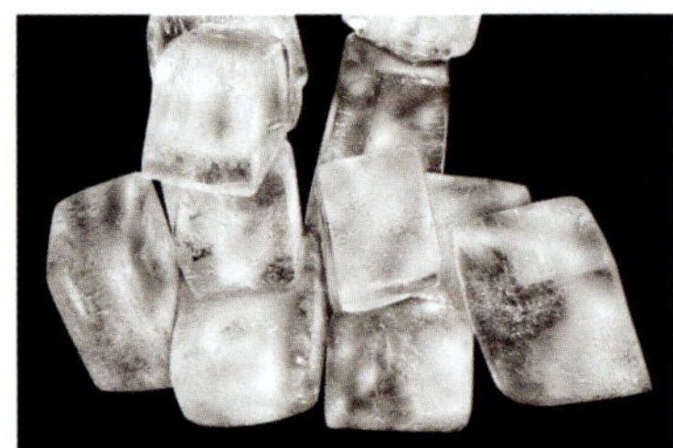

Water can be a liquid, a solid or a gas.

Before we talk about the water cycle, let's remember what you learnt about water in the Year 2 book of this series. Water can exist in three states of matter: as a solid, liquid or gas. The water you drink is a liquid. You know what we call water when it's a solid – ice. When you boil water on a stove, it turns to a gas called steam or water vapour. Water vapour is a gas in the air around you. Now, as we go on to learn about the water cycle, keep in mind that ice, water and water vapour are all water, just in different states of matter. Whether it's in the form of a solid, liquid or gas, water is water.

Evaporation

Think of some places on the earth where you can find water. Did you think of rivers, lakes and, most of all, oceans and seas? There's lots of water on this planet: almost two-thirds of the surface of the earth is covered with water!

The water in rivers, lakes and oceans is liquid. But every day, some of this liquid turns to gas. Every day, as the sun shines down, some of the water

You can try this evaporation experiment.

evaporates: it turns into water vapour and mixes with the air. Do you recognise the word 'vapour' inside that big word 'evaporation'?

Here's a question to think about: where do you think most of the water vapour in the air comes from? Hint: where is most of the water on the earth? That's right, the oceans and seas.

There's water vapour in the air around you. Try this. Put a few centimetres of water in a glass. With a piece of tape or a washable marker, mark a line where the water comes up to. Then put the glass where it won't be disturbed. Every day come back and check how much water is in the glass. What has happened to the water? It has evaporated. It has turned into water vapour and become part of the air around you. Maybe you're breathing it in right now!

At different times, there are different amounts of water vapour in the air. When we talk about the amount of water vapour in the air, we talk about *humidity*. A day with a lot of moisture in the air has 'high humidity'. A day with very little water in the air has 'low humidity'. On a hot, humid summer day, have you ever heard someone complain: 'It's not the heat, it's the humidity'? That means that what makes us feel sticky and uncomfortable on such a day isn't so much the high temperature but instead the high amount of water vapour in the air.

Going Up, Going Down

When it rains hard, puddles of water form on the ground. When it stops raining and the sun starts to shine, what happens to the puddles? Slowly, they get smaller, and then they go away. Where does the water go? Well, some of it evaporates. It turns to water vapour and goes up into the air, just as steam rises from a pan of water that you heat on the stove. But in nature, it's the sun that heats the water and turns it to vapour.

The water that doesn't go up into the air soaks down into the earth. It becomes *groundwater*, which is the name for water found under the ground. When people drill a well, they are drilling down to find the groundwater. Once they dig deep enough to find this underground water, they can put long pipes into the hole and then pump the water up to use in their homes, schools or other places.

After it rains, what happens to the puddles?

Condensation and Precipitation

What happens to the water vapour in the air? Some of it mixes with the air near the ground and some of it rises high into the sky, way up where the air is cooler. In this coolness, the water vapour turns back into little droplets of liquid water. When water vapour turns from a gas back into a liquid, we say it *condenses*.

Here's a way to see condensation happen. Fill a glass with ice and water. Make sure the outside of the glass stays nice and dry. Let it sit for a little while, maybe five or ten minutes. Pretty soon, the outside of the glass will develop a thin coating of water. Feel it – it's wet. Now, where did that water come from? Your glass didn't leak. No, the water came from the air. The ice water made the glass cold, which made the air around the glass cool, just like the air high up in the sky. Then the water vapour in the air condensed – it turned back into liquid – on the outside of your glass.

Up in the sky, when water vapour condenses into droplets of liquid, it forms clouds. Yes indeed, even though they may look like candyfloss, clouds are made of billions of water droplets (or sometimes, if the air is very cold, billions of tiny ice particles). In the clouds, the water droplets bump against each other. But instead of saying 'excuse me' and getting out of each other's way, they join and turn into bigger drops. When the drops get heavy enough, they fall from the clouds – it's raining! Or, if it's cold enough, instead of rain, snow will fall. Snow is water frozen into tiny crystals that fall as snowflakes.

Wispy, feathery clouds are cirrus [SIH-rus] clouds. They form high in the sky and are made of tiny ice crystals.

Big, puffy clouds are cumulus [KYOOM-yuh-lus] clouds. They are usually signs of fair weather.

When a dark layer of stratus [STRAR-tus] clouds covers the sky, it often means rain is on the way.

On television, have you ever heard the weather forecaster say something like: 'Tonight will be cloudy with a chance of precipitation'? That means, there's a chance that water, in some form, is going to fall from the sky. Rain and snow are the most common forms of precipitation, but there are others, such as hail or sleet.

Putting It All Together: The Water Cycle

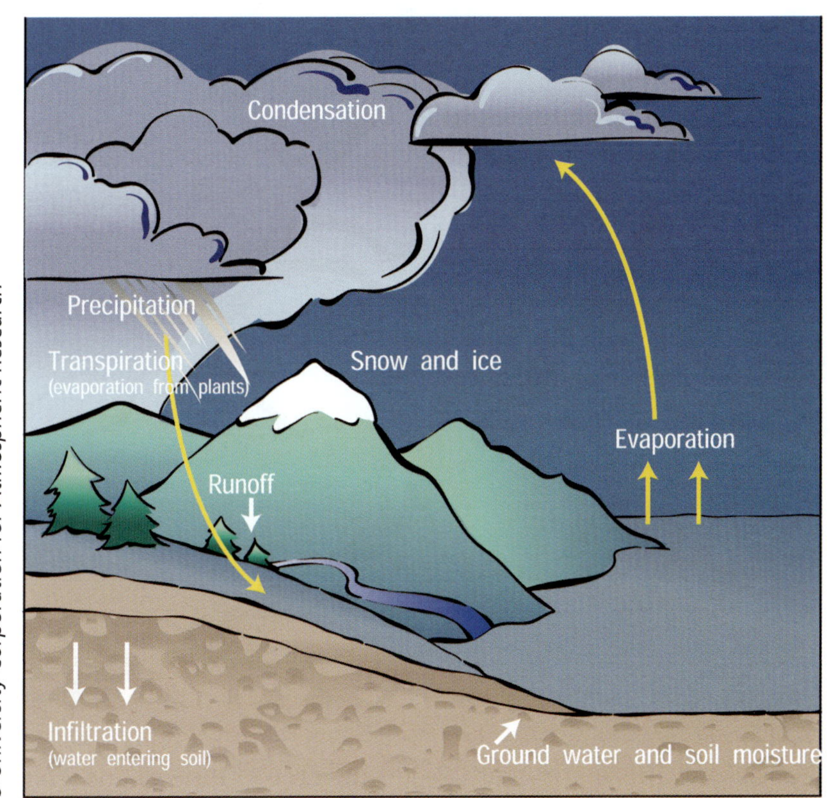

The water cycle

Every day water is evaporating up into the air and then condensing and falling back to the earth. We can draw all these movements of water as a great big circle, called the water cycle.

Every day, water evaporates from the earth, especially from the oceans and seas. As it rises into the sky, the water vapour condenses into little droplets that form clouds. When the droplets get big enough, then the water falls back to the earth as some form of precipitation. It fills rivers, lakes and oceans, and some of it soaks into the earth's groundwater. From the rivers, lakes and oceans, water evaporates and rises into the sky, and you know what happens next! That's the never-ending water cycle: on and on it goes, over and over again.

Insects

Insects Everywhere!

How many insects can you name? Did you think of a fly that bothers you as it buzzes around the room? Or a bee that floats from flower to flower collecting nectar to make into honey? Or a mosquito that can bite you and make you itch? Or a butterfly with beautiful, coloured wings?

Flies, bees, butterflies, ants, ladybirds and stag beetles are all insects.

Did you know that in the UK alone there are over 23,000 different kinds of insects? But that's just the beginning: around the world there are almost a million kinds of insects.

Most are smaller than one of your fingernails. Some are so small that you have to use a microscope to see them. But some, like stag beetles, grow to seven centimetres long. They are Britain's largest beetle.

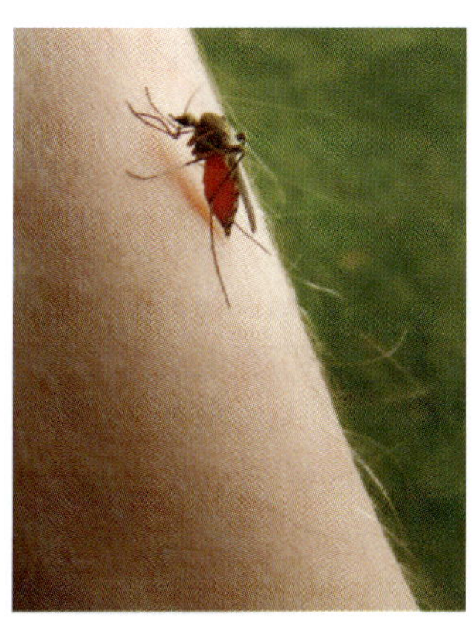

It's lunchtime for this mosquito, who's biting this person's arm.

If a mosquito bites you, you will know that sometimes insects can be harmful to people. Flies carry germs that can spread diseases. Swarms of locusts can destroy a farmer's crops. Tiny aphids can damage or kill plants. Horseflies can give you a painful bite and wasps a painful sting.

But some insects can be very helpful to people. Ladybirds and wasps help us because they eat aphids and other insects that harm crops. Bees make honey. Bees and butterflies help flowers grow when they carry pollen from one flower to another.

Ladybirds munch on some aphids.

What Makes an Insect an Insect?

Hi there! I'm Edward the Ant. You can call me Eddie. They've asked me to tell you what makes me an insect. That's simple. Like all insects, I'm witty, handsome, a great dancer and... What's that? Oh, you want to know the *scientific* facts? Okay, no worries.

I'm an ant, right? And a cricket's a cricket, and a bee's a bee. But we're all insects. Along with butterflies, grasshoppers and, yes, even cockroaches. We're all different in many ways, but here's what we have in common (though I just hate to think about having anything in common with a cockroach – ugh!). Let's start with the legs. How many do you have? Only two? How in the world do you manage with only two legs? You poor creatures. Well, take a look at us insects. Every insect has six legs, three on each side of its body. Count them and see.

Now let's take a closer look at an insect body. A really strong, handsome body – like mine, for example. Every insect, whether it's in your garden or in a jungle halfway around the world, has three main body sections: the *head*, the *thorax* and the *abdomen*.

Do you remember singing the song La Cucaracha (that's 'cockroach' in Spanish) in Year 2?

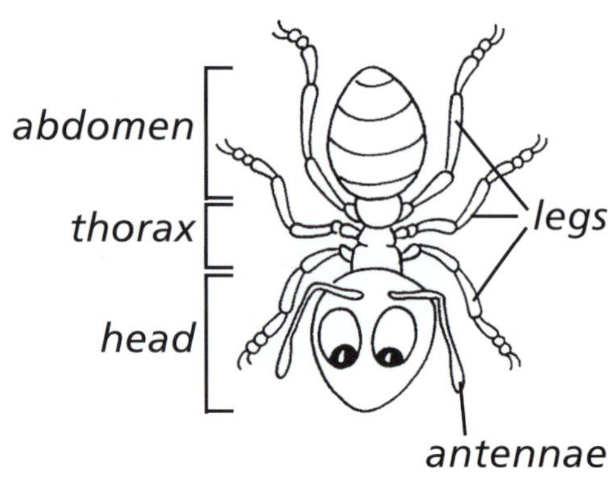

An insect's head is a bit like yours, just not so hairy. Like you, we have eyes and a mouth. And most of us have antennae, or feelers. We use these to feel, taste and smell things.

The middle part of an insect's body is called the *thorax*. That word comes from an old Greek word for 'breastplate'. (How do I know that? Well, I read a poem by the famous ancient Greek poet named Homer at school.) On the thorax most insects have wings. I don't, but some of my fellow ants do.

From the head and the thorax, we move back to the hind part of an insect, called the *abdomen*. You may already know that word because sometimes people use it to refer to their tummy. For us insects, the abdomen is usually the largest of our body sections.

Where's your skeleton? It's inside your body, of course! Well, we insects have skeletons too, but our skeletons are *outside* our bodies. Every insect has an *exoskeleton* – which means an 'outside skeleton'. Your skeleton is made of bones, but not mine. My exoskeleton is made of a material called *chitin* [KITE-in]. It's the hardest part of my body. It's like armour on a Greek soldier.

Inside the chitin, insect bodies are soft. Maybe you've noticed that if you've ever swatted a fly. But yuck, I don't want to think about that. Say – you're not one of those children who goes around stepping on ants, are you? Good, I didn't think so. So, let's review. If it's an insect, you can be sure it has:

- six legs

- three main body sections (head, thorax and abdomen)

- and a hard exoskeleton

Hey, it's been nice talking to you. Maybe I'll see you at your next picnic!

This picture shows a fly's eyes, shown many times larger than their actual size. A fly has eyes made up of many parts. These eyes, called compound eyes, let the fly see all around. Maybe that's why it's so hard to swat a fly!

Are They Insects?

Now you know some characteristics that every insect shares: six legs, three body sections and an exoskeleton. You might think certain creatures are insects, although scientists may not classify them that way. Here are some creatures that might look like insects but they're not. Can you see why? (Hint: Look closely at their bodies and count their legs.)

Ticks, spiders and centipedes are not insects!

At first you might think that caterpillars are not insects because they appear to have more than six legs. But only the first three pairs of legs are true legs, with joints. Further back on their bodies, caterpillars have stubby little bumps called *prolegs*, which help them hold up and move their hind parts but don't count for telling if it is an insect. So, caterpillars really are insects.

Read the story of Arachne on page 76 who wove so beautifully that she was turned into a spider.

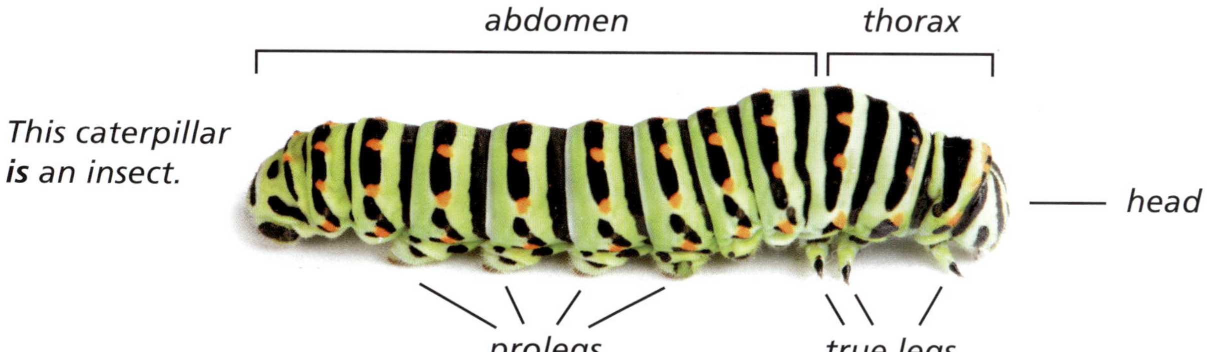

Insect Life Cycles

Nature does some amazing things. For example, who would think that from that a little, crawling caterpillar would come a beautiful butterfly?

That's a very big change! And there's a very big word to describe this kind of change. The word is *metamorphosis* [MET-uh-MORE-foh-sis]. It comes from a Greek word for 'changing shape'.

Let's take a closer look at the big change from a caterpillar to a butterfly.

The stages of caterpillar changing into a butterfly.

A female butterfly lays eggs. They look like tiny beads attached to the bark of a tree or the underside of a leaf. When the eggs hatch, out comes – no, not a butterfly, not yet – but a caterpillar. The caterpillar is the larva [LAHR-vuh], or the baby insect.

The caterpillar crawls up and down the stalks of plants, finding fresh, green leaves to chew on. The caterpillar eats and eats – it's like a little eating machine! – and it grows longer and larger. When the caterpillar matures, it attaches itself to a leaf or twig. It makes a tough, shiny covering that's called a cocoon, and wraps itself completely inside the cocoon. Now the larva has become a *pupa* [PYOO-puh].

From the outside, the pupa looks asleep. It looks as if nothing is happening. But inside, the insect is still growing, and big changes are happening. When the pupa finally opens, the adult insect comes out, but it doesn't look like a caterpillar anymore! Now you can tell it's a butterfly. When it first comes out, the butterfly is weak, damp and crumpled. Then slowly it spreads its wings. When the wings have dried, the butterfly is ready to fly away and flutter from flower to flower to look for food.

So, in growing up, the butterfly has gone through these stages in its life:

$$egg \rightarrow larva \rightarrow pupa \rightarrow adult$$

A Simpler Kind of Metamorphosis

Different insects go through different kinds of metamorphosis. For some insects, like butterflies and ants, when the baby is born it doesn't look anything like the adult. As it grows, it goes through a complete change of shape. But for other insects, the baby can look like a little adult. These insects start small and get bigger, but they don't completely change shape. For example, when baby grasshoppers hatch from eggs, you can tell they're grasshoppers. They just look smaller than the adults. Each baby grasshopper has a rounded head, straight wings and long back legs. It eats whatever leaves and grass it can find, until it's about to burst.

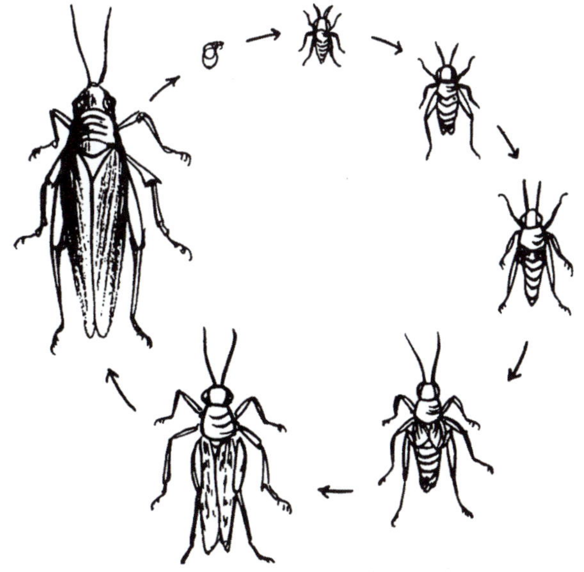

The life cycle of a grasshopper

And in a way, that's what it does. The grasshopper eats and grows until it gets so big that its old exoskeleton splits open and drops off, just like an old coat that doesn't fit anymore. Out climbs a bigger grasshopper. When this happens, we say the grasshopper has *moulted*, which means that it has shed an old exoskeleton and is developing a new one. Grasshoppers moult about five times as they grow from newborn babies to adults.

This picture does not show two insects, but just one dragonfly moulting!

Social Insects

Have you ever seen an ant hill? Then you know that ants don't live alone: they live and work together with other ants. Ants live in groups and they depend on each other to survive. We call ants 'social insects'. Other social insects include bees, termites and wasps.

The word 'social' comes from the word 'society'. A society is a group of beings that live together and generally cooperate with each other to get things done. What other animals do you know that live in a society? Human beings do! We cooperate with each other in all sorts of ways – growing food, building houses, making clothes, teaching each other. We are able to cooperate because we use language to communicate. Do ants speak? No, but they can communicate, as you'll see.

An Ant Colony

A group of ants living and working together is called an ant colony. If you find a few ants in your house or at school, then there must be an ant colony somewhere close by. Ants eat leaves, and they also like sweet things like syrup! If you find ants outside your home or school, put a drop of golden syrup near the ants. You may have to wait an hour, or even a day, but after a while, you will see a parade of ants walking to the drop, like soldiers marching in single file. And another line of ants will be walking away from the golden syrup, back to the colony, each one carrying a tiny droplet of syrup.

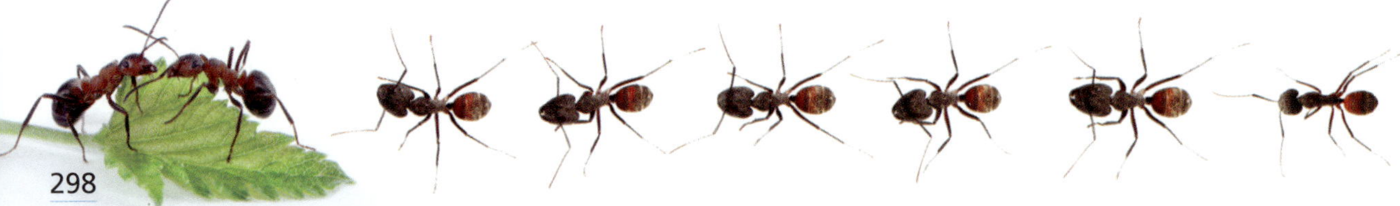

How do the ants tell each other where the syrup is? They don't use language like we do, but their bodies communicate with chemicals. When the first ant found the syrup, it got very excited. That excitement made its body lay down a tiny chemical trail to the food. Other ants sensed that chemical signal, and they followed the trail to the syrup.

Ants cooperate in many other ways, too. They build complicated nests. They share the work of taking care of the babies and young ants. When a special ant, called the queen, lays the eggs, other ants called workers dig tunnels and help keep the eggs clean and warm. When the eggs hatch, the worker ants gather food and help feed the larvae [LARV-eye]; it means 'more than one larva']. Later, they help the growing ants break out of their cocoons. In some colonies, other ants, called soldiers, protect the colony against insect enemies.

In a Beehive

Have you ever tasted sweet, golden honey? Do you know where honey comes from? From the nests of honeybees!

Where do the honeybees get the honey? They make it from the sweet liquid, called nectar that they gather from hundreds of flowers. In their home, called a beehive, the bees feed the sweet honey to the young larvae.

Read the poem 'Bee, I'm expecting you' on page 5.

Beekeepers make special beehives so they can carefully remove some honey that people can eat, but they always leave some honey behind. They know the bees need some honey to feed the larvae so they will grow into adult honeybees. Do you see the beekeeper's protective clothing?

Like ants, honeybees can communicate with each other by giving off a chemical scent. But honeybees can communicate in another way, too. When a honeybee finds a field of flowers with lots of nectar, she can tell the other bees in her hive where to find those flowers. How? By doing a 'waggle dance'!

She turns from side to side, flaps her wings and buzzes. Her dancing imitates how she flew to the flowers. The other bees understand her message and they fly to the flowers. One of the most important things that bees do is to take pollen from one flower and put it on another. Pollination enables the flower to make seeds.

When bees gather nectar from flowers, they also gather a substance called pollen. You can see pollen on this bee's legs, and all over the bee on page 292.

Honeybees are social insects. There are many other kinds of bees, and most of them live alone: they are not social insects.

In a honeybee hive, there are three different kinds of bees. Each hive has one queen bee. She is female, and she grows bigger than the rest. Her job is to lay all the eggs in the beehive. She is the mother of every bee in the hive. In the spring and summer, she can lay as many as hundreds or even thousands of eggs in a single day!

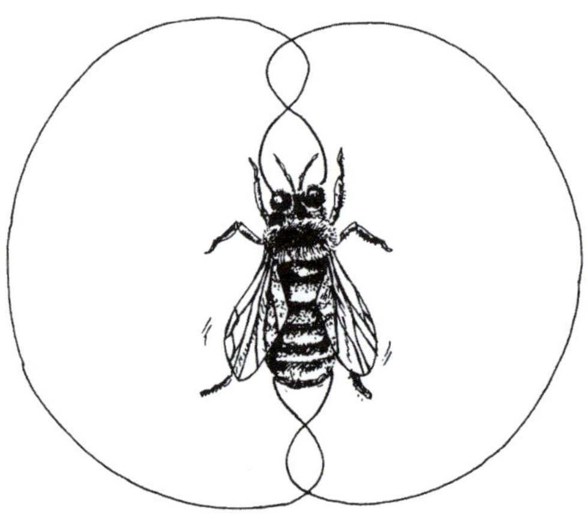

The lines show the pattern of a bee's 'waggle dance'.

In a hive, the queen is surrounded by many bees that are constantly feeding her and cleaning her. These are the worker bees. Most of the bees in a hive are worker bees.

This honeycomb is made of beeswax and is already partially full with honey – what busy bees!

Worker bee

Drone bee

Queen bee

Have you ever been stung by a bee? Ouch! Honeybees only sting to defend themselves if they think you are trying to hurt them or steal their honey. In fact, if a honeybee stings you, it dies soon afterward, because it leaves its sting and part of its body behind.

They are female, but they do not lay eggs (only the queen does that). The workers do a lot more than take care of the queen. From their own bodies they make a special wax that they use to build the honeycombs. These amazing structures have thousands of little six-sided compartments in which the honey is stored. The honey is food for each baby bee growing in one of the little compartments! The workers help take care of the larvae. They fly out from the hive and find flowers with sweet nectar, so they can make honey. Besides the one queen bee and the many worker bees, a honeybee hive has many drone bees. The drones are male. Compared to the female worker bees, drones seem pretty lazy. They do not gather nectar or make honey or help build the hive. Their only job is to mate with the queen to help her make more bees. They are the fathers of every bee in the hive.

How do honeybees start a new colony? First they make a new queen. They pick a baby bee and feed it only special food called 'royal jelly', made from pollen, honey and bee saliva. When the baby queen grows up, she flies away and many bees follow her. When they find a good place with lots of flowers, they start building a new hive. 'Royal jelly! Yummy!'

The Human Body

Cells: The Building Blocks of Living Things

If you have a magnifying glass, look at the back of your hand through it. The hairs look thicker and your skin looks like it has little hills and valleys. Now imagine that you have a super-powerful magnifying glass, and you use it to look at just one hair on your body. It makes the hair look almost like a telegraph pole sticking up out of the ground. And when you look even closer, you see that the hair is made up of many, many little pieces. Each one of those little pieces is called a *cell*.

All living things are made up of cells. Cells are the building blocks of all plants and animals. Every living thing – a flower petal, a maple leaf, a blade of grass, a worm, your body – is made up of cells.

Through your imaginary, super-powerful magnifying glass, you would be able to see that all living things are made up of cells. Well, scientists actually have super-powerful magnifying glasses called *microscopes*. Microscopes help us see things that are much too small to see just with our eyes. Thanks to microscopes, we understand a lot about cells.

A modern microscope

To find out about one of the first scientists to learn a lot with microscopes, read about Antonj van Leeuwenhoek on page 320.

With a very powerful microscope, you can see what some cells look like:

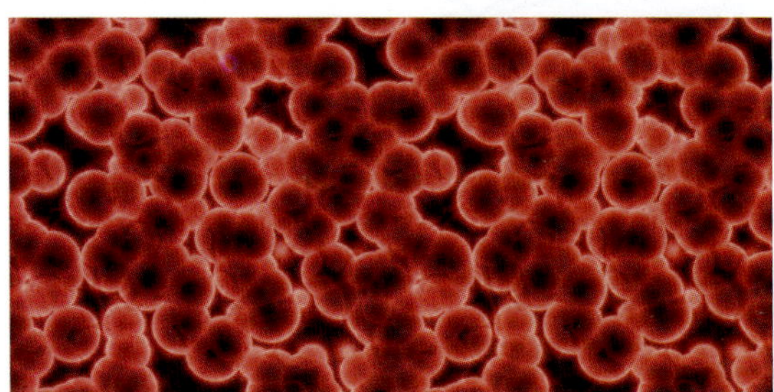

Human blood cells

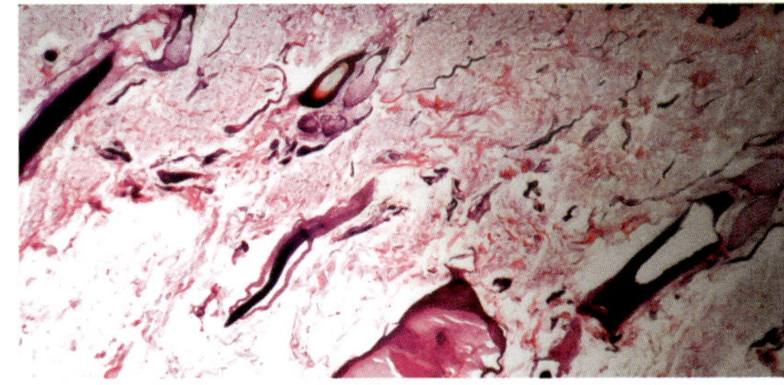

Human hair cells

Cells and Tissues, Organs and Systems

Cells develop into different shapes, depending on what part of a living thing they make up and what job they perform. In your body, there are many different kinds of cells. Your blood cells are very different from your hair cells, which are both different from your brain cells, skin cells or bone cells.

A lot of cells of the same kind join together to form a tissue. No, this isn't the kind of tissue you use to blow your nose! This kind of tissue is a group of the same kinds of cells that work together. These different tissues work together to form organs. Some of the most important organs in your body are your brain, your heart and your lungs.

Some tissues and organs in your body work together like the members of a team. The parts that work together are called a *system*. For example, your mouth, teeth, tongue, stomach and intestines all work together to help you chew and digest your food. They're all important players on the team called the digestive system.

In Year 2, we learnt about some of the most important body systems: the skeletal system, the muscular system, the circulatory system, the nervous system and the digestive system. Now we're going to learn more about the digestive system.

What Happens to the Food You Eat?

Do you remember the saying 'An apple a day keeps the doctor away'?

Eating apples and other healthy foods helps you grow stronger. But how? In order for your body to get what it needs from an apple, it needs to *digest* it. Digesting means breaking food down into little pieces – so little you can't see them with just your eyes – so that your body can take those pieces and use them for energy and for building its own cells, tissues and organs.

Pretend you're holding a big, crisp, juicy red apple. The digestive process begins even before you take a bite. Your eyes, your nose and your fingertips send signals to your brain, and your brain sends a message to your mouth and stomach: *'Get ready, food is coming!'*

When you take a bite of the apple, your tongue tastes the sweetness and tells your brain, 'Mmm, here's something good and sweet'. Then your brain sends an order to the parts of your mouth called the salivary [sal-EYE-verree] glands: 'Get to work!' And they jump to it by making a watery liquid called saliva [suh-LIE-vuh]. You may just call it 'spit', but saliva is an important team player in your digestive process. It helps make the food you eat wet and soft, and it has chemicals that help you digest your food.

On the surface of your tongue there are many tiny *taste buds*. Different taste buds taste different flavours: sweet, salty, sour and bitter. The taste buds send messages to your brain, like 'Yum, this apple is sweet and delicious' or 'This twiglet is salty' or 'What a sour lemon!' or 'Ugh, this is too bitter – spit it out!'

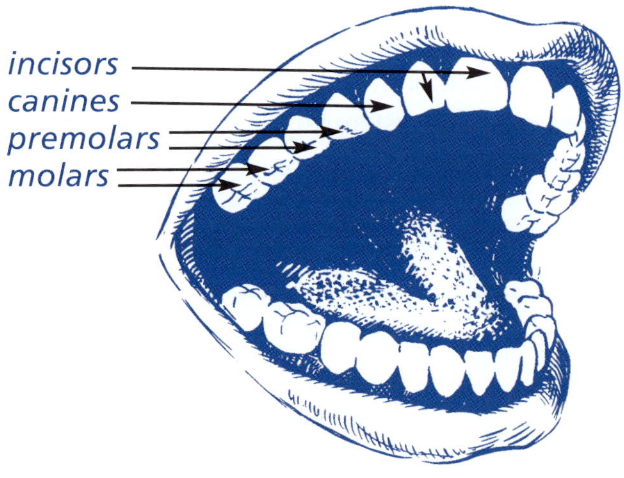

Wash your hands with soap and water, then look in a mirror and try to point to and identify your different teeth.

When you bite the apple, the piece in your mouth is still too big to swallow. So you chew it up. Your teeth are important players on the digestive team as well. They cut, munch and crunch the food into smaller and smaller pieces. Your front eight teeth, four on the top and four on the bottom, are called your *incisors*. To incise means to cut. Growing right next to your incisors are four pointy teeth called your *canines* [KAY-nines]. They tear the food into pieces. By the way, 'canine' is an old Latin word for 'dog'! Why do you think your sharp, pointy teeth are called 'canines'?

After your incisors and canines bite and tear the apple, your tongue pushes the pieces of food to the teeth in the back of your mouth. Your *premolars* have two bumps on them that help crush the apple pieces. Your *molars* have flat tops for grinding the food into pieces small enough to swallow.

Now that you've chewed enough, the apple pieces are small enough to swallow. Gulp! Down they go. Go where? Down your throat, though a tube called the *oesophagus* [e-SOF-ah-gus], and into your stomach.

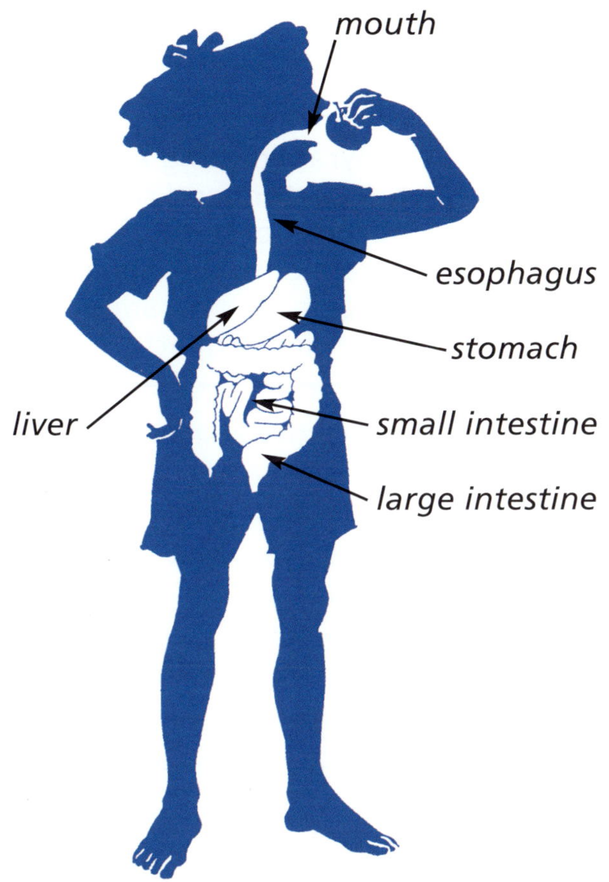

These are some of the major organs in your digestive system.

Maybe someone you know has had an operation to take out their *appendix*. The appendix is a little tube that grows where the small intestine joins the large intestine. Even though it's there, it doesn't really have a job. Usually it doesn't bother anyone, but sometimes the appendix can get swollen and infected. When that happens, a person has to have an operation to have their appendix removed. But it's okay to take it out because you don't really need it.

Do you know where your stomach is? Put your right hand to the left of the centre of your body. Feel your ribs. Your stomach is inside there. Your stomach is a big muscle designed to stir up the food you eat. As it stirs, it adds liquids and chemicals to help digest the food. In your stomach, the bite of apple you took no longer looks anything like an apple. All the grinding, stirring and chemicals make it look like soup.

Now the food is almost small enough for your body to use. From your stomach the soupy stuff moves to the *intestines*. Your intestines are a long, coiled-up tube that winds around inside your tummy. If you stretched them out, they would measure much longer than you are tall. An adult's intestines are about eight metres long! Most of the intestine is like a narrow rope. This is called the small intestine. The last part of the tube is bigger. This is called the large intestine. In your small intestine, the soupy food is mixed with more liquids and chemicals that break down the food into bits too small to see. The good particles, called the *nutrients* [NYOO-tree-uhnts], are then absorbed into your blood. Your blood carries the nutrients to all the cells of your body.

A Healthy Diet: The Food Pyramid

The food pyramid

A pyramid is big at the bottom and small at the top, so the food pyramid has the same shape as the pyramids of ancient Egypt!

Your digestive system breaks down food for your body. For your digestive system to do a good job, you need to give it good food to work with. To be sure you're eating enough of the food that's good for you, take a look at this picture, called the food pyramid.

The food pyramid is divided into four sections with different kinds of foods in each section: the bigger the section, the more of that kind of food you should be eating.

Most of all you need to eat grains, like bread, cereal, rice and pasta. You also need to eat plenty of fruits and vegetables. And you need to eat foods that give you proteins. These foods include dairy products, like milk, cheese and yogurt. You also get protein from meat, fish, eggs and nuts.

See how much smaller the section at the top of the pyramid is compared with all the other sections? This smallest section includes fats, oils and sweets, which means we need very little of these. In fact, if you are eating the foods shown in the bigger sections of the food pyramid, you are already getting some fats and sugars. For example, if you eat a sausage, you're getting some protein, but you're also eating a lot of fat, too. If you eat fried foods like chips and fried chicken, you are eating a lot of fat along with the potatoes or the chicken. That's why the food pyramid says you should eat very few extra fats and sweets. Fats and oils include things like mayonnaise, salad dressing and butter. Your body needs some fats or oils, but just a little bit. Too much fat can do bad things, such as damage your heart.

Does anybody *not* like sweets? They taste so good it's hard to resist them. But be careful not to eat too many sweets, like fizzy drinks, biscuits, cakes, lollies and ice cream. All these sweets are made with lots of sugar. Your body does need sugar for energy. But many of the good foods in the food pyramid, such as fruit and bread, already give your body good, natural sugar. To keep your body strong and healthy, it's best not to eat many sweets or drink a lot of fizzy drinks.

Vitamins and Minerals

You can't see them, but *vitamins* and *minerals* are some of the important nutrients that come to you in good foods, especially in vegetables and fruits. To be as healthy as you can be, your body needs the right combination of vitamins and minerals every day. Without enough vitamins and minerals, you could get very sick.

Vitamins are named with letters of the alphabet, and there are at least 13 that our bodies need. Here are some of them:

- Vitamin A helps the skin, tissues and eyes grow strong. You can get plenty of vitamin A by eating carrots, sweet potatoes and other orange vegetables, and by drinking milk.

- There are eight different vitamins called vitamin B, each with its own role in keeping your body healthy. Most come in meat, and many come in vegetables as well.

- Vitamin C helps cells grow strong, and it helps your body fight against disease. You get plenty of vitamin C by eating oranges, tomatoes and broccoli.

- Vitamin D is important because it helps your teeth and bones grow strong. Your skin absorbs some vitamin D from sunshine, and you also get vitamin D from tuna, egg yolks and milk.

Besides vitamins, your body also needs minerals. Does that mean you have to eat rocks? No, but the minerals your body needs are actually tiny amounts of the same minerals that can be found in the earth. Your body only needs small amounts of these minerals, which you can get from the right foods.

Your body needs iron to build blood cells. When people don't have enough iron in their blood, they feel tired and unwell. Foods with plenty of iron include meat, green leafy vegetables, whole grain cereals, raisins and dried beans.

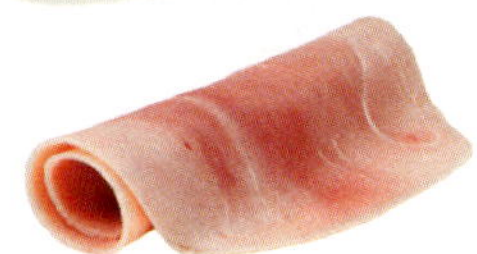

Calcium is a mineral that helps make your bones and teeth strong, and helps your muscles work hard. When people don't have enough calcium, their bones sometimes break easily. Foods with lots of calcium include milk, yogurt, dried beans and green leafy vegetables like lettuce.

Vegetables provide many important vitamins and minerals.

Magnetism

That Special Magnetic Attraction

Put some paper clips on a table. Bring a magnet near them. What happens? The clips almost seem alive as they jump up to the magnet. That's what it looks like, but what *really* happens?

Remember that the magnet exerts a force of attraction on the paper clips. You can't see the force, but it's there, and it's strong enough to pull the paper clips up off the table once the magnet moves close enough to them.

Will the magnet attract everything? For example, will it pull a shoelace or tissue or plastic comb toward it?

No. The shoelace, tissue and comb are not made of iron. But the paper clip is made of steel, a metal that has iron in it. Magnets attract things made of iron. But magnets do not attract copper or aluminium. Bring a magnet close to some aluminium foil and you'll see.

Experiment with Magnetism

Pennies and 2p coins were made of copper until 1992. New coins are mostly steel with a thin copper coating. Which coins will the magnet attract? Try it out at home!

Many magnets that we use today have been manufactured out of metals containing iron. People make some magnets, but others occur in nature. They can be found in stones in the earth called *lodestones*. Lodestones are special pieces of iron ore that act just like the magnets we make. Lodestones are the first magnets that were ever found.

Magnetism is a force all around us. You can't see it, but you can see the way it acts in the world. People use magnetic force every day, whether it's to attach a note to the refrigerator or lift an old, wrecked car at a scrapyard. Magnets work around the home in doorbells, cupboards, headphones, speakers and telephones. Some restaurants put a ring of magnets around the bins to stop staff from accidentally throwing away the cutlery with the waste food.

Magnets come in many shapes and sizes. The horseshoe magnet and bar magnet are common.

Have you ridden on a train? Maybe you've looked at a ticket. The ticket uses magnetic material to store information about where you can get off. That's why you should never put a magnet near a train ticket, because it could wipe off the information stored on your ticket.

Magnetic Poles

Here's an experiment you can do with two bar magnets. Put the two bar magnets on a table. Bring an end of one of the magnets toward an end of the other. What happens? Do they pull together or push apart?

Now turn *just one* of the magnets around, and bring the ends together. What happens now? If your magnets pulled together the first time, then this time they will push apart. If your magnets pushed apart the first time, then this time they will pull together.

Why? To find out, let's look at a bar magnet and its magnetic field. Even though you can't see the forces coming from that magnet, the little lines show them in the picture on the next page. The lines show what's called the magnetic field, which is present in the space around the magnet and where the magnetic force can be felt. If you put a paper clip inside the magnetic field, the magnet will attract the clip.

In the picture, can you see where the magnetic force is strongest? It's strongest at the two ends of the magnet (where the dotted lines are close together). We call those two ends where the magnetic force is strongest the *magnetic poles*.

Even though the poles of a magnet may look the same, they are different. We need names for these two poles so we can tell them apart. We call one pole 'north' and the other 'south'.

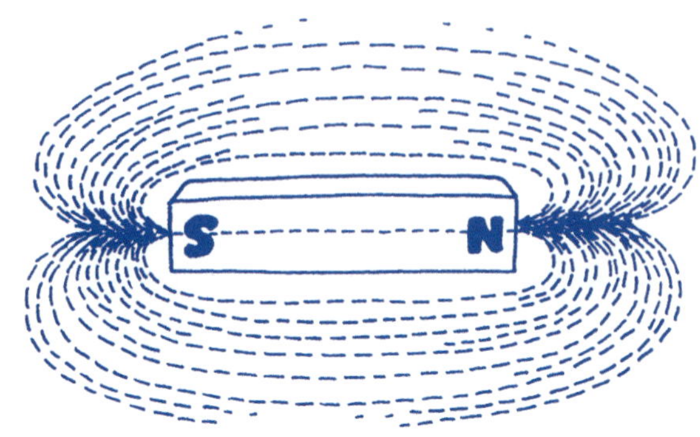

The dotted lines show the magnetic field.

Why are the poles called north and south? For the answer, try this. Take a bar magnet and tie a string around its middle so it balances when you hold it by the string. Tape the other end of the string to something, such as a table, so that the magnet can hang and move freely. Watch what it does when you let it go.

The bar magnet will turn around until it settles in one direction. Notice something in the room that one pole (one end of the magnet) is pointing to, for example, a nearby lamp or picture. Put a little sticker on the end pointing to the lamp or whatever you've chosen. Then gently twirl the magnet. When it stops again, what happens? The pole with the sticker is pointing in exactly the same direction, isn't it?

If you kept doing this experiment with every bar magnet you could find, every one of them would point to the same direction. That's because your magnets are finding the forces of magnetic attraction that exist in nature. They are being pulled by great fields of magnetic attraction that surround the earth.

That's right, the earth is like a great big magnet! The magnetic fields surrounding the earth are strongest very near the North Pole and the South Pole. So, one end of your magnet is pointing north and the other is pointing south. And that's why the poles of your magnet are called north and south.

You can try this experiment with a bar magnet.

Ask an adult to help you to work out if the sticker end of your magnet is pointing north or south. Once you know that, you can label one end of your magnet *north* and the other end *south*.

Now that you know that magnets have different poles, let's go back and think about what happened when you brought the ends of two bar magnets together. Once they pulled towards each other, but once they pushed apart. They were following a rule of magnetic force that says:

unlike poles attract but like poles repel.

'Repel' means 'push away'. The north pole of a magnet pulls or attracts the south pole of another magnet. But if you bring two north poles together, or two south poles together, they repel each other – they push apart. Try it!

Using a Compass

You know that we use magnets in many ways. One of the most useful things a magnet can do is tell us what direction we're going – north, south, east or west. When a magnet is used in this way, we call it a compass.

Compasses help sailors find their way at sea. They help ramblers find their way through forests. They can help you find your way, too.

You learnt the points of the compass in Year 1, and now you know how a compass works.

If you did the experiment of tying a bar magnet to a string, you made a kind of compass. Most compasses have a small magnet in the shape of an arrow, called a needle. This magnetised needle can spin around. When it stops spinning, the needle always points north.

A compass. The red needle is pointing north, and the arrow shows that the mountaintop is south-east of the walker.

Take a compass and turn it around. You'll see that the needle always points the same way – north. But what if you want to go *east*? How would you use the compass to do that?

First, face in the direction of the needle – north. So, what direction is behind you? That's right, south. Which way is east? Is it to your right or your left? East is to your right, and west is to your left.

That's the way maps work, remember? The top is north, the bottom is south, the right is east, the left is west. ('Left' and 'west' sound alike, remember?)

So, if you need to go east, what do you do? Your compass needle points north. East is to the right of where the needle points. So, you can go east by turning yourself until the needle is pointing to your left. Then you march straight ahead, always keeping the needle pointed to your left.

Simple Machines

Tools and Machines

The world we live in today depends on many tools. With tools, we build and dig, we lift and cut, we grip and carry. What tools can you name? Did you think of a hammer, screwdriver or pliers? What's a hammer for? To whack in a nail. What's a screwdriver for? To twist a screw. What are pliers for? To grip and pull. With the right tool, you can do a lot more than you can with just your hands alone.

A screwdriver and a hammer

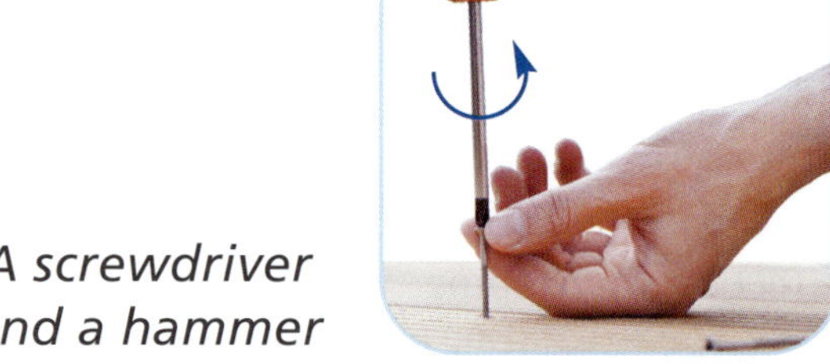

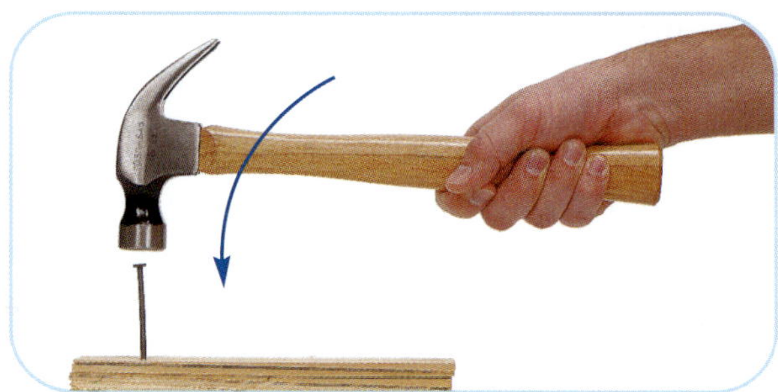

We use tools to help us do things; we also use machines. When you hear the word 'machine', you may think of something like a sewing machine, or a washing machine, or a bulldozer. Those are one kind of machine, but there's another. We call this other kind *simple machines*. They make a lot of work easier for us to do. Let's learn about some of the simple machines that help people every day.

Levers

The simple machine called a *lever* is so simple you might not even think it's a machine. But like other machines, levers help us do work. Levers can help you lift things. You use a lever when you use the claw of a hammer to pull a nail out of a board. You also use a lever when you use an old screwdriver to prise open the lid of a tin of paint. When you push down on one end of the screwdriver, the other end is forced up, which brings the lid up, too.

A screwdriver acts as a lever when you use it to prise open a paint tin.

Take a look at the picture here. This girl had gone for a walk and she found a big rock. She wanted to see what was under it, but it was much too big and heavy for her to lift. So she found a strong stick and a little rock nearby. She pushed one end of the stick under the big rock. Then she supported the stick on the little rock. Clever! She's used the stick as a lever. When she pushed down, then the big rock moved up. With a lever, she can lift something that she could not lift just with her hands.

The big stick acts as a lever, and helps the girl lift the rock.

Wheels

There's something missing in this picture.

You'd have a very hard time pulling your friends in this cart, because the wheels are missing!

The wheel is a simple machine that makes work easier. Wheels turn, and they help us move things. If you have a cart or a toy car or truck, you can see that wheels turn around on something. A wheel turns around on an *axle*, which is like a stick stuck through the middle of a wheel.

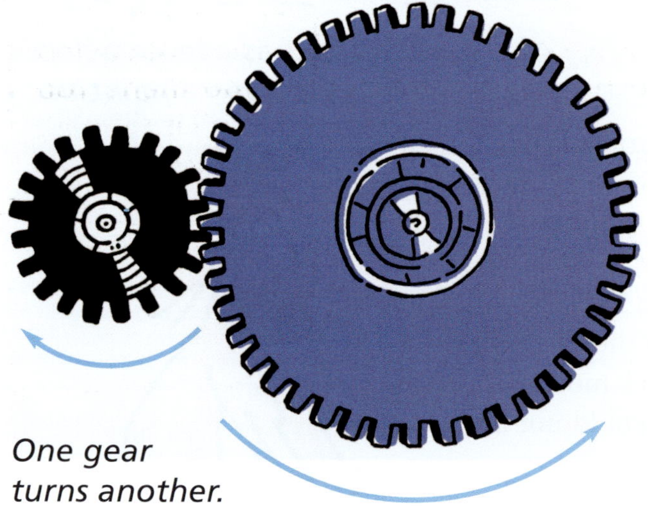

One gear turns another.

An axle can join two wheels together. If you have a cart or toy car, look at how the axle joins the wheels.

A *gear* is a wheel with teeth. The teeth on gears fit together so that one gear can turn another. The gears on a bicycle are connected by a chain. When you pedal, you turn the big gear by moving your feet, which makes the chain move, which makes the gears behind go around, which makes the bicycle start moving.

Do you see how gears work in the picture? When the big gear turns anti-clockwise, the small gear turns clockwise.

Friction

Imagine that you're riding a bike. You're pedalling hard and the wheels are turning quickly. You see a STOP sign ahead, so you put on the brakes. The brakes press against the wheels and stop them from turning.

When the brakes press against the wheels, they cause *friction*. When two surfaces rub against each other, you get friction. You can feel friction. Quickly rub the palms of your hands together, back and forth. Keep rubbing and what do you feel? Heat! This heat is produced by the friction caused when the surfaces of your hands rubbed against each other.

Sometimes friction can be a good thing, such as when you use your brakes to stop a bike, or when you use a rubber on paper to remove a mistake. But sometimes you don't want friction. For example, have you ever started riding a bike and heard a squeaking sound? That squeaking can happen when there's too much friction. What do you do then? You can put a few drops of oil between the wheel and axle. The oil is slippery and *lubricates* surfaces: it cuts down the friction between them.

You can feel how lubrication works. First, rub your hands together. Now, put a few drops of liquid soap in your hands, then rub them together again. Do you feel how the soap lubricates your hands and cuts down the friction between them?

Pulleys

With wheels and ropes you can make another simple machine called a *pulley*. The name, pulley, says what it helps you do – pull. If you've ever pulled on a cord to raise some blinds on a window, then you've used a pulley. When you pulled the cord down, the blind went up – that's because a pulley changes the direction of a pull. If you see a flagpole or a sailing boat, take a close look at it: does it use pulleys to help you raise and lower the flag or sail?

Can you lift 10 kilograms? That's pretty heavy, but this boy can lift that much – he's using a pulley to help him! Pulleys work for

A pulley helps you lift.

us every day. Recovery vehicles use pulleys when they lift cars. Lifts use pulleys to carry people up and down. With several pulleys together, you can lift some very heavy things. Cranes use pulleys to lift huge beams to build a city's tall buildings.

Inclined Planes

Imagine you're pushing a heavy load in a wheelbarrow – maybe your sister and your dog (be careful, now!), or a pile of rubble you've collected. You come to a kerb, and you can see that it's going to be hard to push your loaded wheelbarrow up that kerb. How can you get the wheelbarrow up the kerb easily? Luckily, you see a wooden plank nearby. You place it so that your wheelbarrow can

roll right up the plank and over the kerb. There, that was easier!

When you used that plank, you made a simple machine called an *inclined plane*. 'Inclined' means slanted or leaning. A plane is a flat surface. When you pushed your wheelbarrow up the plank, the inclined plane helped spread out the work of lifting the loaded wheelbarrow over the kerb.

Did you know that a wheelbarrow is also a machine? It is a lever attached to a wheel and axle. The handles are a lever to help you lift the load. The wheel lets you roll the load once you have lifted it. Rolling a wheelbarrow up the plank is three machines working together.

People in wheelchairs also use inclined planes – ramps. Ramps make it possible for people in wheelchairs and for people with baby buggies to get in and out of buildings, and to roll smoothly on or off a pavement. Look for these inclined planes at the buildings near where you live.

Wedges

Have you ever used a V-shaped simple machine called a *wedge*? You can use a wedge to hold something tight. If you slide a wedge under a door, it will hold the door tightly in place. Wedges also help to hold a plane's wheels in place to make sure it does not roll.

These wedges keep the plane's wheels in place.

A wedge can also be used to split things apart. To split a log, you can use a wedge made of metal. You hammer the wedge into the log until the log splits apart.

Take a look at the picture: as you hammer the wedge in from the top, it splits apart the wood from side to side.

What's the name of the tool that has a sharp metal wedge attached to a handle? It's an axe, or a hatchet. Thousands of years ago, people made hatchets with sticks for handles and stones for blades. Today, we make the blades out of steel. Whether it's an ancient hatchet made of stone or a brand-new axe made of steel, the basic tool is the same: a wedge on a handle.

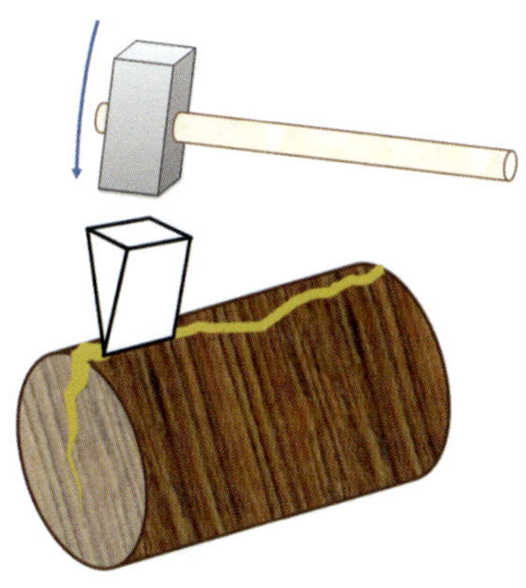

This wedge helps split the log.

This axe's wedge-shape helps the boy split the log.

Screws

A screw

The last simple machine we're going to learn about is the *screw*. Take a look at the kind of screw you can use to hold pieces of wood together. Do you see the slanted ridges going up and down this screw? Those ridges, which are called the 'thread', are really one long inclined plane.

To see how a screw is an inclined plane, try this. On a sheet of paper, draw a triangle like the one below. Make the bottom about 16 centimetres long, and the short side about 8 centimetres high. Use a coloured pencil or marker to draw the long slanted side.

You have drawn the edge of an inclined plane. Now, cut it out and wrap it around a pencil. Do you see how the coloured line you drew looks like the thread of a screw? This shows how an inclined plane curves up and up on a screw.

When you turn a screw with a screwdriver, the thread bites into the wood and pulls the screw a little bit further in. It's a lot easier than trying to push the screw straight in!

A big earth auger also works as a screw. You can use it to dig holes in the ground. As you twist it down into the earth, it pulls soil up and makes a hole.

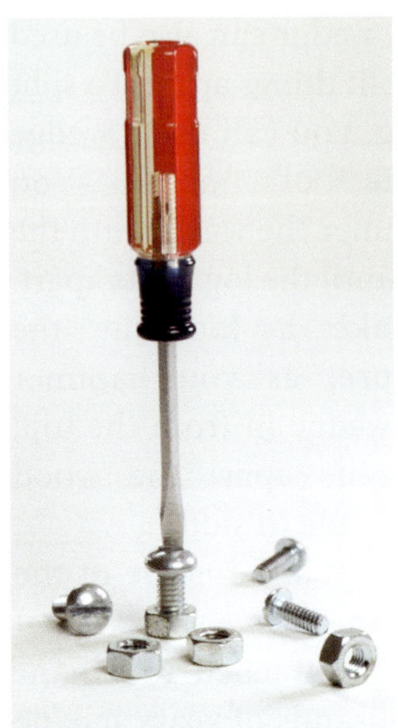

A screwdriver

An earth auger at work

Stories About Scientists

Aristotle

In the History and Geography chapter you were introduced to Aristotle, a great philosopher and scientist who lived in ancient Greece. A philosopher is someone who asks questions about why people do things and why we think certain things are true. Aristotle's father was a doctor. He taught Aristotle about the life cycle and the human body, which you have just been learning about. Aristotle travelled around ancient Greece with his father and looked after people who were ill. He started to learn how to become a doctor.

Sadly, when Aristotle was still young, his father died. Aristotle then lived with his uncle who taught him poetry and other things. When Aristotle was 17, he began studying philosophy with an older philosopher, Plato, at Plato's school in Athens. Aristotle enjoyed learning about philosophy so much that he even became a teacher! He enjoyed asking questions about life and people.

Aristotle's father and uncle both taught him different things that helped him to become a great philosopher, writer and scientist. In ancient Greece, philosophers and scientists were very similar as they both tried to explain why things happened.

One of Aristotle's students was Alexander the Great. Learn about him on page 157.

Aristotle believed in watching and measuring things to find out about them. He made a system of organising things into lists. This is a bit like the sorting and pattern-making we did in maths in Year 1 and Year 2. For example, we know that Labradors are dogs, and we know that dogs are animals. Therefore we also know that Labradors are animals. Aristotle made groups and lists for lots of different types of living things.

Since Aristotle liked sorting things and using a set process for working through his experiments, he created something called the 'scientific method' which you might use when you do investigations in science. His 'scientific method' starts with finding a problem, thinking of an answer, then testing out the answer to see if it is right or wrong. Because Aristotle was the first person to investigate things in this way, he is sometimes called the 'Father of Science'.

Archimedes

Archimedes was born on the island of Sicily a very long time ago, in about 287 B.C. He lived in the town of Syracuse where he solved lots of scientific puzzles.

One puzzle was how to get water out of leaky ships. The answer Archimedes came up with was to make a machine. He put a large screw inside a sloping cylinder and turned it with a handle down the middle. The screw pushed the water up the cylinder whenever someone turned the handle. The cylinder stopped the water spilling off the sides. Archimedes could make water go uphill!

An Archimedes Screw in use today

Archimedes had many other ideas. Hiero, the king of Syracuse, wanted to know how big his crown was. He needed to know the volume. The crown was a funny shape, with too many sides and corners and holes to work out all the measurements with a ruler. Archimedes thought and thought but he couldn't find an answer. He went to the bath-house for a bath. Only the very rich had baths at home then. As Archimedes climbed in, the water rose up and poured over the edge of the bathtub. How much water poured out? The same volume as the volume of Archimedes that was in the bathtub. He wriggled down a bit further and a bit more water overflowed.

This was too exciting. He didn't have to measure the crown. He could measure the water that overflowed from a big bowl when he put the crown in it. 'I've got it!' he shouted, except he spoke Greek so he shouted 'Eureka!' instead, which was their word for the same thing. He knew he mustn't forget the idea before he could write it down. So he jumped straight out of the bath, not even stopping to put his clothes on. He ran all the way home through the streets of Syracuse, still shouting 'Eureka! Eureka!'

Antonj van Leeuwenhoek

Cells, bacteria, plankton – these are just a few of the things that you learn about in science but that you can't see. Even though we can't see these things, we know they exist. Why? Because scientists have seen them – not with their eyes alone, but through a microscope. Have you ever looked through a microscope? If you haven't, maybe you've looked through a magnifying glass or examined the photos taken using a microscope on page 302. Most microscopes use specially made pieces of glass, called lenses, to magnify things. Do you know what it means to 'magnify'? It means to make something appear bigger.

Antonj van Leeuwenhoek

One of the first people to explore the world of tiny things we can't see with our eyes alone was Antonj van Leeuwenhoek [AN-tonn-ee fon LAY-vun-hook]. He was born in Delft, a town in the Netherlands, in 1632. (Can you find the Netherlands on a map?) Delft was also home to the artist Jan Vermeer, whom we learnt about in Year 2. Delft is a seaport and van Leeuwenhoek made his living as a merchant. He also liked finding things out. When he read a book about microscopes, he wanted to try observing things for himself. He found a quick way of making lenses from tiny, clear glass marbles that could make things look hundreds of times bigger. The smaller the marble, the bigger things looked through it. Then he built metal frames for holding everything steady.

Discover more about the Netherlands on page 108.

To try van Leeuwenhoek's experiment yourself, visit the Science Activity section of our website at **www.coreknowledge.org.uk/science.php**

Van Leeuwenhoek looked at a drop of blood through a microscope and could see it clearly enough to describe the round, dented cells within. He put a drop of dirty water under a lens. What do you think he saw? He saw a swarm of tiny, squirming, squiggly shapes. There were living creatures in the water! He scraped some plaque from his own teeth and put it under a lens, and he saw more squirmy, squiggling shapes. There were tiny creatures living in his own mouth!

He called these little creatures 'animalcules'. Scientists today would call them micro-organisms. ('Micro' means small, and an organism is a living thing, so a micro-organism is a small living thing – not small like a beetle or kitten, but *really* small, too small to see with your eyes alone.)

Van Leeuwenhoek built many microscopes. Word got around about the amazing things you could see through them. He shared his observations with leading scientists in London's Royal Society. Even Tsar Peter the Great of Russia came to look through his lenses. But he never told anyone how he had made the lenses and it was many years before anyone else discovered his secret.

The Curie Family

The Curies were a family of scientists. Pierre, the father, and his brother Jacques made a special machine that could measure electricity. Do you remember making a circuit with crocodile clips and a light bulb? It was like this experiment but their machine could measure very, very tiny amounts of electricity.

Try the experiment using a light bulb and crocodile clips in the Year 2 book.

Marie and Pierre Curie at work in their laboratory

Marie Curie, the mother, was born in Poland but she went to France to learn more about science. Both of her parents were teachers, so she had to work hard! When she went to university in 1891 there were not very many women there, only 23 who were learning about science. There were over a thousand men. It was quite unusual for a woman to study science.

Marie met Pierre Curie at her university. He was learning about science too. Marie used the machine that Jacques and Pierre invented to do some of her own experiments. She made an amazing discovery! She experimented with a kind of invisible energy called 'radiation' and discovered two new

Artists painted this mural at Marie Curie's birthplace in Warsaw in 2001. It celebrates the 100th anniversary of her second Nobel Prize, which she earned for her discoveries of polonium and radium.

elements which are like ingredients for everything that exists. She called these elements 'radium' which is like the word radiation and 'polonium' because Marie still loved the country she was born in, Poland. Some of her experiments even glowed in the dark! Unfortunately, Marie and Pierre did not realise that radiation could be dangerous and was making them ill. Now scientists protect themselves with special clothes and equipment when they use radium or polonium.

Radium helped doctors in hospitals to treat people who were suffering from cancer. Marie's discoveries also helped doctors perform X-rays on soldiers who had been hurt in World War One. Marie and her husband Pierre won a special prize for science called the Nobel Prize. In fact Marie won the prize twice! Their daughter Irene, who was also a scientist, won the prize some years later. Marie died of an illness called leukaemia which she most probably got from being too close to those dangerous elements. The Curie family's scientific discoveries have helped doctors treat thousands of people in hospitals all over the world.

Suggested Resources

The Cycle of Life and the Seasons

The Science Behind Growth by Chris Oxlade (Raintree) 2013

The First Flower: How Pollination Works and Why Insects are So Important by R. Beaumont-Parkinson (AuthorHouse) 2009

How Does it Grow: Butterfly by Jinny Johnson (Franklin Watts) 2009

Caterpillars and Butterflies by Stephanie Turnbull (Usborne) 2006

Wildfowl & Wetlands Trust (WWT) website: www.wwt.org.uk, where you can watch animals and birds on webcams

Weather: The Water Cycle and More

Drought (Wild Weather series) by Catherine Chambers (Heinemann) 2008

How The Weather Works by Christiane Dorion and Beverley Young (Templar) 2011

Our World of Water by Beatrice Hollyer (Frances Lincoln) 2009

Clouds (Watching the Weather series) by Elizabeth Miles (Heinemann) 2005

Rain (Watching the Weather series) by Elizabeth Miles (Heinemann) 2005

Where Do Puddles Go? by Fay Robinson (Turtleback Books) 2001

Insects

1001 Bugs to Spot (Usborne 1001 Things to Spot series) by Emma Helborough (Usborne) 2009

Amazing Insects by Laurence Mound (Knopf) 1993

Microlife that Lives in the Soil by Steve Parker (Raintree) 2006

Where to Find Minibeasts series by Sarah Ridley (Franklin Watts) 2011

Bugs and Insects (Usborne Spotter's Guide) by Anthony Wootton (Usborne) 2006

The Human Body

Cells and Tissues by Leslie Jean LeMaster (Children's Press) 1985

Health and Growth (Start-Up Science) by Claire Llewellyn (Evans Brothers) 2004

What Happens to a Hamburger by Paul Showers (HarperCollins) 2001

Magnetism

Experiments with Magnets by Helen J. Challand (Children's Press) 1986

Now You Know Science: Magnet Magic by Terry Jennings (Franklin Watts) 2009

All About Magnets by Stephen Krensky (Scholastic) 1993

Simple Machines

Simple Machines by Anne Horvatic (Dutton) 1989

Very Useful Machines: Pulleys by Chris Oxlade (Heinemann) 2004

Simple Technology: Wheels and Cogs by Mandy Suhr (Wayland) 2009

Illustration and Photo Credits

Jose Armet Portanell (1843-1911). *Education of Alexander the Great* by Aristotle / Private Collection / © Look and Learn / The Bridgeman Art Library: **319 (a)**

Mark Beech: **4**, **5 (a, b)**, **6-7**, **8**, **9 (a, b)**, **11**, **12**, **13 (a-f)**, **15**, **18**, **20**, **35**, **38 (a)**, **42**, **44**, **51**, **52**, **53**, **57**, **58**, **60**, **61**, **63**, **83**, **84**, **85 (a-c)**, **86**, **87**, **88 (a-f)**, **89**, **92**, **93 (a-c)**, **94 (a, b)**, **95 (a, b)**, **96**, **204**, **219**, **220 (a, b)**, **221**, **222**, **223**, **224**, **228 (a, b)**, **288 (d)**, **301 (d)**, **303**, **310 (b)**, **311**, **313 (a, b)**, **314 (a)**, **316 (b)**, **320 (a)**

British Museum Images, *Eglin Marbles* (mesotope coloured), British Museum, London. © The Trustees of the British Museum: **194 (a)**

Paul Cézanne (French, 1839 -1906) *Still-life with apples*, 1877-1878 (oil on canvas). © The Masters and Fellows of King's College, Cambridge. The Fitzwilliam Museum, Cambridge: **189**

Paul Collicutt: **65**, **66 (a-c)**, **67 (a-c)**, **68 (a-c)**, **69 (a, b)**, **70**, **71 (a-d)**, **72 (a, b)**, **73**, **75**, **76**, **77**, **78**, **79**, **80**, **81**

John Constable (English, 1776-1837), *Salisbury Cathedral from the Meadows*, 1831 (detail of 1560). Private Collection / The Bridgeman Art Library: **188**

Walter Crane (1845-1915), *He ran towards the horse and seized the bridle*, illustration from *The Story of Greece* by Mary Macgregor, 1st edition, 1913 (colour print). Private Collection / The Stapleton Collection / The Bridgeman Art Library: **158**

Leonardo da Vinci (Italian, 1452-1519), *Last Supper*, 1495-98 (tempera and mixed media on plaster). Santa Maria delle Grazie, Italy / Photos.com: **185**

Edward Dovey: **101**, **103 (a)**, **113**, **127**, **143**, **148**, **154 (b)**, **160**, **166**

Gerlach Flicke (German, d. 1558), *Thomas Cranmer*, 1545 (oil on panel). National Portrait Gallery, London / Wikimedia Commons: **175**

A.S. Forrest, 'The Days Seemed Very Long and Dreary to the Two Little Boys' from *Our Island Story* by Henrietta Marshall (1905): **171 (a)**

A.S. Forrest, 'There is Time to Finish the Game and Beat the Spaniards too' from *Our Island Story* by Henrietta Marshall (1905): **179 (a)**

Marcus Gheeraerts II (1561–1636), *Sir Francis Drake Wearing the Drake Jewel or Drake Pendant at his Waist*, 1591. National Maritime Museum / Wikimedia Commons: **178**

George Gower (1540–1596), *Elizabeth I of England, the Armada Portrait*, c. 1588 (oil on panel). Woburn Abbey / Wikimedia Commons: **176**

Steve Henry: **229**, **291 (a)**, **293 (c)**, **294 (a)**, **310 (a)**, **314 (b)**, **317 (e)**

Katsushika Hokusai (1760–1849), *The Great Wave off Kanagawa* (Series *Thirty-six Views of Mount Fuji*, no. 21), 1833 (color woodblock print). Library of Congress / Wikimedia Commons **184**

Luke Jefford: **230 (b)**, **231 (a)**, **249 (a-c)**, **250 (a-i)**, **263 (c)**, **268 (c-f)**, **269 (a-h)**, **270 (a-e)**, **272 (a-d)**, **273 (a-c)**, **274**, **275**, **317 (f)**

Richard Kelly: **114**, **116 (a)**, **118-119**

Bob Kirchman: **194 (b)**, **282 (b)**

Paul Klee, *Was fehlt ihm?* ('What's the Matter with Him?'), 1930 (stamped drawing in ink on Ingres paper on cardboard). © Fondation Beyeler, Riehen/Basel. Photography by: Peter Schibli, Basel: **182**

Edward Lear: **14 (a, b)**

Tanya Lubicz-Nawrocka: **137 (a, b)**, **138 (b)**, **265 (a-d)**, **266 (a-c)**, **267**, **268 (a, b)**

Angus McBride (1931-2007), *Martin Luther* / Private Collection / © Look and Learn / The Bridgeman Art Library: **173**

Gail McIntosh: **304, 305**

Gail McIntosh/ Paul Collicutt: **22, 24, 25, 26, 38 (b), 39, 45, 46, 49**

Claude Monet (French, 1840-1926), *Impression, Soleil Levant (Impression: Sunrise)*, 1872-1873 (oil on canvas). Musee Marmottan, Paris / Wikimedia Commons: **107**

Mark Otton: owls *passim*

Giovanni Paolo Panini (1691–1765), *Alexander the Great Cutting the Gordian Knot*, 1718 -1719 (oil on canvas). Walters Art Museum / Wikimedia Commons: **159**

Glyn Warren Philpot, *Richard I Leaving England for the Crusades 1189*, c.1927 (oil on canvas). © Palace of Westminster Collection, WOA 2601 www.parliament.uk/art: **167**

Pablo Picasso (Spanish, 1881-1973), *Mother and Child*, 1922 (oil on canvas), 39 1/2 x 32 1/16 in. (100.3 x 81.4 cm.). © The Baltimore Museum of Art: The Cone Collection, formed by Dr. Claribel Cone and Miss Etta Cone of Baltimore, Maryland, United States. BMA 1950.279. Photography by: Mitro Hood: **183**

Antonio del Pollaiuolo (Italian, 1470-1480), *Apollo and Daphne*, 1470-80 (oil on wood). The National Gallery, London / Photos.com: **191**

Photos.com: **2, 55, 90, 103 (b), 104 (a-c), 105, 106 (a, b), 108, 109 (a, b), 110 (a-c), 111 (a, b), 112 (a-c), 115, 117 (a), 121, 122 (a, b), 123 (a, b), 125, 128 (a), 136, 139 (a), 140, 142, 145, 146 (a-c), 150, 154 (a), 162, 163, 165, 168, 179 (b), 192 (a), 205, 207 (a-c), 209 (b), 210 (a, b), 211 (a, b), 212, 213, 230 (a), 231 (b), 235 (a, b), 236 (a-g), 239 (a-h), 240 (a-i), 244 (a-e), 248, 249 (d), 259, 260 (a-d), 261 (a-c), 262 (a-d), 263 (a, b), 270 (f-k), 277 (a-c), 279, 282 (a), 283 (a-d), 284 (a), 285 (a-d), 286 (a, b), 287 (a, b), 288 (a-c), 289, 292 (a-f), 293 (a, b), 295 (a-d), 296, 298 (a, b), 299, 300 (a, c), 301 (a-c), 302 (a-c), 306, 307 (a-d), 308 (a, b), 309 (a), 312 (b, c), 314 (c), 315 (a-b), 317 (a, c, d), 318 (a, b)**

Raphael (1483 – 1520), *The School of Athens*, 1509–1510 (fresco). Apostolic Palace, Vatican City / Wikimedia Commons: **157**

Mason Robbins: **139 (b)**

Jacob van Ruisdael (1628/29-1682), *The Castle of Bentheim*, 1653 (oil on canvas). National Gallery of Ireland: Beit Collection, presented by Sir Alfred and Lady Beit / Wikimedia Commons: **187**

Dave Thompson / Press Association Images: **202 (b)**

Jan Verkolje I (1650–1693), *Portrait of Anthonie van Leeuwenhoek (1632-1723)*, 1680 (oil on canvas). Museum Boerhaave / Wikimedia Commons: **320 (b)**

Robert Harding World Imagery: **138 (a)**

Robert Whelan: **64, 321**

Robert Whelan and Tanya Lubicz-Nawrocka: **258 (all)**

Franciszek Smuglewicz (1745–1807), *Scythian Emissaries Meeting with Darius*, 1785 (oil on canvas). Wikimedia Commons: **152**

University Corporation for Atmospheric Research (UCAR), *The Water Cycle*, © University Corporation for Atmospheric Research: **291 (b)**

Philipp von Foltz (1805–1877), *The Age of Pericles*, 1853. Wikimedia Commons: **155**

Wikimedia Commons: **116 (b)** (photo by Mick Garratt), **117 (b)** (photo by David Wright), **120** (photo by Anton Obolensky), **124 (a)** (photo by Jlazovskis), **124 (b)** (photo by Justin Watt), **126, 128 (b)** (photo Jorge Royan), **129, 131, 132, 133, 134, 135** (photo by Yann), **141, 144** (from the United States Library of Congress), **147 (a-b), 151 (a)** (photo by Judith Swaddling), **151 (b), 153** (photo by Stéphane Magnenat), **170 (a, b)** and **171 (b)** (illustration by James William Edmund Doyle), **172, 174** (photo by Antony McCallum), **177** (illustration by Anthony Anthony), **192 (b)** (photo by Ryan Kaldari), **193, 195** (photo by Bernard Gagnon), **196, 197** (by Myk Reeve), **198 (a), 198 (b)** (photo by Russ McGinn), **199, 202 (a)** (photo by Chris Nyborg), **201** (photo by Hanay), **206 (a)** (photo by Derek Gleeson), **206 (b), 209 (a)** (photo by Yuichi), **290 (a-c), 294**

(b) (photo by Thomas Shahan), **309 (b)**, **312 (a)** (photo by Audrius Meskauskas), **316 (a)** (photo by César Rincón), **317 (b)**, **319 (b)** (photo by Dirk Ingo Franke), **322 (a)** (scanned photo by Vitold Muratov), **322 (b)** (photo by Nihil Novi)

Oksana Wynnyckyi-Yusypovych, 'Va pensiero scene' from *Nabucco*, 2009, Lviv National Opera and Ballet Theatre, Ukraine. © Oksana Wynnyckyi-Yusypovych: **203**

Text Credits and Sources

Poems

'The Answer' by Allan Ahlberg. Reproduced by permission of Penguin Books Ltd.

'Caracola' ('Conch Shell') by Federico García Lorca and translated by Will Kirkland. © Herederos de Federico García Lorca and William Kirkland. All rights reserved. For information regarding rights and permissions of Lorca's works in Spanish and any other language, please contact lorca@artslaw.co.uk or William Peter Kosmas, Esq., 8 Franklin Square, London W14 9UU, England. Reproduced by permission of William Peter Kosmas, Esq.

'On the Ning Nang Nong' by Spike Milligan. © Spike Milligan Productions. Reproduced by permission of Spike Milligan Productions.

'Rickety Train Ride' by Tony Mitton. © Tony Mitton. Reproduced by permission of David Higham Associates.

Stories, Folktales and Myths

'Beauty and the Beast', adapted from *The Blue Fairy Book* by Andrew Lang,1889, and *Third Year Language Reader*, edited by F. Baker, G. Carpenter and M Brooks, 1919.

A Christmas Carol, adapted from the original Charles Dickens story by Andrea Rowland and John Holdren.

'The Emperor's New Clothes', adapted from *Fairy Tales and Other Stories* by Hans Christian Anderson, translated by W.A. and J.K. Craigie, 1914, and *Everyday Classics Third Reader*, edited by F. Baker and A. Thorndike, 1917.

'The Fisherman and His Wife', adapted from *Grimm's Fairy Tales*, edited by Orton Lowe, 1922, and *Everyday Classics Second Reader*, edited by F. Baker, A. Thorndike and M. Batchelder, 1922.

'How the Camel Got His Hump' from *Just So Stories* written and illustrated by Rudyard Kipling (George S. Morang & Co.) 1902.

'The Magic Paintbrush', retold by John Holdren.

Myths from Ancient Greece, retold by John Holdren, based on multiple sources, including *Old Greek Stories* retold by James Baldwin, 1895; *Thirty More Famous Stories* retold by James Baldwin, 1905; *The Children's Own Readers: Book Four* edited by Mary Pendell and A. Cusack, 1929; *The Merrill Readers: Third Reader* edited by F. Dyer and M. Brady (n.d.); *Everyday Classics Sixth Reader* edited by F. Baker and A. Thorndike, 1921; and *Mythology* by Edith Hamilton, 1942.

'Peter Pan' adapted from J.M. Barrie's 1911 novel *Peter Pan*, which is turn was based on his 1904 play. Reproduced by permission of the Great Ormond Street Hospital.

'Please Look After This Bear' from *A Bear Called Paddington* by Michael Bond and illustrated by Peggy Fortnum (William Collins & Sons, now HarperCollins Children's Books) 1958. Reprinted by permission of HarperCollins Publishers Ltd. / www.paddingtonbear.com.

'Rama and Sita: A Tale from the Ramayana', adapted from *Rama and Sita, Folk Tales of the World* by Govinder Ram.

'The Story of the Seventh Daughter' adapted from 'The Story of Prince Sobur' from *Folk Tales of Bengal* (Richard Clary and Sons, Ltd.) 1883 (1st Edition).

'Talk' from *The Cow-Tail Switch, a collection of West African stories* retold by Harold Courlander and George Herzog (Henry Holt and Company) 1975.

'The Tongue-Cut Sparrow', adapted from the retelling by Yei Theodara Ozaki in *The Children's Hour: Folk Stories and Fables*, selected by Eva March Tappan, 1907.

Music

'Do-Re-Me', © 1959 by Richard Rodgers & Oscar Hammerstein II. Copyright Renewed. International Copyright Secured. All Rights Reserved. Used by Permission of Williamson Music, A Division of Rodgers & Hammerstein: An Imagem Company.

'The Happy Wanderer'. Words by Florenz Siegesmund. English translation by Antonia Ridge. Music by Friedrich Wilhelm Möller. © Copyright 1954 Bosworth GmbH. Bosworth & Company Limited. All Rights Reserved. International Copyright Secured. Used by permission.

'The Hippopotamus Song' (also known as 'Mud, Mud, Glorious Mud'). © the Estates of Michael Flanders & Donald Swann. Reproduced by permission of the Estates of Michael Flanders & Donald Swann.

While every care has been taken to trace and acknowledge copyright, the editors tender their apologies for any accidental infringement where copyright has proved untraceable. They would be pleased to insert the appropriate acknowledgement in any subsequent edition of this publication.

Index

= (equals sign), **238**
> (greater than sign), **238, 255**
< (less than sign), **238, 255, 278**
× (multiplication sign), **235–236, 273–278**
÷ (division sign), **276–279**

Abbreviations
    in addresses, **90**
    for measurements, **262**
Abdomen (of insect), **293–295**
Academy, the, **156**
Addends, **229, 242, 257**
Addressing a letter, **27, 47, 90**
Adjectives, **88**
Aegean Sea, **75, 149**
Aegeus, King, **74–75**
Agriculture, **103, 105, 109, 149**
Alexander the Great, **157–160**
    Bucephalus and, **158**
    empire of, **159–160**
    Gordian knot and, **158–159**
Alps, **104–105, 121**
AM hours, **267**
Amazon River, **123**
Amphibians, **284**
Anglo–Saxons, **162**
Antennae, **294**
Antonyms, **89**
Ants, **292–294, 297–299**
    colonies, **298–299**
Aphids, **293**
Aphrodite, **67, 70, 79**
Apollo, **67, 70, 81**
Apostrophes, **89**
Arachne the Weaver, **76–78, 295**
Arachnids, **278, 295**
Archaeology, **161**
    archaeologist, **126**

Architecture, **126, 192–199**
    architect, **192, 194–195, 197–198**
Ares, **68, 70**
Ariadne, **74–76**
Aristotle, **156–157, 318–319**
Artemis, **67, 70**
Aryans, **126–127**
Ashanti (Asante), **17**
Asian civilisations, **125–146**
Asoka, King, **134–135**
Atalanta, **78–79**
Athena, **69–70, 77, 155**
Athens, **69, 74–76, 148–154, 155–157, 170**
Atlas (book of maps), **83**
Atlas (mythical figure), **82–83**
Attraction, force of, **308, 310**
Augeas, King, **82**
Augers, **318**
Austria, **102, 104, 106–107, 110, 121**
Autumn, **285, 287**
Axes, **317**
Axles, **314–316**
Ayodha, **129, 132**

Babylon, **137, 151, 163**
Bach, Johann Christoph, **212–213**
Bach, Johann Sebastian, **207–208, 212–213, 225–226**
Bar graphs, **230–231**
Bar magnets, **309–311**
Basin, **114, 116–117, 122–123**
Bass drums, **211**
Bass guitars, **209–210**
Beat (music), **211, 214–215**
Becket, Thomas à, **164–165**
Bees, **284, 292–293, 298–301**
    beehives, **299–301**

beekeepers, **299**
honeybees, **299–301**
poem about, **5**
stinging by, **301**
Beethoven, Ludwig van, **106–107, 109, 111, 207–208, 213, 225–226**
Belgium, **102, 106, 109–110**
Bharat, Prince, **130**
Bicycles, **28, 93, 96, 109, 282, 314**
Bitter taste, **304**
Bizet, Georges, **211**
Blocks (musical instruments), **211**
Blood, **302–303, 305, 307, 321**
    blood cells, **302–303, 307**
Boleyn, Anne, **174**
Boys' Day, **146**
Brahman (Hindu god), **127–128**
Brahms, Johannes, **106**
Bronze, **161**
Bucephalus, **158**
Buddha, **132–135, 195**
Buddhism, **132–135, 145, 195**
Butterflies, **4–5, 292–293, 296–297, 323**
    metamorphosis of, **296–297**

Calcium, **308**
Calendars, **263–264**
Camels, **31–34**
Canals, **109, 115, 120**
Canine teeth, **304**
Capital letters, **84–85, 90–91**
Carmen (Bizet), **211**
Carnival of the Animals, The (Saint-Saëns), **210, 225**
Castanets, **211**
Caterpillars, **295–297, 323**
    poem about, **4**

Levers, **313, 316**
Life cycle, **282–288, 296–298**
    chickens, **282–283**
    frogs, **284–285**
    insects, **286, 296–298**
    plants, **284**
Lines
    in geometry, **269–272**
    number lines, **232, 248**
    in visual arts, **181–186, 191, 194–198**
Lions, **135**
Liver, **305**
Locust, **293**
Lodestones, **309**
Lubrication, **315**
Lunar calendar, **139–140**
Luther, Martin, **173**
Luxembourg, **102, 110**
Lyres, **67**

Macedonia, **157–158**
Mackenzie River, **124**
Maracas, **211**
Marathon
    battle of, **153**
    races, **153**
Marimbas, **211**
Mary I, Queen, **176–178, 180**
Matterhorn, **104**
Measurement
    abbreviations for, **262**
    length, **260–262**
    perimeter, **269**
    time, **263–268**
    weight, **262–263**
Mediterranean Sea, **105, 120–121, 149, 151**
Melody, **201, 214, 216**
Metamorphosis, **296–298**
Mice, **6, 13, 62–64, 287**
Micro-organisms, **121**
Microscopes, **292, 302, 320–321**
Migration, **11, 287**

Minerals, **307–308, 322**
Minos, King, **74, 76**
Minotaur, **74–75, 149**
Mississippi River, **124**
Mohenjo-Daro, **126**
Molars, **304**
Monkeys, **13, 86, 130–131**
Mont Blanc, **104**
Monet, Claude, **107–108**
Mongols, **137, 140–142**
Montfort, Simon de, **167–170**
Mosquitoes, **292–293**
Moulting, **298**
Mount Fuji, **142–144, 184**
Mount Olympus, **65, 72, 80**
Mozart, Wolfgang Amadeus, **107, 205–206, 213, 225–226**
Mulberry trees, **138–139**
Multiplication sign, **235–236, 273–278**
Murray River, **123**
Music alphabet, **216**

Nectar, **292, 299–301**
Nemea, **81**
Nemean lion, **81**
Neptune, **50–51, 70**
Netherlands, **102, 104, 108–110, 121, 145, 178, 182, 186–187**
New Year Festival (Chinese), **139–140**
New Year's Day (Japanese), **146**
Nicholas, Saint, **6–7**
Niger River, **121**
Nile River, **114, 120–121, 125, 148, 159**
Normans, **55–56, 162–163**
Northern Europe, **102, 104**
Northern Hemisphere, **102**
North Pole, **102, 310–311**
Notes (music), **210, 212–217**
Nouns, **84–86, 88**
Number lines, **232, 248**

Nutrients, **286, 305, 307**

Ob River, **122**
Oceans, **22, 66, 73, 120–121, 123–124, 144, 177, 287–289, 291**
Oedipus, **73**
Oesophagus, **304**
Oils, **306, 315**
Olympia, **147**
Olympics, **147, 149, 151**
Orchestras, **205–206, 208–211, 225–226**
Organs (musical instruments), **207–208, 212–213, 226**
Organs (of body), **303, 305**
Origami, **146**
Orinoco River, **124**
Ouse River, **100, 117**
Ovule, **284**

Pan, **71**
Pandora, **72**
Paper, invention of, **138, 141**
Parallel lines, **185, 271**
Paraná River, **123**
Parthenon, **155, 192–197, 199–200**
Past tense, **86–87**
Pegasus, **71**
Peninsulas, **149**
Percussion instruments, **209, 211–212, 226**
Pericles, **155**
Perimeter, **196, 269**
Persephone, **79–80**
Persian Wars, **151, 155**
Pheidippides, **153**
Philip, King, **157–158**
Philip II, King of Spain, **178**
Philosophers, **155–157**
Phoebus Apollo, **67, 70, 81**
Pianos, **207, 212–213, 217, 226**
Picasso, Pablo, **183–184, 200**
Pigs, **12, 85**